MW01641435

Security, Development and Human Rights in East Asia

Series Editor
Brendan Howe
Graduate School of International Studies
Ewha Womans University
Seoul
Korea (Republic of)

This series focuses on the indissoluble links uniting security, development and human rights as the three pillars of the UN, and the foundation of global governance. It takes into account how rising Asia has dramatically impacted the three pillars at the national, international and global levels of governance, but redirects attention, in this most Westphalian of regions, to human-centered considerations. Projects submitted for inclusion in the series should therefore address the nexus or intersection of two or more of the pillars at the level of national or international governance, but with a focus on vulnerable individuals and groups. The series targets postgraduate students, lecturers, researchers and practitioners of development studies, international relations, Asian studies, human rights and international organizations.

More information about this series at
http://www.palgrave.com/gp/series/14488

Yoichi Mine • Oscar A. Gómez
Ako Muto
Editors

Human Security Norms in East Asia

palgrave
macmillan

Editors
Yoichi Mine
Graduate School of Global Studies
Doshisha University
Kyoto, Japan

Oscar A. Gómez
Research Institute
Japan International Cooperation
Agency (JICA)
Tokyo, Japan

Ako Muto
Research Institute
Japan International Cooperation
Agency (JICA)
Tokyo, Japan

Security, Development and Human Rights in East Asia
ISBN 978-3-319-97246-6 ISBN 978-3-319-97247-3 (eBook)
https://doi.org/10.1007/978-3-319-97247-3

Library of Congress Control Number: 2018953344

This Palgrave Macmillan imprint is published by the registered company Springer Nature Switzerland AG
The registered company address is: Gewerbestrasse 11, 6330 Cham, Switzerland

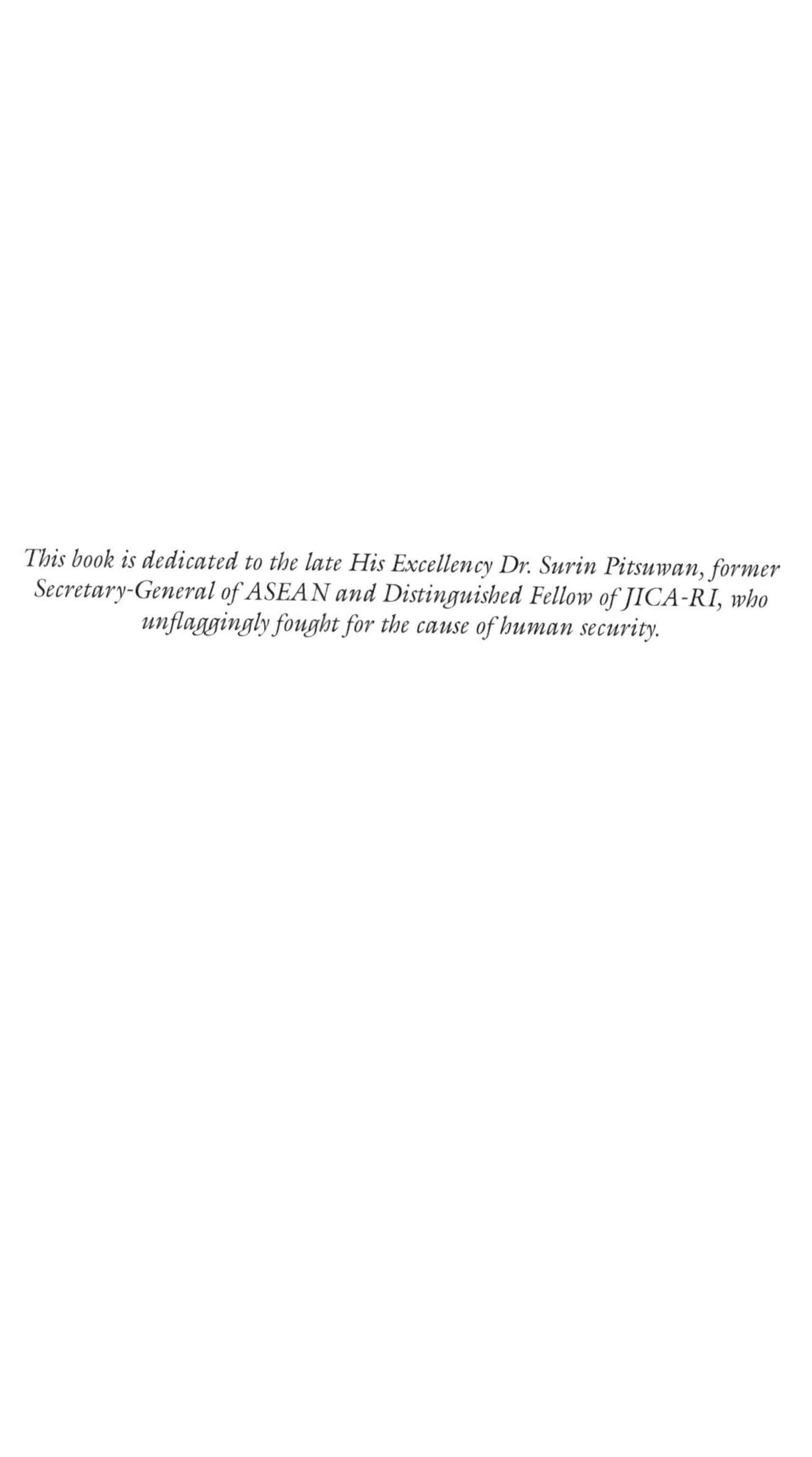

This book is dedicated to the late His Excellency Dr. Surin Pitsuwan, former Secretary-General of ASEAN and Distinguished Fellow of JICA-RI, who unflaggingly fought for the cause of human security.

Foreword

East Asia is a diverse and complex region with multiple challenges and vulnerabilities. Despite enjoying rapid economic development and relative peace after the Cold War, the region continues to face several threats to human security. While the entire East Asian region lacks a formal mechanism for regional collaboration to solve human security issues, the Association of Southeast Asian Nations (ASEAN) has developed its own way of gradual, consensus-based problem resolution, in contrast to aggressive intervention. The geographical proximity of East Asian countries necessitates horizontal collaboration to solve concrete issues and nurture the cultural norms of respecting differences and autonomy, while paying due respect to state sovereignty. Realizing closer regional cooperation means the certain ability to wield a larger international influence and create more effective solutions to regional and global challenges.

This book is the culmination of a five-year research project on how countries in the East Asian region have accommodated the concept of human security since the mid-1990s. The volume shows that the elements of the human security norm, namely, freedom from fear and want and the right to live in dignity, combined with protection and empowerment, are taking root in many East Asian countries. While the concept of human security may still lack the traction needed to integrate these elements into a single prevailing norm in the region, the institutional settings in various countries seem to provide a fertile ground for collaboration to realize human security in East Asia. For our part, JICA has prioritized human security by including it in its organizational mission: "realizing human security and quality growth."

With contributions from 24 East Asia-based scholars providing a kaleidoscopic view of the spread of human security norms in the region, this book is published at a time when globalization is experiencing setbacks and human security norms are being challenged. Learning from the experience of the diverse East Asian countries on how to realize human security will surely contribute to world peace and stability. This book can certainly help in our understanding of the regional dynamics of norm diffusion.

Along with this book that presents country-based research outcomes, another team of East Asia-based scholars is to publish a book on the issue-based state of the art of human security practice in the region, titled *Human Security and Cross-Border Cooperation in East Asia*. These books will, I am sure, complement each other successfully.

Chiyoda, Tokyo, Japan

Shinichi Kitaoka
President
Japan International Cooperation Agency

Acknowledgments

The Japan International Cooperation Agency Research Institute (JICA-RI) initiated the research project, *Human Security in Practice: East Asian Experiences Phase I*, on which the 11 case study chapters of this volume are based. The project would not have come to fruition without the invaluable guidance and cordial support given by successive Presidents of JICA, Madame Sadako Ogata, Dr. Akihiko Tanaka, and Dr. Shinichi Kitaoka, as well as Mr. Hiroshi Kato, Senior Vice President of JICA, and Dr. Naohiro Kitano, former Director of JICA-RI. Our heartfelt gratitude goes to Professor Keiichi Tsunekawa, Director of JICA-RI at the time of the project launch, who supervised this project when it was still a toddling child.

We are thankful to all contributors for their thoughtful and substantial revisions of their original working papers. We convened the first workshop of this project in Tokyo in November 2013, where we received insightful comments from distinguished participants, particularly Dr. Carolina Hernandez, Founding President of the Institute for Strategic and Development Studies (ISDS) Philippines. We could not have organized the project without her continuous engagement and support. We are grateful to the Centre for Strategic and International Studies (CSIS) Indonesia, as well as the ISDS, especially Ms. Clara Joewono for her insightful input to the research design, and to Mr. Allan A. delos Reyes for his logistical assistance. We offer local interviewees and researchers who assisted the chapter authors' research genuine thanks for their significant contributions to this project.

Finally, Mr. Yasuhiko Sato, the editor of JICA-RI, provided professional editorial support. Mr. Ryutaro Murotani and Dr. Atsushi Hanatani skillfully administered the project at JICA-RI. We greatly acknowledge the coordination work performed by JICA-RI Research Fellows, Research Officers, and Research Assistants at various stages, especially Ms. Sachiko G. Kamidohzono, Ms. Naoko Arakawa, Ms. Ayako Kono, and Dr. Rui Saraiva.

Yoichi Mine
Oscar A. Gómez
Ako Muto

Praise for *Human Security Norms in East Asia*

"An impressive array of top-quality case studies. Human security norms are localized and deeply rooted in economic and development strategy in East Asia. It is very timely to reflect the added-value of human security to the Sustainable Development Goals (SDGs): no one left behind."

—Yukio Takasu, *Special Advisor to the UN Secretary-General on Human Security*

"The definitive comparative analysis of the varieties of human security in East Asia over the last quarter-century. Demands by East Asians for dignity and agency advance redefinitions of human security, projecting the new South onto a problematic global scene."

—Timothy Shaw, *Visiting Professor, University of Massachusetts Boston, USA*

Contents

Notes on Contributors

Lina A. Alexandra is Senior Researcher in the Department of International Relations, CSIS, Jakarta. She is undertaking her Ph.D. at the School of Political Science and International Studies, University of Queensland, Australia. Her research areas are conflict resolution and non-traditional security issues. Some of her recent publications include: book chapters on "New Actors and Innovative Approaches to Peacebuilding: The Case of Myanmar" (co-authored with Marc Lanteigne) and "New Actors and Innovative Approaches to Peacebuilding: Indonesia" (both in 2017), and an article on "Indonesia and Responsibility to Protect" in *Pacific Review* 25(1) (March 2012).

Maria Ela L. Atienza is Professor and Department Chair at the Department of Political Science, University of the Philippines (UP) Diliman. She is Editor of the *Philippine Political Science Journal*, member of the Board of Trustees of the Institute for Strategic and Development Studies, former Director of the UP Third World Studies Center (2010–2013), and former President of the Philippine Political Science Association (2007–2009). She obtained her Executive Master's in International and European Relations (with distinction) from the University of Amsterdam, and her Ph.D. in Political Science from Kobe University. Her research interests include local politics, health policy, and human security.

Seon Young Bae graduated with a Master's in International Relations from the Graduate School of International Studies at Ewha Womans University, Rep. Korea, in 2016. She is working as Communication Officer of the International Committee of the Red Cross, Seoul Office. She has a strong research interest in human security and international relations.

Alice Beban is Lecturer in Sociology at Massey University, New Zealand. She holds a Ph.D. in Development Sociology from Cornell University (New York) and a Master's in Development Studies from Massey. Her research addresses land rights, agricultural production, and gender concerns to understand people's relationships with land. Her recent research investigates "land grabs" and land reform in Cambodia, and cross-border migration of smallholder farmers in Southeast Asia. She also works with community activist groups in Cambodia to strengthen people's access to land, and previously worked with Global Focus Aotearoa (New Zealand) and the Cambodian Institute for Cooperation and Peace (Cambodia).

Bich Thao Bui obtained her Master's in the Theory and Practice of Human Rights from the University of Oslo, Norway, in 2017. She participated in teaching activities of the master-level course on Law and Ethnic Affairs at the School of Law, Yunnan University, China. She spent two years working and researching at the Faculty of International Law, Diplomatic Academy of Vietnam (DAV). Prior to working at DAV, she completed the Lawyer Training Program at the Judicial Academy of Vietnam. Her research interests are in Public International Law, Law of International Organizations, Human Rights Law, and Humanitarian Law.

Belinda Chng is Director for Policy and Programs at the Milken Institute's Asia Center in Singapore. Prior to joining the Institute, she spent five years with the Rajaratnam School of International Studies at the Nanyang Technological University in Singapore, most recently as research fellow and program development manager. She has co-authored many analytical articles and reports, including papers commissioned by the Economic Research Institute for Association of Southeast Asian Nations (ASEAN) and East Asia, the JICA Research Institute, and the National Security Coordination Secretariat of Singapore.

Oscar A. Gómez (Ph.D. Tohoku University) is Assistant Professor at the College of Asia Pacific Studies, Ritsumeikan Asia Pacific University, previously Research Fellow at the Japan International Cooperation Agency

Research Institute (JICA-RI). His main interest is in global governance and human security practice, with special emphasis on the environment, migration, humanitarian crises, and international cooperation. He was part of a panel discussion at the United Nations (UN) on human security operationalization in 2013, and co-authored background papers for the 2014 and 2016 Human Development Reports. He has worked as a consultant for several UN agencies in Latin America. Besides this book, he recently co-edited a volume on crisis management beyond the humanitarian-development nexus, and is preparing new research on emerging powers and non-Western humanitarianism.

Sofiah Jamil is in the final stages of completing her Ph.D. thesis on Islamic environmentalism in Indonesia. Prior to pursuing her Ph.D. at the Australian National University, Sofiah was an Associate Research Fellow at the RSIS Centre for Non-Traditional Security Studies. She was conferred an M.Sc. (International Relations) from Nanyang Technological University, Singapore, in 2010. She also served on the Board of Management of the Young Association of Muslim Professionals in Singapore from 2008 to 2016. Her research interests include contemporary Muslim politics, human security, and environmental issues.

Surangrut Jumnianpol is Researcher and Deputy Director of the Chulalongkorn University Social Research Institute (CUSRI). Her areas of specialization are civil society, social capital, social justice, and human security. Her recent research focuses on deliberative democracy and global inequality. She has published several articles in these fields; her recent paper is *Can Deliberative Democracy Be an Alternative for the Twenty-First Century? A Case Study of Thailand in Globalization and Democracy in Southeast Asia* (2016).

Eun Mee Kim is Dean of the Graduate School, Professor and former Dean of the Graduate School of International Studies, and Director of the Institute for Development and Human Security at Ewha Womans University. Her research interests include East Asian development, development cooperation, globalization, multiculturalism, and *chaebol.* Her books include *Promoting Development: The Political Economy of East Asian Foreign Aid* (2017, co-authored with Barbara Stallings); *Big Business, Strong State: Collusion and Conflict in South Korean Development, 1960–1990* (1997). She received the Service Merit Medal from the Republic of Korea in 2012 for her contributions to the Fourth High-Level Forum on Aid Effectiveness.

Kaoru Kurusu is Professor in International Relations at Kobe University, Japan. Her current research interests are in human security, international relations theories, and Japan's multilateral diplomacy. Her publications include "Why Do Companies Join the United Nations Global Compact? The Case of Japanese Signatories," (with S. Miura) in K. Tsutsui and A. Lim eds, *Corporate Social Responsibility in a Globalizing World* (2015), and "Japan as a Norm Entrepreneur for Human Security," in M. McCarthy ed, the *Routledge Handbook of Japanese Foreign Policy* (2018).

Yoichi Mine is Professor at the Graduate School of Global Studies, Doshisha University, Visiting Fellow at JICA-RI, Secretary-General of the Japan Association for Human Security Studies, and Professor Extraordinaire at the Department of Political Science, Stellenbosch University, South Africa. His research interests include human security, international development, and African politics. His English publications include books such as Yoichi Mine, Frances Stewart, Sakiko Fukuda-Parr and Thandika Mkandawire eds, *Preventing Violent Conflict in Africa: Inequalities, Perceptions and Institutions* (Palgrave, 2013), and Scarlett Cornelissen and Yoichi Mine eds, *Migration and Agency: Afro-Asian Encounters* (Palgrave, 2018).

Ako Muto serves as Senior Research Fellow at JICA-RI, involved in research on human security, humanitarian crisis, and gender-based violence under conflict-affected situations. The Japan International Cooperation Agency (JICA) is a wing of the Japanese government tasked with providing bilateral Official Development Assistance (ODA) to developing countries. Prior to her current position, Muto served as Director of Gender Equality Division at the JICA head office and was Senior Representative in its Jordan Office. She obtained a Master's degree in History from the Graduate School of Culture, Keio University, Japan.

Thi Trang Ngo is Lecturer and Researcher at the International Law Faculty of the Diplomatic Academy of Vietnam, Ministry of Foreign Affairs of Vietnam. She has researched extensively on institutional aspects of the United Nations, Vietnamese perspectives on international trade under WTO Agreements, and recent new-generation Free Trade Agreements between Vietnam and its trade partners. She has also participated in projects on disaster risk management and dissemination of international humanitarian law in Vietnam. She holds Master's in International

Law and Economics from the World Trade Institute (WTI), University of Bern, Switzerland.

Ik Tien Ngu is Senior Lecturer in the Department of Chinese Studies at the University of Malaya. She holds a Ph.D. in Political Science. Her research addresses ethnicity, regionalism, and identity politics in Malaysia. Her works have been published in journals such as the *Inter-Asia Cultural Studies*, the *Asia Journal of Social Science*, *Southeast Asian Affairs*, *Universitas*, and others. She has also contributed chapters to the following titles: "Electoral dynamics in Malaysia: Findings from the grassroots" and "Electoral dynamics in Sarawak: Contesting developmentalism and rights," both published by the Institute of Southeast Asian Studies in Singapore.

Ngoc Lan Nguyen is Ph.D. candidate at the University of Cambridge (UK) and graduate research fellow at the Centre for Rising Powers. Before that, she was assisting an LLM class on settlement of disputes on the topic of "Recent Developments in International Dispute Settlement" and was lecturer and researcher at the International Law Faculty of the Diplomatic Academy, Ministry of Foreign Affairs of Vietnam. Her research interests are in Public International Law, Settlement of International Disputes, and Law of the Sea.

Thu Giang Nguyen has been working as a legal official in the Ministry of Foreign Affairs of Vietnam since 2015. There, she focuses on boundary issues and maritime cooperation. She is also Visiting Lecturer at the Diplomatic Academy of Vietnam (DAV), teaching public international law, the law of the sea, and international commercial law. She obtained an LLM in European and International Law from Ghent University, Belgium in 2016.

Nithi Nuangjamnong is Assistant Professor at the Department of Political Science and Public Administration, Faculty of Social Sciences, Naresuan University, in Phitsanulok, Thailand. His research interests cover comparative politics, international political economy, and East Asian studies. He has published more than 30 articles in these fields.

Lan Dung Pham is Secretary-General of the Vietnam Society of International Law and Director General of the Foreign Services Training Center, Diplomatic Academy of Vietnam (DAV). Her research interests lie in the Law of the Sea with respect to South China Sea disputes, legal aspects of the United Nations and its Security Council. She received a

Diploma in International Law from the Moscow State Institute of International Relations in 1993, a Master of Arts in Law and Diplomacy from Fletcher School of Law and Diplomacy, Tufts University, in 2002; and a Ph.D. in International Relations from the DAV in 2014.

Ji Hyun Shin graduated with a Master's in Development Cooperation from the Graduate School of International Studies at Ewha Womans University, Korea in 2016. She has worked at the Korea International Cooperation Agency (KOICA) and the Korea ExIm Bank. She has a strong interest in development cooperation research with a focus on Asian countries and on human security.

Pou Sovachana is Deputy Executive Director in Charge of Research and Publication at the Cambodian Institute for Peace and Cooperation (CICP). He taught at Paññāsāstra University of Cambodia for over four years and Zaman University for more than two years. He is the author of the books *The Voices of Change in Cambodia* and co-author of *Human Security and Land Rights in Cambodia*. He has written extensively, including various book chapters and articles, on the development of Cambodia and the region. His research interests include human capital development, peacebuilding, and human security.

Benny Cheng Guan Teh is Associate Professor at the School of Social Sciences, Universiti Sains Malaysia (USM), Penang, Malaysia. His research interests include East Asian regionalism, Association of Southeast Asian Nations (ASEAN) community building, traditional security, human security, and the politics of free trade agreements. He is the editor of the books titled *Human Security: Securing East Asia's Future* (Springer, 2012) and *Foreign Policy and Security in an Asian Century: Threats, Strategies and Policy Choices* (World Scientific, 2014).

Moe Thuzar is Lead Researcher (socio-cultural) at the Association of Southeast Asian Nations (ASEAN) Studies Centre of the ISEAS-Yusof Ishak Institute. She concurrently holds responsibilities as co-coordinator of the Myanmar Studies Programme at ISEAS. Prior to joining ISEAS, Moe headed the Human Development Unit at the ASEAN Secretariat, which coordinates regional cooperation on social and human development issues. A former diplomat, she is researching Myanmar's external relations in the post-World War II years for her Ph.D. dissertation.

Ren Xiao is Professor of International Politics at the Institute of International Studies (IIS), Fudan University, Shanghai, China, and Director of the Center for the Study of Chinese Foreign Policy. Previously, he was Senior Fellow and Director of the Asia Pacific Studies Department, Shanghai Institute for International Studies (SIIS). He worked at the Chinese Embassy in Tokyo from 2010 to 2012. His work has appeared in scholarly journals such as *The Pacific Review*, *Asia Policy*, *Third World Quarterly*, *Journal of Contemporary China*, and *East Asia: An International Quarterly*. He received his Ph.D. in Political Science from Fudan University in 1992.

List of Abbreviations

AADMER	ASEAN Agreement on Disaster Management and Emergency Response
ADFI	Assisi Development Foundation, Inc.
AFP	Armed Forces of the Philippines
AHRD	ASEAN Human Rights Declaration
AICHR	ASEAN Intergovernmental Commission on Human Rights
AIGE	ASEAN Institute on Green Economy
AMP	Association of Muslim Professionals (Singapore)
AP	Associated Press
APEC	Asia-Pacific Economic Cooperation Forum
APHR	ASEAN Parliamentarians for Human Rights
ARSA	Arakan Rohingya Solidarity Army
ASEAN	Association of Southeast Asian Nations
BR1M	Bantuan Rakyat 1Malaysia
BSPP	Burma Socialist Program Party
CARHRIHL	Comprehensive Agreement on Respect for Human Rights and International Humanitarian Law
CDAC	Chinese Development Assistance Council
CESD	Centre for Economic and Social Development (Myanmar)
CHS	Commission on Human Security
CIDC	Committee for International Development Cooperation (South Korea)
CNRP	Cambodia National Rescue Party
COMMIT	Coordinated Mekong Ministerial Initiative against Trafficking
CPF	Central Provident Fund (Singapore)
CSIS	Centre for Strategic and International Studies (Indonesia)
CSO	Civil Society Organizations

CSR	Corporate Social Responsibility
DDR	Disarmament, Demobilization and Reintegration
DFA	Department of Foreign Affairs (Philippines)
DfID	Department for International Development (UK)
DK	Democratic Kampuchea
DND	Department of National Defense (Philippines)
DPW	Department of Public Welfare (Thailand)
EASE	Enhancement for Active Seniors
EDCF	Economic Development Cooperation Fund (South Korea)
EITI	Extractive Industries Transparency Initiative
FESR	Framework on Economic and Social Reforms (Myanmar)
FGDs	Focus Group Discussions
FSI	Foreign Service Institute (Philippines)
FUNCINPEC	National United Front for an Independent, Neutral, Peaceful and Co-operative Cambodia
GDP	Gross Domestic Product
GIZ	Deutsche Gesellschaft für Internationale Zusammenarbeit (German Society for International Cooperation)
GMM	Global Movement of Moderates
GMS	Greater Mekong Sub-region
GST	Goods and Services Tax
GTP	Government Transformation Program (Malaysia)
HAKAM	National Human Rights Society (Malaysia)
HDB	Housing Development Board (Singapore)
HIV/AIDS	Human Immunodeficiency Virus Infection and Acquired Immune Deficiency Syndrome
HSN	Human Security Network
ICISS	International Commission on Intervention and State Sovereignty
ICRC	International Red Cross and Red Crescent
IDPs	Internally Displaced Persons
IHLCA	Integrated Household Living Conditions Assessment
IOM	International Organization for Migration
IPs	Indigenous Peoples
ISIS	Islamic State in Syria and Iraq
ISO-IPSP	Internal Security Operations-Internal Peace and Security Plan (Philippines)
IUUF	Illegal, Unreported and Unregulated Fishing
JBIC	Japan Bank for International Cooperation
JICA	Japan International Cooperation Agency
KIO	Kachin Independence Organisation
KOICA	Korea International Cooperation Agency

KPNLF	Khmer People's National Liberation Front
LDCs	Least Developed Countries
LGBT	Lesbian, Gay, Bisexual and Transsexual
MDGs	Millennium Development Goals
MEDCo	Mindanao Economic Development Council
MHA	Ministry of Home Affairs (Singapore)
MMO	Malay-Muslim Organization
MNCs	Multinational Corporations
MOFA	Ministry of Foreign Affairs (Japan; South Korea)
MOM	Ministry of Manpower (Singapore)
MOSF	Ministry of Strategy and Finance (South Korea)
MPs	Members of Parliament
MSDHS	Ministry of Social Development and Human Security (Thailand)
MUIS	Council of Islamic Scholars in Singapore
NAPC	National Anti-Poverty Commission (Philippines)
NESDB	National Economic and Social Development Board (Thailand)
NF	National Front (Malaysia)
NGO	Non-governmental Organization
NKRAs	National Key Results Areas (Malaysia)
NLB	National Library Board of Singapore
NLD	National League for Democracy (Myanmar)
NPAD	New Politics Alliance for Democracy (South Korea)
NPC	National People's Congress (China)
NSC	National Security Commission (China)
NSC	National Security Council (Philippines)
NTS	Non-traditional Security
ODA	Official Development Assistance
OECD	Organisation for Economic Co-operation and Development
OECD-DAC	Organisation for Economic Co-operation and Development-Development Assistance Committee
OPAPP	Office of the Presidential Adviser on the Peace Process (Philippines)
PAP	People's Action Party (Singapore)
PMC	Post-Ministerial Conference
PMO	Prime Minister's Office (Singapore; South Korea)
PRC	People's Republic of China
PRK	People's Republic of Kampuchea
PUP	Polytechnic University of the Philippines
R2P	Responsibility to Protect
RGC	Royal Government of Cambodia
SARS	Severe Acute Respiratory Syndrome

SDGs	Sustainable Development Goals
SINDA	Singapore Indian Development Association
SIS	Sisters in Islam (Malaysia)
SLORC	State Law and Order Restoration Council (Myanmar)
SMEs	Small and Medium Enterprises
SPDC	State Peace and Development Council (Myanmar)
SUARAM	Suara Rakyat Malaysia
SUHAKAM	Human Rights Commission of Malaysia
TCG	Tripartite Core Group
TIP	Trafficking in Persons
TPPA	Trans-Pacific Partnership Agreement
UEHRD	Union Enterprise for Humanitarian Assistance, Resettlement and Development in Rakhine
UN	United Nations
UNDP	United Nations Development Programme
UNGA	United Nations General Assembly
UNHCR	United Nations High Commissioner to Refugees
UNIAP	United Nations Inter-Agency Project on Human Trafficking
UNICEF	United Nations Children's Fund
UNODC	United Nations Office on Drugs and Crime
UNWFP	UN World Food Programme
UPR	Universal Periodical Review (UN Human Rights Council)
UPTWSC	University of the Philippines Third World Studies Center
USDP	Union Solidarity and Development Party (Myanmar)
WHO	World Health Organization
WMSU	Western Mindanao State University
WRI	World Resources Institute (Indonesia)
WV	World Vision (South Korea)

List of Figures

List of Tables

CHAPTER 1

Human Security in East Asia: Assembling a Puzzle

Yoichi Mine, Oscar A. Gómez, and Ako Muto

1.1 Human Security and Norm Dynamics

1.1.1 An Indelible Agenda

Human security was advocated by the United Nations Development Programme (UNDP) after the demise of the Cold War (UNDP 1993, 2–3; 1994, Chap. 2). A quarter of a century has passed since then, and some who were once enthusiastic about this concept no longer discuss it. However, when some lost interest, others took up the idea in other places.[1] It may thus seem to have faded out from time to time, but in reality, it did not. Where does this persistence come from?

Y. Mine (✉)
Graduate School of Global Studies, Doshisha University, Kyoto, Japan
e-mail: ymine@mail.doshisha.ac.jp

O. A. Gómez • A. Muto
Research Institute, Japan International Cooperation Agency (JICA), Tokyo, Japan
e-mail: oagomez@apu.ac.jp; Muto.Ako@jica.go.jp

Y. Mine et al. (eds.), *Human Security Norms in East Asia*, Security, Development and Human Rights in East Asia,
https://doi.org/10.1007/978-3-319-97247-3_1

Human security is an international norm concerned with global public interest, or a concept that aims to be an international norm such as human rights, the Sustainable Development Goals (SDGs), and corporate social responsibility (CSR). In general terms, norms denote codes of desirable (or undesirable) behaviors shared in a specific community. One of the strongest norms common in human society is that "homicide is evil." Even when the death penalty and war are allowed, they are considered exceptions to this norm. Written norms become statutes and formal regulations, while social consciousness supporting specific codes of conduct can also be called norms.[2] Normative sciences not only describe facts but also inquire into "how the object ought to be," covering logic, ethics, and aesthetics. The study of norms can be part of such an intellectual exercise: we describe and evaluate what people consider to be appropriate behaviors, nationally and internationally.

Let us try to answer the above question. Why does human security not fade out? It is because the international community needs this concept. Though not explicitly using this term, the UN can be thought of as being originally organized to realize human security beyond international security. The originality of human security as an international norm lies in its attempt to shift the referent object of security from "states" to "individuals" and to urge various actors to conduct themselves accordingly. The two world wars in the twentieth century claimed large numbers of human lives and stripped as many of their dignity and property in the all-out wars between nation states. In order not to repeat such calamities, the UN conferred on its Security Council the authority to limit the sovereignty of states threatening international peace and security and to impose military sanctions under international law. In the UN, state sovereignty is not necessarily an inviolable sanctuary, even though "non-interference" remains a major norm in international society.

It is often assumed that Hobbes' "realism" and Kant's "idealism" are poles apart. However, if the nation-state is invented to overcome the havoc caused by the war of every man against every man (Hobbes 1996 [originally 1651]), and a world federation is shaped to avoid the devastation caused by the war of every state against every other state (Kant 1977 [originally 1795]), these two world views are conterminous in a single spectrum. In this light, the ultimate objective of both nation states and international organizations is to realize the security of individuals by ensuring freedom for all people. Therefore, it is of pressing importance to evaluate government functions on the extent to which they serve this objective. Although we cannot deny the crucial roles of nation states and national governments, the strong nation states are those that effectively serve the security of individuals living in their territories, not those that demand citizens' sacrifice for state security too easily. In a nutshell, the normative message of human security boils down to a powerful proposition that the ultimate objective of governance at all levels is to provide security (or ensure freedoms) for every individual.

1.1.2 *Human Security as a "Norm-Complex"*

The core message of human security is thus very simple, but many other intentions and meanings have been subsumed in this concept along the way. If the objective is the security of individual persons, we must be able to characterize the core constitutive elements of such a secure state, as well as the principal means to achieve that goal, which can be described as norms themselves. Human security is being formed as a "norm-complex" in which different existing norms are combined and nested under the umbrella of human security (Kurusu 2005).[3] This hybrid nature of human security is observable in the consensus-based resolution on the definition of human security adopted by the United Nations General Assembly (UNGA) in September 2012.[4]

That resolution stipulates that human security is "an approach to assist Member States in identifying and addressing widespread and cross-cutting challenges to survival, livelihood and dignity of their people." According to the resolution, a common understanding on the notion of human security includes: "(a) The right of people to live in freedom and dignity, free from poverty and despair. All individuals, especially vulnerable people, are entitled to freedom from fear and freedom from want, with an equal opportunity to enjoy all their rights and fully develop their human potential." The resolution then enumerates certain qualifications of the concept: "(b) Human security calls for people-centred, comprehensive, context-specific and prevention-oriented responses that strengthen the protection and empowerment of all people and all communities," "(c) Human security recognizes the interlinkages between peace, development and human rights, and equally considers civil, political, economic, social and cultural rights," "(d) The notion of human security is distinct from the responsibility to protect and its implementation," and "(e) Human security does not entail the threat or the use of force or coercive measures" and "does not replace State security." Human security thus makes much of "national ownership," local contexts and bottom-up initiatives, and pays respect to all generations of human rights.

Based on the characterization of human security in past documents, including this UNGA resolution as well as the Commission on Human Security (2003) and UNDP (1993, 1994), we defined the practice of human security for the present research as follows: *to ensure three freedoms (freedom from fear, freedom from want, and freedom to live in dignity) for individuals and communities vulnerable to large-scale and cross-border threats, by combining protection from above and empowerment from below.* Although this definition may still feel too complicated, with careful attention, one finds that the concept has been made dynamic by incorporating new elements into a set of established norms. Let us discuss three points.

First, while taking the concept of "freedoms from fear and want" as a given, human security brought in the third element, "dignity." Realizing a world free from "fear and want" is the ideal of the Universal Declaration of Human Rights, and these two freedoms can be represented by civil liberties and socio-economic rights. They are embedded in the national constitutions of many nations as well as in international human rights law. On the other hand, dignity corresponds to a moral attitude when aiming at the realization of these freedoms: to express respect for humanity, recognizing that every human being has intrinsic worth (Rosen 2012). It is impossible to think of the human rights of the dead, even though we do think of the dignity of the dead. This is because dignity is a relational concept, and practical methods to respect the irreplaceability of others depend on local cultural contexts.[5]

Second, while human security does not deny the importance of protection, it incorporates the element of "empowering" people from below as a complement to protecting them from above. Empowerment is a process that enables people to become the masters of their own lives and may require the redistribution of power and resources between the powerful and the powerless. In the context of social development, Friedman (1992) developed a theory of empowerment focusing on community development and livelihood support. Women's empowerment has been incorporated into both the Millennium Development Goals (MDGs) and, more recently, the SDGs. Self-evaluation tools for empowerment processes have also been developed (Fetterman et al. 2015). If practitioners of human security want to translate empowerment into practice, it is important for them to unambiguously respect the agency of local people while avoiding their protracted dependence on assistance wherever possible. By reinforcing the power not only of individuals but also of communities and local governments, the excessive power of national governments can also be effectively checked. In human security, it is important to lower the level of the focus of empowerment from the national to the subnational and down to the community level.

Thus, in the human security discourse, by adding the concepts of dignity and empowerment, the elements of culture and agency have been grafted onto existing norms of human rights and humanitarian intervention. This deserves more attention as a new value that has been added to the human security idea. In East Asia, where social hierarchy is relatively strongly rooted, the concept of dignity based on the premise that individuals are embedded in society can be accepted more easily than the concept of empowerment that might "disturb" public order. However, as a counterbalance to public authorities' sometimes excessively paternalistic protection, the emphasis on empowerment is undeniably of great significance in this region.[6]

The third source of power that can dynamize human security is the awareness that human society is in danger. Mahbub ul Haq, a Pakistani economist and the first advocate of human security in the UN, wrote: "A powerful, revolutionary idea, the emerging concept of human security forces a new morality on all of us through a perception of common threats to our very survival (…) While great religions often move the human spirit through the sublimeness of their messages, they also carry in their messages the fear of eventual punishment. Much human change comes from a fear for human survival (Haq 1995, 116)." We cannot fully control the forces of nature or the fate of humanity. In envisioning a sustainable future for human beings and nature, the human security idea is expected to contribute to the realization of the SDGs through its emphasis on serious and pervasive threats (downside risks) and people's vulnerability to these.

Human security as defined in the UNGA resolution makes much of national ownership in organizing human security action. The implication of this approach will be discussed further in the rest of this volume.

1.1.3 Norm Dynamics

Modern international norms involving many and diverse stakeholders tend to be complex, which relates to the ways a norm is established. There is a normative process of norm-making: in other words, a desirable process that is the standard way of setting a new norm. Wise people may gather to put *bonum commune* of humankind into statutory forms and diffuse this downward. However, the actual processes of norm creation and diffusion are a little different. For an idea to be established as a norm, it must be internalized in the minds of the members of society irrespective of whether it is legally enforced or not. For this purpose, it is desirable for as many parties as possible at the center and at the periphery to actively participate in the process of norm-making instead of passively waiting for the advent of a new norm. In this process, both universal and local values tend to slot into a new norm, thereby making it hybrid, composite, or complex.

International norms are said to have life cycles. At the beginning, "norm entrepreneurs"[7] propose a new norm, which is accepted by several states (the norm emergence stage). Then, after a certain "tipping point," the norm diffuses quickly and prevails throughout international society (the norm cascade stage). Finally, the norm is internalized in every country and becomes "taken for granted" (the internalization stage) (Finnemore and Sikkink 1998). However, as clarified by Amitav Acharya in the case of the security regime in Southeast Asia, foreign norms may be opposed, modified, or displaced by existing local norms in local space. Norms are not simply accepted or rejected but are also localized (Acharya 2004; 2009). Conversely, new norms that are (re)created by local actors in the periphery may eventually reach the core nations and/or challenge global powers (Acharya 2011; Towns 2012). As indicated by the concept of *bricolage* in cultural anthropology (Lévi-Strauss 1962), people living in communities bring together various indigenous and foreign materials to ingeniously create a new modality of life. Proposed norms are to diffuse or fade out while being transformed vertically from the UN headquarters to a small village, and horizontally across diverse world regions and nations.

The process of initiation, diffusion, and regeneration of a norm is called "norm dynamics." As described above, the concept of human security was first advocated by a group of norm entrepreneurs at the UNDP, consisting of Mahbub ul Haq and others. After that, several countries including Canada reinterpreted the human security concept, and this gave rise to an offshoot norm called responsibility to protect (R2P), which defined the conditions for international society to intervene into a sovereign state with military and/or non-military measures to directly protect citizens from the horror of "genocide, war crimes, ethnic cleansing and crimes against humanity."[8] On the other hand, countries including Japan, Thailand, and the Philippines understood the nature of threats in broader and more comprehensive ways and tried to redefine human security to avoid confrontation between state sovereignty and humanitarian imperatives by emphasizing prevention and sensitivity to local contexts.

It should be noted that the comprehensive human security initiative of the latter group, maintaining the universality of UN-based messages, has passed through the process of localization in Asia. A radical change of international norms is often triggered by a dispute or a grave event (Sandholtz and Stiles 2009). The Prime Minister of Japan, Keizo Obuchi, officially advocated human security for the first time in Singapore in 1998 after the Asian financial crisis (he was Foreign Minister at the time) (Kurusu 2011). The Commission on Human Security, which released the final report on the comprehensive human security approach in 2003, was co-chaired by the former United Nations High Commissioner for Refugees (UNHCR) Sadako Ogata and the Nobel Prize-winning economist Amartya Sen, a combination of East Asian and South Asian universal figures (CHS 2003). Pitsuwan and Caballero-Anthony (2014) relate the effects of the financial crises, as well as the multiple humanitarian crises, that have made evident the significance of human security as a "compelling normative framework." Still, they argue "that as far as institutionalizing human security in its security practices, … ASEAN still has a long way to go," particularly because of gaps in economic security, protection from disasters and of minorities and migrants, among others.

In the rest of this introductory chapter, we discuss how the concept of human security has been received in East Asia in terms of the perspective of norm dynamics. What do Asian countries accept, reject, or remodel of the idea of human security born in the UN? In this book, the so-called ASEAN Plus Three countries (the member states of the Association of Southeast Asian Nations (ASEAN) plus China, Japan, and South Korea) is defined as East Asia. In this region that has experienced "miraculous" growth (World Bank 1993), the nexus between economic development and human insecurities is prominent.[9]

1.2 The Localization of Human Security

1.2.1 *Diffusion in Asian Settings*

Japan is not the only country that has accepted the human security norm in Asia. The late Surin Pitsuwan, a member of the Commission on Human Security and Distinguished Fellow of the JICA Research Institute, persevered in his effort to diffuse the concept of human security in Southeast Asia, serving as the Minister of Foreign Affairs of Thailand and then as Secretary General of ASEAN. As discussed in Chap. 11, in 2002 the government of Thailand set up the first government ministry in the world bearing the name of human security: The Ministry of Social Development and Human Security. In Thailand, knowledge on human security had been widely diffused among academic researchers, but the practice of human security canalized by the establishment of this ministry came to focus on the social welfare of the vulnerable: persons with disabilities, the elderly, children, women, and ethnic minorities.

The Philippines also paid attention to human security as soon as the 1994 UNDP report was released, and multiple efforts of localization can be enumerated, including the design of a "human security index." There have been attempts of co-option as well. An antiterrorism law called the "Human Security Act" was enacted in 2007, inviting criticism from Filipino civil society (Chap. 8). Application of the concept of human security in Thailand and the Philippines headed in the opposite directions of benign welfare and hardline public order.

The Chinese government does not often mention human security, but Chap. 3 argues that China articulates a vision similar to this concept and practices it without saying so. That is partly because China, a permanent member of the UN Security Council, is expected to promote international norms embraced by the UN system. The acceptance of human security by way of participation in multilateral stages is applicable to South Korea as well. In 2010, South Korea became a member of the Organisation for Economic Co-operation and Development-Development Assistance Committee (OECD-DAC). In addition, Ban Ki-moon promoted human security in his capacity as UN Secretary-General. Also, the government of South Korea has occasionally referred to the importance of human security in addresses by its President and Foreign Minister (Chap. 10).

Thus, in East Asia, several countries have accepted the concept of human security to varying degrees under government initiatives. In the meantime, local scholars have also accumulated academic inquiries. In addition to two major single-authored books (Howe 2013; Nishikawa 2010), a train of edited volumes on human security in the East Asian contexts has been published (Kassim 2011; Peou 2009; Teh 2012; Tow et al. 2000, 2013; Umegaki et al. 2009). Moreover, with relatively limited circulation, the proceedings, commentaries, and policy recommendations based on international conferences held in Bangkok, Seoul, Jakarta, and so on, have been published one after another (Banpasirichote et al. 2012; Hernandez and Kraft 2012; Thabchumpon 2012; UNESCO 2004, 2007; Wun'gaeo 2004). These publications have shared a certain feature: authors based in East Asia transmit messages mainly to readers within the region.

These earlier studies, especially most of the edited volumes, discuss how concrete issues can be interpreted using the concept of human security and how those issues can be addressed on the ground. However, there is little research that digs into the processes by which individual countries in the East Asian region have accepted the human security norm in their own ways. The country-by-country analyses in this book are expected to fill this gap.

1.2.2 *The Launch of Collaborative Work*

In 2003, when the final report of the Commission on Human Security was published, Sadako Ogata returned to Japan to take the helm of the Japan International Cooperation Agency (JICA). Under her presidency, the human security idea became embedded in the spirit of the agency. When a part of the Japan Bank for International Cooperation (JBIC) and JICA were integrated to set up the new JICA in 2008, the JICA Research Institute was established and launched several international research projects related to human security.

Then, in 2013, a research project to directly investigate the norm dynamics of human security in East Asia was set up. Based on a common questionnaire, researchers from 11 East Asian countries were to work on interview surveys and document research to elucidate the present status of human security in each country (see Fig. 1.1). The researchers participating in the project—the authors of the chapters in this book—are a combination of senior and young scholars specializing in international relations, political science, development studies and other disciplines and working for universities and think tanks in various parts of the region.

The researchers agreed to ask questions about the following three topics in the interviews: first, local perceptions of threats (the ranking of human security issues that are considered important in each country and in the East Asian region); second, the ways of (selective) acceptance of the concept of human security (the understanding of freedoms from fear, from want and to live in dignity, the strategy for combining protection and empowerment, and the understanding of preparedness for calamities, and so on); and third, the question of national sovereignty (whether to allow foreign actors to operate within the country in case of natural disasters and violent conflict, as well as whether to take action in territories of other countries in such a case). At the same time, respondents were allowed to change the combination of interview questions to adapt to their countries' unique circumstances. In addition, it was agreed that the researchers would welcome responses criticizing human security.

Fig. 1.1 Countries where case studies were conducted (Japan, China, South Korea, and several ASEAN countries: Indonesia, Cambodia, Singapore, Thailand, the Philippines, Vietnam, Malaysia, and Myanmar)

The interviewees included government officials, lawmakers, researchers at universities and think tanks, nongovernmental organization (NGO) activists, religious leaders, journalists, business persons, and international organization staff. Though they were not necessarily statistically representative, in-depth interviews were conducted (some of the survey activities included anthropological interviews with villagers in the countryside and focus group discussions). The interviews reached more than a hundred, and two workshops for chapter authors were organized in Tokyo and Manila. In the next section, we put together the research outcomes in the light of norm dynamics, including the localization processes.

1.3 The Current Status of Human Security in East Asia

1.3.1 Perceptions of Threats

First, let us think about what threats to human security we face. Classifying the sources of threats to human security into those derived from the physical system (the earth), from the living system (animals and plants), and from the social system (human beings), Akihiko Tanaka called for a clearer understanding of the mechanism in which these threats bring about human insecurities. To that end, close collaboration between different academic disciplines including the natural sciences and engineering, the biological and ecological sciences, and the social sciences and the humanities is required (Tanaka 2015).

In our surveys of the 11 East Asian countries, local experts were asked to enumerate the threats to human security. Though priority ranking varies from country to country, an integrated list of threats arranged according to the above three systems can be as follows: climate change, typhoons/cyclones, floods, volcano eruptions, earthquakes, tsunami, infectious diseases such as Severe Acute Respiratory Syndrome (SARS), avian influenza and HIV/AIDS, food crises, lack of basic health and education, environmental pollution, urbanization, extreme poverty, unemployment, migration, human trafficking, violent conflicts, interstate military conflicts, religious intolerance, organized crime, oppression from the government, and so forth.

Meanwhile, the UNDP's *Human Development Report 1994* listed seven main categories of human security: economic, food, health, environmental, personal, community, and political security (UNDP 1994, Chap. 2). In the case studies of Cambodia (Chap. 2), Thailand (Chap. 11), the Philippines (Chap. 8), and Vietnam (Chap. 12), human security challenges are classified in line with these seven categories. These areas correspond not only to the divisions of the UN Specialized Agencies but also to government ministries, so that the classification could be accepted as familiar and practical.

Such a diversity of threats largely overlaps with the so-called non-traditional security (NTS) issues. While military threats from foreign states are considered "traditional," many threats that simultaneously affect multiple countries are of a non-military nature and fall into the category of "non-traditional" threats. As pointed out in the cases of China (Chap. 3),

Indonesia (Chap. 4), Malaysia (Chap. 6), the Philippines (Chap. 8), South Korea (Chap. 10), and Vietnam (Chap. 12), there is growing interest in NTS among policymakers and researchers in China, South Korea and in the ASEAN countries, which seems to have contributed to the acceptance of human security in the region (Caballero-Anthony et al. 2006; Caballero-Anthony and Cook 2013; Li 2010). However, there is substantial difference between the NTS and the human security approach: while the actors that address such diverse threats still concentrate on the national governments in the former, more emphasis is placed on peer collaboration between states and other actors in the latter. The role of national armies in coping with human security challenges should be limited. Chapter 4 presents the opinion of an Indonesian military officer who argued that the term "security" should not be used until the poverty level or the impact of a disaster exceeded a certain threshold and becomes a real threat to the survival of all citizens. If every threat was considered a security challenge, the military would be overwhelmed by the resulting deluge of duties.

Human security is regarded as a principle of official development assistance (ODA) policies in Japan, and to a lesser extent, in South Korea. As described in Chap. 5, in Japan, the idea to combine efforts toward development and peacebuilding has gradually taken root under this framework. As an added value of human security, Japanese interviewees emphasized the importance of a "comprehensive approach" in which diverse actors (including NGOs and private firms) cooperate, as well as the significance of working among grassroots people and paying more attention to real needs in the field. Meanwhile, most experts pointed out that human security challenges lie on the domestic front, too. People who were familiar with the concept of human security interpreted the Great East Japan Earthquake and the resultant Fukushima disaster as a typical human security issue. In addition, the aging population and a possible collapse of social security in the future can also be serious domestic human insecurity issues.

In terms of domestic human security challenges, the case of Singapore as presented in Chap. 9 is also revealing. While Singapore has achieved a high degree of human security as a developed country in Southeast Asia, this small city-state is also going through acute human insecurities such as growing inequalities, increasing psychological stresses on citizens, the survival race between small enterprises, and discrimination against migrants and minorities. Here, social media cuts two ways by spreading messages virally: it can mobilize good will but may also deeply wound people. In Singapore, with strong administrative control from above, empowerment is supposed to be of great significance. Besides, Singapore assists neighboring countries in the form of philanthropy, even though this is not officially classified as ODA. It is pointed out that the Philippines has also provided humanitarian assistance while receiving assistance itself (Chap. 8). In the Great East Japan Earthquake, Japan, a major provider of ODA, received goodwill support from many countries including recipients of Japan's assistance (Chap. 5). It is noteworthy that the line separating providers from recipients of ODA is blurred in the case of humanitarian crises.

A country that has faced a series of exceptionally acute threats to human security is Cambodia (Chap. 2). This country is considered "a showcase of human insecurities" that started with the genocide under the Pol Pot regime (it is said that around 2 million people were killed in a country with a population of 8 million). The interviewees enumerated contemporary sources of threats in Cambodia such as the government, natural disasters, diseases, political insecurity, and land issues. Some respondents pinpointed the problem of the "government approach, relying on the heavy presence of security forces and legal means to threaten and detain people." It is widely perceived that Cambodian society has been destabilized and that human security has been threatened despite (or due to) recent economic growth.

One of the topical concerns in East Asia that has wider political implications is the North Korean issue (Chap. 10). An emergency on the Korean Peninsula could bring about an exodus of refugees and other situations, which may potentially give rise to grave human insecurities both regionally and globally. The risk of military conflict over maritime interests could also be a threat to human security, as voiced by several countries. The necessity to address cross-border issues such as human trafficking, air pollution, infectious diseases, food security, and cybersecurity was also pointed out by many interviewees.

1.3.2 *The Parts and the Whole*

How far has the concept of human security permeated East Asian countries so that stakeholders can jointly address the multiple threats described thus far? As pointed out in those chapters that discuss the experiences in the Philippines (Chap. 8), Malaysia (Chap. 6), and Thailand (Chap. 11), East Asian experts did not fully understand the difference between human security and human rights or human development, while activists in civil society tended to use the discourse of human rights more often than that of human security. However, even though the human security norm has not prevailed in East Asia, the concept has been accepted at least partially, as argued in several of the case study chapters.

The survey carried out in Vietnam (Chap. 12) broke down human security into the seven security categories of the UNDP and found that all these elements were inscribed into the Vietnamese Constitution and other laws. In addition, even when interviewees were not familiar with the concept of human security, they "were able to quickly connect the abstract concepts of 'freedom from fear', 'freedom from want', and 'freedom to live in dignity' to specific examples in their lives." Human security in Vietnam "can be said to be a jigsaw puzzle, in which the pieces are identified, but have not been put together." The surveys in Indonesia (Chap. 4) and South Korea (Chap. 10) also found, by examining official documents, that the elements of human security defined in this chapter, such as the three freedoms, protection, and empowerment, were all written into these documents to varying degrees (the former in domestic policies and the latter in ODA policies). In addition, people who were interviewed in Cambodia pointed out that the three freedoms were closely linked to each other in substance (Chap. 2).

What is the most important element among the components that make up human security? The study of Japan (Chap. 5) presented the expert opinion that the third "freedom to live in dignity" could be a real added value of the human security approach, indicating that "dignity is an idea of waiting and caring." The survey in the Philippines also mentioned that the concept of dignity had potential to lead human security to a higher dimension and emphasized the importance of local contexts. Moreover, people in Cambodia said that having dignity is associated with "having a moral character; with notions of respect, pride, and having value and independence; and of helping others and having an honest character." A rural resident made a candid remark: "Dignity is most important because it is about no discrimination, having rights to do what we want, not being looked down upon by wealthy people."

While the expectation of state protection was found in many interview results, empowerment was mostly referred to in general terms. However, protection and empowerment make an effective pair in reality. Empowerment leads to a series of concepts that value people's agency, such as ownership, self-help support, resilience, and capacity development in the practice of development cooperation, while the same concept is expected to promote collaboration between governments and civil society in domestic policies. Given that the Asian approach to human security tends to give relative weight to the role of states as discussed below, the counterbalance of empowerment is needed all the more in this region.

1.3.3 *Human Security and State Security*

In many countries, we also asked the interviewees whether foreign support should be accepted in case their own country suffers an uncontrollable crisis due to a natural disaster or violent conflict (and whether their country should support neighboring countries in case the latter suffers the same situations). The common pattern of responses to these hypothetical situations was that foreign support was undesirable during political unrest but welcome when a natural disaster occurs. It was also preferred that the support should be provided in multilateral rather than unilateral frameworks, as mentioned in the studies on Malaysia (Chap. 6), the Philippines (Chap. 8), and Vietnam (Chap. 12). These reactions illustrate that East Asians tend to think that state security could be compromised in favor of humanitarian concerns in certain emergency situations, especially in case of natural disasters. It should be remembered that Sadako Ogata stressed that human security and state security complement one another (Ogata 2003).[10]

As to the role of states in realizing human security, both a loose consensus and a subtle disagreement could be found among East Asian countries. The case study of China argues as follows (Chap. 3). On the one hand, we can establish the causal connection that state security contributes to human security. The idea that people should not be easily sacrificed for national objectives is absolutely correct because human beings are not means but ends in themselves. On the other hand, national security and personal security can be compatible. The perception that states are a "necessary evil" is not a Chinese but a Western idea. East Asians naturally expect a great deal from their governments: people expect the governments to protect them just like parents protect their children. This represents a view of states as benevolent and "paternalistic." The relationship in which a stable state guarantees people's security is also expressed in the case study of Vietnam (Chap. 12).

On the "right" of this view of states, there is another understanding that human security is part of state security, that is, state security subordinates human security, not vice versa. In this research project, such a view was expressed by government officers from Indonesia (Chap. 4) and Malaysia (Chap. 6). From the government side, however, some added that the role of the military in human security should be strictly limited. Indonesian interviewees opined that military operations should be firmly placed under civilian control, even though the military effectively responded to the earthquake and tsunami in 2004. This is because they consider that the military is essentially not trained to respond to non-military threats, and it is often better to entrust the duty of maintaining public order to police forces in disaster situations.

On the "left" side, there are countries with impressive traditions of civil society activism such as the Philippines (Chap. 8) and Thailand (Chap. 11), which have strongly influenced the trajectories of acceptance of human security. In the case studies of Malaysia (Chap. 6) and Singapore (Chap. 9), dynamic and strained relationships between the government and civil society are vividly depicted. The chapter on Malaysia places expectations in consolidating human security through empowerment of local governments, more active dialogues between the government and civil society, and regional cooperation through the networks of ASEAN and NGOs, against the backdrop of the government repression of free speech, religious intolerance, and the surge of Rohingya refugees.

When severe threats to human security are actualized, the relationship between state sovereignty and human security may become extremely tense. As described in Chap. 7, when Cyclone Nargis hit Myanmar in 2008, the military government refused to accept foreign aid, even while lowland residents were caught in the flooding. It is said that the dead and missing persons numbered nearly 140,000. Though Western countries such as France threatened to make a R2P-type humanitarian intervention, the government of Myanmar rejected such operations and instead decided to accept coordinated assistance from organizations such as ASEAN and the UN. This multilateral collaboration has become a model for humanitarian operations in East Asia.

The case study of Japan (Chap. 5) warns that the concept of human security could be "politicized" in the contexts of domestic debates on security and securitization. In contrast, the study of Thailand (Chap. 11) voices concern that human security is now too "depoliticized," arguing that the concept has been reduced to the practice of social welfare and is now rarely discussed in Thai diplomatic contexts. However, behind the activities of the Ministry of Social Development and Human Security seeking to improve the well-being of the socially vulnerable seems to lie the Buddhist concept of mercy as well as an attempt to integrate human security with the concept of sufficiency economy advocated by King Rama IX. These dynamics of politicization, depoliticization, and local reinterpretation are interesting in terms of the "norm localization" discussed in this chapter.

Keeping in mind the urgent problems including land grabbing and King Sihanouk's political legacy in Cambodia, Chap. 2 emphasizes the importance of "cooperative leadership" based on the spirit of tolerance and compromise. The key to ensuring human security in Cambodia is to realize voluntary collaboration among opposing political parties, between the government and civil society, and between the central and local governments, and to make the government listen to the voice of the people.

Different countries have different perceptions as to which state and non-state actors should be valued as against others. However, we can safely say that there is a shared understanding in the region that diverse actors, including national governments, should coordinate each other's activities to secure freedoms and development for individual persons in the face of serious and pervasive threats.

1.4 Conclusions

Just as a world where autonomous villages cease to make decisions on their own affairs is hard to imagine, it is unlikely that the governments of nation states will cease to make their own decisions. National governments are important because most of them have strong powers and the authority to ensure security for individuals by utilizing well-developed institutions, resources, and national cohesion. However, overly powerful state security mechanisms require an antidote, which can be the human security norm. As history illustrates, when pluralist thinking that endorses critical roles played by non-state actors is denied, the world as well as national politics go awry.[11]

The purpose of the association of world peoples is not only to promote the security of nations but also to ultimately promote the security of all human beings. In this sense, the Security Council of the UN could be renamed a Human Security Council. In the practice of human security, neither "Western individualism" nor "Oriental despotism" is required in their pure forms; it seems that Asian versions of human security have begun walking along the middle road between the two. In East Asian nations, perceptions of diverse threats as sources of insecurities largely overlap, and therefore the conditions for collective action to address common threats also seem to be maturing.

Even though the term human security is not officially used very often, in this research it was found that the constituent elements of human security, namely, the three freedoms as well as protection and empowerment, have been accepted more or less in all parts of East Asia. If regional spaces for dialogues are provided, the human security idea may diffuse in the short term like a cascade. An international network of experts sharing the value of a specific norm and assuming key roles in its diffusion as well as policy coordination is called an epistemic community (Haas 1992). In the process of this research, we witnessed the emergence of a bridged community with a shared interest in human security in East Asia. The process of this research endeavor itself might be part of the formation of such a community.

Lastly, we would like to pay notice to the fact that the outcomes of this research reflect not only East Asia's potential unity but also its actual diversity. Once we zoom in to the regional space of East Asia, we can see a kaleidoscopic diversity of human security stakeholders and their values. This is the reason why this book is entitled *Human Security Norms* rather than *The Human Security Norm*. The latter is only in the making: there remain forces that resist the idea of human security, while East Asian nations are developing their own human security norms with different interpretations and preferences.

The country-by-country analyses in subsequent chapters are based on independent research, which seems to have succeeded in shedding light upon the diversity of the history, society, and political economy of the region. The chapters are arranged in the alphabetical order of countries, so readers can start with any chapter while referring to the comparative analysis in Chap. 13. We return to the issue of East Asia's diversity in Chap. 14, in which we will suggest a direction to proceed with the practice of human security in this region.

Notes

1. Martin and Owen (2014) present a stock-taking collection of reflections on the concept and its application. Bourbeau (2015) captures the multidisciplinary nature of the study of security, including human security.
2. In international relations, norms are defined as "shared expectations about appropriate behavior held by a community of actors" (Finnemore 1996, 22) or "collective expectations for the proper behavior of actors with a

given identity" (Katzenstein 1996, 5). Criticizing the proposition that human rights make sense only when they are legally guaranteed, Amartya Sen argues that strong moral imperatives of what to do and not to do make up human rights. These imperatives may call for legislation, but legal provision is not a prerequisite for human rights (Sen 2009, 355–87). As in the case of human rights, a set of moral judgments often precedes the formalization of norms.

3. See also the discussions of "composite norms" in Betts and Orchard (2014).
4. United Nations General Assembly, Follow-up to paragraph 143 on human security of the 2005 World Summit Outcome, 6 September 2012, A/66 L.55/Rev.1. See also the website of the UN Trust Fund for Human Security: http://www.un.org/humansecurity/
5. For this reason, when translating the notion of dignity into practice, it is essential to gain insights into non-Western value systems, as demonstrated by Debes (2017) and Düwell et al. (2014). The concept of dignity was explicitly introduced to the human security discourse in the Commission on Human Security (2003) as one of the triad of "survival, livelihood and dignity."
6. Dignity has long been debated in bioethics and philosophy of law, but it has not yet permeated the study of development and peace building. However, Annan (2005) has introduced "freedom to live in dignity" into the agenda of the UN reform, and Tadjbakhsh and Chenoy (2007) have attempted to incorporate dignity fully into the human security perspective. On the other hand, while the concept of empowerment is widely diffused in social movements in the Americas and South Asia, East Asians still seem to be hesitant to fully discuss its implications.
7. After a norm is established by idealistic "norm entrepreneurs," a different group of pragmatic actors called "message entrepreneurs" start negotiating a consensus to give a concrete shape to the norm (Fukuda-Parr and Hulme 2011), as the drafters of the 2012 UNGA resolution did in the UN.
8. United Nations General Assembly, 2005 World Summit Outcome, 15 September 2005, A/60/L.1, paras. 138–9.
9. Human development and human security correspond to the upside and the downside of economic growth, and to the dual policy challenges of "growth with equity" and "downturn with security" (Sen 2003). See also Chap. 13.
10. For the role of states to promote human security, see Bae and Maruyama (2015), a collaborative work by American and Japanese scholars of human security.
11. The criticism of political pluralism by Carl Schmitt (Schmitt 1976 [originally 1932]) was typically a product of the time of state nationalism on the eve of the Second World War.

References

Acharya, Amitav. 2004. How Ideas Spread: Whose Norms Matter? Norm Localization and Institutional Change in Asian Regionalism. *International Organization* 58 (2): 239–275.

———. 2009. *Whose Ideas Matter? Agency and Power in Asian Regionalism.* Ithaca: Cornell University Press.

———. 2011. Norm Subsidiarity and Regional Orders: Sovereignty, Regionalism, and Rule-Making in the Third World. *International Studies Quarterly* 55: 95–123.

Annan, Kofi A. 2005. *In Larger Freedom: Towards Development, Security and Human Rights for All: Report of the Secretary-General.* New York: United Nations Department of Public Information.

Bae, Sangmin, and Makoto Maruyama, eds. 2015. *Human Security, Changing States and Global Responses: Institutions and Practices.* Abingdon, Oxon: Routledge.

Banpasirichote, Chantana, Philippe Doneys, Mike Hayes, and Chandan Sengupta, eds. 2012. *Mainstreaming Human Security: Asian Perspectives.* Bangkok: Chula Global Network and International Development Studies Program, Chulalongkorn University.

Betts, Alexander, and Phil Orchard, eds. 2014. *Implementation and World Politics: How International Norms Change Practice.* Oxford: Oxford University Press.

Bourbeau, Philippe, ed. 2015. *Security: Dialogue across Disciplines.* Cambridge: Cambridge University Press.

Caballero-Anthony, Mely, and Alistair D.B. Cook, eds. 2013. *Non-Traditional Security in Asia: Issues, Challenges and Framework for Action.* Singapore: Institute of Southeast Asian Studies.

Caballero-Anthony, Mely, Ralf Emmers, and Amitav Acharya, eds. 2006. *Non-Traditional Security in Asia: Dilemmas in Securitization.* Aldershot: Ashgate.

CHS (Commission on Human Security). 2003. *Human Security Now.* New York: Commission on Human Security.

Debes, Remy, ed. 2017. *Dignity: A History.* Oxford: Oxford University Press.

Düwell, Marcus, Jens Braarvig, Roger Brownsword, and Dietmar Mieth, eds. 2014. *The Cambridge Handbook of Human Dignity: Interdisciplinary Perspectives.* Cambridge: Cambridge University Press.

Fetterman, David M., Shakeh J. Kaftarian, and Abraham Wandersman, eds. 2015. *Empowerment Evaluation: Knowledge and Tools for Self-Assessment, Evaluation Capacity Building, and Accountability.* 2nd ed. Thousand Oaks: Sage.

Finnemore, Martha. 1996. *National Interests in International Society.* Ithaca: Cornell University Press.

Finnemore, Martha, and Kathryn Sikkink. 1998. International Norm Dynamics and Political Change. *International Organization* 52 (4): 887–917.

Friedmann, John. 1992. *Empowerment: The Politics of Alternative Development.* Cambridge, MA: Blackwell.

Fukuda-Parr, Sakiko, and David Hulme. 2011. International Norm Dynamics and the 'End of Poverty': Understanding the Millennium Development Goals. *Global Governance* 17 (1): 17–36.

Haas, Peter M. 1992. Introduction: Epistemic Communities and International Policy Coordination. *International Organization* 46 (1): 1–35.

Haq, Mahbub ul. 1995. *Reflections on Human Development*. New York: Oxford University Press.

Hernandez, Carolina G., and Herman Joseph S. Kraft, eds. 2012. *Mainstreaming Human Security in ASEAN Integration* (three volumes). Quezon City: Institute for Strategic and Development Studies.

Hobbes, Thomas. 1996. *Leviathan*. Oxford: Oxford University Press.

Howe, Brendan. 2013. *The Protection and Promotion of Human Security in East Asia*. Basingstoke: Palgrave Macmillan.

Kant, Immanuel. 1977. Perpetual Peace: A Philosophical Sketch. In *Kant's Political Writings*, ed. H.S. Reiss, 93–130. Cambridge: Cambridge University Press.

Kassim, Yang Razali, ed. 2011. *Strategic Currents: Issues in Human Security in Asia*. Singapore: S. Rajaratnam School of International Studies and Institute of Southeast Asian Studies.

Katzenstein, Peter J. 1996. Introduction: Alternative Perspectives on National Security. In *The Culture of National Security: Norms and Identity in World Politics*, ed. Peter J. Katzenstein, 1–32. New York: Columbia University Press.

Kurusu, Kaoru. 2005. Development of Human Security 'Norm' and Global Governance: How is a Norm-Complex Constructed in World Politics? *Kokusai Seiji (International Relations)* 143: 76–91.

———. 2011. Japan as an Active Agent for Global Norms: The Political Dynamism Behind the Acceptance and Promotion of 'Human Security.' *Asia-Pacific Review* 18 (2): 115–137.

Lèvi-Strauss, Claude. 1962. *La pensée sauvage*. Paris: Plon.

Li, Mingjiang, ed. 2010. *China and Non-Traditional Security in Asia*. London: Routledge.

Martin, Mary, and Taylor Owen, eds. 2014. *Routledge Handbook of Human Security*. London: Routledge.

Nishikawa, Yukiko. 2010. *Human Security in Southeast Asia*. London: Routledge.

Ogata, Sadako. 2003. Human Security and State Security. In *Human Security Now*, ed. Commission on Human Security, 5. New York: Commission on Human Security.

Peou, Sorpong, ed. 2009. *Human Security in East Asia: Challenges for Collaborative Action*. London: Routledge.

Pitsuwan, Surin, and Mely Caballero-Anthony. 2014. Human Security in Southeast Asia: 20 Years in Review. *Asian Journal of Peacebuilding* 2 (2): 199–215.

Rosen, Michael. 2012. *Dignity: Its History and Meaning*. Cambridge, MA: Harvard University Press.

Sandholtz, Wayne, and Kendall Stiles. 2009. *International Norms and Cycles of Change*. New York: Oxford University Press.

Schmitt, Carl. 1976. *The Concept of the Political*. Trans. George Schwab. New Brunswick: Rutgers University Press.

Sen, Amartya. 2003. Development, Rights, and Human Security. In *Human Security Now*, ed. The Commission on Human Security, 8–9. New York: Commission on Human Security.

———. 2009. *The Idea of Justice*. Cambridge, MA: Belknap Press of Harvard University Press.

Tadjbakhsh, Shahrbanou, and Anuradha M. Chenoy. 2007. *Human Security: Concepts and Implications*. Abingdon, Oxon: Routledge.

Tanaka, Akihiko. 2015. *Toward a Theory of Human Security*, JICA-RI Working Paper 91. Tokyo: JICA-RI.

Teh, Benny Cheng Guan, ed. 2012. *Human Security: Securing East Asia's Future*. Dordrecht: Springer.

Thabchumpon, Naruemon, ed. 2012. *Critical Connections: Human Rights, Human Development and Human Security*. Bangkok: Chula Unisearch, Chulalongkorn University.

Tow, William T., Ramesh Thakur, and In-Taek Hyun, eds. 2000. *Asia's Emerging Regional Order: Reconciling Traditional and Human Security*. Tokyo: United Nations University Press.

Tow, William T., David Walton, and Rikki Kersten, eds. 2013. *New Approaches to Human Security in the Asia-Pacific: China, Japan and Australia*. Harnham: Ashgate.

Towns, Ann E. 2012. Norms and Social Hierarchies: Understanding International Policy Diffusion 'From Below. *International Organization* 66 (2): 179–209.

Umegaki, Michio, Lynn Thiesmeyer, and Atsushi Watabe, eds. 2009. *Human Insecurity in East Asia*. Tokyo: United Nations University Press.

UNDP (United Nations Development Programme). 1993. *Human Development Report 1993*. Oxford: Oxford University Press.

———. 1994. *Human Development Report 1994*. Oxford: Oxford University Press.

UNESCO (United Nations Educational, Scientific and Cultural Organization). 2004. *Proceedings of the International Conference on Human Security in East Asia*. Seoul: Korean National Commission for UNESCO.

———. 2007. *Proceedings of the ASEAN-UNESCO Concept Workshop on Human Security in South-East Asia*. Jakarta: ASEAN-UNESCO.

World Bank. 1993. *The East Asian Miracle: Economic Growth and Public Policy*. Oxford: Oxford University Press.

Wun'gaeo, Surichai, ed. 2004. *Human Security Now: Strengthening Policy Networks in Southeast Asia*. Bangkok: Center for Social Development Studies, Chulalongkorn University.

CHAPTER 2

Human Security Problems in Cambodia: Far from Over

Pou Sovachana and Alice Beban

2.1 Introduction

Perhaps no other country on earth has suffered so much from as many forms of human insecurity as Cambodia has. The list of atrocities from the 1970s is a showcase of human insecurities: massive bombardments, civil and interstate wars, the "killing fields," human rights violations, disease, starvation, displacement of people, one of the world's highest rates of deforestation, grinding poverty, as well as land grabs have ravaged this once-proud and influential country of Southeast Asia. Conflict plagued Cambodia from the 1970s to the late 1990s. Today, if we use traditional security measures that focus on stability and freedom from violence and conflict, Cambodia might seem like a secure country. Nonetheless, hundreds of thousands of people have been forcibly removed from their land

P. Sovachana (✉)
Cambodian Institute for Cooperation and Peace, Phnom Penh, Cambodia
e-mail: cicp01@online.com.kh

A. Beban
School of People, Environment and Planning, Massey University Albany, Albany, New Zealand
e-mail: a.beban@massey.ac.nz

Y. Mine et al. (eds.), *Human Security Norms in East Asia*, Security, Development and Human Rights in East Asia,
https://doi.org/10.1007/978-3-319-97247-3_2

and lack the means of subsistence, while still more die every year from preventable illnesses, lack of sanitation, and food insecurity. People suffering from a precarious existence are unable to enjoy full security in their lives. Thus, a human security approach can reveal the interconnected threats that prevent people in Cambodia from realizing their full human potential (UNDP 1994).

In this chapter, we aim to understand how the Cambodian people perceive and interpret human security and insecurity. We argue that interconnected, multidimensional insecurities in Cambodia can be revealed by taking a broad approach to human security. It is by recognizing the interdependent relationships between "freedom from fear" and "freedom from want," and in the added dimension of "freedom to live in dignity," that we believe the concept of human security is most useful in Cambodia (Nishikawa 2009, 2010).

Below, we first explore the human security situation in Cambodia today by tracing human security issues from the Khmer Rouge regime until the present. The second section presents our findings from primary research. We conducted semi-structured interviews and focus group discussions to understand how different groups perceive the human security concept and threats to it, and how they feel human security threats can be mitigated. This study was limited by time and geographic constraints, and the results are not generalizable to Cambodia's population. Rather, we analyze some of the main themes that arose from this exploratory research and suggest future policy and research priorities.

2.2 The Continual Unraveling of Human Security in Cambodia

The Khmer Rouge isolated Cambodia from much of the world, destroying key social-cultural institutions and economic activities in a reign of terror and violence between 1975 and 1979. Between 1.7 million and 2.5 million people out of a 1975 population of roughly 8 million lost their lives (Heuveline 1998, 52). This tragedy continues to live on in the hearts and minds of many Cambodians and, when added to its aftermath, has had dire consequences in terms of human security. In December 1978, the Vietnamese invaded Cambodia, ousted the brutal regime, and installed a new government in Phnom Penh. Throughout the 1980s, government forces engaged in frequent and fierce battles with Khmer Rouge units, which continued to terrorize the Cambodian countryside. The Khmer

Rouge, as well as the successive Heng Samrin and Hun Sen regimes, planted millions of land mines across the country and continued to displace citizens.[1]

Political instability and human insecurity did not end with the Vietnamese ouster of the Khmer Rouge but persisted throughout socialist rule. Vietnamese forces pulled out of Cambodia in 1989. After years of tense negotiations, the United Nations broached a peace agreement in Paris on October 23, 1991, between the People's Republic of Kampuchea (PRK) and the three resistance factions: National United Front for an Independent, Neutral, Peaceful and Co-operative Cambodia (FUNCINPEC) founded and led by Norodom Sihanouk, the Khmer People's National Liberation Front (KPNLF) led by former Prime Minister Son Sann, and Democratic Kampuchea (DK) led by Pol Pot. This treaty enabled the United Nations Transitional Authority in Cambodia (UNTAC) to undertake a massive peacekeeping operation, and to call and supervise a national election in May 1993. From a human security perspective, the Paris Peace Agreement promised to usher in a brighter chapter in Cambodian political history. However, UNTAC was not completely successful in its mission for peace and disarmament (Sundaranaman 1997).

In the aftermath of the 1993 election, a coalition government headed by a system of two incompatible prime ministers was formed between the FUNCINPEC and the Cambodian People's Party (CPP). In 1997, Second Prime Minister Hun Sen used his loyal military force to oust First Prime Minister Prince Norodom Ranariddh, which resulted in the death, torture, or arrest of more than 200 people loyal to the prince (Reaksmey 2014). Conflict between the two main political parties persisted, and security threats from the Khmer Rouge remained high until its final disintegration in early 1999 and the monopolization of power by Prime Minister Hun Sen.

Cambodia's long-desired peace ushered in an era of rapid economic development. Economic growth averaged 7.9 percent during 2000–2012 (CDRI 2014), and the poverty rate dropped drastically from 47.8 percent in 2007 to about 14 percent in 2017 (ADB 2017), making Cambodia one of the best performers in poverty reduction worldwide. Cambodia's improvement in economic growth and poverty reduction is, however, precarious. A World Bank Poverty Assessment report warns that, despite impressive reductions in poverty, these hard-won gains are fragile. Many people who have escaped poverty are still at high risk of falling back into poverty. For example, the loss of just 1200 Riels (about $0.30) per day in income would throw an estimated 3 million Cambodians back into poverty, doubling the poverty rate to 40 percent (World Bank 2014, 1).

The human security concept itself is not well known in Cambodia and the discourse is little used in policy, but human security-related concerns are considered by the Royal Government of Cambodia (RGC) to be the highest priority. According to the Ministry of Planning Guidelines for Formulating the National Strategic Development Plan (NSDP 2014–2018), the Government of Cambodia is committed to ensuring a better quality of life for its people, and to building a democratic, rule-based society, with equitable rights and opportunities for the population in terms of economic, political, cultural, and other spheres (Ministry of Planning 2014). In 2013, a workshop on human security in Phnom Penh brought together policymakers and academics for the first time to discuss the concept and its implementation in Cambodia. The ruling party chairman of the Commission of Human Rights was positive about the concept being a "social revolution for the 21st Century" with its focus on "problems of individual life and dignity rather than weapons" (Southeast Asia Weekly 2013).

Human security issues remain, however, and are becoming harder to disguise under the veil of economic advancement. Despite strong economic growth indicators and sensitive government policies, the cost has been rapid environmental degradation, limited liberties, and a profoundly unequal distribution of wealth. The overall development of human security in Cambodia remains far from ideal and thus requires an explanation (Peou 2014). There are profound and widening inequalities of wealth between rich and poor, and rural and urban areas. Social injustice also continues to be a common experience in the daily life of the people due to a lack of proper individual protection and ineffective governance. For years, Transparency International (2014) has ranked the country as one of the most corrupt nations in the world. Furthermore, Cambodia's judicial system is generally recognized as lacking both legal know-how and political independence. In recent years, there has been a surge in forced displacement of rural and indigenous communities resulting from large-scale land concessions granted by the government for agribusiness, what scholars and activists term "land grabs." Since 2000, Amnesty International estimates, about 420,000 people have been affected by forced evictions to make way for development projects that are said to be in the "national interest" but are invariably also very much in the business interests of senior members of the regime (Gregory 2013, 1). This land-grabbing issue is the latest example of the state struggling to meet the needs of its citizens and the growth expectations of the international community. Community needs as basic as providing clean water, decent housing, health care, social justice, and education are undercut by the need to increase gross domestic product (GDP) and to de-regulate social services.

Political insecurity and human rights abuses are also currently evident. After the national election in 2013, post-election violence led to the death of seven people and to dozens more being injured. And in 2014, garment workers, a group who suffer from poor work conditions as global garment manufacturers leverage cheap Cambodian labor, went on strike to demand a living wage of $160. The protests turned fatal as the military police used AK-47 rifles to fire bullets directly into a crowd, some of whom were throwing rocks and Molotov cocktails (Pheap 2014). In 2017, in the lead up to the 2018 national election, the ruling party arrested the opposition Cambodia National Rescue Party (CNRP) leader Kem Sokha, shut down human rights non-governmental organizations (NGOs) and independent media outlets, and stepped up its surveillance of activists. As the campaign against civil society and free expression intensified in November 2017, the Supreme Court made a landmark decision to dissolve the CNRP and banned 118 senior political party officials from engaging in politics for five years. This final dismantling of the only real challenger to Hun Sen's grip on power has serious implication for Cambodia's democratic development and creates grave consequences for human security. Political repression and military intervention might stop the uprisings, but stability established by using direct oppression and bullets is unlikely to last for long.

In summary, according to the government and the international community, the indicators for human security in Cambodia are positive. One might conclude that more Cambodians have enjoyed better security in the last two decades in terms of freedom from fear and freedom from want. But the reality on the streets is different for many people. Rapid and unchecked economic growth in the absence of pro-poor policies continues to threaten the lives and livelihoods of Cambodian people in ways that do not correspond with the positive reports of rising GDP and per-capita income levels. In a public forum on land issues, one indigenous representative summarized the gravity of another type of human suffering in Cambodia by saying: "All this development is destroying our lives."[2]

2.3 Methodology

We undertook focus group discussions and in-depth interviews to understand how human security and its threats are perceived and interpreted by different stakeholders in Cambodia. One methodological issue was related to how the concept of "human security" should be translated into Khmer. The Khmer language has several words that can be translated as security, but each has different nuances. These include *santesok* (referring to peace, and freedom from violence and fear), *sawatapeap* (safety), and *sekadae sok* (a deeper, broader concept of security encompassing spiritual dimensions). We focused on *santesok* as participants were comfortable discussing this concept, but we used all three terms during interviews to elicit responses that covered a broad understanding of security. Interview participants included:

- Three key policymakers from the central government, including both ruling party (CPP) and opposition party (CNRP) members of the National Assembly;
- A rural village chief;
- Three academics who teach and conduct research in Phnom Penh;
- Three civil society organization representatives working on programs relevant to human security;
- Four media representatives who report on areas relevant to human security;
- A focus group comprising six monks from a Phnom Penh temple and an interview with a senior monk;
- A focus group of four university students in Phnom Penh and two interviews with rural and urban university students; and
- Three focus groups; each composed of between 8 and 12 people from lower socio-economic strata. One group discussion was held in Phnom Penh and two held in rural areas of Kampong Chhnang Province, an area that faces multiple human security threats, including climate change-related threats, poverty and land dispossession, and deforestation.

In Cambodia's increasingly repressive political situation, our research participants took risks in openly sharing their views with us. To protect their anonymity, we have chosen not to provide full references of names and job titles for our research participants.

2.4 Knowledge and Definition of the Human Security Concept

2.4.1 *Knowledge*

Most research participants had not heard of the human security concept. A Member of the National Assembly suggested that the concept is gaining traction in Cambodia in some areas of government, as he has now heard the term used in political debate several times after first hearing it two years ago: "It gives voice to concerns we already had but did not have a name for." He described Cambodia as being on track to implement human security in the post-conflict shift from concerns over stability to concerns for people, and noted that Cambodia has "reached the first step" of putting the concept into the constitution: "Article 20 and Chapter 3 talks about the security of the people in the form of human rights, right to live, right to survival, and right to have good health, and the right to speak." He recognized, however, that the challenge (as also voiced by those in other sectors) is putting the policy into practice: "This just gives us a road map; now, how do we get there?"

The human security concept was most familiar to civil society organizations with ties to international human rights-based donors. One NGO director said that she was familiar with the concept and had used it to frame a program that encompassed land rights and environmental activism. The director of an international NGO with a country office in Phnom Penh said the NGO has established the position of "Human Security Officer" in Cambodia, following a directive from its head office. This position was originally conceived to encompass a broad scope including natural disasters, conflict and violence, and human rights advocacy. However, the NGO found it difficult to work with such a broad concept and gradually shifted the position to focus on natural disasters. The director noted: "Like the word accountability, human security sounds good in theory but is difficult to work with in practice." She suggested that the term needs to be well defined for specific contexts so that it does not become mainstreamed "without real meaning."

2.4.2 *Definitions of Human Security*

Among the government representatives, the notion of state protection was central to their definitions of human security: "Human security is everything we do to guarantee the well-being, the safety, the needs, or the survival of the people" (Member of the National Assembly, CPP). A Member of the National Assembly from the opposition party (CNRP) reflected on human security as intimately tied to economic development—"the prosperity of the nation." While other participants' definitions also focused on economic security, freedom from fear was also emphasized. One journalist from the Phnom Penh Post described human security as "being free from danger and fear, both social and human," and another journalist noted that "even if we have money, if we have fear we cannot have security." These narratives suggest a tension between the state's goals for economic development and poverty reduction, and the negative impacts of these same development processes for social and environmental justice.

The notion of people's participation in governance was a common theme in definitions of human security. A reporter from The Phnom Penh Post defined human security as "referring not to the armed forces but to the participation of the people," and others talked of "being able to have a voice in our country" and "feeling safe to speak out." Safety in daily life was another central theme; rural focus groups talked of human security as the ability to "go anywhere without fear of harm of violence" and as having "no gangsters in our community." Definitions of human security as security from threats by wealthy people and government officials were expressed in all three focus groups consisting of lower socio-economic urban and rural people.

For many people in our study, the cultural and moral dimensions of security were central. Participants described human security not only in terms of "freedom from…" but also in positive terms: rural focus groups spoke of "helping, supporting and loving each other," and the urban focus group described charity, tolerance, and honesty as central aspects. People's strength and resilience came through strongly in the focus groups; for example, a participant from one rural focus group who was struggling with land eviction said that despite their fear of land loss, "they have fifty percent security because they love and support each other." While "empowerment" and "protection" are often thought of in secular terms, several participants focused on spiritual and religious discourse, and the notion of culturally specific moral codes to define human security. When asked to define human security, one economics professor described the concept as an "outside power, physical power, spiritual power, and soul power"; another professor described it as "every institution that relates to life including food, spirit, emotional, and physical matters." This points to the importance of trust and solidarity in making people feel secure, notions which are often minimized by the human security concept's focus on "freedom from…." Indeed, the human security concept offers little guidance on how to move beyond "not fearing people" to trusting them to act responsibly and in one's interests.

2.4.3 *The Three Dimensions of Human Security*

We asked participants to discuss which aspect of human security they emphasized the most (freedom from fear, freedom from want, or freedom to live in dignity), and categorized responses into four categories as shown in Fig. 2.1.

Participants often described "freedom from want" as the most pressing of the concerns. One Member of the National Assembly for CPP said: "Countries that are in conflict need to focus on freedom from fear, but now in Cambodia we need to focus on freedom from want first, and freedom to live in dignity. The government is pushing this through the economic growth strategy." Health concerns were also a common reason for

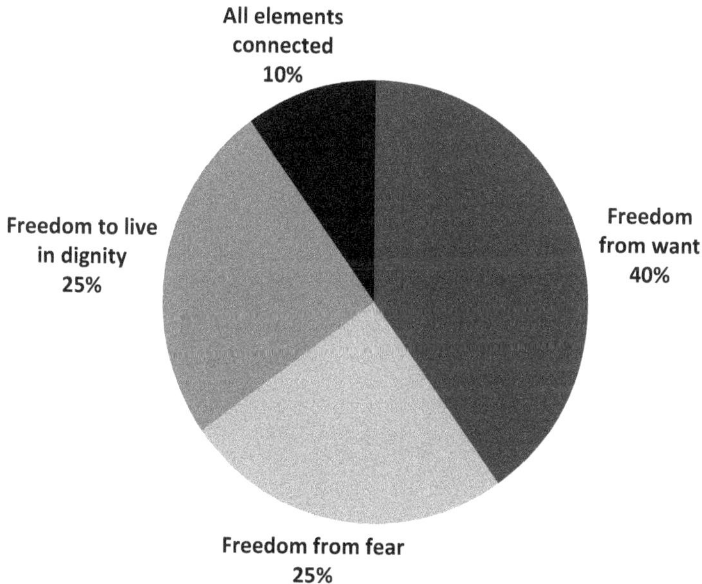

Fig. 2.1 Interviewee responses to the question: Which element of human security do you emphasize? (N = 42)

people emphasizing freedom from want. Rural focus group participants suggested that: "Freedom from want is most important for daily life, including having enough money to afford health care, good food, and being free from illness and disease."

Freedom from fear was also emphasized, and many participants in all sectors described the fear they feel in daily life. One academic voiced an opinion we heard often: "Freedom from fear is most important because fear could cause people to lose everything, including fear to speak, to stand up for our rights." A monk described his fear of being threatened by government officials and suggested that, "while the people and monks are being threatened, the freedom to live in dignity cannot happen." For him, as for some other participants, fear of large-scale conflict has declined since the 1990s, but fear of speaking openly is still felt strongly due to the threat of violence.

Several respondents felt that dignity is at the core of the concept of human security. Having dignity was associated by many participants with having a moral character, with notions of respect, pride, and having value and independence, and of helping others and having an honest character. One rural focus group participant suggested: "They are connected; if there is no fear, we can have dignity. Dignity is most important because it is about no discrimination, having rights to do what we want, not being looked down upon by wealthy people." Participants in the lower socio-economic urban focus group recalled times when they lost their dignity, such as begging for loans or money, and noted that, "when people are in need, they also lose their dignity."

Given the continued prevalence of poverty in Cambodia, it is not surprising that many participants suggested freedom from want is most important. As Nishikawa (2009, 213) notes in her analysis of human security in Southeast Asia, the Cambodian government has explicitly focused on freedom from want rather than freedom from fear; this has the benefit of reducing poverty rates and maintaining a high economic growth rate. However, this has been achieved in part through the creation of fear rather than through lessening fear in society. One civil society representative described this situation as the government focusing only on protection rather than on the bottom-up empowerment aspect of security: "Security in Cambodia is seen as the need to protect. Security equals military. This is the same for all ASEAN countries… Security is fear. Hun Sen uses infrastructure and security as his political manifesto when he says that at least things are better now than under Pol Pot. But people won't accept this anymore, they want more than this." A large part of this shift is the huge cohort of young people who have no memories of the Khmer Rouge period or even of civil war. In this way, both socio-economic class and generation play into perceptions of desirable security.

An important question that arose in these narratives is the interconnections between the three dimensions of human security, and whether there are trade-offs to be made by focusing on one or the other dimension. The CPP Member of the National Assembly suggested that there is a necessary trade-off between the three dimensions: "It's three-dimensional… If you push too hard, then the freedom from fear relaxes and what happens then? And if you focus on the right of expression, then you lose the freedom from want." We interpret this perspective as suggesting that freedom of expression may hinder development goals. This view could be seen, for example, in concerns from some government participants that ongoing public demonstrations by garment workers demanding higher wages may scare investors away. However, other participants felt that the different dimensions can be mutually strengthening, because when they can avoid poverty and fear, they will have freedom to live in dignity. Students spoke about the connections of these elements in the difficulties facing young people in Cambodia today: "They are all connected… After we graduated from school, we don't know where we should go and what we should do, the public service is not transparent; we face discrimination in getting public sector jobs. The problems of daily living and security will affect the next generation."

2.5 Human Security Threats in Cambodia

We asked participants whether they felt secure and what were the most important urgent and long-term human security threats facing Cambodia. No participant said they felt completely secure; participants spoke ambivalently of their relief that the country is no longer in conflict and has achieved stability, and of their continued insecurity in daily life. When asked if they felt that human security was better now than five years ago, participants offered conflicting responses, with around half of the participants feeling that the situation now was better and half feeling that it was unchanged or worse. We analyzed the key themes in people's descriptions of human security threats (Fig. 2.2). The major threats identified include: fear of government authorities/powerful people, and threats of natural disasters, poor health, political instability, as well as land shortages. It is interesting that more people raised fear-related threats as the biggest

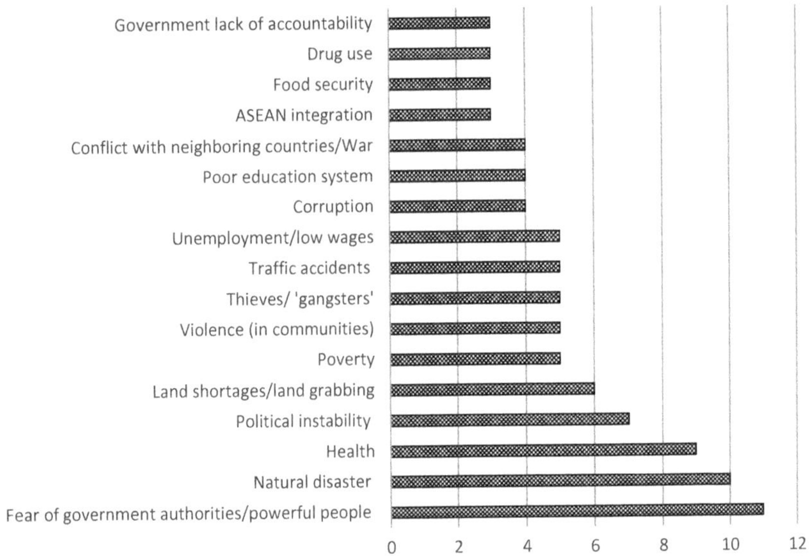

Fig. 2.2 Interviewee responses to the question: "What are the biggest threats to human security in Cambodia?" (N = 42)

threat to human security (such as fear of authorities and powerful figures), even though more participants prioritized "freedom from want" rather than "freedom from fear." However, we see this not so much as a contradiction but as a response to the way the state uses a fear-based government approach, relying on the heavy presence of security forces and legal means to threaten and detain people who protest the government's development objectives.

2.5.1 *Fear of Authorities*

The most common threat was fear of government authorities and powerful people, and fear of speaking out. Several participants described this fear as in part stemming from the aftermath of the Khmer Rouge regime, such as a newspaper reporter who said: "People are fearful; this is left from the period of conflict…At the same time, Khmers help each other." One academic described this threat as stemming from a lack of moral values: "I don't have any individual security because I live with fear; I'm afraid of the authorities not respecting human rights. Cambodians do not give value to Cambodia itself." Closely connected to this threat, many participants talked about the threat of political instability. A student described the situation as "getting more violent; the police and army are using more and more violent means to stop the protesters, but the protesters are desperate, they demand change… This relates to the security of the country, and to the security of the people. And it relates to freedoms; because the people are protesting to have freedom from want (proper wages, land) but when the government cracks down on the protest, people can't have freedom."

Several participants connected their discussion of fear of authorities with the threat of corruption. A journalist suggested that "the main threat comes from the society that teaches us that power comes through corrupt practices and nepotism," and one student echoed many participants' connections between corruption and inequality: "Here there is too much freedom in the sense that some people have freedom… the wealthy have freedom in the law… Even if we have the courage to complain, they know that probably nothing will happen… So, Cambodia is a great place to live for the wealthy. And a difficult place to live for the poor." While most participants focused on the role of the state in corruption and nepotism and instability, one civil society representative spoke reflectively of the role of the international community in promoting development policies "aligned with the neoliberal belief that GDP trickles down when the country isn't ready."

2.5.2 *Natural Disasters*

Both rural focus groups discussed the threat of natural disasters, including climate change, and specifically floods and drought, as among the greatest threats they faced. Indeed, the country was recently rated as the most vulnerable country in the world to the effects of climate change (Morton 2014). A ruling party Member of the National Assembly also suggested that humans create the threat of "natural" disasters through natural resource extraction, arguing that "people are responsible. When they want something too fast it destroys the balance of nature." This Member of the National Assembly said that people can adapt when natural disasters happen slowly, such as in droughts, but in a sudden disaster, the government and international community need to step in. One NGO director argued that in fact it is the slow disasters that are most threatening over the long term: "People are usually more resilient to flooding because they are used to it, but not droughts. That's what drives internal migration the most. There is no government support for this long-term problem of drought. And it impacts women the most."

2.5.3 *Health Threats*

All three of the lower socio-economic focus groups focused heavily on health concerns as threats. This was not only the threat of becoming sick but also connected with the fear of abuse by powerful people, as several people revealed a lack of trust in the medical system, and the high costs of health care. The rural focus groups discussed fear of doctors refusing to treat them if they could not pay, of distrust for the medical system, of overworked medical personnel, and most importantly, of lacking the money to be treated. A specific health concern mentioned by several participants was the threat of traffic accidents. This can be understood given the context of Cambodia's high rate of road accidents and deaths. Traffic accidents have increased by more than 200 percent in recent years and on average almost five people die in traffic accidents each day, with increasing numbers of automobiles and lax enforcement of traffic laws taking their toll (Cambodia Ministry of Public Works 2012).

2.5.4 *Land Shortages/Land Grabbing*

In most rural focus groups and among state and civil society stakeholders, many people spoke of the threats of land shortages and land conflicts and discussed the long-term consequences of land grabbing and land shortages for their children's futures, particularly as these issues intensified migration out of the country. In one rural commune where land had been confiscated for a state development project, the participants said they lack security due to their land being confiscated so they are concerned about having no land to give to their children. One civil society representative described how the notion of a rural safety net promoted by some donor agencies is becoming less viable as many people lose access to land. She suggested that the country needs to prioritize investment in agriculture for smallholder farmers, then some people can "stay in agriculture and make a decent living, and others can have a platform to move out."

2.5.5 *Political Instability*

Several participants in media, government, and student sectors focused primarily on the threat of political instability. For some participants, it seems that political rivalry (arguably born of democratization) is perceived as a threat rather than as a part of the democratization process. Participants, from government to rural focus groups, spoke of the need for reconciliation between the two main parties, with the focus largely on compromise as the way forward rather than ongoing oppositional politics or debate. Some argued that the increasing number of young people and rising unemployment/low-wage employment creates frustration and the potential for increased violence and instability. Some people tied the issue of youth unemployment and instability to problems within the education system: "The biggest long-term security issue is the young population; the population is growing, but there are no jobs" (NGO director).

2.6 Achieving Protection and Empowerment: Whose Responsibility Is Human Security?

Those attempting to operationalize human security at the national and international level disagree on what the concept encompasses, how it should be achieved, and about who should be responsible for it. The Commission on Human Security (2003) suggests "protection" (shielding people from danger) and "empowerment" (ensuring people develop human potential and participate in decision making) strategies to achieve human security. We asked participants whom they felt was most responsible for ensuring human security, and what the role of different stakeholders should be.

Most participants felt that the state is most responsible for ensuring human security, although some saw the state's role as a protector and others emphasized the need for the state to promote empowerment for people to actively participate in mitigating threats. Several people likened the state to a parental figure whose duty it is to protect the population: "Whenever the children have an argument, the parents have to reconcile and that is the responsibility of the government" (a journalist). This recalls the paternalism that the former popular Cambodian King Sihanouk played to and suggests a cultural value of a benign paternalistic monarch that does not necessarily mesh with Western ideas of empowerment.

Others portrayed a very different way of understanding government responsibility, speaking of the need to participate in elections and protests to increase respect for rights, and to encourage the government to respect the law. Young people, and educated urban people, were particularly strong in their notions of holding the government to task for its actions. Others argued that "we can't always rely on the State, so we have to learn how to act on our own" (a journalist) and that the government needs to "create an enabling environment for people to act" (an NGO member). Many of the participants suggested ways that they themselves and people in their communities could mitigate threats to human security, including participating in civic affairs. Both rural focus groups suggested that they could help mitigate threats by reducing chemical use in agriculture, sharing ideas and advice to solve common problems, communicating with local authorities, and generally being tolerant and supportive of others. The lower socio-economic focus group in Phnom Penh spoke of their capacity to reduce violence and of the need for people to join together to strengthen their voices, but they also felt their power is limited and good leadership within the central government is most important.

Many participants suggested that both government and people themselves are responsible for human security, and it is the cooperation and interdependence of people and the state that is most important. This theme of cooperative, interdependent relationships for human security came through in many interviews, with participants in civil society and government describing the need for linkages between local, national, regional, and global partnerships, and the need for truly global relationships to tackle global challenges such as climate change. One NGO director suggested that many of Cambodia's human security issues cannot be solved domestically, for they are linked to global flows of trade and aid such as land grabbing linked to international investment and commodity consumption. Therefore, more cooperation and pressure on global players to adopt socially and environmentally just practices need to be part of a broad strategy to ensure human security. The rural focus groups expressed similar concerns that their own actions were insufficient due to global commodity flows. As one farmer said, even if they reduce chemical use, the country still imports chemical-heavy fruit and vegetables from other countries, so the agricultural policy needs to change if the farmers are going to be able to change themselves.

2.7 The Need for Cooperative Leadership

Many participants, such as those in the urban focus group, described the need for cooperation and tolerance between the political parties, and between civil society and government to mitigate threats of political instability. Participants described themes of "cooperative leadership," "compromise," "engagements," and "recognizing the constraints of others" as essential for moving toward a system where different interests can work together. This non-confrontational, conciliatory attitude has a long history in Cambodia, and was used famously by King Sihanouk to attempt to avoid becoming drawn into conflict by cultivating relationships with both sides, and by Hun Sen to bring the former Khmer Rouge into the folds of government after the civil war. More generally in Cambodian society, conciliation and harmony are valued highly, and outright debate and hostility is discouraged (Gellman 2007).

We feel that there is an important lesson here for the human security discourse, for in stressing the need for tolerance and compromise, along with the paternalistic notion of government, some participants were essentially describing political rivalry itself as a human security threat rather than as a sign of a participatory democracy. This is perhaps not surprising given Cambodia's long history of hierarchical, authoritarian monarchs and leaders, and its desire to avoid further conflict; it suggests that Western notions of democratic leadership may not be understood in the same way in this very different cultural and historical context. This strategy can successfully reduce conflict, but it can also breed frustration since anger may be buried and resurface later. A Member of the National Assembly said: "We have to eliminate all the misunderstandings between the two parties, then the two parties have to listen to the people, then you come up with something that could serve the benefit of the people." The member was unclear, however, about how "misunderstandings" would be resolved in a way that promotes multiparty democracy and debate rather than continued one-party dominance.

Many stakeholders spoke of the need for continued strengthening of competent leadership in Cambodia. Leadership in this case was described not only as Western values of engagement, transparency, and responsibility, but also as Buddhist values of morality and notions of patrimonial protection. Several interviewees argued that developing more rules and laws was not enough, because without good morals to underpin them, people would twist the laws to their benefit. These moral values were described by monks in the focus group as "starting from yourself, with a good education, morality and mind." One older monk described the basis of good morality from Buddhist discourse as central to effective leadership, which includes (1) avoid taking the life of beings; (2) avoid stealing; (3) avoid sexual misconduct; (4) avoid telling lies; and (5) avoid taking intoxicating substances.

Some participants linked the need for the government to listen to the voices and concerns of people with long-term threats to the broader Cambodian economy. One student suggested that the government must hear what the people want. "People have things they lack and those that they want. If we do not have secure communities, the investment will not come, the factories will go elsewhere, people will be poorer. So, having a more responsive government is the main thing, and the freedom of speech to tell the government what we think."

To achieve human security through cooperative leadership, several people talked about the importance of education, including both a quality, inclusive formal schooling system and informal, community-based knowledge sharing to be aware of rights and responsibilities and to better communicate with other stakeholders. Several participants described the need to up-skill the population before ASEAN integration, to reduce the risk of further out-migration of low-skilled Cambodian workers. Students in a focus group suggested that improving education and wages were essential for reducing the urban/rural achievement gap, with one saying that: "I strongly believe that if people are paid a fair wage, they would not have to engage in so much corruption. And we must improve the wages at the same time as we put more effort into improving the quality of education, especially for rural children so they can achieve the same as the urban children."

2.8 Conclusions

Our research suggests that replacing older realist discourses of state security with the concept of human security provides a promising way to open new kinds of conversations with local people about the insecurities they experience, and the hopes they hold for the future. In general, all of those whom we asked about the relevance and usefulness of the concept of human security for Cambodia found it helpful for identifying their security concerns and reflecting upon their aspirations for a better future. Many referred to issues such as freedom of speech, human rights, and lives of dignity as important for a peaceful future in Cambodia. Clearly shifting the focus of security from being a referent object of the state to that of the individual human being has strong resonance for people from all walks of life.

Despite its rhetorical appeal, though, there are problems with the concept of human security. First, several of our respondents pointed out that the real difficulty lies in putting the concept into practice, not only by designing policies and regulations, but by translating these into human behavior. As some of our informants indicated, the problem is not a lack of laws and regulations but the lack of shared values. As consumerist values seep into every area of Cambodian life, many Cambodians continue to refer to the Buddha's teachings as a moral compass for the control of greed and for the creation of an inclusive "imagined community" for Cambodia's future. This sort of attitude should alert us to the risks of Eurocentric attitudes in the concept of human security, and to the importance of listening to indigenous experience and ways of formulating hopes of a more secure future.

Second, it is clear from our interview material that the concept of human security means different things for differently positioned people in Cambodia today. Factors such as age, background, and access to social capital shape the "wants" that people express. It is hardly surprising that a middle-aged rural farmer, who has memories of war, views political rivalry in the distant capital with dread, and simply wishes for stability in order that (s)he can get on with the business of making a living. However, for today's swelling group of young students in the capital, who are Internet savvy and cognizant of the structural hindrances to their own advancement, securing the future may mean challenging the status quo through protests and demands for a regime change. If both these positions are to be respected, then Cambodia's leaders are going to need to find a way to respond to challenges and enact change without resorting to violence, threat, and coercion

This brings us to the third problem that our material brings to light, the fact that the concept of human security embraces several intertwined and sometimes contradictory aspirations. The "freedom from want" element has clearly been adopted by some stakeholders as justifying neoliberal reforms and trajectories of development that satisfy the demands of a global marketplace and elites. However, addressing want in this globally endorsed way, without simultaneously implementing inclusive, pro-poor policies for wealth redistribution and protection of rights, clearly increases "fear" as well as want for large groups of people. The current struggle over land in Cambodia is perhaps the most alarming example of this. There are now strong global incentives that encourage elites to enforce stability to encourage investors while ignoring democratization and respect for the needs and rights of those who get in the way of the elite's development agendas. Indeed, it could be argued that the very notion of freedom from want is something of an oxymoron since the engine of global consumer culture is the continual generation of new wants for new consumer items.

While much of today's debate about human security is focused on either protection or empowerment of individuals, our data suggest that people themselves present a far more complex and sometimes conflicting range of ideas about how their future well-being may be secured. A perspective that focuses on people's lived experience as "active participants in the making of their own lives in the effort to survive the interim" (Umegaki 2009, 11) is needed to alert us to policies that ignore or imperil certain sections of the population now in the pursuit of long-term freedom from want. Above all, we propose that ordinary people wish to have their needs, as they themselves experience them, listened to and responded to by leaders they regard as responsible and morally dependable. In this way, they are requesting the right to be treated with respect and live in dignity.

In sum, we contend that by inviting reflection upon the precariousness of individual lives, the concept of human security is helpful for enabling people to communicate the kinds of problems they are experiencing in countries like Cambodia, where poverty, corruption, and human rights abuses continue to create insecurity. The challenge remains, however, for the proponents of human security to draw up concrete strategies for ensuring that government, and national and international elite actors behave responsibly toward ordinary citizens, particularly the most vulnerable. Given the growing tensions in Cambodia today, the Royal Government of Cambodia now bears a particularly heavy burden of responsibility to its people for ending corruption and incorporating all Cambodians into a more just and equal society. While they may have been expedient in the past, the ruling party's methods for addressing want and fear in Cambodia over the past three decades will need to be adapted to suit the changing ethos among Cambodian people. As a new generation of the Cambodian electorate comes of age, the leaders may find that they can no longer enforce stability using time-tested practices of rewarding supporters and intimidating opponents. More politically mature methods of open dialogue about visions of the future, a willingness to share and to compromise, and the establishment of a strong and independent judiciary are all key to the building of lasting peace and security in Cambodia.

Notes

1. The Cambodian Mine Action Centre (CMAC) estimates that there may still be 4–6 million mines and other pieces of unexploded ordnance in Cambodia (CMAC 2014).
2. Comment made at a meeting of the Prey Lang Network at the Foreign Correspondents' Club, Phnom Penh, June 19, 2014.

References

ADB (Asian Development Bank). 2017. *Basic Statistics*. Manila: ADB.

Cambodia Ministry of Public Works. 2012. *Annual Report on Traffic Accidents 2012*. Phnom Penh: Ministry of Public Works.

CDRI (Cambodia Development Research Institute). 2014. *Annual Development Review 2013–2014: Development Inclusiveness, Sustainability and Governance in Cambodia*. Phnom Penh: CDRI.

CMAC (Cambodia Mine Action Center). 2014. *Ten Years: Achievements and Perspectives*. Phnom Penh: CMAC.

Gellman, Neesha. 2007. Powerful Cultures: Indigenous and Western Conflict Resolution Practices in Cambodian Peacebuilding. *Journal of Peace, Conflict and Development* 11: 25–36.

Gregory, Peter. 2013. Cambodian Government Must Reform Land Rights Laws. *Cambodia Daily*, June 6.

Heuveline, Patrick. 1998. Between One and Three Million: Towards the Demographic Reconstruction of a Decade of Cambodian History (1970–79). *Population Studies* 52: 49–65.

Ministry of Planning. 2014. National Strategic Development Plan 2014–2018. http://mop.gov.kh/Home/NSDP/NSDP20142018/tabid/216/Default.aspx. Accessed 24 Oct 2015.

Morton, Eddie. 2014. Cambodia Most Vulnerable to Climate Change: Study. *Phnom Penh Post*, June 12.

Nishikawa, Yukiko. 2009. Human Security in Southeast Asia: Viable Solution or Empty Slogan? *Security Dialogue* 40 (2): 213–236.

———. 2010. *Human Security in Southeast Asia*. London: Routledge.

Peou, Sorpong. 2014. Human Security in Post-Cold War Cambodia. In *Post-Conflict Development in East Asia*, ed. Brendan M. Howe, 117–136. Burlington: Ashgate.

Pheap, Aun. 2014. Unions Tell Garment Workers to Suspend Strike. *The Cambodia Daily*, January 8.

Reaksmey, Hul. 2014. CNRP Promises Museum to Document 'Criminal' Acts by CPP. *Cambodia Daily*, July 7.

Southeast Asia Weekly. 2013. Cambodia Starts Focusing on Human Security. *Southeast Asia Weekly*, December 29.
Sundaranaman, Shankari. 1997. Cambodia Since the UNTAC: Deep into the Quagmire. https://www.idsa-india.org/an-sep-8.html. Accessed 25 Oct 2014.
Transparency International. 2014. Cambodia: Corruption Concerns Amid Hopes for the Future. *Transparency International*, February 20.
Umegaki, Michio. 2009. Introduction: East Asia in a Human Security Perspective. In *Human Insecurity in East Asia*, ed. Michio Umegaki, Lynn Thiesmeyer, and Atsushi Watabe, 1–19. Tokyo: United Nations University Press.
UNDP (United Nations Development Programme). 1994. *Human Development Report 1994*. New York: Oxford University Press.
World Bank. 2014. *Poverty Has Fallen, Yet Many Cambodians Are Still at Risk of Falling Back into Poverty, Report Finds*. Washington, DC: World Bank.

CHAPTER 3

Human Security in Practice: The Chinese Experience

Ren Xiao

3.1 Introduction

Human security was defined as freedom from want, freedom from fear, and the centrality of dignity by the Commission on Human Security (2003). This was subsequently endorsed by the United Nations (UN) General Assembly when it referred to the "right of people to live in freedom and dignity" (UNGA 2012). Although the actual term "human security" (人的安全 in Chinese) has not been widely used thus far, similar ideas or practices have been flourishing in China. In response to the questions underlying the emergence of human security norms, this chapter attempts to elaborate on China's experience and progress with regard to human security by, respectively, dealing with three major issues, namely, how the idea of human security is understood or defined by the government and social actors; the ways in which the distinctions between the "protection" and "empowerment" aspects of human security are understood and accepted; and what particular downside risks

R. Xiao (✉)
Institute of International Studies, Fudan University, Shanghai, China
e-mail: renxiao2006@fudan.edu.cn

Y. Mine et al. (eds.), *Human Security Norms in East Asia*, Security, Development and Human Rights in East Asia,
https://doi.org/10.1007/978-3-319-97247-3_3

are perceived as pressing human security issues in China. The chapter concludes with a discussion of the overall human security practices and shows that, based on current indicators, China is heading in a healthy direction in terms of promoting human security.

3.2 The Understanding of Human Security in China

3.2.1 *A New Consensus*

In China, the government is often wary of new academic terms and tends to avoid using them directly. However, the findings from our previous study (Ren and Li 2013) clearly showed that the country is following a trajectory of increasingly attaching more importance to human (both individual and collective) security. Much greater attention has been paid to mitigating threats to human security, and practical measures are being taken to fulfill the mandate. We emphasized the convergence of the human security idea and China's practices (Ren and Li 2013). Our findings disprove the following statement: "the very notion of 'human security' has so far not appeared in the Chinese language in any possible translation, and the People's Republic of China (PRC) has not even accepted or adopted the concept of human security in either domestic development papers or foreign policy guidelines..." (Wu 2013, 1). Our examination suggests otherwise. Though the Chinese government has only used the term "human security" on a few occasions, China is definitely engaged in the enterprise of enhancing human security.

The fact that China is becoming more open and receptive to human security is strongly related to its experience within the UN system. As one of the five permanent members of the UN Security Council, China has long been supportive of the UN, the most important international organization in today's world, and the country has played a proactive role in various UN activities such as peacebuilding, development, and global governance (Breslin and Ren 2018). Over the years, the UN has been subjected to criticisms and it is widely believed that reforms are needed, which China supports. Nevertheless, Beijing continues to show a belief that the UN plays an irreplaceable role in global governance, and China has endeavored to support this by encouraging the UN to play its role well (Kim 1999). This has remained an unchanged priority in China's foreign policy agenda.

China's steady backing has boosted the status of the UN in world affairs, at a time when the world is faced with growing global challenges in the first decades of the twenty-first century. Meanwhile, the UN has taken the lead in advocating and/or spreading norms and principles, and this has affected and helped to shape China's ideas (Kent 2014). Usually, UN initiatives or proposals attract China's attention, and prompt Beijing to have a closer look at them before taking actions to adapt to the new norms or principles (Morton 2009, 75–76). For example, China was involved in the deliberations and adoption of the UN World Summit Outcome Document in 2005. Although it is not the same thing as the "responsibility to protect" idea proposed by the International Commission on Intervention and State Sovereignty (ICISS 2001), to some extent the Outcome Document is consistent with this idea in terms of thinking on protection. The Outcome Document attempts to strike a balance between the need to protect innocent people around the world from being harmed while avoiding the abuse of external intervention or selfish behavior in the name of protection. For this, the Outcome Document imposes limitations by listing four specific crimes against which the international community should act to prevent people's lives from being jeopardized: genocide, war crimes, ethnic cleansing, and crimes against humanity. In this way, the Outcome Document has become a new international legal document. China was involved in this process and made its own contribution. Thus, involvement in global or regional institutions has pushed China to clarify or develop its own thinking on human security.

Against the backdrop of the great earthquake and tsunami that devastated Japan's Tohoku region, the Ministerial Millennium Development Goals Follow-up Meeting was held under the UN framework in June 2011 in Tokyo, Japan. China sent Vice Foreign Minister Cui Tiankai to attend the meeting. In the speech he delivered, Cui, as the representative of the Government of China, stated:

> To discuss the MDGs from the angle of human security offers a thought-provoking perspective. We believe that the MDGs and human security are interrelated and should be mutually reinforcing. The MDGs embody so many aspects of human security, while the realization of MDGs aims at greater well-being and security of more people in the first place. (T. Cui 2011)

Cui pointed to the fact that the general picture of global security remains disturbing: "Civilians in North Africa and the Middle East continue to bear the brunt of turmoil, and innocent women and children are still being displaced or killed in armed conflicts in various parts of the world." Cui concluded that:

> These give rise to the call for *a new concept on security* and an international political order where the United Nations should play a central role. We strongly believe that the purposes and principles of the UN Charter should be upheld, and Security Council resolutions should be implemented in a faithful manner. …In a word, if human security in the larger sense of the term is still so much threatened, there is little hope for better individual security. (T. Cui 2011)

This is an illuminating example of how China has clearly and definitively adopted and used both the idea of and the actual term "human security" in the context of a formal UN meeting. Although it was an event on MDGs and not specifically on human security, the term "human security" was explicitly employed to express China's opinion and position.

This discourse was reinforced by further developments. In February 2014, Ms. Fu Ying, Chairperson of the National People's Congress Foreign Affairs Committee, was invited to and spoke at the Munich Security Conference. She argued that the security necessary for people to survive and develop is fundamental to any security. The core of the Chinese Dream of the revival of the Chinese nation proposed by President Xi Jinping is to have the 1.3 billion Chinese people live a happy life. In other words, all ordinary people have the right and are entitled to live with dignity in a secure environment. This is the attraction of China's success story to the world, as well as the charm of the Chinese dream.[1] This line of thinking has many elements in common with the widely shared "human security" idea. For instance, both place emphasis on individuals and their happiness, and this must be fulfilled together with national development. Ends and means should be consistent, and the persistent value is that people themselves are the end and they should not be sacrificed for arbitrary national goals.

The key point here is that China's security concept is undergoing a profound transformation. A new consensus has emerged that assumes security does not equal military security, and security should not only be comprehensive but also people-centered (*yi renmin wei zhongxin*): "national security" now has new connotations.

3.2.2 *The Third Plenum*[2]

During the landmark Third Plenum, which was held in November 2013, a major resolution to comprehensively deepen China's reform was deliberated and passed. The long reformist document has 16 parts and 60 items. The decision to create a new National Security Commission (NSC) was announced as a component of the 13th part on the new social governance system. The purpose of the NSC is to improve the relevant institutions and strategy to better safeguard China's national security. According to the explanatory speech President Xi Jinping gave, reform and development are conditional on national security and social stability, without which reform and development cannot be advanced further.[3]

At present, China is faced with the dual pressure of safeguarding national sovereignty, security, and development interests externally, and maintaining political security and social stability internally (Xi 2017, 411). All kinds of risks that can or cannot be foreseen are clearly increasing, while the country's institutions and security mechanisms are insufficient to adequately meet the need of maintaining national security. This has resulted in demands to set up a powerful and capable platform to coordinate all work on national security. The responsibilities of the NSC include formulating and implementing national security strategies, advancing the construction of national security rule of law, deciding national security guidelines and policies, and studying and addressing major issues in the national security work.[4] Quite understandably, this major decision drew considerable attention both at home and abroad.

In April 2014, the first meeting of the new NSC was held. According to the speech President Xi Jinping delivered, the security of the people must be its core purpose. State security should in every sense serve the people and rely on the people. The mass foundation of state security must be laid and consolidated.[5] This means that state security and human security are not confrontational but rather that the two can and should coexist.

Internally, China is undergoing a modernization process and the number of contradictions is growing. In this time of rapid economic and social development, a series of social problems have been accumulating that have not been "digested" well. For some Chinese observers, "group incidents" resulting from unbalanced distribution of interests frequently break out, negatively affecting social stability. Externally, as China continues to grow, some powers and neighboring countries have been hedging against China, and as a result, contradictions or frictions in China's neighborhood have been increasing. Moreover, challenges to social stability and security, from home and abroad, have been affecting each other, and they are interlinked. Coping with them is becoming a more difficult job. In the current era, the concept of national security is becoming richer in depth and wider in breadth, involving a range of issues in a variety of areas. Increasingly complex problems cannot be dealt separately by foreign affairs, national defense, and security departments but rather are demanding that more agencies, social organizations, and even the whole society work together (Hu and Wang 2013).

Since the initiative to create China's NSC appears in the "social governance system" section of the November 2013 resolution, its domestic and internal security dimension is self-evident. In the meantime, the commission's work involves two dimensions (both external and internal) rather than just one. Thus the "security" the initiative refers to is of a comprehensive nature. It is not difficult to come to that conclusion if we simply recall the July 5, 2009, incident in Xinjiang, the riots in Tibet and Tibet-related self-immolations in its neighboring provinces, and the horrible killing at the Kunming Railway Station on March 1, 2014. During all these incidents, innocent people were killed or injured, and some of the incidents resulted from the actions by hostile external forces. That is why it was widely believed that internal security would be the dominant concern for China's NSC, at least in its early stage. When ordinary people can be unexpectedly harmed by violent terrorist attacks in any situation and without warning, a sense of insecurity arises, and this can be frightening. Thus, even though freedom from want is no longer a problem in today's China, ordinary people should also be able to live their lives free from fear. A broad concept of security of this kind logically became the goal for China's NSC.

In fact, as Cui Shunji of Zhejiang University points out, since the initiation of reform, at the highest levels, attention has been placed on poverty reduction, the pursuit of a sustainable development model, and China's proposals for constructing a "harmonious society" and a "harmonious world." These goals indicate that China regards the guaranteeing of basic human needs, social justice, and harmony as well as sustainable development as important parts of a continuum of national security (S. Cui 2014, 68–69). "Letting people live a happier life with more dignity" has become the goal of national development, which indicates that China's recognition of human security has been elevated to the political level. Putting people first and "governing for the people" have become the new thinking for governing the country. As a reflection of the foreign policy changes, handling foreign affairs for the state is shifting to handling foreign affairs for the people (S. Cui 2014). This was reinforced at the 19th Party Congress, held in October 2017, which emphasized the need to regard people's interests as paramount and let the achievements of reform and development benefit everybody more and fairly.

3.2.3 *The "Non-traditional Security" Discourse*

In China's research community, "human security" is often discussed in terms of the discourse on "non-traditional security." For years, Chinese researchers have utilized the term "non-traditional security" to distinguish the so-called non-traditional matters from more traditional matters. Traditional security usually refers to military security, namely, assuring national security through boosting military power. However, after the end of the Cold War, threats to security have increasingly come from non-military domains in the form of unconventional or non-traditional security threats. Such issues include financial crises, terrorism, transnational crime, environmental degradation, the spread of HIV/AIDS, scarcity of water resources, food insecurity, and so forth.

According to the summation by a leading Chinese researcher, non-traditional security is broad-based, complex, and multi-dimensional. Examining each in turn, while traditional security falls into military, political, and diplomatic areas, and its supreme value is the pursuit of peace and the elimination of war or the possibility of war, a broad-based non-traditional security is more about economic, social, cultural, and environmental threats as well as the emerging cyber security and space issues. In addition to peace, non-traditional security relates more to risk, crisis, emergency, and daily threats to life. It relates more to natural disasters, accidents, emerging public health incidents, and major public security events.

Second, non-traditional security is complex. Threats to non-traditional security are mainly the threats to "societal security" and "human security." Society and people are the chief referent objects of non-traditional security, and a "safe China" has societal and human dimensions. For individuals, safety means that the security of people is guaranteed: namely, individuals enjoy a state of existence in which a person's body is not injured, their mind is not harmed, they are not deprived of their property, and their living environment is not undermined.

Third, non-traditional security is multi-dimensional. According to the place and origin of non-traditional security events, threats to non-traditional security facing a country can be divided into four categories: (1) exogenous non-traditional security threats which take place abroad and chiefly require diplomatic negotiations; (2) endogenous non-traditional security threats which take place at home and chiefly require domestic interventions; (3) "bi-dogenous" (双源性) non-traditional security threats which take place in peripheral areas, necessitating both domestic and international management; and (4) "multi-dogenous" (多源性) non-traditional security threats that involve both traditional and non-traditional security issues requiring the involvement of the military in addition to other organizations (Yu 2013, 3–6).

Throughout the above process of ideational transition, a few landmark crises have affected China deeply, including the 1997 Asian financial crisis that highlighted the importance of financial security, the 2003 SARS crisis that highlighted public health security, and the March 1, 2014, terrorist attacks at the railway station in Kunming, the capital of Yunnan Province. The horrible March 1 violence against innocent people especially highlighted the serious security threat that ordinary people could encounter in their daily lives. This genuine risk could give rise to a widespread sense of fear.

As noted, earlier conceptions of security in China were mainly focused on state security, the importance of which remained unquestioned. Now that human security has been put forward, and given its undeniable value orientation, support for the concept is gaining momentum. In fact, Chinese scholars speak highly of human security and argue that it goes beyond the limits of state-centric traditional security research and is the least traditional theory among the non-traditional security domains (Yu 2014, 18). Human security research explicitly sees people as a collectivity and individuals as the referent object of security. This transcends the dilemma of more traditional security theory, since the state can bring about insecurity to its citizens. Such a possibility raises questions concerning the relationship between state security and human security. In general, Chinese researchers do not endorse the view that human security overrides state security or that the two are confrontational, but rather affirm the reasonableness and value of state security at the same time.

For example, Shi Bin, a professor at Nanjing University, asserts that the human security idea is a focal embodiment of non-traditional security and new security concepts, and yet the relationship between human security and state security is much more complicated (Shi 2014, 97–100). Shi argues that both state security and human security, in terms of their security concerns and value pursuits, have legitimate claims. However, there is no reason for either of them to become totally dominant. Human security is of course the fundamental goal and ultimate value of human development. The value orientation of putting people first, with human security at the center, provides it with the moral high ground and legitimacy. However, a person has both individuality and sociality, and individuals are often weak and helpless. Resisting foreign military invasion and safeguarding national sovereignty and territorial integrity are therefore in the nation's common interest. Nonetheless, the traditional state-centric security idea and strategy indeed ignores the security needs of many non-state or sub-national entities and cannot adequately deal with external non-military threats such as environmental degradation and pandemic disease.

Second, Shi Bin articulates that, although there is a tension between "human security" and "state security" and the two may conflict in practice, they can still be mutually accommodating and complementary if handled and balanced well. Therefore, this can provide a favorable opportunity for upgrading the overall security level of all entities. People's security and welfare, and the improvement of their living conditions and quality of life, are an important base for national identity, social stability, and political legitimacy. In this sense, human security and state security are not necessarily contradictory. For Shi, the human security discourse has a tangible Western value orientation bearing liberal colors; consequently, in practice, it tends to override the security interests of the sovereign state. The acclaimed paradigm shift from the state to individuals excessively downgrades the positive role of the state in dealing with various security challenges.

For Zhang Yunling of the Chinese Academy of Social Sciences, the rise of non-traditional security issues does not mean that traditional security is no longer important. The appearance of non-traditional security on the agenda and the fact that it is stressed imply that it has been included in the category of security, and therefore the formation of a "comprehensive security" concept includes both traditional and non-traditional security as well as the corresponding security policies (Y. Zhang 2012).

Taken together, with "non-traditional security" increasingly becoming part of the mainstream discourse in China, researchers tend not to deny the value of state security but rather see human and state security as being mutually accommodating. Nevertheless, the theoretical shortcomings of non-traditional security, as Guoguang Wu rightly points out, are obvious, when it is narrowly framed as oppositional to traditional security, without any positive and substantive defining of the contents and nature of new "securities" (Wu 2013, 5).

The relationship between state security and personal security is not a zero-sum one though. More state security does not mean less personal security, and vice versa. The goal should be a calibrated balance between the two. Moreover, the increasing tendency to securitize many issues and aspects of life may not be entirely beneficial. An overemphasis on discussions of security may imply a growth of insecurity. For example, in China food safety was previously not discussed often but was later widely talked about. This indicated that food safety was not formerly an issue, but it became such an issue. The deterioration of food safety was a negative development that involved the need for moral reconstruction in the society.

As shown above, the Chinese research community has attached increasing importance to the issue of human security. Meanwhile, they are not just following in others' footsteps, but rather have developed their own analyses and views. Some researchers have stressed that individuals are both the starting point and the ultimate purpose of any society. The emancipation of human beings should be the fundamental goal of any social emancipation. It is people who are the final objective of the concept of human security, and this is the core value any security is supposed to protect, while the state provides the means or temporary purpose (J. Li 2013, 74–75). The establishment of "people are the purpose" as a value grew to have great significance for Chinese society after the community had drawn lessons from the history of the People's Republic since 1949.

During the Cultural Revolution period, many innocent people were attacked, detained, or persecuted illegally and immorally; rights were ignored, and people were harmed. After a disastrous decade, many people reflected on their painful experiences and thought about the phenomenon of imposing horrible acts on innocent individuals, something that should never recur. In the early reform period, there emerged a movement in China's intellectual community that began to discuss the issues of humanism (*rendao zhuyi*) and alienation (*yihua*). During this time, many intellectuals affirmed the significance of humanism and argued for the promotion of human values. Some of them cautiously adopted the term "Marxist humanism" or "socialist humanism" to distinguish from the so-called capitalist doctrine. Not long after, the debate abruptly came to a halt due to a political intervention. However, along with further economic reform and considerable social development, the awareness of the value of the individual human being in China was reawakened and the value of people confirmed. The initiative for humanism in the 1980s was in fact later accepted by the whole of Chinese society. This was also reflected in the discussions and research on human security, since it was made clear that guaranteeing human security is the value base for maintaining non-traditional security. The protection of people and human development should be set as the ultimate goals of any security course. Obviously, this progress is precious for Chinese society and deserves appreciation by the outside world.

The paradigm of human security opposes the harming of the human freedoms and rights to promote economic growth or social stability. Nor does it favor the pursuit of economic benefits and communitarian policies at the expense of sacrificing the security and dignity of the individuals or the nation. The fundamental reason for this lies in enhancing the value of people, which is the key and ultimate goal, and there is no higher goal than this.

The previous practices of both "collective security" and "common security," Yu Xiaofeng, a leading scholar in human security, argues, could not have avoided the limitations of regarding the state as the chief actor (Yu 2014, 33). By contrast, "shared security," which he has proposed, regards the human community as occupying the central position of security, the protection of human life as the value base of security, social safety and prosperity as the priority goals of security, and harmony and cooperation as the supreme principles for security interactions between the states (Yu 2014, 33–34). This moves the discussion beyond the traditional security discourses and has the potential for further theoretical development.

3.3 Protection and Empowerment

According to the *Human Security Now* report (CHS 2003) and the October 2012 resolution adopted by the UN General Assembly as a follow-up to Paragraph 143 on human security of the 2005 World Summit Outcome, as well as the definition and design of this book, human security has two dimensions: protection and empowerment. In China, the dimension of protection has drawn much attention, epitomized in the doctrines of "putting people first" (*yiren weiben*) and "diplomacy serving the people" (*waijiao weimin*), which I discussed in a detailed way in an earlier study (Ren and Li 2013). The findings from this earlier study have been reinforced by recent evidence. For example, a Chinese newspaper correspondent wrote of his impressions when reporting from the National People's Congress (NPC) sessions. He was deeply impressed by the attention the NPC delegates paid to the concrete issues concerning people's daily lives, including social insurance, income distribution, rights of peasant workers, food safety, unreasonably high drug prices, and protection of stakeholder interests. In his view, those kinds of issues had never before been so meticulously discussed at the NPC (Yuan 2005). The changes the correspondent detected indicate ongoing healthy trends in human security terms.

A harmonious society is one that puts people first, which means people's everyday life is a priority for the society. A government that puts people first is a government that represents people's interests. Economic and social development should put human development at the center, and human development is the ultimate value judgment for social progress (Yuan 2005). Meanwhile, the achievement of human security is a cooperative venture between the individual, society, and the state (Bedeski 2013, 29). Government as a "necessary evil" is very much a Western invention and is not a Chinese idea. Traditionally, people in China often have wishes for their government, and they want it to do good things for them. Compared to Western political culture, they have less vigilance but higher expectations of the government. One revealing example is the use of the term "parent officials" (*fumu guan*) to refer to government officials, with people expecting them to play a paternalistic role. Without cooperative ventures, human security cannot be achieved.

On the protection side, while people-oriented ideals might be considered noble ones, challenges come from the process of implementation. Not surprisingly, many problems are persistent. One prominent example is the matter of government land appropriation and relocation of residents. Sometimes the failure to protect the rights and interests of the ordinary people has led to acute standoffs and conflicts, and in some cases even extreme acts of protest. When property development businessmen and arbitrary power coalesce, together they can undermine the interests of the ordinary people who are affected. Protecting people's legitimate interests has become an outstanding issue in China's human security amid the drastic social changes and urbanization of recent decades.

Moreover, the Chinese leadership came into office with a promise to narrow the widening gap between rich and poor, and to shift to a more environmentally and economically sustainable growth model. Since gross domestic product (GDP) became the brand of accomplishment for many government officials, "GDP worship" has prevailed. Local officials tended to initiate projects that show their "achievements" and promote their image to the public. When poorly planned, such projects led to unexpected outcomes and environmental damage. When this became obvious, a strategic shift had to be undertaken. “No GDP growth at the expense of the environment” is becoming a new norm and “ecological civilization” the new banner, which was again stressed in the 19th Party Congress Report of October 2017.

The reform era has been characterized by remarkable success in terms of rapid economic growth and the improvement of living standards. After three decades of successful economic development, the country is standing at a new starting point. If the ruling party’s historical promise to “let some people get rich first and eventually arrive at common prosperity” was a prerequisite for the reforms to unfold, and if four decades later this historical task has been basically fulfilled, what the reform enterprise must accomplish now is the other half: namely, to realize a common prosperity. This is a goal that will justify and inform further reforms. The reaffirmation of realizing common prosperity in line with the principles of governing for the people and building a comprehensive and balanced well-off society will guide future reform with a clear direction.[6] To fulfill its pledge to narrow the gap between rich and poor and to “unwaveringly pursue common prosperity,” the leaders have to place the people in their hearts and take their needs seriously in order to realize the goal of the “Chinese dream.” After the 18th Party Congress in 2012, the new General Secretary Xi Jinping expressed his view that “to fulfill the people’s desire for better lives is what we shall strive for.”[7] This statement sounded dear and close to the ordinary Chinese people.

On the empowerment side, there have also been several measures. Only when a person has the capability for survival and development can he or she enjoy real freedom. The capacity for development is what empowers an individual. Thus, a modernized China should not only accept empowerment through protection but also appreciate its importance in realizing human freedom and guaranteeing human security. Education as a right is the fundamental and most significant form of empowerment, as the human experience has repeatedly revealed. Thus, educational development is a significant way to empower people, especially compulsory education. China has reason to be proud in this regard. It has a tradition that puts significant emphasis on education, in which parents always try their best to pave the way for their children to receive a good education, and often they are willing to make sacrifices. In China, nine-year compulsory education has been in force for years. In 1989, Project Hope was set up as an educational support supplement, which later became well known throughout Chinese society. It was initiated by the Central Youth League and the China Juvenile Development Foundation as a philanthropic enterprise to help less developed areas to establish primary schools, to financially support children who have dropped out of school in the poorer regions to return to school, and to improve education in rural areas. The project received society-wide attention and support. Implemented successfully, the project has positively changed the fate of hundreds of thousands of children of poor families and has also beefed up the whole society's awareness of the importance of education, thereby improving China's fundamental education.

As a major initiative for the future, the Third Plenum set the aim of modernizing China's governance system and governing capability, a long-term goal for China. An important part of it is to reshape a new social governance system. During the 2014 National People's Congress session, President Xi joined the Shanghai delegation for a deliberation of the government's work. For him, the key to future social governance is institutional innovation, and its core lies in people. Only when people are living harmoniously can society be operating in a stable and orderly manner. For Han Zheng, the party secretary of Shanghai, social governance was up to everybody, and the governing process should serve the all-round development of people. Rule of law is the foundation of social governance, without which there can be no base for long-standing good governance and robust stability.[8] For that matter, among other things, it is necessary for grass-root cadres to regard people's concerns as their own matters, while always trying to understand their feelings and demands. Again, the key challenge is to make this happen in real life. Fortunately, in China there have been local autonomous grassroots organizations that play an intermediate role and serve to help in addressing problems at the grassroots level. They assist ordinary people who encounter difficulty, and they also, for example, mobilize donations to help people in the regions that have been struck by earthquakes or other natural disasters. The work of these local self-help organizations has proved to be useful and reassuring in terms of social governance.

3.4 Prominent Human Security Threats and the Chinese Responses

Since 'human security' is central to non-traditional security, it is concerned with all kinds of factors that directly threaten human security" (Zhou 2012, 255–256). In today's China, prominent direct threats include air pollution, food safety, and cyber security. This section examines each of these in turn.

The seriousness of the problem of air pollution first became apparent right all across China in 2013. Heavy smog emerged not only in North and Northeast China but also was reported in other regions. Many people were alarmed by the situation, including concerns expressed by China's neighbors, Japan and South Korea. The spread of the smog made it obvious that the environment in which people were living was deteriorating, a red-light signal providing a warning on the existing pattern of economic growth, which was consuming a great amount of energy and yielding considerable waste. While many people were already aware of the issue, the shocking reality of the situation in 2013 and its related risks served to awaken people as never before. With many people walking in the streets wearing masks, the sense of insecurity was palpable and imminent. In this context, the specific threat of air pollution became the number one threat to people's security.

To cope with this threat, in June 2013, China's State Council laid out ten measures to prevent and combat air pollution. As a follow-up, in September, China released an Action Plan to implement this, which was a blueprint to fight against air pollution by 2017. Since then, further work has been undertaken. In his Government Work Report delivered in March 2014, Premier Li Keqiang swore to "fight pollution like fighting poverty." When he was looking around the city of Beijing, President Xi emphasized that the sprawling pattern of urban development had to be contained and steps should be taken to deal with smog pollution and improve air quality. Among the five requests Xi made, one was logically to reinforce the measures to rein in air pollution. The top priority to combat air pollution and improve air quality was to control PM2.5, with major steps that included reducing the burning of coal, strictly limiting growth in the number of cars, adjusting industries, tightening management, and executing joint prevention and control.[9] Xi's move clearly sent a signal that the government was committed to taking measures for better air quality.

The Chinese leadership had previously pledged to launch a revolution in energy production and consumption and said that urbanization must be balanced with ecological security (Hook 2012, 1). However, pollution was worsening and was posing a serious threat to human health and social stability. To reduce air pollution and carbon emissions, Beijing (population 20 million) is attempting to phase out coal-fired power plants within the city's urban core, replacing them with cleaner-burning natural gas power plants. These measures are also basically valid for other cities. After all, fighting pollution is relevant to everybody's security, a point that has attracted a high-degree of consensus within Chinese society. Similarly, China's energy sector had a watershed year in 2013. Reforms that could have a profound impact on China's environment and energy policy were floated. With concerns over air pollution mounting throughout the year, the country is poised to shift away from its reliance on coal and toward use of cleaner forms of energy, including natural gas. Shale gas exploration is making progress in the country. Driven by crises, a true transformation is under way but surely will take time to complete.

The second human security concern among the Chinese people is that of food safety. In recent years, a series of food contamination incidents occurred throughout the country, causing serious concern. A 2010 poll by *Xiaokang* (小康 [Moderately Well Off]) magazine and Tsinghua University conducted in 12 Chinese cities found that food safety ranked number one of all social concerns among those surveyed, reflecting mounting anxiety after the 2008 melamine crisis (Z. Zhang 2010; Wishnick 2013, 256). Within this context of growing concern over food safety, the government has not been unaware or insensitive. Appearing at a press conference, Premier Li Keqiang responded by stressing that "food safety is of utmost importance."[10] Answering a different question concerning the missing MH370 aircraft, he stressed that "any case involving human life has to be treated with the utmost care" (*renming guantian*). As with the issue of air pollution, the 2014 Government Work Report promised to adopt the strictest surveillance, the most severe punishment, and the most serious accountability measures to resolutely govern pollution at the meal table and reassure people of "security on the tongue tip" (K. Li 2014). In fact, there is a widely shared consensus in China on the need to make efforts to ensure food safety.

Specialists distinguish between two separate food-related issues: the first is related to food security or ensuring sufficiency in the quantity of food; the other concerns food safety, which refers to the quality of food. While the former involves the question of whether there is sufficient overall provision of food, an area in which China has vowed to "hold the bowl firmly in our own hands," the latter involves the question of whether people can be assured that the food they eat every day is safe. Formerly, the issue of food scarcity trumped food safety. But today the main problem in China lies in food safety, with people alarmed by reports of different kinds of contamination.

In recent years, this has even spilled over into China's foreign relations, and was epitomized in the spoiled *jiaozi* (dumpling) incident between China and Japan. The incident originated in Hebei Province. An employee in the Tianyang food factory was resentful over his low income. In revenge, he deliberately poisoned *jiaozi*, and the contaminated products were exported and sold in Japan. Some customers bought and ate them, becoming ill. On investigation, pesticides found in the frozen dumplings were traced back to China. This was a single case of a crime that resulted in grave consequences. The reputation of China's food products was seriously damaged, and the Sino-Japanese relationship was also somewhat affected. This incident once again highlighted the close links between domestic and international affairs.

In the final analysis, the root cause lies with individuals, and the issue of "moral collapse" has been used to refer to this situation. To what extent this is true can be debated. There was a belief that overuse of fertilizers and pesticides was rampant, and that growers distinguish between what they themselves eat and what is sold in the market, even if they know the latter is not suitable to be eaten. Again, how widespread the phenomenon is can be discussed, yet reports on these kinds of practices result in people feeling that the food they eat may be unsafe.

As a result, in China there was an obvious lack of public trust in food safety. Tighter regulations must be implemented. Greater transparency helps to build public trust, including more official data and statistics about the improvement (or deterioration) in food safety, increased freedom for media and civil society to verify the official data, more effective actions from the government in handling the corruption and malfeasance involved in food safety issues, stronger protection for whistle blowers who uncover production of unsafe food and, more importantly, removal of the corrupt officials involved. Further measures must be taken to improve China's food safety regulations, consumer education levels, and supply chain traceability and sustainability.

The third and final issue is that of cyber security. The use of the internet has increasingly become a part of everyday life in China. By 2013, there were over 600 million internet users in the country, and mobile internet users reached 461 million, making the community of Chinese "netizens" (*wang min*) the world's largest. With this growth, cyber security has become a prominent issue. In fact, China is one of the major victims of cyber-attacks. The covert activities revealed by Edward Snowden highlighted the vulnerability of nations and individuals who are monitored illegally and immorally (Meng 2014). At the government level, a Central Small Leading Group on Cyber Security was created, which held its first meeting in February 2014. It was emphasized that cyber security involved national security and development, as well as the careers and everyday lives of a vast number of ordinary people. It was therefore a major strategic issue.[11] The breakdown and vulnerability of the internet can have a widespread impact on people and their lives.

3.5 Conclusions

This chapter has addressed the three research questions the research project raised by elaborating on how the idea of human security is understood or defined by the government and social actors, the ways in which the distinctions between the "protection" and "empowerment" aspects of human security are understood and accepted, and what downside risks are perceived as pressing human security issues in China. The major ones discussed here included air pollution, food security, and cyber security.

As has been indicated in this chapter, although human security as a term is not frequently used, there have been various human security practices in China. The idea of human security has been firmly established and threats to human security have been detected. Such problems result from China's still unfinished process of industrialization, urbanization, and drastic social change. The good news is that progress is being made, and theoretically, globally accepted values often exist at the individual level. With this comes occupancy of the moral high ground. China has gone far beyond the lip service level of cheaply talking about people's interests. This deeper approach can be fully integrated into human security in its holistic sense. Threats to human security can be domestic risks, yet they often are transnational ones such as air pollution and sand storms. They require different sectors of the society and neighboring countries to work together.

Over 20 years ago, the Commission on Global Governance drafted a report that emphasized the distinction between the security of states and the security of peoples (CGG 1995). Twenty plus years later, the security of peoples has gained momentum. This is also true in China, the most populous country in the world. China's practices have considerably reinforced the overall trends of affirming the value of people, protecting their lives, ensuring their legitimate interests and dignity, and empowering them not only to survive but also to live a respectful life. What is happening in China is indicating a healthy trend in this direction.

Notes

1. "Fu Ying Attends the Munich Security Conference," see http://www.fmprc.gov.cn/ce/cehu/hu/zgyw/t1128210.htm
2. Each year the Communist Party of China Central Committee holds an annual plenum to deliberate what it believes to be the most important issues.
3. For the full text of the Resolution and Xi's explanation, see *Renmin Ribao*, November 13, 2013.
4. Ibid.
5. See *Renmin Ribao*, April 16, 2014.
6. "Editorial," *Ershiyi shiji jingji baodao* [21st Century Economic Report], October 16, 2003, 2.
7. Xi's remarks at the closing of the 18th Party Congress in November 2012.
8. See *Wenhui Bao* [Wenhu Daily], March 7, 2014, 1.
9. *Renmin Ribao*, February 27, 2014.
10. Li's remarks at the 2013 National People's Congress press conference held in March.
11. *Renmin Ribao*, February 28, 2014, 1.

References

Bedeski, Robert E. 2013. Anthropocentric Theory of Human Security. In *China's Challenges to Human Security – Foreign Relations and Global Implications*, ed. Guoguang Wu, 28–53. London/New York: Routledge.

Breslin, Shaun, and Xiao Ren. 2018. China and Global Governance. In *International Organization and Global Governance*, ed. Thomas G. Weiss and Rorden Wilkinson. London/New York: Routledge.

CGG (Commission on Global Governance). 1995. *Our Global Neighborhood: The Report of the Commission on Global Governance*. Oxford: Oxford University Press.

CHS (Commission on Human Security). 2003. *Human Security Now*. New York: Commission on Human Security.

Cui, Tiankai. 2011. *From Commitment to Concerted Action*. Remarks by Vice Foreign Minister Cui Tiankai of China at the Ministerial Follow-up Meeting, 2 June 2011, Tokyo, Japan. http://www.fmprc.gov.cn/eng/wjdt/zyjh/t827392.shtml

Cui, Shunji. 2014. Ren de fazhan yu ren de zunyan: Zaisi ren de anquan gainian [Human Development and Human Dignity: Rethinking the Concept of Human Security]. *Guoji Anquan Yanjiu* [Journal of International Security Studies] 1: 63–77.

Hook, Lesley. 2012. Battle to Balance Urbanization with Ecological Sustainability. *Financial Times Special Report – China*, December 12: 1.

Hu, Hao, and Wang Dong. 2013. Ruhe kandai sheli guojia anquan weiyuanhui [How We Should Perceive Creating the National Security Commission]. *Liaowang xinwen zhoukan* [Liaowang News Weekly], November 18: 30–31.

ICISS (International Commission on Intervention and State Sovereignty). 2001. *The Responsibility to Protect*. Ottawa: The International Development Research Centre.

Kent, Ann. 2014. China's Participation in International Organizations. In *Power and Responsibility in Chinese Foreign Policy*, ed. Yongjin Zhang and Greg Austin, 132–166. Canberra: Asia Pacific Press.

Kim, Samuel. 1999. China and the United Nations. In *China Joins the World: Progress and Prospects*, ed. Elizabeth Economy and Michel Oksenberg, 42–89. New York: Council on Foreign Relations.

Li, Jia. 2013. Ren de anquan: Fei chuantong anquan nengli jianshe de xinshijiao [Human Security: A New Perspective on the Non-traditional Security Capacity Building]. In *Zhongguo fei chuantong anquan nengli jianshe* [Non-traditional Security Capacity Building in China], ed. Yu Xiaofeng, 106–121. Beijing: Zhongguo shehui kexue chubanshe.

Li, Keqiang. 2014. Zhengfu gongzuo baogao [Government Work Report]. *Renmin Ribao* [People's Daily], March 14.

Meng, Wei. 2014. Wangluo anquan: Guojiazhanlue yu guoji zhili [Cyber Security: National Strategy and International Governance). *Dangdai Shijie* [Contemporary World] 2: 46–49.

Morton, Katherine. 2009. *China and the Global Environment: Learning from the Past, Anticipating the Future*. Sydney: Lowy Institute for International Policy.

Ren, Xiao, and Yanxing Li. 2013. A Return to People: China's Approach to Human Security. In *New Approaches to Human Security in the Asia-Pacific: China, Japan and Australia*, ed. William T. Tow, David Walton, and Rikki Kersten, 31–42. Farnham: Ashgate.

Shi, Bin. 2014. 'Ren de anquan' yu guojia anquan ['Human Security' and National Security]. *Shijie Jingji yu Zhengzhi* [World Economics and Politics] 2: 85–110.

UNGA (United Nations General Assembly). 2012. *Resolution 66/290. Follow-up to Paragraph 143 on Human Security of the 2005 World Summit Outcome*. New York: United Nations.

Wishnick, Elizabeth. 2013. Food Security and Food Safety in China's Foreign Policy. In *China's Challenges to Human Security – Foreign Relations and Global Implications*, ed. Guoguang Wu, 245–260. London/New York: Routledge.

Wu, Guoguang. 2013. Human Security Challenges with China. In *China's Challenges to Human Security – Foreign Relations and Global Implications*, ed. Guoguang Wu, 1–27. London/New York: Routledge.

Xi, Jinping. 2017. *The Governance of China II*. Beijing: Foreign Languages Press.

Yu, Xiaofeng. 2013. Fei chuantong anquan zhili yu 'hemei zhongguo' [Non-traditional Security Governance and a 'Safe China']. In *Zhongguo fei chuantong anquan yanjiu baogao, 2012–2013* [Report on China's Non-Traditional Security, 2012–2013], ed. Yu Xiaofeng, 1–50. Beijing: Shehui kexue wenxian chubanshe.

———. 2014. Gongxiang anquan: Fei chuantong anquan yanjiu de zhongguo shiyu [Shared Security: A Chinese Perspective on the Study of Non-Traditional Security]. *Guoji anquan yanjiu* [Journal of International Security Studies] 1: 4–34.

Yuan, Xialiang. 2005. 'Ren' de daxie ['People' Amplified], *Wenhui Bao* [Wenhui Daily], March 8: 3.

Zhang, Zhiwei. 2010. Food Security Tops People's Concern in Survey. *China Daily*, June 30. www.chinadaily.com.cn/china/2010-06/30/content_10042303.htm.

Zhang, Yunling. 2012. Preface. In *Zhongguo fei chuantong anquan yanjiu baogao, 2011–2012* [Report on China's Non-Traditional Security Studies, 2011–2012], ed. Yu Xiaofeng, 1–4. Beijing: Shehui kexue wenxian chubanshe.

Zhou, Jiehong. 2012. Zhongguo shipin anquan wenti yu qushi [Food Security in China: Issues and Trends]. In *Zhongguo fei chuantong anquan yanjiu baogao, 2011–2012* [Report on China's Non-Traditional Security Studies, 2011–2012], ed. Yu Xiaofeng, 254–276. Beijing: Shehui kexue wenxian chubanshe.

CHAPTER 4

Perceptions on Human Security: An Indonesian View

Lina A. Alexandra

4.1 Introduction

Since its introduction in the *Human Development Report* in 1994, the concept of human security has been variously interpreted. Due to its association with development or socio-economic concerns, civil society actors tend to view human security as an effective tool for raising various issues or challenges to be taken up as security concerns. Meanwhile, other stakeholders, notably government officials, still have reservations about including issues traditionally considered to be social or economic under the term "security," since such action may entail significant consequences, for example, the use of extraordinary measures, including military means.

I thank Rocky Intan, Junior Researcher at the Centre for Strategic and International Studies (CSIS) Indonesia, for his assistance during the interviews and in writing parts of the chapter.

L. A. Alexandra (✉)
Department of International Relations, Centre for Strategic and International Studies (CSIS), Jakarta, Indonesia

Y. Mine et al. (eds.), *Human Security Norms in East Asia*, Security, Development and Human Rights in East Asia,
https://doi.org/10.1007/978-3-319-97247-3_4

Despite its relatively stable economic growth, Indonesia continues to face human security challenges. A disaster-prone country, Indonesia has struggled with reconstructing many areas devastated by natural calamities; among these were the 2004 tsunami in Aceh, the Yogyakarta earthquake (2006), volcanic eruptions in some areas, and the Jakarta floods in early 2013. The country has also faced global pandemics such as avian flu and continues struggling to reduce the spread of HIV/AIDS. In recent times, Indonesia has also witnessed escalating religious tension in some areas, which has resulted in the persecution and displacement of some minority groups.

This chapter elaborates on how human security is perceived in Indonesia and how different stakeholders view its challenges, thus contributing to the overall understanding of East Asian countries' interpretations of human security. The study further delineates the prevailing perceptions of actors regarded as responsible for dealing with the challenges and their readiness for the task. The research employed two methods: (1) a document analysis designed to evaluate various regulations relating to human security issues and (2) in-depth interviews with 12 respondents from diverse backgrounds (including government, military, academicians, and activists representing various non-governmental organizations [NGOs]). Due to time and budget constraints, the interviews were limited to respondents in Jakarta. Nevertheless, we managed to interview one Yogyakarta-based respondent via Skype.

4.2 Overview of Human Security Conditions in Indonesia

In Bahasa Indonesia, human security is translated as *keamanan manusia* or *keamanan insani* (*manusia/insani* = human; *keamanan* = security). The term *kesejahteraan* (welfare) is also used as an equivalent for security since *keamanan* generally refers to hard security with a heavy military emphasis. Discussions addressing new security challenges also often refer to other terms such as "non-traditional security" and "transnational threats," with human security considered as encompassing those kinds of threats (Sukma 2010).

The country hardest hit by the 1997 Asian Financial Crisis, Indonesia has since made great strides in poverty eradication. Between 1998 and 2013, the percentage of the population living below the national poverty line dropped from 24 percent to 11 percent (CSA 2014a). Considerable improvement was also observed in the unemployment rate, which fell from 9 percent to 6 percent in 2000–2013 (CSA 2014b). In the health sector, the percentage of infants under the age of five receiving polio immunizations increased from 86 percent in 1999 to 90 percent in 2012 (CSA 2014c).

However, the perception abounds among Indonesians that they still face numerous human security threats. In a separate national survey conducted by CSIS in March 2014, despite steady fall in unemployment, 32 percent of 1,200 respondents cited lack of a job as the most daunting threat, followed by lack of basic food (17 percent). Perceptions of the most important security threats are shown in Fig. 4.1. The threat of communicable diseases also featured prominently in respondents' answers, with 59 percent saying that they did not feel protected from this risk (CSIS 2014).

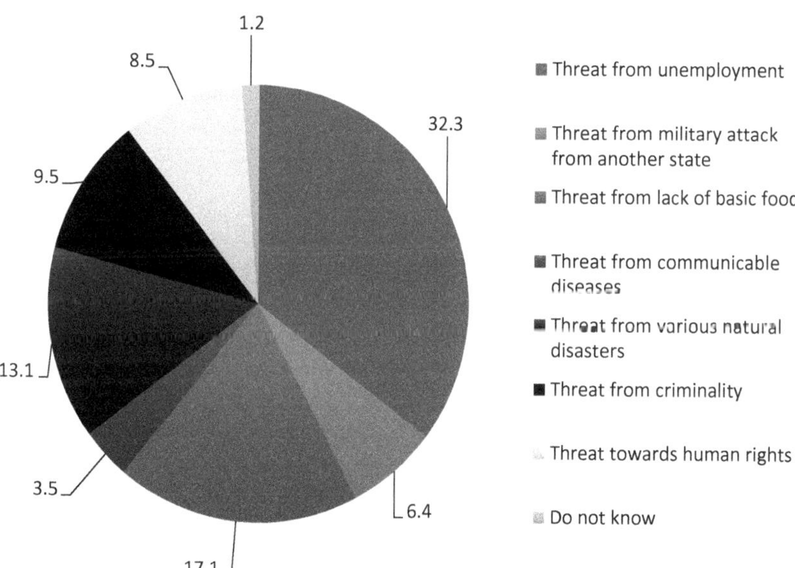

Fig. 4.1 Perceptions of the most important security threats in Indonesia. (Source: CSIS National Survey, March 2014)

Paradoxically, Papua, one of the most energy-rich areas of the country, still struggles with many human security problems, ranging from poverty to pressing public health issues. The percentage of people living below the poverty line in Papua and West Papua stood at 30.05 percent and 27.13 percent, respectively, in March 2014 and was more than double the national average of 11.25 percent (CSA 2014d). The employment situation was marginally better, with unemployment recorded at 3.63 percent and 5.49 percent in Papua and West Papua, respectively, in August 2012 (CSA 2014e). This compared favorably with the national average of 6.14 percent. The public health situation, however, was different; approximately 2.4 percent of the population aged 15–24 suffered from HIV/AIDS, according to a 2012 report by the Joint United Nations Program on HIV/AIDS, noticeably higher than the national average of 0.3 percent (IRIN News 2013).

4.3 Discourses on Human Security in Various Regulations

The term "human security" is seldom explicitly spelt out in formal regulations in Indonesia. A notable exception would be the draft of the National Security Act 2012. Article 5 of the Bill lists human security among the four types of national security (alongside public, internal, and external), while the Appendix includes the following as human security issues: pandemics, extreme hunger, natural disasters resulting in mass casualties, abject poverty, crimes against humanity, and extreme stress. Article 16 also lists "humans" among the referent objects of national security, without discriminating between Indonesian citizens and foreigners present in the country.

Article 17 of the draft distinguishes between military, armed, and non-armed threats. Military threats are perceived as external threats coming from another country's military intent on attacking Indonesia's sovereignty, while armed threats and non-armed threats both fall within internal threats that can also threaten humans. Armed threats to human security include terrorism, separatism, and armed separatist struggles, as well as armed hijacking. The list of non-armed threats to humans that can be included in both public and human security ranges very widely from horizontal/communal conflicts, natural disasters and transnational crimes, to unhealthy trade practices and elimination of national moral and ethical values.[1]

Despite the absence of the term "human security" from most official documents, several articles in the Constitution highlight various rights that can be strongly linked to its elements. Article 27 delineates a citizen's right to a decent job and living. Article 28A talks about the right to life and to maintaining life. Article 28H ensures the right to physical and social welfare and to receive social security. Article 34 ensures state provision for poor and abandoned children. All these relate to state efforts to ensure freedom from want. Article 28A also guarantees freedom from fear. More specifically, Articles 28E and 29 uphold religious freedom, which is of crucial importance, as the past decade has seen a growing level of violence against minorities. Article 28G stipulates individual rights to protect against and be free from torture or ill treatment that undermines human dignity. Finally, Article 28I reiterates the right to live, and not to be tortured.

Aside from the Constitution, there are various specific regulations that ensure protection of human security, namely: Act No. 36/2009 on Health, Act No. 11/2009 on Social Welfare, Act No. 39/2004 on Placement and Protection of Indonesian Migrant Workers Abroad, Act No. 21/2007 on Eradication of Human Trafficking Criminal Practice, Act No. 24/2007 on Disaster Management, Act No. 7/2012 on Social Conflicts Management, and Act No. 40/2008 on Elimination of Racial and Ethnic Discrimination. While these acts do not explicitly mention the term "human security," each refers to its elements, albeit under different notions, such as welfare, human rights, and social protection.

Act on Health 36/2009

This Act's Introduction recognizes health as an element of human rights and welfare. Articles 1 through 4 elaborate the right of all people to gain health physically, mentally, and spiritually, to enable them to live productive lives in both social and economic terms. Articles 14 through 19 state that the government is responsible for ensuring the provision of health in an equal and accessible manner. The government has implemented a social safety system in which the provision of health services comprises a significant component.

Act on Social Welfare 11/2009

This Act mandates the state to provide services to enable a decent and dignified life, as well as to fulfill citizens' rights to basic needs. State provision is closely linked to social welfare, defined as the fulfillment of material, spiritual, and social needs so that people may sustain their lives, be able to develop themselves, and perform societal functions. Article 4 of this Act articulates clearly that the government bears responsibility for organizing matters related to social welfare. Management of social services, both at national and local levels, includes rehabilitation, empowerment, protection, and provision of a social safety net. Protection refers to efforts to prevent and absorb risks from social shocks or susceptibilities. Empowerment aims at assisting citizens in meeting basic needs. Article 5 enumerates target groups prioritized for social services: (1) the poor, (2) the displaced, (3) the disabled, (4) the isolated, (5) the socially disabled, (6) disaster victims, and (7) victims of torture, exploitation, and discrimination.

Act on Placement and Protection of Indonesian Migrant Workers Abroad 39/2004
This Act recognizes the right to work as a human right that needs to be respected and protected. Article 5 obligates the government to regulate, conduct, and monitor the placement and protection of migrant workers abroad. Article 6 reaffirms the government's responsibility to enhance protection efforts. Article 8 mandates legal protection to each worker from disgraceful acts and violations of their rights. Protection of migrant workers' rights are expected to be better due to the recent Government Regulation 4/2015, which has been issued to specifically monitor such process on the ground.

Act on Eradication of Human Trafficking Criminal Practice 21/2007
This Act's Introduction discloses trafficking as a modern form of slavery, which strips human beings of their dignity. Article 59 asserts the necessity for international cooperation, bilateral, regional, and multilateral, in effectively preventing and eradicating trafficking. Article 61 obligates the government to open access for community participation, at both national and international levels, in efforts to combat trafficking. That Indonesia has this specific anti-trafficking law signals its clear recognition of one of the most serious human security threats.

Act on Disaster Management 24/2007
This Act's introduction acknowledges that geographical, geological, and demographic factors contribute to community vulnerability to disasters. Disasters, whether natural or man-made, may claim human lives. Policymakers must identify downside risks to be able to undertake preventive measures

and implement early-warning systems to mitigate possible future damage. Article 6 delineates the government's responsibility in disaster management, which includes risk reduction, incorporating such efforts into development programs, protecting society from impacts, and meeting the needs of victims/the displaced. Article 30 allows international and non-governmental organizations to participate in relief efforts and to receive government protection while conducting their tasks. This indicates acceptance, to a certain degree, of external intervention in responding to disasters.

Act on Social Conflicts Management 7/2012
This Act outlines comprehensive measures to respond to all stages of social conflict, starting from prevention (early-warning system), management (cessation of violence/hostilities), and resolution (post-conflict peace-building, reconstruction). It also lays out mechanisms for settlement, including establishment of an ad hoc task force. The Act reiterates the goal to protect the nation, including ensuring safety and security as well as the need to be free from fear to attain social welfare (as the Constitution mandates). Again, the State is held fully responsible for protection and promotion of human rights. This Act notes how ethnic, religious, and cultural diversity overlaps with injustice and the development gap, as well as social, economic, and political disparities in ways that carry the potential to cause conflict.[2]

Act on Elimination of Racial and Ethnicity Discriminations 40/2008
This Act stipulates the elimination of racial and ethnic discrimination through protecting and ensuring equality before the law (Article 5). Article 9 decrees that all citizens must be accorded equal and non-discriminatory treatment in attaining their civil, political, economic, and social rights. Article 8 further mandates the National Human Rights Commission to monitor efforts toward protection against discrimination, including conducting fact-finding investigations, which may be opened on government institutions suspected of discriminatory acts. Article 13 articulates the right of individuals to file a lawsuit in the face of any discriminatory treatment that causes certain loss.

4.4 Perceptions of Human Security

Human security is a very broad concept perceived differently by different individuals. This section elaborates how stakeholders from various backgrounds (i.e. government officials, ex-military, academics, and NGO staff) view human security and its threats/challenges. For the purposes of this chapter, human security is considered from the following aspects:

1. Elements of human security based on the *Human Development Report 1994*: freedom from fear, freedom from want, and freedom to live in dignity;
2. Response to human security challenges, whether geared toward protection (top-down) or more empowerment-oriented (bottom-up);
3. Preparedness for downside risks, beyond reactive or emergency responses; and
4. Policies to cope with both cross-border and domestic risks.

4.5 General Knowledge/Understanding of Human Security

In general, stakeholders in Indonesia have some knowledge of human security. At the very least, they retain basic understanding of what human security is—a concept that addresses issues related to the basic needs of human beings or individuals beyond a traditional security framework focused on military threats. However, very few of the respondents could articulate human security in similar terms to the framework provided by the *Human Development Report 1994*. Some had heard of the promotion of human security by the United Nations but were unable or unwilling to delve deeper into how the concept has developed.

While most respondents did not problematize the human security concept, one ex-military respondent commented on how its logic followed a path that is entirely separate from the traditional ("military") security idea. He argued that prioritization of certain problems to become a human security threat often occurs "by default," meaning that this happens due to the escalation of certain social problems, and then necessitates certain extraordinary measures to handle them, rather than being deliberately planned by the government from the outset. According to him, when certain non-military problems worsen to the extent that this situation goes beyond a certain threshold of threat to state security, then the government declares it as a human security issue.[3] This mirrors the argument of another respondent, an NGO activist, who said that human security is still mainly viewed in terms of the national security paradigm.[4]

The ex-military respondent cited two criteria that must be met in classifying an issue as a security threat. First, it must pose an existential danger, such as threatening the very survival of the people; second, it must establish a need to respond with extraordinary measures. The interviewee also pointed to the ambiguity in the human security concept, noting that there is no indicator available so far that would allow us to distinguish human security from human development. While acknowledging that threats to human security are real, he viewed that the Indonesian policymakers' understanding of human security remains lacking. This observation has some validity and was vindicated by the difficulty displayed by another respondent in distinguishing human security threats from problems relating to interpersonal relations (e.g. the injured dignity and sense of societal exclusion felt by an individual not invited to a wedding party).

Similarly, a high-ranking government official claimed that while he had no objection to the concept, he considered it very vague. He showed how the term human security has attracted criticism and rejection due to the political circumstances surrounding its inception, which prevented its inclusion into the report submitted by the High-Level Panel for the Millennium Development Goals in Post-2015. He warned against rushing to put everything under the term "human security." He regarded issues such as poverty, natural disasters, and religious conflicts as serious challenges, but considered them as falling within the social realm and not as security issues. A human security issue entails deliberate action by authorities to threaten the safety and security of its own people, namely through specific regulations that clearly limit freedoms (from want/fear and to live in dignity). When this does not occur, an issue remains in the social or economic realm and should not be treated as a security matter.[5]

While governmental and non-governmental actors understand the concept differently, both comprehend that human security extends beyond traditional security (linkage to military dimension/defense issues). Some respondents referred to the term "non-traditional security threats" when identifying human security threats. Civil society respondents believed that the government has considerable knowledge of human security (its definition, threats, and challenges), and there is the possibility that some human security elements have been considered or incorporated into policy frameworks. However, high-ranking officials may have a better understanding than lower-ranking officials, and this might have repercussions at the implementation level.

4.5.1 *Human Security as a Policy Framework*

The respondents generally agreed, however, that human security is a useful policy framework, especially when used to raise security issues that threaten individuals in dimensions beyond the military. However, the use of a human security framework has not automatically led to comprehensive policies. An NGO respondent focusing on poverty alleviation illustrated how in relation to this issue policies tend to be constructed from the philanthropic or charity lens, instead of as a set of comprehensive measures, resulting in reactive rather than preventive and sustained responses.[6]

Another challenge comes from the ineluctable political calculation within the decision-making process. An issue will be attended to only when there are political benefits to be gained from it. This could be observed especially in the lackluster efforts to protect religious freedom. Defending minority interests does not necessarily serve leaders' interests, quite the reverse, it might be counterproductive (leading to a vote backlash in future elections or challenging their political legitimacy). Similarly, on the issue of deforestation, an emphatic stress on preventing more conversion of land for industrial purposes might risk antagonizing investors (e.g. palm oil companies) who may provide job opportunities to locals.[7]

Finally, incorporation of human security as a policy framework is not enough. Strong political will is still required. This is clearly missing in the government's response to the migrant workers' issue. Despite awareness of actual problems, the government appears reluctant to criticize or negotiate with host countries where violations and abuse of workers persist, preferring not to disrupt bilateral relations and hence, focus on protecting the state (i.e. sovereignty/state dignity) rather than the human (worker rights).

4.5.2 *Priority Issues in Human Security*

Regarding the question of which element of human security is a priority for Indonesia, a bias is apparent toward the issues that respondents focus on, which covers a wide variety of areas, such as environment/climate change/deforestation, health, religious freedom, horizontal conflicts, land struggles, women, and migrant workers protection. Concerns relating to economic security are (income gap/inequality, unequal distribution of welfare/resources) also featured frequently.

Respondents generally regarded the three elements of human security, that is, freedom from fear, freedom from want, and freedom to live in dignity, as interrelated. This interlinkage is illustrated by a respondent who asserted that due to the land's association with identity, land grabbing represents not only a threat to freedom from want but also to the freedom to live in dignity. Similarly, the Papua crisis signaled not only the need to pay attention to economic security (freedom from want) but also to dignity because this is what is being seriously undermined in the Papuan case. Moreover, poverty, closely associated with freedom from want, receives special attention as it is likely to lead to other kinds of threats (terrorism, radicalism, extremism). Climate change is also perceived as carrying spillover risk potentials, such as food insecurity, and the propensity to extreme weather.

Regarding freedom from fear, some respondents argued that the situation has improved compared to the New Order era (1967–1998), which saw limited freedom of expression under an authoritarian rule. Others suggested that a different kind of threat is present in the post-*Reformasi* era, which stems from the government's ignorance of its duty to protect minorities. Prioritizing these threats is affected by very real dilemmas. As has been briefly touched upon, in dealing with deforestation, a potential clash is presented between prioritizing environmental security (preventing more forest conversion) over the need to achieve economic security. The latter might require allowing more palm oil production, for example, to increase to meet consumption level. There is high domestic demand for palm oil and it is a significant export commodity for Indonesia.

Regarding issues of human security, some respondents rather disagree with the idea of treating these social and environmental problems as security threats as we have seen. The ex-military respondent cautioned against conceptualizing certain issues as human security problems. For example, famine should be assessed first through its scale, to show whether the level of incidence is widespread, and hence endangers the whole society. Otherwise, it cannot be categorized as a human security threat. Infectious diseases should also first be subjected to evaluation, to determine severity as well as the speed at which the infection spreads to decide whether immediate and extraordinary measures should be used. If such measures are not needed, it cannot be defined as a human security threat. While agreeing that human security is part of national security, he said that there should be a clear understanding of whether or not a certain issue is really a security threat or not to decide what measures should be taken. If an issue does not present any existential threat (does not threaten to destroy human lives), it should not be considered as a human security threat. In a related argument, another high-ranking official surmised that there are no human security challenges in Indonesia. In his view, challenges are not inherent, but lie rather in the way people fail to position themselves *vis-à-vis* challenges. He explained that people become victims of natural disasters when the local government fails to properly impose an effective "zoning" system that maps disaster-prone areas and prevents people from living within them, or when there is refusal to follow official instructions to vacate the said areas.

4.5.3 Protection and/or Empowerment

There is a shared perception that the government, at both national and local levels, is the actor most responsible for dealing with human security threats. Respondents alluded to the government's resources and capacities as main modalities that allow it to empower civil society, so that the latter might work alongside the government in addressing challenges. More broadly, beyond the government-civil society partnership, high-ranking official respondents acknowledged that it is indeed the government's obligation toward its citizens to facilitate their self-empowerment, especially through the provision of health and education.

Opinions were split on the issue of protection, with academic and NGO respondents claiming that the government still failed the people in various ways. For religious freedom, for example, protection is practically non-existent. Even worse, rather than protecting religious freedom, the government, especially at the local level, often acts as the violator of this right. The government continues to advance official discourse on maintaining "religious harmony" (*kerukunan beragama*), and preserving stability, disregarding situations in which minority groups or those who interpret mainstream religions differently are required to "adjust" accordingly (to the dominant convention of the majority). In various cases of violent attacks against minority groups, either intra-religious (persecution of the Shi'ites and Ahmadiyyah, e.g.) or inter-religious, the government overlooks the problem by either feigning ignorance or failing to recognize the threats posed to human security (Halili and Naipospos 2013). This denial validates views criticizing the government's absenteeism or evasion of responsibility.

Government respondents said in response that they have made serious efforts to address human security challenges through the implementation of various policies to improve health, reduce environmental degradation, assist communities in coping with climate change impacts, and alleviate poverty. They also emphasized that the government has indiscriminately provided equal opportunities to all citizens in pursuing economic and social rights and extending public services such as health provision. Some respondents had a more nuanced perception of the government's efforts in protecting against climate change. One NGO activist respondent argued that despite adoption of many policies to mitigate impacts, great challenges remain at the implementation level. For example, monitoring Indonesia's forest areas presents an arduous task due to their size. Maintaining updated statistics is greatly challenging since data collection can take almost a year. By the time they are available, data are usually outdated.

One main issue regarding protection, pertaining to the previous discussion on prioritization, concerns whose security should be emphasized in which area. The main challenge in the issue of deforestation concerns the impasse between protecting the environment and protecting local livelihoods. Providing access to forests is crucial since activities such as clearing the forest for farming and collecting wood and other resources are central to economic security. One respondent highlighted the importance of finding a balanced solution, which simultaneously sustains the palm oil industry and mitigates negative impacts.

On the issue of migrant workers, instead of protection, collusion between state and non-state actors (agencies that engage in sending workers abroad) has resulted in workers' commodification. The government and the labor agencies prioritize placement, mainly treating labor out-migration as a business transaction. The practice persists as most agencies are owned by politically powerful individuals. Furthermore, very few respondents responded to the question on empowerment. When asked about the role of civil society, the activist respondent from the World Resources Institute (WRI), an organization concerned with deforestation, criticized prominent NGOs' failure in considering the problem holistically. For instance, Greenpeace takes a strong stand against the palm oil industry, but fails to find viable, alternative solutions to safeguard economic security. The WRI activist shared a best practice where people living around protected forest areas are hired professionally as rangers to monitor potentially harmful activities while ensuring that some zones along the forest borders are reserved for local farming.[8] Finally, for religious freedoms, the situation is markedly different. Rather than empowering civil society, the government often attempts to repress critical groups. One activist respondent remarked that civil society actors are still largely excluded from the decision-making process and often seen as troublemakers.

4.5.4 *Downside Risks: How Prepared Are We?*

Several respondents were unclear as to what comprises "downside risk," despite prior explanation being provided to them (the term was defined as "certain conditions which may, if ignored in the mid- or long-term, develop into serious human security threats"). Some of them regarded income gap/inequality as an urgent downside risk. Meanwhile, one scholar respondent contended that land conflicts and conflict/competition over resources should be considered mid-term risks as the number of incidences has risen and claimed significant loss in terms of property and human lives.

Regarding health, government respondents claimed they have sufficiently acknowledged the importance of prevention measures. For example, the Ministry of Health has initiated reproductive health education for the public. However, this program attracted strong criticism and demands for cancelation from radical groups, claiming that it would encourage people to engage in pre-marital sex. Similarly, distribution of needles and condoms as part of HIV/AIDS prevention was viewed as promoting drug abuse and risky sexual behavior.[9]

On migrant workers' protection, one respondent stated that it is fairly easy to identify downside risks as persisting issues remain, such as forged documents, recruitment of underage workers that leads to child labor, abuse of tourist visas, and deployment of untrained workers who are vulnerable to exploitation. To date, serious efforts toward finding solutions have been lacking, which results in the recurrence of problems.[10] On religious freedom, legal recognition of only six religions and the government's discourse on religious harmony in the name of stability have sown the seeds of conflict, resulting in attacks against those minorities perceived to be religious deviants. One scholar focusing on this issue passionately admonished that it is not for the government to decide which religions or teachings are correct or incorrect.

One scholar respondent pointed to unemployment as a contributing factor to the easy recruitment of youth by terrorist groups, as observed in Poso, an area where communal conflict has previously occurred. She considered the government's strategy to be short sighted and merely focused on stopping direct violence. Absence of mid- and long-term planning forges the potential for further cycles of violence. To give another example, in Aceh, after the peace agreement was signed, the government discontinued policies that addressed human security challenges, such as food insecurity (McCarthy 2013). On the other side, several scholars highlighted that the government's inability to handle downside risk is strongly linked to failure to facilitate and support research in institutions/universities, as well as lack of a comprehensive database to support it. Even if research were conducted, the government would be reluctant to use the results as the basis for generating policies, preventive measures, or long-term roadmaps.

Another main problem concerns the proclivity for a one-size-fits-all policy, which disregards the importance of identifying the distinct characteristics of each human security challenge within the context of the area where it occurs. This was the case with the official approach to land conflict in Jambi, where the government's solution was a simple return of the land, which was not supported by any investigation of the actual matter at hand. Human security efforts are also often hampered by lack of coordination. For example, during the land conflict in Mesuji, the local government did not carry through with directives issued by the Coordinating Minister for Political and Security Affairs to relocate encroachers into the protected area to prevent further conflicts. The ex-military respondent lamented the dissolution of the Coordinating Agency for National Stability (*Bakorstanas*), a previous instrument used to monitor potential internal threats.[11] The disbanding of this body, according to him, led to coordination problems. Nowadays, the police and armed forces often clash with each other at crucial times when a joint response is needed. A scholar respondent focusing on conflict resolution, however, contradicted this view and argued that a Violence Monitoring System (*Sistem Nasional Pemantau Kekerasan/SNPK*)[12] has been developed under the coordinating efforts of the Ministry of Welfare.

4.5.5 *Cross-Border Issues, Sovereignty, and Military Involvement*

Issues emerging from the interviews were mainly domestic. Discussion of cross-border risks was limited, with the exception of the mention of the need for international cooperation in combating human trafficking. There was consensus among respondents on the importance of sovereignty, although the majority also emphasized cooperation with other countries and international organizations. Cooperation in dealing with HIV/AIDS, malaria, and tuberculosis was cited as an important example. Concerning disaster management, one high-ranking official, who was directly involved in coordinating the post-tsunami efforts in Aceh, strongly dismissed the portrayal of foreign humanitarian assistance as intervention.[13]

Respondents displayed divergent views regarding religious conflict. One respondent expressed the opinion that interventions are needed, although they should not necessarily be military in form. Instead of praising Indonesia as a model for democracy and diversity, foreign leaders, especially those from major countries, should pressure the government by condemning its lackluster response to the increasing violations of religious freedom. Mechanisms such as the Universal Periodical Review (UPR) could also be utilized.[14] Another respondent preferred non-intervention, as religious discord is customarily considered a domestic problem. Foreign countries claiming to be democracies tend to use such issues to pursue their own agendas over weaker countries. According to him, it is possible for intervention to occur at the societal level. Groups with ties/affiliations to minority groups in country X can call on their own government to wield influence over the government in country X to stop violations against its minority. This could be observed in the way his people have rallied for the Palestinian, Bosnian, and Kashmiri causes.[15]

Another respondent pointed to the Rohingya issue, which has emerged as a regional concern. Considering that a fraction of the Rohingya did travel to Indonesia and requested support from radical groups, as well as the fact that there were threats directed at Buddhist worship houses and the Myanmar Embassy in Jakarta, serious regional cooperation is indeed needed.[16]

Finally, most respondents agreed that involving the Indonesian military in addressing some human security threats (e.g. natural disasters) is acceptable if the ultimate decision on action lies with the civilian government, in this case the president. It is not within the military's own discretion to decide to intervene. Military response is not always appropriate: the police should be the main agency deployed to restore order. Military engagement should be limited, as they are not trained to counter non-military threats.

4.6 From Yudhoyono to the Jokowi Era: More Promising?

During his administration, President Yudhoyono carried out initiatives that to a certain extent addressed human security problems. An example is the issuance of the Perppu 1/2008, which granted Special Autonomy status to West Papua to accelerate development and infrastructure building at the local level. Toward the end of Yudhoyono's second term, the Village Act (Undang-undang Desa) 6/2014 was passed to drive decentralization down to the most local level, marking a crucial recognition of the village as a traditional governmental unit, which has often been marginalized in national development. The presidential succession in 2014 raised high expectations, particularly for more "down-to-earth" political leadership as the elected president, Joko Widodo, or Jokowi, as he is more affectionately called, is widely regarded as exemplifying a leader hailing from the common people. High hopes mounted for a more humanist, less elitist approach during his term.

There are several indicators to refer to how a human security perspective has been better reflected and elevated to priority focus under Jokowi's administration. The first is the nine-priority agenda, dubbed "*Nawa Cita.*" Introduced during his presidential campaign (Jokowi 2014), it centers on enhancing people's quality of life and assisting the marginalized. Upon Jokowi's election, the agenda was immediately adopted and elaborated in the Mid-Term National Development Plan (*Rencana Pembangunan Jangka Menengah Nasional/RPJMN*) 2015–2019, and can be seen as another indicator of commitment to human security.

Among the many programs outlined in this development plan, several could be considered groundbreaking. The first is the administration's "asymmetric decentralization," which transforms the previous centralized development approach into a policy pathway that gives more attention to remote/outer areas, including border regions, to create equitable development, and more responsiveness to specific needs at the local level. This has mainly been translated into an acceleration of infrastructure development, that is, the building of roads, seaports, airports, and railroads to open up access and enhance economic interaction. Another breakthrough is the launch of a series of programs to improve health and educational provisions, create job opportunities, increase subsidized housing, and implement land reform. In health provision and employment protection, the government has intensified delivery of services through the Agency of Social Security (*Badan Penyelenggara Jaminan Sosial/*BPJS). To make this universal coverage scheme work, the administration has re-enunciated the participatory obligation of all citizens under the existing Act No. 24/2011. The third major breakthrough is the political commitment to solve past human rights violations and protect the marginalized. The third indicator of more commitment toward improving human security is the recent attention toward the Sustainable Development Goals (SDGs), especially through the issuance of the Presidential Regulation 59/2017 on the Implementation of SDGs. This regulation provides legal basis for the establishment of a national coordination team for SDGs under the Minister for National Development Planning, the development of the roadmap as well as the national and regional action plan, and the accompanying reporting and financing mechanisms.

Finally, the fourth indicator is the increasing attention on Papua. Within months after his inauguration, President Widodo made a visit to Papua in December 2014 to spend New Year's Eve there. This gesture symbolized his intent to shift focus toward this long-neglected region. Widodo has since made subsequent visits to the provinces, even to the conflict areas, the last one undertaken in May 2017 to monitor the Trans Papua road construction. For 2017, the government increased its budget allotment, to a total of IDR 8.2 trillion for Papua and IDR 3.3 trillion for West Papua.[17] At the beginning of his administration, Jokowi had proclaimed his intention to implement a comprehensive approach in Papua, which would balance development ambitions (building infrastructure) and humanist concerns. This has been translated into breakthrough policies such as adjusting the fuel price in Papua to the same level as Java, lifting restrictions on foreign journalistic coverage of Papua, as well as the release of political prisoners involved in the Free Papuan Movement (Organisasi Papua Merdeka/OPM).

While Jokowi's policies seem to indicate a positive outlook toward greater incorporation of human security in the policy framework, limitations remain. The main problem lies in the heavy focus on the economic sector; though it is important to close the infrastructure gap, particularly to accelerate economic development in marginalized areas, human security, as elaborated earlier, also entails other dimensions, including the political and socio-cultural. It is imperative that equal commitment be given to resolving political issues, especially as Indonesia is seeing growing religious intolerance, which often intensifies during local and national election periods. The people also await the government's firm resoluteness in addressing unresolved past human rights abuses, such as the communist purge in 1965, the anti-Chinese riots in May 1998, and the Tanjung Priok tragedy. With regard to the 1965 tragedy, while the government has shown goodwill in its initiative to organize a national symposium facilitating dialogue with the victims (alleged members of or sympathizers with the purged Indonesian Communist Party), significant follow-ups have been stalled by strong pressures from different elements within the society, as communism is still widely perceived as the biggest threat to the country. Finally, with regard to Papua, despite many efforts as well as additional funds poured into the region to accelerate development, a comprehensive approach which balances economic and humanist approaches remains to be seen as referendum calls persist, evident in the recent petition to the United Nations, which was signed by 70 percent of the locals (it has now been dropped) (Doherty and Lamb 2017; Hawley 2017).

4.7 Conclusions

While human security is widely known and various stakeholders have a general comprehension of the concept, it has not been fully incorporated into policy frameworks or optimized as an effective tool in addressing "new security threats/challenges." Interviews with the elites highlight a concern about regarding human security as a "foreign" concept that requires clarification and further discussion in the Indonesian context. Before it can be adopted, it needs to be adapted to the context and complexities at the local level. While elements of human security are touched on broadly in several regulations, they do not offer deeper elaboration regarding how it should be adopted as a full policy framework. They do not expand on aspects such as empowerment and downside risks, focusing only on ad hoc and immediate measures rather than developing instruments to identify preventive actions.

We noticed some differences between the national survey and the stakeholder interviews. Whereas the national survey pointed to unemployment and food shortage as the two most crucial challenges, interviewees tended to view challenges in more abstract terms, such as inequality and poverty. Survey respondents also focused more on direct causation, while the interviewees took indirect causation into consideration (displaying a more holistic examination of a problem). For example, survey respondents regarded natural disasters as a human security threat in themselves, while the interviewees saw beyond disasters per se, viewing them rather as consequences of more fundamental threats, such as environmental degradation or, even, poverty.

Stakeholders tended to identify issues of their own focus/interests as the most significant human security challenge. Some actors still have reservations about the human security concept, particularly since it may dilute the criteria for security definition. Several would even argue that there are currently no serious security threats in Indonesia since existing issues do not gravely threaten the survival of individuals. Regarding protection and empowerment, most stakeholders agreed that the government has only made minimal efforts in safeguarding freedom from fear/want/

to live in dignity. On certain issues such as religious discord, the government could even be regarded as the perpetrator. Relating to empowerment, the non-government stakeholders' view that the government still does not provide enough support for civil society contrasted with the government stakeholders' opinion that empowerment should come from individuals themselves. Most respondents fell short of elaborating on the cross-border dimensions of human security, highlighting concerns that are mostly domestic or national in scope, although human trafficking and migrant workers protection did get mentioned. Relating to sovereignty, most stakeholders did not interpret cooperation or assistance from other countries as intervention; rather, they saw it as necessary, especially when the government is unable to deal with an issue effectively. All interviewees strongly underlined that military involvement should be limited and subject to civilian control, particularly as the military is not equipped to deal with non-military threats.

In the end, reflecting on the Jokowi administration, there is a slight promise for a better incorporation of the human security framework in future policy-making processes. However, we need stronger political will from the government, especially in addressing harder issues beyond the current economic focus. While it is necessary to improve material welfare, a comprehensive approach that equally addresses other dimensions, the political and socio-cultural, is crucial.

Notes

1. This chapter addresses both potential and actual threats. "Potential" refers to threats that have not previously occurred or have very rarely taken place while at the same time carrying the potential, should such events take place, to threaten the existence and security of the state. "Actual" refers to threats that have previously taken place and are likely to recur.
2. A closer observation reveals how this Act is charged with anxiety over the heightened possibility of intervention in the context of a globalizing world. For countries undergoing democratic transition like Indonesia, foreign interference is a potentially aggravating factor, particularly in horizontal conflicts.
3. Military Source #1.
4. Civil Society Source #1.
5. Government Source #1.
6. Civil Society Source #2.
7. Civil Society Source #3.

8. Civil Society Source #3.
9. Government Source #2.
10. Civil Society Source #4.
11. Aside from ministry representatives, this institution is comprised of retired military officers.
12. *Sistem Nasional Pemantauan Kekerasan* (SNPK) is an information system that provides data and analysis on incidents of conflict and violence that are taking place in different areas of Indonesia. The main activities are to collect detailed and periodical data on when, where, how, and why violence is taking place as well as the impacts of such violence. The data serve as basis for policy analyses and designing conflict management and prevention.
13. Government Source #3.
14. Civil Society Source #5.
15. Civil Society Source #6.
16. Civil Society Source #7.
17. The budget comprises of the special autonomy and additional budget for infrastructure development. Ministry of Finance, *National Budget Information 2017* (Informasi APBN 2017).

References

CSA (Central Statistics Agency). 2014a. *Number of Poor People, Percentage of Poor People, and the Poverty Line, 1970–2013*. Jakarta: Central Statistics Agency.

———. 2014b. *Number of Labor Force, Labor, Unemployment, TPAK and TPT, 1986–2013*. Jakarta: Central Statistics Agency.

———. 2014c. *Health Indicators 1995–2012*. Jakarta: Central Statistics Agency.

———. 2014d. *Numbers and Percentage of People Under Poverty, the Poverty Line, Poverty Depth Index, and Poverty Prevalence Index by Provinces, March 2014*. Jakarta: Central Statistics Agency.

———. 2014e. *Unemployment Rate and Workforce Participation Rate by Provinces, 2002–2012*. Jakarta: Central Statistics Agency.

CSIS (Centre for Strategic and International Studies). 2014. *National Survey March 2014*. Jakarta: CSIS.

Doherty, Ben, and Kate Lamb. 2017. Banned West Papua Independence Petition Handed to UN. *The Guardian*, September 27.

Halili, and Bonar Tigor Naipospos. 2013. *Stagnasi Kebebasan Beragama: Laporan Kondisi Kebebasan Beragama/Berkeyakinan di Indonesia Tahun 2013* [Religious Freedom Stagnation: A Report on the Condition of Religious Freedom in Indonesia]. Setara Institute. http://www.setara-institute.org/sites/setara-institute.org/files/Reports/140522-buku%20laporan%20kbb%20 2013%20SETARA%20INSTITUTE.pdf. Accessed 31 July 2014.

Hawley, Samantha. 2017. West Papua Independence Petition Does Not Exist, United Nations Says. *The ABC News*, September 29. http://www.abc.net.au/news/2017-09-29/west-papua-independence-petition-reports-false-say-un/9001538.

IRIN News and Analysis. 2013. Growing HIV/AIDS Awareness in Indonesia's Papua Region. *IRIN News and Analysis*. http://www.irinnews.org/report/98245/growing-hiv-aids-awareness-in-indonesia-s-papua-region. Accessed 28 Oct 2014.

Jokowi, J.K. 2014. *The Way of Change for a Sovereign, Independent, and Personable Indonesia – Vision, Mission, and Action Program Jokowi-Jusuf Kalla* [Jalan Perubahan untuk Indonesia yang Berdaulat, Mandiri, dan Berkepribadian – Visi Misi, dan Program Aksi Jokowi-Jusuf Kalla], Jakarta, May. http://kpu.go.id/koleksigambar/VISI_MISI_Jokowi-JK.pdf. Accessed 20 Dec 2014.

McCarthy, John. 2013. *Learning from Disaster: Why Does Food Insecurity Persist in Post Tsunami Aceh?* Development Policy Center, November 6. http://devpolicy.org/learning-from-disaster-why-does-food-insecurity-persist-in-post-tsunami-aceh-20131106/. Accessed 2 July 2014.

Ministry of Finance. 2017. *National Budget Information 2017*. Jakarta: Informasi APBN 2017.

Ministry of National Planning. 2014. *Mid-Term National Development Plan 2015–2019*. Jakarta: Kementerian PPN/ Bappenas.

Sukma, Rizal. 2010. Indonesia's Security Outlook, Defence Policy, and Regional Cooperation. In *Asia Pacific Countries' Security Outlook and Its Implications for the Defense Sector*, NIDS Joint Research Series, ed. The National Institute for Defense Studies, Japan, vol. 5, 3–24. Tokyo: The National Institute for Defense Studies.

UNDP (United Nations Development Programme). 1994. *Human Development Report 1994*. New York: Oxford University Press.

Interviews

Military Source #1. 2014. Interviewed by author in Jakarta, June 6.

Civil Society Source #1. 2014. Interviewed by the author in Jakarta, June 16.

Government Source #1. 2014. Interviewed by the author in Jakarta, June 6.

Civil Society Source #2. 2014. Respondent from SMERU Research Institute. Interviewed by the author in Jakarta, June 6.

Civil Society Source #3. 2014. Respondent from World Resources Institute (WRI). Interviewed by the author in Jakarta, May 20.

Government Source #2. 2014. High-rank official from Ministry of Health. Interviewed by the author in Jakarta, June 30.

Civil Society Source #4. 2014. Respondent from Migrant Care. Interviewed by the author in Jakarta, June 16.

Government Source #3. 2014. High-ranking official previously in charge on the Rehabilitation and Reconstruction Agency for Aceh. Interviewed by the author in Jakarta, June 17.

Civil Society Source #5. 2014. Human rights activist from Human Rights Watch. Interviewed by the author in Jakarta, June 16.

Civil Society Source #6. 2014. Respondent from Indonesian Consortium for Religious Studies (ICRS). Interviewed by the author in Jakarta, May 20.

Civil Society Source #7. 2014. Human rights activist from Institute for Policy Analysis of Conflict (IPAC). Interviewed by the author in Jakarta, May 20.

CHAPTER 5

An Analysis of Japanese Stakeholder Perceptions

Kaoru Kurusu

5.1 Introduction

A variety of human security issues have emerged in the field of international public policy over the past two decades. The notion of human security was first highlighted in the *Human Development Report* 1994 (United Nations Development Program 1994), and since then has been discussed and developed in a series of reports, declarations, and resolutions of the United Nations (UN) and other regional organizations (G8 1999; APEC 2004; UNGA 2005, 2012). The report of the Commission on Human Security (CHS), *Human Security Now* specifically elaborated the concept in a way that a human-centered approach could be put into practice (CHS 2003).

The commission's report focuses on the following key elements: (i) the goal of human security is to assure the three freedoms, freedom from want, freedom from fear, and freedom to live in dignity; (ii) human security pays attention to the aspect of downside risks; (iii) human security helps individuals and communities not only cope with actual threats but

K. Kurusu (✉)
Graduate School of Law, Kobe University, Kobe, Japan
e-mail: kurusu@dragon.kobe-u.ac.jp

Y. Mine et al. (eds.), *Human Security Norms in East Asia*, Security, Development and Human Rights in East Asia,
https://doi.org/10.1007/978-3-319-97247-3_5

also works to prevent them. To prevent risks to human survival, strengthening the "resilience" of people and society is the key; (iv) the goals of human security would be better achieved by combining protection and empowerment; (v) the human security approach stresses the significance of a multi-sectoral approach since most human security issues are crosscutting in nature; and (vi) the goals of human security would be better achieved by approaching not only individuals but also communities.

The concept elaborated by the CHS went through further elaboration and review processes from 2005 through 2012 and was developed into the resolution adopted by the UN General Assembly (UNGA) in 2012. Then, has the introduction of "human security" brought about any value to our well-being and security? To give a preliminary answer to this question, this chapter focuses on the case of Japan. Japan is a special case due to its explicit stance of having accepted and promoted the concept of human security from the very outset.

Academic literature on human security is abundant (Paris 2001; Newman and Richmond 2001; King and Murray 2001; Tadjbakhsh and Chenoy 2007). However, despite Japan's status as one of the main advocates of human security, empirical analyses on its commitment to human security have been limited in number. Studies of the Japanese government's human security policy have been undertaken (Tan 2010; Edström 2008; Gilson and Purvis 2003; Soeya 2005; Fukushima 2010; Bosold and Werthes 2005). Their studies present interesting analyses of policy processes, but systematic analyses of Japanese stakeholders' perceptions of human security are scarce. Therefore, this study collected data from interviews of key Japanese stakeholders on their perceptions of the utility of the human security concept.

This research aims to depict the characteristics of the key Japanese stakeholder perceptions of human security, while leaving room for incorporating specificity and details of their discourse by utilizing their narratives. For this purpose, "semi-structured" interviews were conducted.[1] Interviews were conducted with ten major individuals not only from the government sector but also from academia, civil society, and business. The selection of interviewees was not based on representativeness among a population, but on their significance for the research theme itself (key informant interviews). They have either been involved in policymaking and implementation or written about human security. Ordinary people or beneficiaries of human security projects overseas were not included.[2]

In each interview, we raised six clusters of questions: (i) understanding of human security; (ii) human insecurities in East Asia and Japan; (iii) cross-border responses to human security, including the cases of accepting assistance and providing assistance, involving the issue of state sovereignty; (iv) human security in practice, especially on protection and empowerment; (v) the conceptual basis of human security, that is, on freedom from fear, freedom from want, and freedom to live in dignity; and (vi) their views on the added value of human security.[3] We made it clear if their statements were based on their personal viewpoints or representing their organization.

In the next section, a brief overview of how Japan's human security policy has evolved will be presented. The subsequent sections will analyze the perceptions of key stakeholders along the line of the above six questions.

5.2 Human Security in Japan's Foreign Policy[4]

Around the time when the Human Development Report was published in 1994, the definition and usage of the term human security by Japanese policymakers was far from settled. For instance, during this period some parliamentarians used the notion in the context of domestic issues such as the government's response to the Great Hanshin Awaji Earthquake of 1995, and social welfare policy, whereas others referred to human security in debating foreign policy.[5] Only after Prime Minister Keizo Obuchi came to power did the Japanese government start to regard human security as its main foreign policy tool. From 1997 through 1998, Japan sought an appropriate policy concept that succinctly expressed the philosophy behind the country's assistance to people suffering from the Asian economic crisis. Since then, the Japanese government has engaged itself in promoting and implementing the concept, one step toward this was the establishment of the United Nations Trust Fund for Human Security in 1999 (Kurusu 2011a). Gradually from this period onward, human security has become a term that the government has used primarily in promoting development assistance policy and foreign policy in multilateral organizations.

While the Japanese government pursued human security in issues related to official development assistance (ODA) and global issues, the Canadian government also used human security to denote its policies when campaigning for the treaty banning anti-personnel landmines and later in establishing the International Commission on Intervention and State Sovereignty (ICISS). This was done to discuss the crucial issue of transcending sovereignty in cases of large-scale loss of life with genocidal intentions or in the failed state situation (McRae and Hubert 2001; Smith 2006). In short, it explicitly articulated "freedom from fear" as a policy priority. Japan took the initiative of establishing the CHS partially due to the need to address the gap between the two governments' stances toward human security (Kurusu 2011a). The commission reconsidered the concept of human security holistically and submitted a report to the UN Secretary General (UNSG) in 2003.

After the report was published, the Japanese government introduced its main ideas into the revised ODA Charter of 2003 and since then human security has become one of the fundamental principles of Japan's ODA (Ministry of Foreign Affairs 2003). The Japan International Cooperation Agency (JICA), under the new leadership of Sadako Ogata, a former head of UNHCR and co-chair of the CHS, also began to incorporate its ideas into the organization's principles. In 2004 JICA presented its revised policy pillars: "on the ground," "efficacy, benefit, speed," and "human security." To realize these policy pillars in actual projects, JICA introduced the "Seven Aspects of Human Security."[6] The CHS report was so influential that it encouraged Japanese stakeholders, though mainly governmental actors, to rethink or confirm their views on human security (Kurusu 2011a). The Japanese stakeholders' understanding of human security converged around the ideas presented in the commission's report.

Though progressing more slowly, human security started to be incorporated into other foreign policy fields than development assistance. Human security came to be implemented in a manner closely related to the peacebuilding activities that the Japanese government launched at the beginning of the 2000s. In the 2003 ODA Charter introduced above, the Japanese government made clear that its overseas assistance would be used for peacebuilding activities, i.e. "consolidation of peace" and "state-building" in Japanese terminology (MOFA 2003). Human security and peacebuilding were expected to add new official flavors to Japan's foreign policy posture by expanding areas of activities for "international contribution."

Within the Foreign Ministry, human security has tended to be regarded as a matter to be dealt with mainly by bodies such as the International Cooperation Bureau. From the mid-2000s onwards, the International Cooperation Bureau started to actively disseminate the human security notion in the UNGA. Such initiatives led to the inclusion of a paragraph on human security in the final document of the World Summit in 2005 and adoption of a resolution on human security in 2012 (UNGA 2012).

It was a highpoint in Japan's understanding of human security as its foreign policy tool (Kurusu 2018).

After 2012, there were two developments that drove Japanese stakeholders to reconsider the meaning and utility of human security. First, since the government has achieved its tentative goal of acquiring the UNGA resolution, it is now faced with a situation in which it might lose further impetus in the field of human security. Second, the Japanese stakeholders were moved by the experience of the Great East Japan Earthquake in March 2011 and the radioactive contamination subsequently caused by Fukushima Daiichi Nuclear Power Plant. It has become more common to hear the argument that human security should be applied throughout Japanese society as well (Katsumata 2011).

5.3 The Conceptual Interpretation of Human Security

With regard to the characteristics of the usage of the human security concept in Japan, the previous literature points to the following: human security has been regarded as a governmental policy; it is a broad and comprehensive conception; and state security and human security are complementary. In this section, I will further elaborate such features mainly based on our interviews. In addition to the above characteristics, the Japanese government has tried to ensure that state sovereignty be respected and that non-military approaches to human security are prioritized. This aspect will be further elaborated in Section 5.5.

As discussed above, in Japan, human security has been regarded as part of the Japanese government's foreign policy agenda. For the foreign ministry, it is regarded as one of its foreign policy pillars and a guiding principle for international cooperation. For the current ruling parties (Liberal Democratic Party and Komeito, as of November 2017), human security is likewise one of the policy pillars. The concept of human security has gained nearly non-partisan support to date in Japan.[7] However, at the same time, there has been strong criticism against the above idea of "human security as government policy"; that is, the government has been criticized for using the notion of human security just as a "slogan" to advertise its foreign policy. By contrast, Japanese civil society organizations seldom use the term "human security." Though their tasks and approaches could quite often be suitably expressed by the notion of human security, they have found limited utility in the concept thus far.

With the above tendency in mind, our interviewees emphasized future possibilities. One acknowledged that many non-governmental organization (NGO) activities fall within the scope of human security, and that human security, by putting the human being at the center, can become a novel concept that encourages consideration of problems in a comprehensive way (Civil Society Sector Source #1). However, it requires collective contributions from various actors based on a multi-sectoral approach. Another interviewee suggested that private corporations could also be involved in human security issues, either on their own or in partnership with actors in other sectors (Private Sector Source #1). These comments suggest that, whether or not the notion of "human security" is used by various non-governmental actors, such actors have been active in human security issues for a long time. And there is the possibility that the human security notion could serve as the glue to bring various actors together to cope with such issues by using a comprehensive approach.

The second generally known characteristic is that Japanese actors have understood human security as a broad and comprehensive concept. Issues related to "freedom from want," such as poverty alleviation and coping with global issues of infectious disease and natural disasters, have been the main targets of Japan's human security policies. More issues, however, have gradually started to be counted as relating to "freedom from fear." These include the removal of anti-personnel landmines, the consolidation of peace, and state-building. At the same time there has also been a growing recognition that both "freedoms" are interrelated. According to most interviews, human security is indeed mostly perceived as a broad and comprehensive concept. A staff member of an aid agency explained that human security is a broad concept and that a variety of JICA projects fall generally under this concept (Aid Agency Source #3).

The third typical characteristic of the Japanese actors' understanding of human security concerns the relationship between human security and state security. Human security and state security are often seen as being at opposite ends of a continuum in their approach to security considerations. However, this does not necessarily mean that state security and human security are contradictory; rather, it is that on many occasions when the state functions well these concepts can complement each other. Of course, if a government is not functioning and thereby unable to provide security for its people, or the government itself undermines people's security, then enhancing state security undermines or is unrelated to people's security. Among our respondents, there was a common recognition of these points as well.

There are other characteristics that can be drawn from the interviews. Many of the interviewees attached a practical meaning to human security. Interviewees stressed that the actual humanitarian result is more important than term usage of human security (Academic Sector Sources #1 and #2). Then what are the characteristics of the human security concept when considered in a more practical sense? For one JICA staff member, the introduction of human security induced JICA to implement projects directly accessible to people, and that they should not only build the capacity of governments but also empower people and communities through the grassroots level based on "bottom-up" approaches (Aid Agency Source #3). On the other hand, an interviewee from an NGO stated that, for NGOs, human security is not new at all, since the human-centered approach is the *raison d'etre* for many NGOs. However, it can become innovative and has strength when it encourages a multi-sector/agency approach based on a more comprehensive examination of a problem that cannot be realized by a single NGO (Civil Society Sector Source #1).

5.4 Risks in East Asia and Japan

5.4.1 *A Variety of Human Security Risks in East Asia*

According to our interviews, human security risks in the East Asia can be categorized into several groups of issues. These are (i) natural disasters and environmental risks, (ii) interstate relations, (iii) intrastate or regional conflicts, and (iv) social issues. First, almost all the interviewees responded that natural disasters, such as earthquakes, tsunamis, typhoons, and floods, would continue to be short term as well as long-term risks in the region. This suggests that natural disasters, a distinguishing characteristic of this region, are widely perceived as risks.[8] Natural disasters affect people's lives in various ways. Disaster prevention/reduction has become and will continue to be a crucial agenda item and is in most cases a cross-cutting issue.

One interviewee argued that the causes and outcomes of natural disasters in this region demonstrate their complex nature. East Asian countries now face a growing level of urbanization. As urbanization accelerates, ways of controlling and mitigating the risks emanating from natural disasters in densely populated urban areas will become a serious issue. Another interviewee pointed out that natural disasters are likely to cause social instability in some cases as well as degradation in the quality of lives (Aid Agency Sources #1 and #2).

Second, one of the distinctive characteristics in East Asia is how growing tensions in interstate relations impinge on human security. Three interviewees referred to interstate and international system-level relations as urgent sources of human insecurity that deserve attention (Academic Sector Source #2; Government Sector Source #2; Civil Society Sector Source #1). The fluctuating relations of major power rivalries are likely to intensify regional instability, which could cause serious human insecurities (Government Sector Source #2). Third, about a half of the interviewees pointed out that intrastate conflicts, such as in Myanmar and Mindanao, are likely to continue to be a source of human insecurity. Armed conflicts are likely to lead to a degradation of the quality of lives: people may have to flee as refugees or otherwise become internally displaced; and landmines continue to affect people even after a peace agreement is signed (Aid Agency Sources #2 and 3; Academic Sector Source #1; Government Sector Sources #1 and 2).

Fourth, several respondents stated that social risks stemming from economic or financial crises and the growing wealth gap are likely to affect the most vulnerable groups in society. Especially in China and the ASEAN countries, with their rapid economic growth, a gap between the rich and poor is likely to increase human security risks (Aid Agency Sources #2 and #3; Government Sector Source # 1).

5.4.2 Human Security for a "Developed" Country

When we look at the case of Japan, the idea of human security has been exclusively applied to foreign policy and development assistance. Against such tendencies in the past, all interviewees stressed that human security should be used as a notion to consider and deal with domestic issues in Japan as well. The respondents mentioned that they would feel uncomfortable if the notion was applied only to overseas assistance policies for developing countries, adding that human security should be applied to all individuals regardless of levels of economic development (Government Sector Source #3; Academic Sector Source #1). However, the Japanese government regards human security as something to be dealt with only by the foreign ministry. The concept has therefore not been well recognized among other ministries dealing with related concerns, and close coordination among related agencies, a distinctive characteristic of human security, has not been activated (Civil Society Sector Source #1).

There are some human security issues that have been systematically left behind as policy priorities even in Japan; these are in areas especially related to women, children, and the younger generation (Government Sector Source #2). Most of the interviewees pointed out that certain social issues that are typical for developed countries are likely to continue to be human security risks in Japan. The inadequacy of the social welfare system is becoming a serious issue when the society is faced with a growing aging population and decreasing birth rates. The interviewees highlighted recent social issues especially for the younger population. These include the so-called working poor, who earn low levels of income despite long working hours, "black companies" that exploit employees, and, consequently, the poverty of the younger generation, as well as poverty among children.

Half of our interviewees mentioned that natural disasters are and will continue to be a major source of human insecurity in Japan. Because of the Great East Japan Earthquake, 15,891 people died and 2584 are still missing (as of March 2015) (Asahi Shimbun 2015). Linked with this, following the subsequent tsunami and nuclear power plant crisis in Fukushima, many people have been forced to live away from their homes. With the number of these people remaining at 200,000 (as of August 2015), we should consider referring to those who were forced to leave their homes as "internally displaced persons" (IDPs). Earthquakes not only cause loss of lives and damage infrastructure but also destroy the communities in which people live.

Some of the interviewees said that hazards and insecurities emanating from modernization, such as nuclear power plants, are also especially a growing concern for advanced societies. Japan's experience of the Great East Japan Earthquake in 2011 and subsequent radioactive contamination in Fukushima served as a serious opportunity for reconsideration of this aspect of human security (Academic Sector Source #1 and #2; Government Sector Source #1; Private Sector Source #1; Civil Society Sector Source #1).

5.5 Cross-Border Responses to Human Security

5.5.1 *Accepting Assistance*

As natural disasters continue to be one of the major sources of threats to human security for Japanese society, methods for tackling human insecurities at every stage of natural disasters should be a policy priority for the Japanese government. This naturally would include improving policies for the acceptance of international assistance from overseas actors. The following observations are timely in view of the Great East Japan Earthquake that occurred in 2011. Not a small amount of literature has focused on Japan's acceptance of foreign assistance in the case of natural disasters (Yanagisawa 2013; Katayama 2013; Watabe et al. 2013).

We asked if Japan should accept overseas assistance in cases where Japan has been affected by a massive natural disaster such as an earthquake and tsunami and is faced with serious damage that is beyond the capacity of the government. After asking about the case of a natural disaster, we then asked for their views on a case that involved an escalation of violence. Though in contemporary Japan intrastate conflicts are unimaginable, Japanese society did experience a serious terrorist attack carried out by the Japanese *Aum Shinrikyo* cult in 1995, so the question is not totally inappropriate.

All the interviewees responded in the affirmative to both these questions, though to varying degrees and with different emphases. According to the interviews, from a humanitarian point of view, Japan should accept overseas assistance. One respondent described it concisely: in view of the Great Hanshin Awaji Earthquake of 17 January 1995, regrettably, Japan's domestic system was unable to cope with overseas offers of assistance effectively, yet there had been some improvement by the time of the Great East Japan Earthquake of 2011 (Academic Sector Source #1). However, at the earlier time the Japanese government was not well prepared to accept such offers of assistance and it took a substantial amount of time before the decision was made to accept it.

The earthquake, which took place in a densely populated and advanced city area in Western Japan, caused the deaths of more than 6000 people and destroyed core urban infrastructure in Kobe city and neighboring municipalities. On the day the earthquake hit Japan, the Japanese government responded negatively to foreign governments' offers to send rescue teams, saying that foreign rescue teams were not necessary since Japan could afford enough of its own. The Governments of Switzerland, France and the UK finally succeeded in gaining Japan's consent after repeated attempts to persuade the government (Yanagisawa 2013, 57–58). By contrast, in March 2011, following the earthquake and tsunami in the Eastern region of Japan, the government quickly decided to accept foreign assistance and consequently received rescue teams from 17 countries while several overseas NGOs were also active in the region. The assistance provided by the US military in Operation *Tomodachi* (friend) amounted to about 24,000 personnel with accompanying vessels and aircraft (Yanagisawa 2013, 62).

If we reconsider Japan's response to foreign assistance, it has been often pointed out that greater coordination is indispensable, including coordination between the tangible foreign assistance offered and real needs on the ground. To mitigate human insecurities quickly and effectively, one interviewee noted that taking any offers could easily lead to confusion, and effective coordination is necessary (Academic Sector Source #1). Another interviewee remarked that, since the scale of the disaster was unexpectedly huge, even local governments could not function. Manuals and know-how on how to deal with such situations should be prepared in advance (Government Sector Source #3).

If we look at interviewee responses to the question related to cases of terrorism or armed conflict, Japan should also accept foreign assistance. An interviewee mentioned that it should accept overseas assistance only when the purpose is humanitarian, and as a last resort.[9] Another interviewee said that if we are to accept foreign military personnel, it should be based on mutual confidence and trust in existing bilateral relations, such as bilateral alliances and other established institutional relations (Government Sector Source #2).

5.5.2 *Providing Assistance*

The next question concerned the case of a massive natural disaster that is beyond the control of the national government. If the government of the affected country is reluctant to accept assistance from overseas, how should the situation be dealt with? We asked the same question in the case of an escalation of violence as well. These questions are linked to the issue of state sovereignty. According to previous research, Japan's government actors have been skeptical about linking human security to interventions that extend beyond state sovereignty, even in case of humanitarian emergencies (Kurusu 2011b). One interviewee likewise mentioned that human security as a notion tends to "securitize" various threats to human beings. Securitization, as a merit, brings attention to specific issues. However, usage of the term might invoke politicization, and those who would be assisted might as a result become too cautious to accept even a potentially beneficial project for them (Academic Sector Source #1).

Japan has its "peace constitution" and has long-term experience of bilateral official economic assistance based on "requests" by the recipients.

In addition, the Japanese government is concerned about opposition from developing countries to the transcendence of sovereignty, especially to the "responsibility to protect" (R2P) concept. In promoting resolutions in the UN General Assembly in 2005, 2009, and 2012, Japan's foreign ministry made every effort to differentiate between the two concepts so that human security did not include R2P (Kurusu 2018).

In the case of natural disasters, our respondents' main stance was that assisting human security in foreign countries should be based on the "recipient country's request or consent." When the government is reluctant or not functioning, we should first analyze the situation to understand the reasons for its sensitivity and should then "persuade" it to accept foreign assistance. Foreign aid without the recipient government's consent is unlikely to be effective and "if we intervene without the recipient country's consent, the negative impacts of doing so could be greater" (Aid Agency Source #1). In some cases, we might be able to avoid directly bringing sovereignty to the center of the agenda by approaching the country through quiet diplomacy. One interviewee suggested:

> Before taking these measures, as a premise, how come they are so reluctant? We must thoroughly analyze the reasons for their sensitivity. Then, if we find some areas or fields able to cooperate, we could start with these. As a rule, I believe that we should not give up by saying to ourselves. "This is an issue of sovereignty, so that there is no hope of resolving it." But, I would rather think that more and more analysis is desirable. (Academic Sector Source #1).

Another interviewee suggested that Japan, at the time of the Great Hanshin Awaji Earthquake, had also experienced a situation in which the government itself was thrown into a panic. It would hold true even for a country that suffers from internal political tensions. Japan should build reliable relations with those countries on a day-to-day basis so that an offer might be accepted without skepticism (Government Sector Source #2).

Second, when a recipient government is reluctant, the non-governmental sector can be much better suited to the task of assisting people in that country. Japan can assist people indirectly through NGOs or international humanitarian organizations by giving them financial support and so on (Aid Agency Sources #2 and 3; Government Sector Source #1). Private companies can contribute by the division of roles in which they build partnerships with NGOs and the Japan Platform,[10] in addition to giving financial and other resources to them (Private Sector Source #1).

In cases where there has been an escalation of violence, the basic position of respondents was like that seen in the case of natural disasters. Assistance should be based on the "recipient country's request or consent." Some expressed their private views that in an extremely serious humanitarian crisis due to escalation of violence, international society should intervene. One of the interviewees, however, noted that forceful intervention does not always guarantee a better humanitarian consequence (Academic Sector Source #2). In such cases, what the Japanese government can do is to "indirectly" assist the country by giving financial support through the UN. Alternatively, Japan could contribute more in terms of conflict mediation as a third party (Government Sector Source #3). Japan can also approach such cases by setting up international conferences so that the recipient government is assured of the continued commitment and involvement of international society (Academic Sector Source #2). Another way to be involved in such a situation is to provide specialized knowledge and know-how in areas where Japan has a comparative advantage. For instance, in the Syrian case, Japan has a specialized capability for the disposal of chemical weapons and could play a role in securing human lives in situations involving these weapons (Government Sector Source #2).

5.6 Human Security in Practice: On Protection and Empowerment

There is a shared perception among interviewees that both approaches of protection and empowerment are important and closely connected to each other. Most of the interviewees mentioned that protection is more important in a life-threatening emergency, but that to make human security "sustainable," empowerment is indispensable (Academic Sector Sources #1 and #2; Government Sector Source #1). Protecting people affected by a tsunami is crucial, but what is more essential is to help people so that they can rebuild their own lives and thus to assure "resilience." For such a purpose, we also have to empower "communities" (Government Sector Source #3).

JICA, as an implementation agency for ODA, has mainly focused on the improvement of the people's daily lives, based on "empowerment" approaches. One staff member asserted that approaches promoting "empowerment" have become even stronger since the introduction of the human security concept (Aid Agency Source # 3). In a practical sense, "emphasis on (either aspect of) human security varies among JICA's internal departments" (Aid Agency Source #3). JICA had not previously dealt so much with issues in areas of "protection" proper, namely, protection of people in cases of emergencies such as armed conflict. Nonetheless, it is interesting to point out that JICA interprets the meaning of "protection" in such a way that it fits with JICA's previous principles and activities. A staff member of JICA argued that "protection" means creating national "frameworks."

> JICA regards them (i.e., protection and empowerment) both as important. Providing assistance to national framework building is regarded as protection. Great emphasis is placed on this point (Aid Agency Source #3).

Another interviewee also gave a similar view:

> Historically, JICA has employed bottom-up approaches by sending specialists to long-term projects. However, such an approach is not sustainable without protection by the recipient government. Both approaches are necessary (Aid Agency Source #1).

For JICA staff, projects involving "protection" have mainly targeted the building of recipient governments' administrative and legal frameworks for this purpose. This is a distinctive interpretation of "protection" developed in a way that fits the customs or norms of an implementation organization for development assistance.

5.7 The Conceptual Basis of Human Security: The Three Freedoms

Human security highlights the "universality and interdependence of a set of freedoms that are fundamental to human lives: freedom from fear, freedom from want and freedom to live in dignity" (UNSG 2012). However, there has been some debate on which element should be prioritized. The disagreement between the governments of Canada and Japan at the beginning of the 2000s was over whether a narrower approach with a focus on freedom from fear, or a broader approach should be taken. As we know, the CHS report was written so that co-chairs, Sadako Ogata and Amartya Sen, could represent the efforts to realize freedom from fear and freedom from want, respectively. Apart from previous debates on the freedom from want and fear, "freedom to live in dignity" has started to gain attention recently.

We first asked questions on the relationships between these elements. Our interviewees for the most part agreed that all the elements are co-related (Aid Agency Source #3; Academic Sector Source #1; Government Sector Sources #1 and 2; Private Sector Source #1). "These three components are part of a comprehensive perspective," and encouraging people to think that the three elements are interrelated is the very innovative aspect of human security (Academic Sector Source #1).

Then we asked about the meaning of adding "dignity" into the debates on human security. The dignity aspect appeared in the CHS report of 2003 and was also included in UN Secretary General Kofi Annan's report of 2005, *In Larger Freedom*, as one of the three pillars of the UN activities (UNSG 2005). In answer to this question, interestingly, most of our interviewees responded quite positively and gave their own views. An interviewee stated that even if the other two freedoms are met, this is insufficient for improving human security; the freedom to live in dignity also must be fulfilled. According to his/her view, the final purpose of human security amounts to dignity. Even if our needs for goods and education opportunities are met, if a person feels he/she is needed by no one and left out of the group, we do not think his/her human security has been achieved (Government Sector Source #1). Another interviewee cited a phrase from the Christian bible: "Man shall not live by bread alone," indicating that as a human being, the spiritual aspect is more important in the end (Academic Sector Source #2).

5.8 The Added Value of Human Security

Lastly, we examine the added value, if any, of human security. While human security as a notion has been criticized as something that merely gives old issues a new label (Paris 2001), there have been efforts to find its added value component. For instance, at the UN General Assembly, a meeting on "added value" in the work of the UN took place during May 2008, and the Secretary General's report in 2012 considered the matter (UNGA 2010; UNSG 2012). In both cases, they discussed the added value of human security in a practical sense, and what it would bring to the UN tasks.[11]

For our interviewees, first, there was apparent interest in the instrumental utility of the human security concept. Some of our interviewees pointed out that the introduction of human security as a new concept has some appeal for both international audiences and domestic constituencies (Government Sector Source #1). Similarly, for JICA for instance, utility can be found in putting emphasis on the difference between JICA's approach and other donors' methods of assistance (Aid Agency Sources #1 and #2). Our interviewee from a private company said that human security as a concept, together with the concept of human development, can be used to place the company's corporate social responsibility activities within a broader picture. Private companies have their own comparative advantage in contributing to either human development or human security (Private Sector Source #1).

Second, the concept has brought the following changes to Japan's Aid Agency. For some staff of JICA, human security was felt to have brought nothing new to an organization already engaged in implementing official development assistance. There was a relatively strong feeling that those "Seven Aspects of Human Security" discussed earlier in this chapter had existed previously in more vague ways within JICA's practice (Kurusu 2011a). But for others, human security has brought new perspectives. For example, the practice of targeting its assistance not only at governments but also to people and communities is comparatively new (JICA 2007). In addition, as already discussed, the approach of empowering people has become stronger since the introduction of human security. Another point suggested in our interviews and other literature is that, previously there were many instances of established projects that did not reach the people in need (JICA 2006b), but this has changed since the introduction of human security as a principle. One interviewee said:

> I also had the impression that the organization had begun to emphasize onsite needs and people-related needs more, or to focus on the bottom-up approach, although I believe this could be attributed to the influence of President Ogata as well as the idea of human security. (…) A bottom-up approach had been advocated. However, instead of just being advocated, it was put into action, such as by allocating more people to field sites. This was a new movement.[12]

Third, some pointed out that human security's comprehensive nature and its multi-sector approach are innovative, especially in achieving human security on the ground (Civil Society Sector Source #1). NGOs usually engage in a single issue or a limited number of specific issues. However, if they are to deal with the abolition of anti-personnel landmines, not only by advocating as such but also employing broader and cross-cutting approaches, such as linking their approach to a development perspective, may be more effective.

Human security is a comprehensive idea that brings together all the related issues that have been formerly dealt with in isolation (Aid Agency Source #1).

Fourth, the additional element of "dignity" was considered as part of the added value of human security (Aid Agency Source #3). A parliamentarian indicated that although the freedoms from want and fear were the main challenges in the twentieth century, we should seek "dignity" in the twenty-first century (Government Sector Source #2). Thus, in all probability, dignity is an idea of waiting and caring. Putting aside exceptional humanitarian crises such as genocide and massive violations of human rights, when cooperating through the provision of assistance, we should not violate the feelings of people in recipient societies and should respect what they value in the ways that they organize their cultural, religious, and social lives. With this approach, we may be able to integrate respect for cultural and religious differences into human security practice while recognizing the dignity of the recipient community.

5.9 Conclusions

While the Japanese government has successfully promoted the notion of human security in the resolutions of the UNGA, the concept has yet to be fully accepted in Japanese society itself. Meanwhile, our interviewees have found essential meaning in the approach that the human security notion might bring. Japan would be able to contribute more in areas of human security, if it introduces a stronger cross-sectoral/interdepartmental approach. Japan can also do more by collaborating with civil society organizations and humanitarian international organizations in situations, especially where a recipient state's sovereignty is at issue.

The findings of this analysis may sound relatively unexciting, for instance, compared with the way the emerging norm of "responsibility to protect" challenges state sovereignty. Indeed, responsibility to protect might have an impact on exceptional cases of humanitarian crises if properly implemented. However, in many cases, human insecurities take place in day-to-day situations. In such cases, finding vulnerable groups and individuals, finding comprehensive solutions, by considering local political, social, and cultural contexts, and coordinating appropriate approaches beyond various sectors, actors, and donors are indispensable but require a time-consuming effort. Though such approaches do not bring about instant and drastic impacts on humans in situations where they are at risk, a longer-term strategy based on human security principles would be better at ameliorating these situations and building societies resilient to such risks.

Notes

1. See Brinkmann and Qvale (2009), Dexter (2012).
2. The author thanks the reviewer for raising this question. For evaluations of actual projects on the ground done by the UNTFHS, see JCIE (2004), Hubbard and Suzuki (2008).
3. These six clusters are the result of several rounds of discussion and experimental interviews within JICA-RI.
4. For a detailed analysis of Japan's foreign policy making, see Kurusu (2011a).
5. Available from the following data search system: http://kokkai.ndl.go.jp/.
6. The seven aspects are: (1) reaching those in need through a human-centered approach; (2) empowering people as well as protecting them; (3) focusing on the most vulnerable people; (4) comprehensively addressing both "freedom from want" and "freedom from fear;" (5) assessing and addressing threats through flexible and inter-sectoral approaches; (6) working with both governments and local communities; and (7) strengthening partnerships with various actors to achieve higher impact (JICA 2006a).
7. Opposition parties, such as the Democratic Party of Japan, also regard human security as one of their foreign policy pillars. See DPJ (2009).
8. The United Nations Office for Disaster Risk Reduction found that increasing disaster risks in Asia-Pacific region are driven by the twin challenges of increasing exposure of its people and economic assets, and the inability of the most vulnerable groups to cope with disasters (UNISDR, 23 October 2012, http://www.unisdr.org/archive/29286)
9. The interviewee has been kept anonymous at his/her request.
10. Japan Platform is a framework in which NGOs, the business community and the foreign ministry work together for prompt implementation of emergency aid. It also offers financial support to Japanese NGOs through ODA funds as well as inviting donations from the private sector http://www.japanplatform.org/.
11. The SG report raises three examples of climate change, post-conflict peacebuilding, and economic crisis.
12. The interviewee has been kept anonymous upon his/her request.

References

APEC (Asia Pacific Economic Cooperation). 2004. *Joint Statement: One Community, Our Future*. Presented at the 2004 APEC Ministerial Meeting, Santiago, Chile, November 17–18.

Asahi Shimbun. 2015. Higashinihon Daishinsai Kara Yonen: Hinan 23 Man Nin, Seikatsu No Fukko Michinakaba [Four Years from the Great East Japan

Earthquake: 230 Thousand People Are Still Displaced, Still Half Way to Recovering Their Daily Lives]. *Asahi Shimbun Digital*, March 11.

Bosold, David, and Sascha Werthes. 2005. Human Security in Practice: Canadian and Japanese Experiences. *Internationale Politik und Gesellschaft* I: 84–101.

Brinkmann, Svend and Steinar Qvale. 2009. *Interviews: Learning Craft of Qualitative Research Interviewing*. Los Angeles: Sage Publications.

CHS (Commission on Human Security). 2003. *Human Security Now*. New York: Commission on Human Security.

Democratic Party of Japan. 2009. *Index 2009*. Tokyo: DPJ.

Dexter, Lewis Anthony. 2012. *Elite and Specialized Interviewing*. Colchester: ECPR Press.

Edström, Bert. 2008. *Japan and the Challenge of Human Security: The Founding of a New Policy 1995–2003*. Stockholm-Nacka: Institute for Security and Development Policy.

Fukushima, Akiko. 2010. *Ningen no Anzenhosho* [Human Security]. Tokyo: Chikura Shobo.

Gilson, Julie, and Phillida Purvis. 2003. Japan's Pursuit of Human Security: Humanitarian Agenda or Political Pragmatism? *Japan Forum* 15 (2): 193–207.

Hubbard, Susan, and Tomoko Suzuki. 2008. *Building Resilience: Human Security Approaches to AIDS in Africa and Asia*. Tokyo: Japan Center for International Exchange.

JCIE (Japan Center for International Exchange). 2004. *Human Security in the United Nations*. Tokyo: JCIE.

JICA (Japan International Cooperation Agency). 2006a. *Poverty Reduction and Human Security*, March.

———. 2006b. *Monthly JICA*. Tokyo: JICA, October.

———. 2007. *Monthly JICA*. Tokyo: JICA, February.

Katayama, Yutaka. 2013. Higashinihon Daishinsai ji no Kokusai Kinkyu Shien Ukeire to Gaimusho [International Emergency Assistance During the Great East Japan Earthquake and the Ministry of Foreign Affairs]. *Journal of International Cooperation Studies* 20: 60–62.

Katsumata, Makoto. 2011. Gaiko Seisaku Toshiteno Ningennoanzenhosho: Jinkentaikoku Heno Rodomappu [Human Security as Foreign Policy: A Roadmap to a Human Rights Great Power]. *Kokusaimondai* (International Affairs) 603 (July–August): 25–35.

King, Gary, and Christopher Murray. 2001. Rethinking Human Security. *Political Science Quarterly* 226 (4): 585–610.

Kurusu, Kaoru. 2011a. Japan as an Active Agent for Global Norms: The Political Dynamism Behind the Acceptance and Promotion of 'Human Security'. *Asia Pacific Review* 18 (2): 115–137.

———. 2011b. Gendankai no Ningen no Anzenhosho, (Human Security at this Stage). *Kokusai Mondai* (International Affairs) 603 (July–August): 5–14.

———. 2018. Japan as a Norm Entrepreneur for Human Security. In *The Handbook of Japanese Foreign Policy*, ed. Mary McCarthy, 321–336. London: Routledge.

McRae, Rob, and Don Hubert, eds. 2001. *Human Security and the New Diplomacy: Protecting People, Promoting Peace.* Montreal: McGill-Queen's University Press.

MOFA (Ministry of Foreign Affairs of Japan). 2003. *Japan's Official Development Assistance Charter.* Tokyo: Government of Japan.

Newman, Edward, and Oliver Richmond, eds. 2001. *The United Nations and Human Security.* New York: Palgrave.

Paris, Roland. 2001. Human Security: Paradigm Shift or Hot Air? *International Security* 26 (2): 87–102.

Smith, Heather. 2006. Diminishing Human Security: The Canadian Case. In *A Decade of Human Security*, ed. Sandra Maclean, David R. Black, and Timothy M. Shaw, 73–84. Aldershot: Ashgate.

Soeya, Yoshihide. 2005. Japanese Security Policy in Transition: The Rise of International and Human Security. *Asia-Pacific Review* 12 (1): 103–116.

Tadjbakhsh, Shahrbanou, and Anuradha Chenoy. 2007. *Human Security: Concepts and Implications.* London: Routledge.

Tan, Hsien-Li. 2010. Not Just Global Rhetoric: Japan's Substantive Actualization of Its Human Security Foreign Policy. *International Relations of the Asia-Pacific* 10 (1): 159–187.

G8 (Group of Eight). 1999. *The Conclusion of the G8 Foreign Ministers' Meeting.* Released at the Finance Ministers Meeting, "Gürzenich," Cologne, 10 June 1999.

UNDP (United Nations Development Program). 1994. *Human Development Report 1994.* New York: Oxford University Press.

UNGA (United Nations General Assembly). 2005. *2005 World Summit Outcome*, A/RES/60/1. New York: United Nations.

———. 2010. *Panel Discussion on the Theme "People-Centred Responses: The Added Value of Human Security*," A/64/701. New York: United Nations.

———. 2012. *Follow-up to Paragraph 143 on Human Security of the 2005 World Summit Outcome*, A/RES/66/290. New York: UN.

UNSG (United Nations Secretary General). 2005. *In Larger Freedom: Towards Development, Security and Human Rights for All*, A/59/2005. New York: UN.

———. 2012. *Follow-up to General Assembly Resolution 64/291 on Human Security*, A/66/763. New York: UN.

Watabe, Masaki, and Takeo Murakami. 2013. Kokusai Jindo Shisutemu no Hatten to Higashinihon Daishinsai [Development of the International Humanitarian System and the Great East Japan Earthquake]. *Sekaiho Nenpo* 32: 195–215.

Yanagisawa, Kae, ed. 2013. *Daisaigai ni Tachimukau Sekai to Nihon* [The World and Japan that Challenge Great Disasters]. Tokyo: Saiki.

Interviews

Aid Agency Source #1. 2013. Interviewed by author, Yoichi Mine, Ryutaro Murotani and Sachiko Goto in Tokyo, September 26.

Aid Agency Source #2. 2013. Interviewed by author, Mine, Murotani and Goto in Tokyo, September 26.

Aid Agency Source #3. 2013. Interviewed by author, Mine, Murotani and Goto in Tokyo, September 26.

Academic Sector Source #1. 2013. Interviewed by author in Osaka, November 12.

Academic Sector Source #2. 2013. Interviewed by Mine, Murotani and Goto in Tokyo, November 11.

Civil Society Sector #1. 2014. Interviewed by Goto in Tokyo, April 17.

Government Sector Source #1. 2014. Interviewed by author and Goto in Tokyo, February 26.

Government Sector Source #2. 2014. interviewed by author and Goto in Tokyo, February 26.

Government Sector Source #3. 2014. Interviewed by author in Tokyo, March 10.

Private Sector Source #1. 2014. Interviewed by author in Tokyo, March 10.

CHAPTER 6

Perceptions and Practice of Human Security in Malaysia

Benny Cheng Guan Teh and Ik Tien Ngu

6.1 Introduction

At its core, the essence of security is protection. The role of the state, therefore, is to provide protection for its constituents. This is traditionally understood as putting in place proper rules and laws and ensuring that they are efficiently enforced to keep society safe so that people do not live in constant fear. While the ability of states to fulfill this role has varied throughout history and between regions, the more recent waves of globalization and the enthusiasm of developing nations to liberalize their economies and integrate into the wider international community have not only created challenges for states to keep abreast of the demands arising from rapid societal changes, but have also meant that they must appropriately

B. C. G. Teh (✉)
School of Social Sciences, Universiti Sains Malaysia, Penang, Malaysia
e-mail: ben@usm.my

I. T. Ngu
Department of Chinese Studies, Faculty of Arts and Social Sciences, University of Malaya, Kuala Lumpur, Malaysia
e-mail: tngu@um.edu.my

Y. Mine et al. (eds.), *Human Security Norms in East Asia*, Security, Development and Human Rights in East Asia,
https://doi.org/10.1007/978-3-319-97247-3_6

shield their societies from external destructive forces. This has even become the source of insecurity for some states.

Increasingly integrated and competitive, Malaysia is equally exposed to such challenges. The shift in economic policies from an agriculture-based to an industry-based export-oriented economy began in the 1970s and further developed over the last four decades in accordance with the country's Vision 2020 policy of becoming a developed nation. This development has brought with it various security challenges, especially for a country with a multicultural society. The May 1969 racial riots, caused by violent clashes between the Malays and Chinese right after the general election, prompted the state to introduce an affirmative action program to eradicate poverty and achieve national unity by reconfiguring the socioeconomic structure of its society. The framing of this program as necessary to prevent further racial violence could thus be seen as a desire to incorporate elements of human security.

Although Malaysia's security and its national survival were put to the test due to *Konfrontasi* (Indonesia-Malaysia Confrontation, 1963–1966), it has not experienced any interstate conflicts since then. However, understanding the domestic security situation through the traditional lenses of state security would arguably be insufficient in addressing a myriad of issues and concerns ranging from food and health securities to personal and economic securities. While these may not threaten the survival of the state, they could adversely affect the security and well-being of both individuals and communities.

Focusing specifically on Malaysia, this chapter seeks to discuss three key questions: How is human security understood or perceived by different stakeholders in Malaysia? What are the primary and secondary threats that lead to human insecurity in the country? And, have there been any measures of protection and empowerment taken by the different stakeholders to improve the level of human security in Malaysia? The discussion is concluded by highlighting several salient points and providing suggestions on ways forward.[1]

6.2 The Conceptualization of Human Security and Its Understanding in Malaysia

6.2.1 *Human Security as a Conceptual Framework*

The call for a more human-centered conception of security came from the realization that traditional security, regardless of whether it is defined as cooperative security or comprehensive security, is incapable of addressing the atrocities committed within the boundaries of the state. The 1994 United Nations Development Program (UNDP) Human Development Report was instrumental in reevaluating how the term "security" is understood. This sets in motion the later refinements of the concept, with Canada, Norway, and Japan taking the lead (Teh 2012). The expansion of threats such as communicable diseases, food shortages, and environmental degradation has culminated in the notion of non-traditional security (NTS). Although NTS is often used interchangeably with human security, it is not the same, with the former continuing to be state-centric. The involvement of non-state actors in the decision-making process and the need to empower them are central to the tenets of human security.

In Southeast Asia, the challenges posed by globalization and regional integration have compelled ASEAN leaders to expand their security lexicon to cover several NTS issues that have been prevalent in the region. Various statements and declarations have been issued in recent years, and cooperation in the areas of transnational crime, infectious diseases, humanitarian assistance and disaster relief, and maritime security has increased (Rolls and Teh 2014). The preparedness of ASEAN countries to engage in NTS issues reflects Malaysia's acceptance of NTS. Nevertheless, regional cooperation in NTS has remained largely a top-down endeavor with limited participation from civil society groups (Rolls and Teh 2014).

There have been several efforts to mainstream human security in the ASEAN region, although these have not as yet produced any concrete results. Attempts to do so have come from both policymakers and scholars. In 1998, a proposal was made for the creation of an ASEAN-PMC Caucus on Human Security at the Post-Ministerial Conference in Manila.[2] In 2006, the ASEAN Secretariat partnered with UNESCO to discuss the relevance of the human security concept in Southeast Asia. From 2009 to 2012, a joint project titled "Mainstreaming Human Security in ASEAN Integration" under the auspices of JICA-RI culminated in a three-volume publication. In 2014, a High Level Advisory Panel on R2P in Southeast Asia was established, resulting in a report on ways to build up acceptance of R2P in the region.

Despite such efforts, the term "human security" continues to remain absent from official ASEAN documents. The interest shown by ASEAN leaders in shedding its elitist image and moving toward a people-oriented organization was, however, seen as a positive step in promoting human security in the region. Yet, the creation of an ASEAN Charter, the formation of an ASEAN Intergovernmental Commission on Human Rights (AICHR), and the successive adoption of the ASEAN Human Rights

Declaration (AHRD) failed to receive the strong endorsement of civil society organizations (CSOs) (Peck 2009; Teh 2009). The AHRD, for example, was denounced by regional CSOs as a "declaration of government powers disguised as a declaration of human rights" (Human Rights Watch 2012).

6.2.2 *Differing Interpretations and Understandings of Human Security in Malaysia*

In Malaysia, the official definition of security has been based around the concept of comprehensive security. Unlike the Japanese version of comprehensive security, which focuses on the protection of state interests from external military and non-military threats, ASEAN governments, according to Amitav Acharya, consider the term "as a framework for coping with the danger of insurgency, subversion and political unrest" with "the attainment of performance legitimacy through economic development" as its main element (Acharya 1999, 69). Broader in scope and in line with the country as a small power, the understanding of security extends beyond military defense. In 1992, then Malaysian Defense Minister Najib Tun Razak captured the essence of Malaysia's security understanding when he stated that "…the term security is seen in a very broad manner which encompasses both military and non-military elements. Comprehensive security covers political, economic and defense dimensions. Therefore, to us, to achieve security, it has to be comprehensive, i.e. it has to be politically stable, economically strong and resilient, its population, united and strong-willed, and last, but not least, it has to be militarily sufficient" (Razak 2001, 72).

Almost two decades later, in September 2000, Najib Tun Razak put forward a similar definition, explaining that, "our economic prosperity would be fragile if we lack political stability and that all this would be threatened if we do not have the ability to defend our wealth" (Razak 2001, 55). This echoed then Prime Minister Mahathir Mohamad's earlier definition of security in 1986 as the interweaving between national security and "political stability, economic success and social harmony" (quoted in Mak 2004, 129). Comprehensive security in formal terms has thus been about national resilience: military and "nonmilitary means of empowering and securing the state," and therefore the role of the society and the individual citizens of Malaysia, are to maintain the overall security of the country (Razak 2001, 57; Mak 2004, 129).

The expansion of threats under the rubric of NTS falls comfortably within the framework of comprehensive security instead of human security. It will remain so for as long as the approach is top-down (elite-driven). The compatibility of NTS and Malaysia's comprehensive security explains Kuala Lumpur's active role in promoting NTS at the ASEAN level and beyond (Haniff 2015). By further incorporating NTS concerns under the existing security framework, the government could proclaim its "people-oriented" policies and circumvent the need to adopt a new security approach based on the UNDP definition of human security, as that could shift the focus away from the state and lead to stronger active participation from CSOs in the development of national policies and governance. This may ultimately challenge the regime's capability to exert control and maintain its political dominance.

Since independence, the National Front (NF) has successively won all the general elections in the country. In the 2004 general election, for example, the share of seats obtained by the NF reached 90 percent, yet in the subsequent 2008 and 2013 elections, the NF still managed to win but saw its share of seats reduced significantly.[3] The ability of the opposition coalition to pull their strengths together and deny the NF its traditional two-third majority could perhaps be traced back to the public outcry and call for *Reformasi* (reformation) in 1998. The opposition has succeeded in raising questions over regime legitimacy (Collins 2005, 80), even putting in motion the prospect of political change. *Reformasi* has further given rise to political protests by diverse civil society movements (Islamist and non-Islamist groups) concerned with issues of injustice, eroding democratic values, immorality, and bad governance (Hamid 2009). They were able to traverse their own differences in becoming democratizing agents to challenge the dominance of the NF (Case 2003).

The introduction of *Islam Hadhari* (civilizational Islam) and pursuit of good governance under the premiership of Abdullah Badawi (2003–2009) further encouraged CSOs to play a bigger role in nation building. *Islam Hadhari* contained ten main principles that reflected human security considerations such as a just and trustworthy government, a good quality of life, protection of the rights of minority groups and women, protection of the environment, a free and independent people, and balanced and comprehensive economic development. The concept was meant to imbue people with the right ethics and empower them with a global mindset to be globally competitive and reduce overdependence on government handouts (Chong 2006). It therefore could be said that there was a noble intention to shift from a strong developmental state to a more regulatory-type state where there would be a vibrant and strong civil society.

However, weak leadership was blamed for Badawi's inability to fulfill his electoral promises of tackling corruption and making his government more accountable (Zain and Yusoff 2015). There were limitations in operationalizing his brand of "civil Islam" and promoting it through government policies. His willingness to allow more space for civil society movements, and the increasing role of the Internet in promoting civic discourse was coupled with various unresolved deep-seated issues such as money politics, racial tensions, the increasing cost of living and street crime, and selective persecution of dissidents under his administration.

Due to the dismal performance of the ruling coalition in the 2008 election and the need to shore up its legitimacy, Najib Tun Razak, who took over the helm from Badawi in April 2009, decided to embark on a Government Transformation Program (GTP) based on the philosophy of "people first, performance now" to address people's grievances and improve government services. Public feedback was considered, and the issues raised were categorized into seven National Key Results Areas (NKRAs), namely, reducing crime, fighting corruption, improving student outcomes, raising living standards of low-income households, improving rural basic infrastructure, improving urban public transport, and addressing the cost of living. The GTP report released by the government for 2014 indicated positive results with the key performance indicator for the NKRAs exceeding 105 percent (Sun Daily 2015). While statistics may show a reduction in the crime rate of 40 percent since 2009, Malaysians in general continue to feel unsafe. This perceived insecurity, according to Amin Khan, Director of Pemandu's Reducing Crime NKRA, is due in part to a quarter of crimes going unreported, particularly petty crimes such as common assault and theft (Khan 2015).

The government has yet to adopt a human security approach in its domestic or foreign policy. Kuala Lumpur's position on the concept of human security and the R2P was well spelled out by Malaysia's permanent representative to the UN, Hussein Haniff in 2012, when he stated that:

> Human security should also not replace state security. We agree that governments should retain the primary responsibility for ensuring the survival, livelihood and dignity of their people and population…We also take note that the notion of human security is distinct from the responsibility to protect.

> However, the distinction should not only be confined to the application of the notion but should also shun the possibility of using force or the threat of force on a State or its people...Malaysia's own national development experience has always taken into account the elements of economic and social development, with the welfare of the people consistently at the forefront of policy considerations. At the heart of those policies is the need to distribute the benefits of economic growth equitably to overcome potentially dangerous national rifts. (Haniff 2012)

Haniff's statement demonstrates Malaysia's apprehension toward human security, viewing it as a potential antithesis of state security. However, the two concepts are not essentially contradictory. The role of human security is to reprioritize the understanding of security itself. As Amartya Sen explained in 2015, "...security ultimately is a matter in which the leading concern should be around human life. So, if we are speaking of security, it must be human security. Since this also means security from external threats and violence, what we call national security is only one of the constituent factors in human security" (Haniff, quoted in Sampath 2015). This brings into the picture a stark contrast between comprehensive security that focuses on the survivability of the state with the role of its citizens as defenders of the nation's interests, and human security that emphasizes the value of individual human life with state security as only but one of the components.

Meanwhile, CSOs, at least those interviewed, found the concept of human security lacking clarity as it is too broad to be understood and properly employed as a working framework. Some of the CSOs are well established, from the period even before the advent of human security, and their activities tend to focus more on the championing of human rights. Aliran, for example, is a national reform movement set up in Penang in 1977 with an aim to raise social consciousness, and although their activities are not couched in a human security term, they are connected to it since the organization prioritizes individuals at risk and helps to address their insecurities. Aliran, according to its then president Francis Loh "is involved in the struggle for freedom, justice and solidarity but we don't really look at it from the point of view of human security as such... It is not one of our agendas" (CSO #1 2016). When questioned whether Aliran practices human security, Loh adds, "Of course we do. One of the biggest issues that we are very concerned about now is forced migration. Many of our members and Aliran itself have been working with the forced migrants in terms of trying to fight for a better deal for foreign workers... especially [the] Rohingya" (CSO #1 2016).

Debbie Stothard, a Malaysian and founder of the Bangkok-based ALTSEAN-Burma, echoes this view, noting that most CSOs are human rights organizations trying to address individual elements of human security without necessarily referring to the concept: "It's not very high up in the public sphere" (CSO #2 2016). Charles Santiago, a Malaysian parliamentarian and the Chairperson of the ASEAN Parliamentarians for Human Rights (APHR) admitted that Malaysian society has had little discussion on the concept in comparison to neighboring countries like Indonesia and the Philippines (Parliamentarian #1 2016). Others like Marina Mahathir, a respectable Malaysian socio-political activist and columnist, only learned about the concept of human security through international forums and conferences. Although she has not used the term in her advocacy for women's rights, she agreed that it encompasses a wide range of issues involving human well-being (CSO #3 2016).

Despite showing some uncertainties about the meaning of human security, CSOs agreed with the essential moral values and norms conveyed by the term, which they claimed were equivalent to those of human rights. However, they prefer to employ the term "human rights" since they believe it is broader in scope compared to human security which they see as focusing more on socio-economic interests. Some even regarded human security as a component of human rights. In relation to fundamental human rights, CSOs subscribed to the provisions stipulated in several universal declarations and conventions on human rights. For instance, the International Covenant on Civil and Political Rights was frequently referenced in regard to the protection of human life along with the right to live in dignity, as well as anything that is related to human security. Regarding social and economic interests of the people, conventions such as the International Covenant on Economic, Social and Cultural Rights would become the point of reference.

Aegile Fernandez of Tenaganita, a Malaysian NGO founded in 1991 and concerned with the rights of women, migrants, and refugees, was more knowledgeable of the term. She stated that the introduction of human security in the 1990s was a step forward as it indicated a shift in public attention from national security to individual security. Prior to that, people associated national security issues with war and genocide, but human beings deserve more than survival. The concept is important because it reminds people of the need to protect the well-being of individuals and vulnerable communities. The ultimate aim for her is for human beings to live in dignity, which is obviously a key feature of human security (CSO #4 2016).

6.3 Threat Considerations by Different Stakeholders in Malaysia

Considering that Malaysia is a developing nation, political and economic situations shape the perceptions of local stakeholders in terms of the immediate and major human security threats to the country. Malaysia's economic growth has been affected by both internal and external dynamics. Externally, this was a result of the 1997 Asian financial crisis, followed by the 2008 financial crisis and, more recently, China's economic slowdown. Internally, government debt remains at a very high level and falling oil prices and currency depreciation have not helped improve the situation. The political challenges that the NF government faced from the opposition, and criticisms over the use of controversial laws to clamp down on civil disobedience, have further compounded the situation.

6.3.1 Economic Concerns

Human rights bodies such as the Human Rights Commission of Malaysia (SUHAKAM), APHR, and IKRAM have invariably expressed concerns over the current economic situation in Malaysia. For them, poor economic management and market-oriented economic policies are the fundamental reasons for people living with insecurity. Growing insecurities may lead to religious extremism, and racial disharmony or intolerance. Hafidzi Mohd Noor, the Chairman of MyCare (a humanitarian agency of IKRAM), warned that the voices of extremism can be contagious. Instead of working to contain the situation, he saw some politicians as being inclined to incite hatred between different segments of society (CSO #5 2016).

The economic issues raised by the interviewees include the implementation of a goods and services tax (GST), the Trans-Pacific Partnership Agreement (TPPA), and economic mismanagement. There are concerns that the realization of the TPPA would favor multinational corporations more than local small and medium enterprises (SMEs). With numerous challenges lying ahead, local stakeholders are disheartened that policymakers have yet to introduce feasible long-term policies to empower local SMEs and social communities. Several anti-GST protests have also been held in the capital city to express displeasure (Anand 2016).

In January 2013, the NF government introduced a new scheme called BR1M (Bantuan Rakyat 1Malaysia) to provide cash handouts to help ease the rising living costs of the lower income groups. As it was an election year, the scheme was viewed by critics as a vote-buying tactic.[4] Furthermore, some local stakeholders are dissatisfied with policymakers who, while denying that there has been an increase in poverty cases, have used the economic crisis as an excuse to relinquish their obligation to the people, thus leaving them to bear the costs by themselves. This has led to complaints against the government for its lack of responsiveness to the economic woes faced by the people. SUHAKAM, for example, has called on policymakers to take a people-centered or bottom-up approach in the process of formulating and implementing policies. Mohamad Azizi of SUHAKAM wanted the government to engage and consult more with the people, professionals and civil society groups at different levels of the decision-making process (Government #1 2016).

6.3.2 Mistreatment of Minority Groups

Several stakeholders have expressed concerns over minority rights in the country. Ambiga Sreevanesan, president of the National Human Rights Society (HAKAM), stated in a speech in 2015 that "freedom from fear is what we don't have here in Malaysia. Here, we are not caring enough for the minorities and lack understanding for liberty… With all the denied human rights that we have in Malaysia, I believe we still have a long way to achieve freedom from fear. So, this is where civil society plays an important part in achieving it" (Alegria 2015). She was referring particularly to the Muslim transgender group and the indigenous (Orang Asli) community in Malaysia, who she felt had been mistreated and oppressed. Suara Rakyat Malaysia (SUARAM) shares her concerns; its 2014 human rights report outlined the major threats toward minority groups, namely, court rulings against transgender people, economic and socio-cultural insecurities of indigenous peoples, and the intolerance of religious extremists toward religious minorities (SUARAM 2014).

Other groups who live in fear are refugees and victims of trafficking. SUARAM's report highlights that Malaysia's rankings in the US State Department's *Annual Trafficking in Persons* Report and the *Global Rights Index: The World's Worst Countries for Workers* have dropped to a record low (2014, viii). The Committee on the Rights of the Child, which monitors the implementation of the United Nations Convention on the Rights of the Child, has called on the government to urgently devise a legislative framework to protect refugee and asylum-seeking children who have been found to be susceptible to arrest, detention, and deportation (SUHAKAM 2015b).

Tenaganita's Fernandez notes that Malaysia has yet to develop a protection mechanism for the victims of human trafficking. She said: "We are not looking at these victims as survivors. Here there is no protection mechanism… we need to handle it not because it is our problem that we are not protecting people, but because the US said we have to" (CSO #4 2016). Debbie Stothard of Altsean-Burma shares the same concerns, adding that while advocacy by CSOs on the treatment of the Rohingya boat people[5] has led to a policy turnaround by Malaysia, and those fleeing were allowed into the country, the issue is viewed as an immigration concern instead of a human security issue, and thus there remains a lack of capacity for operationalizing and implementing commitments for human security (CSO #2 2016).

6.3.3 *Suppression of Freedom of Expression*

In the last few years, the move to suppress freedom of expression has been a huge concern for local CSOs. SUARAM's (2014) report showed that the number of people being investigated, charged, or convicted under the Sedition Act 1948 for 2012, 2013, and 2014 was 7, 18, and 44, respectively (SUARAM 2014). They included, among others, activists, academics, journalists, law practitioners, students, and elected representatives. In 2015, the number increased sharply to 220 people (SUARAM 2015). A Universiti Malaya law lecturer, Azmi Sharom, for example, was charged under the Sedition Act in 2014 in relation to an alleged seditious statement.[6] Local prominent academics such as Terence Gomez, a professor of Political Economy at Universiti Malaya, were highly concerned about the incident, fearing that such acts would stifle academic freedom and obstruct intellectual inquiry critical to the production of good scholarship (Gomez 2014). Citizens would need to be more cautious in exchanging ideas and opinions over public issues, particularly those pertaining to the government's actions and policies.

6.4 Addressing Threat Issues Through Multiple Platforms

6.4.1 *Different Initiatives Pursued by Stakeholders*

The approaches taken by stakeholders to pursue their causes are shaped by the nature of the organizations and the resources available to them. Organizations such as IKRAM, Tenaganita, and Sisters in Islam (SIS) employ both protection and empowerment approaches to assist their "clients." Although both approaches are essential, they hold the view that protection is crucial especially when their clients encounter an immediate threat. Effective empowerment could only take place when sufficient protection is enabled.

One of Tenaganita's missions is to promote and protect the rights and dignity of women, migrants, and refugees. It has four major programs—migrant rights protection, anti-trafficking in persons, refugee action programs, and shelters for trafficked women and children—with each program consisting of rights protection, training and education, and consciousness building. These programs are carried out through case management, workshops, and other activities. Each program also aims to address bigger social problems and to advocate for institutional and structural change (Tenaganita 2015, 117). Fernandez believes that protection should come before empowerment. Empowerment can be achieved once the basic needs of people such as food and security are met (CSO #4 2016).

On community participation in policymaking, Tenaganita is part of the National Security Council for Human Trafficking and works closely with the Ministry of Human Resources on the issue of providing legal protection for migrant and domestic workers. Through its collaboration with government agencies, Tenaganita has tried to introduce the concept of human security to government officials (CSO #4 2016). IKRAM also engages government agencies in providing humanitarian aid to groups facing serious risks such as the 2015 Rohingya migrant boat crisis. At home, IKRAM is concerned with worsening ethnic relations. Hafidzi concurs with the findings of human rights reports that ethnic and religious extremism is growing in Malaysia and certain parties could be taking advantage of the situation (CSO #5 2016). To address this concern, IKRAM engages with various parties to seek common ground and resolve differences through dialogue.

For SIS, of which Marina Mahathir is a board member, top-down and bottom-up approaches are equally vital. SIS has a legal unit that provides free legal advisory services to women and men on their legal rights under the Islamic Family Law and the Shari'ah Criminal Offences Law. These laws include inheritance law, divorce and child custody, polygamous marriage, and so forth. In addition to these services, SIS conducts legal training programs and forums for different groups of people such as journalists, activists, artists, and writers. They also make an effort to conduct awareness programs for Muslim women and engage with religious authorities and conservative groups, but so far, responses to the latter have been fairly discouraging.[7]

Advocacy for policy change and collaboration with policymakers are key approaches taken by local stakeholders in protecting as well as empowering their subjects. Marina Mahathir believes that Muslim women can be better protected by making changes to existing laws and policies (CSO #3 2016). This belief motivates SIS to undertake research on Islamic law and develop alternative interpretations to counter the official and mainstream understanding of Islam. A draft family law has been submitted to the NF government for consideration, but the organization has not received a response.

At the state level, Penang, for example, which was under the administration of opposition parties and has limited jurisdiction to promote good governance due to political centralization, has taken several initiatives to empower its people to speak up and express their concerns. According to Zairil Khir Johari, then Chief Executive Officer of the Penang Institute and Member of Parliament, the state government has established two speakers' corners—one on the island and the other on the mainland—to encourage people to express their opinions without fear of oppression. It also passed the Freedom of Information Enactment in 2010 to "allow greater democratization and transparency of information," start engaging with the public to listen to their grievances and receive feedback on policy matters through town hall sessions (Parliamentarian #2 2016).

6.4.2 *Push for Stronger Political Will and Better Governance in Malaysia*

Certain stakeholders such as opposition leaders and CSOs attribute the current plight of Malaysia to poor governance and weak leadership. SUARAM's report showed that out of the 232 recommendations for human rights improvements made by the United Nations Human Rights Council to Malaysia, only 150 were accepted by the government, with the rest rejected, including the recommendation "to review the consistency of SOSMA and PCA with international human rights law" (SUARAM 2014, 2). SUHAKAM's human rights report shares the same tone of disappointment. None of its annual reports submitted to parliament as required by Section 21 of the Human Rights Commission of Malaysia Act 1999 (Act 597) has ever been debated in Parliament

(SUHAKAM 2015b). In its report, SUHAKAM identified two laws—the Sedition Act 1948 and the Prevention of Crime (Amendment and Extension) Act 2013—that it deemed problematic, as they do not fully comply with international norms and are inconsistent with established human rights principles. Despite the fact that the purpose of SUHAKAM is to safeguard the promotion and protection of human rights in Malaysia, it was never consulted or referred to before the amendments to laws or passing of new laws that have a direct impact on human rights, namely, the Prevention of Terrorism Act 2015, Sedition (Amendment) Act 2015, Prevention of Crime (Amendment and Extension) Act 2013, Security Offences (Special Measures) (Amendment) Act 2012, Criminal Procedure Code (Amendment) Act 2004, and Penal Code (Amendment) Act 2003 (SUHAKAM 2015a). Critics like Zairil Khir Johari view some of these laws as "illiberal legislation" that comprise both urgent and long-term threats to the fundamental liberties and human rights of the people in the country (Parliamentarian #2 2016).

A worrying trend in recent years has been an increase in cases of racial and religious hate speeches and hate crimes. Although none of our interviewees specifically raised the issue, some acknowledged the increase in racial and religious tensions in the country and attributed the problem to the heightened sense of economic insecurity among the people. A recently published report titled "Malaysia Racial Discrimination Report 2015" notes the correlation between ethnic relations and the socio-economic policies that have been implemented within "the prevailing culture of racial politics" (Pusat Komas 2016, 7).

In addressing human security issues, there is thus a need to move away from a racial or religious lens to a more practical approach free from the influence of race or religion (CSO #2 2016). In 2013, a National Unity Consultative Council (NUCC) consisting of diverse individuals from various backgrounds was set up, and the council members came up with three draft bills, namely, the National Harmony and Reconciliation Bill, the National Harmony and Reconciliation Commission Bill, and the Racial and Religious Hate Crimes Bill. These bills were meant to serve as a legal means for addressing ethnic and religious discontent and to replace the Sedition Act 1948 (Sipalan 2014).[8] It has been reported that the NF government was in the final stages of drafting a new National Harmony Bill (Bernama 2016). While it remains unclear whether the NUCC's recommendations were taken into consideration, the new proposed bill failed to materialize and replace the Sedition Act as demanded by SUHAKAM and other CSOs.

6.4.3 *Going Beyond National Boundaries and the Challenges Faced*

6.4.3.1 Humanitarian Aid

The Malaysian government has been actively engaged in disaster relief efforts through cross-country cooperation such as the tsunami disaster in Aceh and the Tohoku earthquake in Japan. At home, local stakeholders generally welcome humanitarian aid provided by foreign countries and organizations when large-scale disasters take place. While some local stakeholders do express reservations over the involvement of foreign religious organizations if they carry an intention to proselytize for their religions, Hafidzi claimed that MyCare has collaborated several times with Tzu Chi, a Buddhist organization from Taiwan. He insisted that people should overcome their ideological, ethnic or religious differences when it comes to issues involving humanitarian assistance and disaster relief. Human security should after all be the main concern of all religious bodies (CSO #5 2016).

6.4.3.2 Expectations of Regional and International Organizations

The 2015 Rohingya refugees have drawn international attention to the humanitarian disaster occurring in Myanmar. Neighboring countries—especially Indonesia, Malaysia, and Thailand, that initially declined to host Rohingya refugees—eventually gave in under international pressure. The influx of refugees from Myanmar to these countries has raised the concerns of local governments, civil society groups, and the public. In Malaysia, IKRAM has been working closely with the Immigration Department of Malaysia in aiding the Rohingya people. Their role is to make sure the refugees have access to basic food and medical treatment. However, Hafidzi admitted that hosting Rohingya refugees is a burden on the society and the national healthcare system, and it is unfair to expect the host country to bear the burden alone. Hafidzi urges ASEAN and the UN to come out with more effective mechanisms to resolve the problem (CSO #5 2016).

Aegile Fernandez also expressed her unhappiness with ASEAN's indifference. She said if ASEAN continues to remain indifferent, our neighbor's problems will one day become our own. She observed with disappointment that the governments of ASEAN countries seemed keener on negotiating trade deals than in protecting their own nationals (CSO #4 2016). Fernandez's observation was reiterated by Charles Santiago who criticized ASEAN's non-interference principle as an opportunistic policy. He claimed that ASEAN member countries conveniently use the non-interference principle when it encompasses political matters but not when making economic deals (Parliamentarian #1 2016). Among others who share similar views is Saifuddin Abdullah, the former chief executive officer of the Global Movement of Moderates (GMM), who believes that the principle is an old idea and should be readdressed to reflect current realities (Jalil 2015).

However, local stakeholders generally agree that military intervention should not be used as the way to tackle domestic calamities, be it natural disasters or violent conflicts. Hafidzi asserted that military intervention should not come into the picture because it would not resolve the problems. Referencing the war in Syria, he indicated that foreign interventions have made the situation worse (CSO #5 2016). However, regarding human disasters such as genocide, some stakeholders noted that they would consider military intervention if it is sanctioned by the UN.

6.5 Conclusions

Twenty-four years after the introduction of the concept of human security, the term remains elusive to Malaysian policymakers and CSOs, albeit for different reasons. The NF government appeared to approach the concept cautiously, preferring instead to promote and engage in non-traditional security at the regional and international levels primarily because it falls within the framework of comprehensive security that Malaysia has adopted in its security approach.

While the central government continues to see its role as the main provider of security, it does aim to practice elements of human security by providing greater space for the development of civil society movements. This can be seen particularly under the leadership of Abdullah Badawi and his concept of *Islam Hadhari*, but also through the GTP and its NKRAs under the leadership of Najib Tun Razak.[9] Other stakeholders, primarily CSOs, have not adopted the term 'human security' in their approaches, as they are either unaware of it or lack a clear understanding on how to operationalize the term. Some even viewed it as focusing more on freedom from want than freedom from fear. Since most CSOs are concerned with the violation of human rights, they find the term 'human rights' more suited to their cause, although in practice, they are addressing certain strains of human security. Their focus is on the individual, and their concerns are related to the insecurities faced by marginalized groups, not only within the local population but also for documented and undocumented foreign workers and refugees. CSOs that are committed to helping individuals overcome insecurities regardless of race, gender, sex, class, religion, color, creed, age, disability, and even national origin would naturally value humanity and would undoubtedly align their practices with those of human security.

CSOs wanting to affect policy changes in helping to secure the well-being of the marginalized still experience an uphill battle due in part to the lack of good governance. Poor governance may reflect the lack of political will in prioritizing and emphasizing human security in government policies. Providing cash handouts for lower income groups, for example, has been viewed by some stakeholders as a populist move and, while it may produce temporary financial relief, it creates dependency instead of empowerment in the longer term. Empowering the poor, the destitute, the oppressed and the sidelined to lift themselves out of insecure conditions requires substantial political will in committing to reforms. Effective political, economic, and social reforms entail genuine understanding and active collaborations between the various levels of stakeholders with the ultimate goal of achieving social equality.

With the historic change of regime on May 9, 2018, there has been a renewed hope for a more responsive and accountable government. The new government, which saw a coalition of opposition parties sweeping to power at the 14th general election and replacing the NF for the first time in 61 years since independence, is now entrusted to carry out the needed reforms. Politicians, policymakers, CSOs, and the general public have lauded the peaceful power transition and the quick measures being taken to address a number of pressing issues particularly graft, misappropriation of public funds, reopening investigations of past high-profile cases, and repealing certain unpopular laws. While these moves will bode well in restoring the rule of law and improving good governance, it is still too early to ascertain the impact of regime change on policies pertaining to human security.

The term 'human security' still lingers at the periphery. To mainstream human security in Malaysia, overall awareness of the term and its significance needs to be considerably enhanced. More discussions and debates at the national level need to be generated, particularly on how the concept of human security relates to other concepts that have been in use in the country, such as national security, national resilience, non-traditional threats, human development, and human rights. As one of the founding members of ASEAN, Malaysia should take the lead in making human security the cornerstone of its domestic and foreign policies.

Notes

1. This chapter predominantly employs a two-pronged qualitative research method—document analysis and structured interviews. While the initial idea was to approach a wide range of stakeholders from differing backgrounds, we ended up with a higher concentration of interviewees from civil society movements mainly due to the number of positive responses to our interview request.
2. The proposal was toned down to an ASEAN-PMC Caucus on Social Safety Nets but still failed to receive the endorsement of ASEAN leaders (see Cheeppensook 2007).
3. In the 2013 general election, the NF recorded its lowest percentage of 59.9 percent and saw its popular vote dip below half to 47.38 percent for the first time, compared to the opposition's 50.87 percent.
4. Malaysia's 13th general election was held in May 2013.
5. Over the last five years, there has been a mass migration of Rohingya people from Myanmar and Bangladesh to Southeast Asian countries. In 2015 alone, about 25,000 fled by boat to Malaysia, Indonesia, Thailand, and other neighboring countries. However, they were generally denied settlement in these countries. Malaysia has been one of the intended destinations partly due to its Islamic heritage. In May 2015, more than 3000 boat people were stranded on beaches around Southeast Asia for weeks, capturing the headlines of international and local media.
6. The charge against him was finally withdrawn by the Attorney General in February 2016.
7. SIS has been labeled by a Selangor state religious authority *fatwa* (religious edict) as "deviant" and by some local religious leaders as "insolent" and "extremist."
8. SUARAM's 2014 human rights report provides a long and detailed list of incidents. Some of them include the controversy surrounding the use of the word "Allah" by Malaysian Christians, the continued raids and seizures of bibles, the throwing of Molotov cocktails at a church in Penang, and the cases of unilateral conversions in relation to the conversion of children in custody cases, which led to JAIS stopping a Hindu wedding (SUARAM 2014, 88–103).
9. The NKRAs were cultivated through lab sessions and town hall meetings, allowing the public to become involved in the formulation process.

References

Acharya, Amitav. 1999. Culture, Security, Multilateralism: The 'ASEAN Way' and Regional Order. In *Culture and Security: Multilateralism, Arms Control and Security Building*, ed. Keith R. Krause, 55–84. London: Frank Cass.

Alegria, Kyra. 2015. Civil Society Plays Major Role in Defending Human Rights in Malaysia. *The Rakyat Post*, December 10. http://www.therakyatpost.com/news/2015/12/10/civil-society-plays-major-role-in-defending-human-rights-in-malaysia/.

Anand, Ram. 2016. Thousands Attend Anti-GST Protest, Police Lock Down Dataran Merdeka. *Malay Mail Online*, April 2. http://www.themalaymailonline.com/malaysia/article/police-lock-down-dataran-merdeka-as-anti-gst-protest-starts-to-form.

Bernama. 2016. National Harmony Bill in Final Drafting Stage, Says Minister. *Malaysiakini*, January 11. https://www.malaysiakini.com/news/326377.

Case, William. 2003. Thorns in the Flesh: Civil Society as Democratizing Agent in Malaysia. In *Civil Society in Asia*, ed. David C. Schak and Wayne Hudson, 40–58. Hampshire: Ashgate.

Cheeppensook, Kasira. 2007. The ASEAN Way on Human Security. Paper presented at the *International Development Studies Conference on Mainstreaming Human Security: The Asian Contribution, Bangkok, Thailand, October 4–5, 2007.*

Chong, Terrence. 2006. The Emerging Politics of Islam Hadhari. In *Malaysia: Recent Trends and Challenges*, ed. Saw Swee-Hock and K. Kesavapany, 26–46. Singapore: ISEAS.

Collins, Alan. 2005. *Security and Southeast Asia: Domestic, Regional, and Global Issues.* New Delhi: Viva Books Private Limited.

Gomez, Terence. 2014. Don't Curb Intellectual Discourse. *Kinibiz Online*, September 8. http://www.kinibiz.com/story/opinions/106573/don%E2%80%99t-curb-intellectual-discourse.html.

Hamid, Ahmad Fauzi Abdul. 2009. Islamist Civil Society Activism in Malaysia Under Abdullah Badawi: The Angkatan Belia Islam Malaysia (ABIM) and the Darul Arqam. *Studia Islamika* 16 (3): 439–470.

Haniff, Hussein. 2012. Statement by H.E. Ambassador Hussein Haniff, Permanent Representative of Malaysia to the United Nations, on Agenda Items 14 and 117: Integrated and Coordinated Implementation of and Follow-up to the Outcomes of the Major United Nations Conferences and Summits in the Economic, Social and Related Fields; and Follow-up to the Outcome of the Millennium Summit: Report of the Secretary-General (A/66/763), at the Plenary of the 66th Session of the United Nations General Assembly, New York, 4 June 2012. https://www.un.int/malaysia/sites/www.un.int/files/Malaysia/66th_session/66unga83_1417.pdf4. Accessed 20 June 2017.

———. 2015. Statement by H.E. Ambassador Hussein Haniff, Permanent Representative of Malaysia at the Security Council Open Debate on 'Inclusive Development for the Maintenance of International Peace and Security' New York, January 19. https://www.un.int/malaysia/sites/www.un.int/files/Malaysia/2015-Statements-Security-Council/2015-01-19_-_unsc_open_debate_-inclusive_dev_for_maintenance_of_int_peace_and_security-_f.pdf. Accessed 25 June 2017.

Human Rights Watch. 2012. Civil Society Denounces Adoption of Flawed ASEAN Human Rights Declaration. November. https://www.hrw.org/news/2012/11/19/civil-society-denounces-adoption-flawed-asean-human-rights-declaration.

Jalil, Haikal. 2015. Time for ASEAN to Review Non-interference Policy in Light of the Rohingya Issue. *Sun Daily*, May 22. http://www.thesundaily.my/news/1427817

Khan, Amin. 2015. Throwing Light on Crime Statistics. *The Star*, April 19.

Mak, J.N. 2004. Malaysian Defense and Security Cooperation: Coming Out of the Closet. In *Asia-Pacific Cooperation: National Interests and Regional Order*, ed. Tan See Seng and Amitav Acharya, 127–153. New York: M.E. Sharpe.

Peck, Grant. 2009. Activists Call New SE Asia Rights Body Toothless. *Newsday*, October 23.

Pusat Komas. 2016. *Malaysia Racial Discrimination Report 2015*. Petaling Jaya: Pusat Komas Malaysia.

Razak, Mohamad Najib Abdul. 2001. *Defending Malaysia: Facing the 21st Century*. London: ASEAN Academic Press.

Rolls, Mark G., and Benny Teh Cheng Guan. 2014. ASEAN's Role in the Development of Non-Traditional Regional Security. In *Volume 1: Foreign Policy and Security in an Asian Century: Threats, Strategies and Policy Choices*, ed. Benny Teh Cheng Guan, 213–234. Singapore: World Scientific Publishing.

Sampath, G. 2015. Amartya Sen: National Security Is One Component of Human Security. *The Hindu*, September 6. http://www.thehindu.com/opinion/interview/interview-with-prof-amartya-sen-national-security-is-one-component-of-human-security/article8022388.ece.

Sipalan, Joseph. 2014. Unity Council Presents Three Draft Bills to Replace Sedition Act. *Malay Mail Online*, June 6. http://www.themalaymailonline.com/malaysia/article/unity-council-presents-three-draft-bills-to-replace-sedition-act.

SUARAM. 2014. *Malaysia Human Rights Report 2014*. Petaling Jaya: Suara Inisiatif Sdn Bhd.

———. 2015. *Human Rights Report 2015 Overview: Civil and Political Rights*. Petaling Jaya: Suara Inisiatif Sdn Bhd.

SUHAKAM. 2015a. Throwing Light on the Aim and Mandate of Suhakam. *Malaysiakini*, June 1. https://www.malaysiakini.com/letters/300337.

———. 2015b. *SUHAKAM Annual Report 2014*. Kuala Lumpur: Human Rights Commission of Malaysia.

Sun Daily. 2015. GTP, ETP Showing Positive Results. *Sun Daily*, April 29.

Teh, Benny Cheng Guan. 2009. ASEAN Rights Panel Offers Scant Defense of Victims. *Japan Times*, August 28.

———. 2012. Introduction: Human Security Development and the Future of East Asia. In *Human Security: Securing East Asia's Future*, ed. Benny Teh Cheng Guan, 1–14. Dordrecht: Springer.

Tenaganita. 2015. *The Revolving Door: Modern Day Slavery (Refugees)*. Petaling Jaya: Tenaganita Sdn. Bhd.

UNDP (United Nations Development Program). 1994. *Human Development Report 1994*. New York: Oxford University Press.

Zain, Zawiyah Mohd, and Mohammad Agus Yusoff. 2015. The Emergence of Civil Disobedience: A Comparison during Dr. Mahathir and Abdullah Badawi's Era. *Mediterranean Journal of Social Sciences* 6 (1): 279–285.

Interviews

CSO Source #1. 2016. Francis Loh, then president of Aliran. Interviewed by authors, March 17.

CSO Source #2. 2016. Debbie Stothard, founder of ALTSEAN-Burma. Interviewed by authors, March 21.

CSO Source #3. 2016. Marina Mahathir, board member of Sisters in Islam. Interviewed by authors, March 22.

CSO Source #4. 2016. Aegile Fernandez, director of Tenaganita. Interviewed by authors, January 20.

CSO Source #5. 2016. Hafidzi Mohd Noor, Chairman of MyCare, IKRAM. Interviewed by authors, February 22.

Government Source #1. 2016. Mohamad Azizi bin Azmi, principal assistant secretary at SUHAKAM. Interviewed by authors, February 24.

Parliamentarian Source #1. 2016. Charles Santiago, member of parliament for Klang. Interviewed by authors, January 29.

Parliamentarian Source #2. 2016. Zairil Khir Johari, then member of parliament for Bukit Bendera. Interviewed by authors, April 4.

CHAPTER 7

Human Security and Development in Myanmar: Issues and Implications

Moe Thuzar

7.1 The Context for Human Security and Development

The United Nations Development Program (UNDP)'s *Human Development Report 1994* first highlighted the nexus between human security and development, shifting focus from state security to more concrete deliverables for the security of individuals within a nation-state. Proposing "a new concept of human security" that acknowledges "people's security," encompassing job security, income security, environmental security, and security from crime, conflict, repression, and social disintegration (UNDP 1994, 3), the report also made the argument for human security as an "upstream" intervention that requires long-term development support (UNDP 1994, 3).

Human Security Now, the 2003 report of the independent Commission on Human Security, further elaborated the concept of people-centered human security, stating that "Human security [...] requires both shielding people from acute threats and empowering people to take charge of their

M. Thuzar (✉)
ASEAN Studies Centre, ISEAS-Yusof Ishak Institute, Singapore, Singapore
e-mail: moe_thuzar@iseas.edu.sg

Y. Mine et al. (eds.), *Human Security Norms in East Asia*, Security, Development and Human Rights in East Asia,
https://doi.org/10.1007/978-3-319-97247-3_7

own lives" and called for "integrated policies that focus on people's survival, livelihood, and dignity during downturns as well as in prosperity" (Ogata and Sen 2003, iv), thus bringing together all the issues involved in human security, human rights, and development (Ogata and Sen 2003, 4). Building on this, UN General Assembly Resolution 66/290 on September 10, 2012, established a common understanding of human security, which was essentially freedom from fear, freedom from want, and a life with dignity. The successful pursuit of human security will thus result in an absence of threats to individuals and communities for their survival, livelihoods, and dignity.

Following this, Howe and Jang examined the mutually reinforcing nature of the relationship between human security and development, positing that conflict retards development and underdevelopment can lead to conflict (Howe and Jang 2013, 120–143). This certainly seems to resonate with the experience of Southeast Asian countries, where human security policies and practices emphasize development, whether on the part of the government responsible for ensuring the human security of its populace or on the part of the partner or donor prioritizing human security as an overseas development tool. The underlying notes of conflict and instability from which human security concerns arise, and to which lack of human security could lead, also provoke a sense of urgency for governments to consider human security priorities in their development agendas. This has proved true for Myanmar, even as the transition from state security to human security continues to be in a state of flux in the country.

In this chapter, the broad conceptual approach of human security is used to assess current attitudes toward, and the practices (where relevant) relating to, human security in Myanmar, bearing in mind the legacy of past military regimes which focused mainly on state (and regime) security. Responses in six areas—environment and climate change, migration, urbanization, peace, poverty, and health and education—seem to indicate that the development approach to human security may find greater traction in Myanmar. The current tensions in Rakhine State over the recent exodus of Rohingya communities to Bangladesh, the largest number to date,[1] show that Howe and Jang's assessment of development and conflict has been taken up in Myanmar's human security debate. The situation, though far from ideal, does seem to highlight some opportunities. In addition, the chapter suggests that the Japanese "maximalist" approach to human security (Obuchi 1998) will work better in Myanmar through development cooperation that helps to build a culture of trust. The complexities surrounding the human security, and the more immediate humanitarian needs following the August 2017 military crackdown in Rakhine State, and the ongoing peace negotiations with ethnic armed groups (where issues of trust, and sensitivities over perceptions of which ethnic minority is privileged over others) require more detailed study of how regional cooperation, using the maximalist approach to human security, can play a greater role than before in addressing Myanmar's human security challenges.

7.2 Perceptions and Practices Relating to Human Security in Myanmar

Maung Zarni has pithily noted that the modern history of Burma has been conflict-soaked from 1947 to the present (Zarni 2013). These conflicts have occurred along multiple lines: class and ideology, civil society and the military, and between ethnic groups. Unresolved conflicts from precolonial and colonial eras gave rise to a new set of conflicts upon Burma's independence in 1948. This unbroken line of conflicts in the country, leading to broken trust across the different interest/stakeholder groups, has colored perceptions of human security and responses to human security needs, especially by the ruling elites, at any given point in time in the country. Tin Maung Maung Than contextualizes this in analyzing the human security dimensions within "Myanmar's overwhelmingly state-centered national security perspective" (Than 2007, 176).

The historical roots of human security perceptions in colonial Burma seem to illustrate this point. The earliest organized movements for human security in pre-independence Burma can be found in the motivation of Western-educated young men using Western organizational and institutional forms to protect the people from what they saw as the "encroachment" of Christian missions and other "Westernizing" influences as well as economic exploitation of Burma's natural resources. The early social movements in Burma in the 1900s were aimed at bettering the lives of the Burmese and were mainly rooted in Buddhist civic action. The humanitarian or social actions of these organized movements and civil society associations to protect "national interests" and the security of the local (Burmese) communities politicized issues of concern and promoted nationalism.[2]

Burma/Myanmar's history of the authorities' response to human security concerns also had mainly political underpinnings. Spontaneous action was strictly regulated by the colonial, and later the military, regime. The focus of collective movements was more on civic and humanitarian action via state-organized youth and social welfare organizations, rather than on proactive policies that address human security and developmental needs. In 1950s post-independence Burma, social and business associations, which addressed human security situations as a continuation of the pre-independence movements, were affiliated with (and operated through) the Anti-Fascist People's Freedom League (AFPFL) machinery. Civil and political rights advocacy took a backseat to the growing concerns over the emerging insurgencies that began almost immediately after independence. The insurgency situation led to the overwhelming emphasis, spanning the decades up to the present day, on national (state) security and protecting the state from any enemy or threat. This later became conflated with regime security, particularly after 1962.

After Ne Win took over the powers of the state in 1962, the Burma Socialist Programme Party (BSPP) created institutions for social movement and action while restricting political and economic organizations. The overarching attitude was to strive for self-protection and sufficiency. The BSPP organized local people's militia-type structures to "prepare" the populace against the threat of insurgencies, and formed social organizations, such as the Lanzin Youth and the Peasants' and Workers' Unions, under the aegis of the BSPP ideology. Yet, local social welfare and religious organizations continued to function quite freely, creating favorable conditions for the norms that encourage and promote social collective action (Hlaing 2007), thus keeping alive the spirit of collectively protecting human security needs.

However, when the State Law and Order Restoration Council (SLORC) took control in 1988 after a bloody repression of pro-democracy movements, it had a hostile attitude toward civil society organizations and spontaneous collective action or movements of any sort. But, despite restrictions, many civil society organizations continued to exist, including native place and ethnic organizations, religious organizations, alumni associations, and local business associations in both formal and informal structures. They provided the social networks through which humanitarian issues were communicated and addressed, mainly for localized events and needs. This was in part due to the heavy restrictions placed by the military government on assembly and gatherings. Throughout the mid- to late-1990s, however, the military government gradually allowed operations of civil society organizations that focused mainly on social, health, and later, environmental issues (notwithstanding the political nature of these problems). This helps to explain why many civil society organizations in Myanmar today focus on these topics. They provide a ready base for human security responses in areas or sectors where government capacity to respond is low and/or slow.

The importance of human security in several of its dimensions was driven home to the military regime when Cyclone Nargis struck Myanmar's delta area in 2008. The then Prime Minister Thein Sein realized the importance of constructive partnerships in bridging development and information gaps. Since 2008, Myanmar's political landscape has undergone an important change. The military-led State Peace and Development Council (SPDC) ceded power to a "civilianized" government elected in November 2010. But the 2010 elections were largely decried as a "sham," as they elected the Union Solidarity and Development Party (USDP), which was simply a reformulation of the military regime's social mobilization arm. The main opposition party, the National League for Democracy (NLD) led by Daw Aung San Suu Kyi, did not participate in the election. Daw Suu[3] herself was still under house arrest. This was lifted on November 13, 2010, five days after the elections. U Thein Sein, formerly the Prime Minister and public face of the SPDC, became President of Myanmar and led the USDP government for a five-year term starting on March 30, 2011. He initiated steps to pave the way for the opposition to rejoin the political process, via landmark by-elections on April 1, 2012, when the NLD won most of the seats.

The General Election of November 2015, widely anticipated as the litmus test for the country's democratization process, saw the NLD win an overwhelming majority, enabling it to nominate both the President and one of the two Vice-Presidential posts. Daw Suu could not be nominated to either of these posts under the restrictive provisions of the 2008 Constitution. To circumvent this, the NLD government's first legislative act after taking power on March 30, 2016 was to create the position of State Counselor, which bridged the executive and legislative roles of government, for Daw Suu. She is now treated at home and abroad as Myanmar's de facto leader.

After the first flush of a peaceful handover from the military-backed USDP administration to a civilian government, deep-seated legacy issues from previous administrations have beset the NLD government's performance even up to its mid-term mark. A positive move for human security by the NLD government in its first year in power included repealing repressive legislation such as the 1950 Emergency Provisions Act, which the military junta had used to criminalize freedom of expression. But continued fighting between ethnic armed groups and government forces in Northern Myanmar, the reversal of an uneasy peace in Rakhine State in the wake of militant attacks on border security posts, and the shocking murder of prominent NLD legal advisor U Ko Ni marred efforts to ensure greater personal security. There were also frustrations expressed over the slow pace of the government policy machinery in the economic sphere. Still, Daw Suu's nationwide televised state of the union speech on March 30, 2017, marking the NLD's first year in government, acknowledged that her government was aware of the need to listen to the people, and to "keep trying" to be a government for the people.

The year 2017 presented several challenges. In addition to dealing with the differing views over ceasefire negotiations, and efforts to attract more investments for socio-economic development across the country, the NLD government also faced mounting international criticism over the Rohingya refugee crisis that arose from the harsh military operations responding to attacks on security posts along the border by the Arakan Rohingya Solidarity Army (ARSA) in August 2017. The intransigent attitude toward the Rohingya crisis by a large majority of the population, and the attendant anger in Myanmar toward the international criticism of the NLD government's handling of the issue propelled Daw Suu into a dual position of riding a strong wave of support domestically but facing her strongest criticism to date internationally. The government's interactions with foreign partners now have the additional dimensions of having to explain the complexities of the Rohingya situation and the need to seek support for humanitarian assistance and resettlement in Rakhine State.

The challenges besetting Myanmar today underscore the fact that human security considerations need to form the core of a development policy that is appropriate to the specific circumstances of the country. Ensuring human security for the population should no longer be a matter of debate or choice for Myanmar's policy makers.

7.3 Key Human Security Concerns in Myanmar

Under the USDP administration, the Ministry for National Development and Economic Planning launched their *Framework on Economic and Social Reforms* (FESR) in January 2013. The three-year framework was intended as a "reform bridge" linking to Myanmar's 20-year National Comprehensive Development Plan. The NLD government has also highlighted the importance of an economic policy that supports the government's overarching goal of national reconciliation (Kyaw and Hammond 2016). This includes implementing the NLD's election commitment to ensure, among other priorities, the "freedom and security to prosper" within a "system of government that will fairly and justly defend the people" (NLD 2015). The NLD government recently launched the Myanmar Sustainable Development Plan, linking the priorities for peace and economic stability with people-centered goals. (Aung San Suu Kyi 2018).

Indeed, the NLD government has a unique opportunity to engender people-centered programs and projects in its priority plans. The post-2015 Development Agenda objectives provide additional inspiration, as they call for a "truly integrated people-centered approach" in pursuing inclusive social development, inclusive economic development, environmental sustainability, and peace and security (UNHSU 2014, 17).

7.3.1 Environment and Climate Change[4]

Environmental concerns can provide the impetus for an intersectoral approach linking environmental and human rights. During its tenure of the 2014 ASEAN chairmanship, Myanmar took the lead in adopting an East Asia Summit Declaration on Climate Change (as an input to the international climate change discussions led by the UN) and proposed to host the ASEAN Institute on Green Economy (AIGE). The AIGE was formally launched in February 2018 (Green Economy Growth 2018).

Cross-sectoral cooperation on environment and climate change issues is still weak regionally and nationally. This implies that national efforts (and the national interest) are still the main drivers for regional or global action. Yet, human security concerns are coming to the fore in these areas, with increasing calls for environmental governance in different ASEAN countries to discuss the legislative and judicial frameworks for access rights and public participation in environmental decision-making. There is a nascent environmental justice movement in ASEAN countries with transboundary relevance that requires future monitoring. With major infrastructure projects now being implemented to support closer connectivity among the ASEAN countries, especially in the Greater Mekong Sub-region (GMS), the emerging issues of procedural rights across borders for displaced or relocated local communities are related to environmental and community security. This has been played out at the local level in Myanmar by way of community protests against the Dawei Deep Sea Port project in southern Myanmar.

Human security concerns are also embedded in compliance requirements for the Extractive Industries Transparency Initiative (EITI),[5] to which Myanmar became a candidate country in July 2014. EITI is a voluntary initiative that ensures greater accountability and transparency in reporting revenues from extractive industries. Myanmar's EITI candidacy provides a window to address corruption issues in the country and to gauge the extent to which local communities and the public in general benefit from the "gains" from extractive industries.

Myanmar's EITI compliance preparations group learnt a sad lesson from the harsh security-related responses to community protests over the Letpadaungtaung Copper Mine project, a joint venture between Myanmar and Chinese companies.[6] Protests started in 2012 over land compensation and relocation disagreements, escalating into a crackdown by security forces that severely injured several protesters, including monks. The tensions continued to simmer even after an investigation commission headed by Daw Suu recommended greater compensation, environmentally sustainable practices, and greater corporate social responsibility, among other things. The recommendations did not include the halting of mine operations, and protests returned with the resumption of the mine's operations in 2014,[7] resulting in the death of a villager (Mar 2014).

7.3.2 Urbanization

Myanmar's urban population is roughly one-third of the country's total population.[8] UN statistical data estimates urban population growth at 2.5 percent and rural population growth at –0.1 percent.[9] Rural-urban migration has become one of the contributing factors to Myanmar's urbanization challenges. Migrants usually have the intention to return to their place of origin, but only a few actually return. If they support relatives in their place of origin or intend to spend their savings there, their disposable urban income is often very low, forcing many to share rental rooms or live in informal settlements. Over the years, they become part of the urban population, but their lack of income and access to basic infrastructure services, such as clean water and sanitation, and to power and decision-making processes, renders them vulnerable to the changes and renewals taking place in urban areas in Yangon and other parts of the country.

The country's commercial hub, Yangon, is confronted with the challenge of upgrading its infrastructure and facilities to meet the requirements of ASEAN connectivity, while at the same time dealing with the lack of space, land, and basic social services to accommodate all urban residents adequately. The continued existence of slums or squatter settlements is a result of inadequate housing. There is no security of tenure for a large portion of the urban population, as the government, which technically owns all land in the country, can site new venues for major development projects (such as industrial and/or special economic zones) around major urban agglomerations. Yet many squatters continue to live under the continuing threat of eviction, and with inadequate water and sanitation.

In early 2016, just before the transfer of state power to the NLD, news reports highlighted the increase in the slum population in Yangon, attributing the increase to rural-urban migration and lack of cheap housing (MacDonald and Thiha-Cho 2016). After the NLD took office, the Yangon State Government came into the spotlight over plans to move squatters to "rehabilitation camps" (Y. Mon 2016).

7.3.3 *Migration*

Myanmar has become the country with the highest numbers of migrants in the GMS (IOM 2015). This is mainly a result of people fleeing the conflict in the border areas between armed forces and insurgent groups, as well as semi- and unskilled workers seeking what they perceive as an attractive income in the labor-scarce higher-income ASEAN economies. The NLD government has taken on a more coherent policy approach to addressing the concerns of migrant workers, including registration of employment agencies, establishment of hotlines, and bilateral negotiations with countries where there are large numbers of Myanmar migrant workers. But the migration challenge lies more in the repatriation of refugees and displaced persons, with most of the international attention focused on the Rohingya.

Intercommunal tensions and an overriding focus on the security dimension of migration in Rakhine State have led to displacement and exodus in Rohingya communities. The USDP government started a phased citizenship project in 2014 but ran into some controversy over its insistence on verifying the Rohingya as Bengali. The NLD government relaunched the citizenship process in June 2016 (Maung 2016), but this again stalled with the military retaliation to the October 2016 and August 2017 militant attacks on border security posts and regional security headquarters. The August 2017 attacks, in particular, were termed by the Myanmar military as "terrorist" attacks, and military operations were mounted in response to these, causing the largest exodus of Rohingya communities across the border to date. The United Nations Office for the Coordination of Humanitarian Affairs estimates that there are now over 800,000 Rohingyas in camps in Bangladesh (UNOCHA 2018). At the time of writing, the governments of Myanmar and Bangladesh have signed a Memorandum of Understanding on repatriating the refugees. There are different expectations on the implementation, as well as the human security concerns, of the repatriation process.

To a large extent, Myanmar's responses to the Rohingya exodus and the international backlash to it (with an attendant hardening of nationalist sentiments within Myanmar), has become a test case for how state-led mechanisms and policies can address issues of personal security. But the focus on the Rohingya has lessened international attention on the displaced communities in Kachin State[10] as well as on the ongoing repatriation of refugees and migrants from Thailand. While ceasefire negotiations between the Kachin Independence Organisation (KIO) and the Myanmar government are still ongoing, the Governments of Myanmar and Thailand have coordinated the repatriation of displaced persons along the Thai-Myanmar border, most of whom are in refugee camps or live as undocumented workers in Thailand. Since June 30, 2014, the Ministries of Labor of both countries launched a process to work toward documenting and eventually repatriating the undocumented Myanmar migrant workers in Thailand. The first pilot voluntary returns of refugees from Thailand started in October 2016 (UNHCR 2016), but by May 2017, there were reports of repatriation challenges, mainly in terms of opportunities and social services for the returnees to resettle in Myanmar (Corben 2017).

Government responses to migration still require some policy coherence, although the Office of the State Counsellor seems to be emerging as the overall coordinator (and arbiter) of government responses that vary according to whether the communities in need are returning migrants, refugees, or internally displaced persons (IDPs). The migrant worker issue is dealt with mainly by the Ministry of Labor and Immigration, which has no jurisdiction over IDPs, and which provides peripheral inputs to the negotiations on the liberalization of controls on the movement of skilled professionals. The resettlement of IDPs comes under the mandate of the Ministry for Social Welfare, Relief and Resettlement, as do current efforts for resettlement of the returned Rohingya. The Ministry of Foreign Affairs is in direct discussion with its counterpart in Bangladesh for repatriation of Rohingya and is also the main interlocutor with ASEAN countries regarding humanitarian and capacity-building assistance on the issue, but it is not involved in actual implementation. International humanitarian organizations and related UN agencies have shouldered most of the work in assisting the Myanmar government. In the wake of the Rakhine/Rohingya issue, the Myanmar government has taken the lead in establishing a Union Enterprise for Humanitarian Assistance, Resettlement and Development in Rakhine (UEHRD), which seeks private sector participation as well as external donations to boost Rakhine's socio-economic conditions.[11] The coordination and delivery of humanitarian assistance on the ground is now carried out mainly by the International Red Cross and Red Crescent (ICRC) (ICRC 2018). These efforts—and external interventions, if any—could consider building on the potential of local civil society's capacity to take on a larger bridge-building role in post-conflict peacebuilding and reconciliation efforts.

7.3.4 *Peace*

In August 2011, then President Thein Sein and Daw Suu publicly shared their joint commitment to work together on the decades-long national reconciliation challenges, including building trust among and with the different ethnic minorities and interest groups. These groups each have different sets of concerns over their security and survival beyond ceasefire settlements. Concerns range from resettlement, rehabilitation, and reintegration for citizens affected by the ethnic conflict, as well as disarmament, demobilization, and reintegration (DDR) requirements for armed groups to rejoin the political process. The USDP government pushed for a nationwide ceasefire agreement (NCA) as part of its performance agenda but failed to get 8 of the 16 armed ethnic groups to agree to sign the NCA in October 2015. Inheriting this imperative for continuing the political dialogue toward national reconciliation, the NLD government affirmed its commitment to the peace process and initiated the first in a series of biannual 21st Century Panglong Conferences, August 30 to September 1, 2016. This first conference renewed the commitment to continue ceasefire negotiations with the remaining non-signatories and recognized the need to address multiple stakeholder (including civil society) concerns.

A second conference, scheduled for February 28, 2017, was finally held on May 29, 2017 due to divergent views on the non-secession of states and a federal army structure. Even then, some ethnic armed groups such as the Wa, who had stormed out of the September 2016 conference, attended the May 2017 conference only at China's behest (Htut 2017). This indicates the long reach of Beijing's influence in the Myanmar peace process. China is one of several external interlocutors in this peace process, the others being the United States, the European Union, and Japan (Htut 2016). It has asserted its mediating role in several situations, including the hosting of peace talks in 2013 between the USDP and the KIO negotiating teams. This assertion of influence in the peace process has had some repercussions. China was accused of "meddling" in the finalization of the October 2015 NCA, to block the inclusion of Japan and "Western nations" as international observers as well as to influence some of the armed ethnic groups not to sign the NCA (Wee 2015). China has yet again asserted its mediator role in the three-point proposal put forward by Chinese Foreign Minister Wang Yi (Lee 2017) to resolve the Rakhine/Rohingya issue (Nitta 2017).[12]

China's approach can be contrasted with that taken by Japan. Japan's contributions are mainly through the activities of the Nippon Foundation, focusing on humanitarian assistance in the conflict areas, longer-term capacity support in the health, education, and social welfare sectors, regional development projects in the post-conflict areas, and leadership training programs for administrative officials of the Ministry of Border Affairs. In 2013 a Cabinet decision appointed Mr. Yohei Sasakawa as Special Envoy for National Reconciliation in Myanmar. Mr. Sasakawa's role builds on his earlier efforts to facilitate dialogue and humanitarian assistance to conflict areas in Northern Myanmar and is modeled on an earlier initiative by the Government of Japan to support peace and reconstruction in Sri Lanka in 2002 (Nippon Foundation 2013). Starting in 2012, the Nippon Foundation's Myanmar program initiated the building of elementary schools in Rakhine State (Nippon Foundation 2017) to provide a safe and secure learning environment as well as a shelter in times of disaster.

A third Panglong conference was held in July 2018, and two more ethnic armed groups—the New Mon State Party and the Lau Democratic Union—both based near the Thai-Myanmar border, have signed the NCA. This development gives a boost to the NLD government's peace and reconciliation efforts, but analysts observe that political dialogue remains a challenge (Nitta and Htway 2018), while Myanmar policy think tanks also admit that there is "still a long way to go to reach the goal of a domestic conflict-free country."[13]

The Myanmar government and its interlocutors view poverty reduction as an important part of minimizing conflict as the country moves toward greater personal and economic security.

7.3.5 Poverty Reduction

Prior to 2015–16, Myanmar lacked up-to-date nationwide statistics on poverty and household welfare, apart from the Integrated Household Living Conditions Assessment (IHLCA) conducted with the assistance of the UNDP in 2004–05 and 2009–10. The IHLCA-I in 2004–05 defined poverty incidence as the "proportion of population of households with insufficient consumption expenditure to cover their food and non-food needs." Poverty incidence at the national level dropped from 32.1 percent during IHLCA-I to 25.6 percent in IHLCA-II. However, there were rural-urban,[14] as well as regional, disparities. For example, Rakhine State was ranked the country's second poorest region with an estimated 43.5 percent living below the poverty line, compared to the national average. Nevertheless, the overall reduction in the incidence of poverty nationally encouraged the USDP administration to set the ambitious target of further reducing the poverty incidence to 16 percent by 2015. IHLCA-II also highlighted Rakhine as the country's second poorest region,

Building on the IHLCA data and methodology, the World Bank's 2017 Myanmar Poverty Assessment (World Bank 2017) identified the trends that should be monitored. While 37 percent of the population still live near or below the poverty line of $1.25 a day, the overall poverty incidence decreased to 19.4 percent in 2015. But the decline in poverty rates has been more rapid for urban areas, which have felt the effects of Myanmar's economic opening up the most.

As the 2014 census placed the total population at about 52 million, many people in Myanmar, especially in rural areas, may continue to exist just above the poverty line. The World Bank has highlighted the need to update the country's poverty measures to reflect current living standards data and the changes in living conditions and needs of the poor. The USDP administration established a poverty reduction fund in 2011 as part of the decentralization process. In their report assessing state and regional governments in Myanmar, the Centre for Economic and Social Development (CESD) and the Asia Foundation cited the initiative as "the only fully devolved resource transfer from the union to state and region level." Under this initiative, about 1 billion kyat (roughly US$1 million) was allocated (in FY2012–13) to each state or region, and Chin State—due to its extreme remoteness and lack of facilities—received triple this amount. But the USDP's poverty reduction efforts lost some momentum in the latter part of its administration, notwithstanding a significant push by Japan to ramp up assistance to Myanmar through several channels, including rural poverty reduction and improving HIV/AIDS care via the Asian Development Bank's Japan Fund for Poverty Reduction. In 2014, this fund proposed a US$12 million program for rural poverty reduction, and another US$10 million toward programs for better access and quality to health and HIV/AIDS services (K.H. Mon 2014).

7.3.6 Health and Education

The USDP reforms highlighted health and education as important areas for the empowerment and development of people and their capacity to participate in the country's development. Even so, Myanmar's public spending on health and education ranked lower than other ASEAN countries, according to a study carried out in early 2014 by Action Aid Myanmar (MM Business News 2014). For the 2014–15 budget year, defense spending (12%) was more than the combined allocations for education (6%) and health (3%) (Toe Lwin 2014). The high defense allocation (13%) continued for the FY2016–17 budget, the last approved by the outgoing government. The NLD government's first budget for FY2017–18 continued with a similar allocation for defense, but larger shares for planning and finance (23%), and electricity and energy (21.5%). Allocations for education (8%) and health (5%) also increased (Thant 2017).

Health and nutrition security is paramount for young children (especially those under five years of age) and their mothers in Myanmar. There are twin challenges of lowering the infant and maternal mortality rates, as well as reducing malnutrition in children, particularly those living in rural and remote border/ethnic populations. Public health solutions such as increasing the number of auxiliary health workers and midwives in villages and providing free health care for under-five children have shown results and need to continue. It will also be important to improve/raise the health facility-to-population ratio according to WHO standards (Government Source #1).

About education, there are access, quality, and governance issues affecting primary, secondary, and tertiary education. To address these challenges, a new education law was enacted on September 30, 2014, outlining a decentralized structure and greater space for private or alternative education. Education reforms at the primary and secondary levels will need to break the current vicious cycle of overloaded curriculum, predominance of private tuition, and the poor quality of the teaching-learning process. The ongoing ceasefire negotiations are expected to have a positive impact on the teaching of local languages and culture in ethnic areas. The main challenge for tertiary education reform lies in ensuring that education outcomes match job market requirements as Myanmar develops. Concerns continue over job-skills mismatch and the low quality of tertiary education (Mooney 2014).

7.4 Opportunities and Challenges of Constructive Engagement

SLORC's bloody coup in 1988, and its targeted antagonism toward Daw Suu and the forces for democracy, led to international sanctions against the military junta. Asian, particularly ASEAN, governments did not join the sanctions regime, instead advocating a constructive engagement approach to bring about change in Myanmar. Japan applied limited sanctions while continuing to be a major source of foreign aid to the country (Zarni 2005).

This illustrates the dissimilarities in the Canadian and Japanese approaches to human security. Howe and Jang explain that Canada's human security perspective is associated with conflict and violence-related threats to individuals and allows for "vigorous action" including coercive measures such as sanctions and military force in pursuing the human security agenda. Japan's human security perspective, on the other hand, is rooted in the "heart to heart" Fukuda doctrine, which is essentially anti-military and pro-economic in practice. Learning from the bitter experience of World War II, Japan's human security concept embraces both freedom from fear and freedom from want. This was later expanded to include freedom to live in dignity, building on the "comprehensive security" policy of the 1980s that was inclusive and emphasized multilateralism. This became a key foreign policy perspective for Japan in the 1990s under Prime Minister Keizo Obuchi, and a main objective of Japanese overseas development assistance (ODA); highlighting the notion of a strategic link between development, human security, and Japan's foreign policy (Howe and Jang 2013). Japan's ODA policy also reinforces this notion by emphasizing that human security is one of the "basic policies" of ODA and is a "first priority issue." ODA implementation thus requires assistance programs that put people "at the center of concerns." The revision of Japan's ODA Charter in 2003 saw an increased focus on programs that address basic human needs, including basic social services and emergency aid (Howe and Jang 2013, 131). Japan's approach has since found greater traction among the policy elite in Myanmar (Government Source #2 and #3).

The response to human security and humanitarian needs that arose in the wake of the devastating Cyclone Nargis in 2008 provides a good example of tackling human security concerns through development assistance. The tripartite collaboration among the Myanmar government, the UN, and ASEAN to coordinate post-cyclone international assistance is cited as a best practice for working around the then military government's reluctance to accept aid. International reporting on the Nargis fallout focused more on this reluctance. But the ASEAN Foreign Ministers' special meeting on May 19, 2008, persuaded Myanmar to accept aid through ASEAN's coordination. The ASEAN and UN Secretaries-General also exercised personal diplomacy with the military leadership. This led to an agreement on May 23, 2008, that Myanmar would allow all aid and relief workers into the country "regardless of nationality." Two days later, Yangon hosted the ASEAN-UN International Pledging Conference. ASEAN Foreign Ministers established an ASEAN Humanitarian Task Force to coordinate relief and recovery efforts. A Tripartite Core Group (TCG), comprising representatives from ASEAN, the Government of Myanmar, and the UN, carried out on-the-ground coordination. This created an opportunity for non-government actors, both local and international to work together. It also brought into focus ASEAN's efforts to engage with its members on human security issues.

Attempts to achieve a similar response to human security and recovery needs in Rakhine State over the Rohingya issue have proved more challenging. It is difficult to recapture the spirit of impartial collaboration and apply it to situations of human insecurity such as those that occurred in the wake of the June 2012 clashes between the Rohingya and Rakhine residents in Rakhine State, and, more recently after the August 24, 2017 attacks and the ensuing military crackdown. The 2012 clashes led to religion-based violence in central parts of Myanmar, as well as displacing communities in their aftermath. Hard attitudes toward communities perceived as "others" have lingered. In response to the concern expressed by the international community over the situation in Rakhine State, and the ethno-nationalist tensions today, Myanmar has reverted to placing sovereignty over intervention. Myanmar has also indicated a clear preference for negotiating bilateral measures with individual ASEAN members and other partners rather than consider a full-blown regional approach (Thuzar and Reiffel 2018). Human security issues in ASEAN member states are usually not part of the grouping's formal discussion agendas, although the topic(s) are raised in the corridors or bilaterally. The Rakhine/Rohingya issue has broken this mold, however, as there was an unprecedented move to convene an informal meeting of the ASEAN foreign ministers in Yangon in November 2017 to discuss the Rakhine issue (Chongkittavorn 2016). This was in addition to the briefing that Daw Suu gave to her counterparts during the Leaders' retreat at the 30th ASEAN Summit in the Philippines in November 2017, and the recent appeals for capacity-building assistance at the recent ASEAN-Australia Summit in Sydney, Australia in March 2018 (Yahya 2018). There is some room for optimism that the human security dimensions of the issue may find greater traction with the NLD government's responses to the issue. Singapore, as Chair of ASEAN for 2018, has worked with the Jakarta-based ASEAN Coordinating Centre for Humanitarian Assistance on disaster management (AHA Centre) to facilitate the provision of humanitarian assistance for the displaced communities in Rakhine State.[15] Even as ASEAN has been criticized for not being able to bring about concrete solutions in tackling the plight of the Rohingya, the grouping continues to operate on its regional mandate of supporting the humanitarian response to the issue on regional and bilateral fronts. The Myanmar President's Office announced on May 31, 2018 that an Independent Commission of Enquiry would be formed to investigate human rights violations and related issues following the August 2017 attacks.[16] This announcement was preceded by the signing of a Memorandum of Understanding between the Myanmar Government, the UNDP, and the United Nations Refugee Agency (UNHCR)[17] to facilitate the repatriation and resettlement of refugees. At the time of writing, details of how these arrangements will be implemented on the ground have yet to be further clarified, amidst a general atmosphere (internationally) of skepticism, while perceptions toward the government's human security responses are mixed regarding the detention of and legal proceedings against two Myanmar journalists working for Reuters over their investigation into the killing of Rohingya men in a village in Rakhine State.[18] If anything, the Rahine/Rohingya crisis highlights that the national security narrative will still take precedence.

7.5 Conclusions: Future Human Security Approaches for Myanmar

The success of policies and projects aimed at improving human security in Myanmar lie in greater inclusion and participation of various groups in their formulation and implementation. Inclusion would need to occur at several levels, and participation would need to cut across several sectors. Myanmar has also highlighted an emphasis on improving those socio-economic conditions where intervention is needed the most. It is interesting that the UEHRD concept is premised on Howe and Jang's argument about the development-conflict-security nexus. Nowhere is this nexus more evident than in Myanmar's Rakhine State, where the Rakhine and Rohingya communities are locked in recurring negative cycles of fear and hate, compounded by decades of polarization. The Myanmar government admits the humanitarian dimensions of the situation but maintains that the Rohingya situation is Myanmar's internal affair. Earlier the USDP government rejected several proposals to set up tripartite talks based on the Nargis modus operandi.[19] The late Dr. Surin Pitsuwan, former ASEAN Secretary-General and a Thai Muslim, had been working on possible pathways to achieve a peaceful resolution to the Rohingya crisis, up to his untimely demise on November 30, 2017 (Vatikiotis 2017). He exhorted stakeholders and commentators alike not to put a religious slant on the issue. Yet, the Rakhine situation is still interpreted by many as a conflict between Buddhists and Muslims. The complexities of the situation have been compounded by decades of manipulation by dictator regimes. The many layers to this issue, including national identity and citizenship, corruption and the lack of proper rule of law, and, perhaps most importantly, the problems of poverty alleviation and access to basic social services, all present formidable human security challenges that confront and, to some extent, threaten Myanmar's nascent transition to change. At the core of these issues are the people. This is where their capacity for change can be assisted via civil society organizations designed to bridge tensions over issues of broken trust and continuing feelings of insecurity among the different communities. Civil society groups (especially interfaith groups) in Myanmar have taken some initial steps toward this difficult role. Low-profile mediation efforts for inter- and intra-communal understanding in Rakhine are focusing on boosting the capacity of community leaders and civil society, on learning from other countries' experiences with multicultural, multi-racial policies, and on building bridges at both policy and research tracks. Engaging political parties in Rakhine and the legislators of these parties in the various regional and central-level parliaments is also crucial in framing perceptions and responses. However, it will probably take decades to undo negative perceptions (Than and Thuzar 2012, 1–7) and reestablish a modicum of trust.

Disasters and conflicts thus underscore an urgent need for "bridge-builders" for human security and for building the capacity of individuals and organizations who would take up this role. The situation in Myanmar illustrates that trust is essential for formulating integrated responses to human security needs. Further research should continue to explore whether Myanmar's fellow ASEAN members as well as ASEAN's Dialogue Partners that have bilateral country programs in Myanmar can leverage the regional cooperation mechanisms and utilize the approach of development diplomacy to provide bridges to this end. In an era where the region and the world at large are witnessing more transactional approaches to diplomacy and dialogue, and where domestic priorities are placed above regional and international commitments, bilateral approaches to human security, albeit under the larger regional umbrella, may yet prove the way to go. ASEAN and the international community's past experiences in dealing with Myanmar have shown that quiet diplomacy, accompanied by capacity-building support and advice have been more effective than megaphone interventions (Thuzar and Htut 2017).

Notes

1. The United Nations Office for the Coordination of Humanitarian Affairs (UNOHCA), which tracks new arrivals to the camps in Bangladesh, periodically updates the numbers. As of January 2018, there had been 688,000 new arrivals since August 25, 2017 (see UNOCHA 2017).
2. The history of humanitarian action in Burma has drawn from the analyses of U Maung Maung (1976), *From Sangha to Laity: Nationalist Movements of Burma 1920–1940,* unpublished master's thesis, Australian National University, and Kyaw Yin Hlaing (2009), "Social Capital, Civil Society Organisations and Cyclone Nargis," unpublished paper presented at Workshop on Lessons from Nargis: Disaster Management in Southeast Asia, March 5–6, 2009, Institute of Southeast Asian Studies, Singapore.

3. I refer to Aung San Suu Kyi as Daw Suu hereafter, as there is a popular preference on referring to her with the Daw honorific rather than as "Suu Kyi."
4. The discussion under this heading is based on the author's participation in a workshop on "Human Rights, Environment, Climate Change" in Yangon on September 13–15, 2014.
5. To be EITI compliant, candidate countries are required to have in place a functioning multi-stakeholder group that includes civil society participation, among other key requirements.
6. The joint venture partners are the Union of Myanmar Economic Holdings (UMEHL), a state-owned enterprise with military backing, and Wan Bao Mining, a subsidiary of a Chinese state-owned arms firm.
7. The protestors' concerns were on environmental damage and lack of full compensation. In 2014, three workers were kidnapped by opponents of the mine (The Economist 2014).
8. In 2013, the percentage of the urban population was 33.8, according to UN estimates.
9. Data available at the United Nations Statistics Division, UN data website (accessed 15 October 2014).
10. Some 100,000 people were displaced as a result of the hostilities between the KIO and the Myanmar armed forces.
11. The UEHRD ambit falls under the Office of the State Counselor, and has its own website: http://rakhine.unionenterprise.org/
12. See also Nitta (2017).
13. Remarks made by the Chairman of the Myanmar Institute for Strategic and International Studies at a by-invitation workshop on "Strategies for Peace, Harmony and Development" held in Yangon on February 21, 2018. The author was a panelist at this workshop.
14. In 2009–10, the rural poverty incidence (29.2%) was almost double the urban rate (15.7%).
15. See https://ahacentre.org/press-release/press-release-aha-centre-facilitates-humanitarian-assistance-between-singapore-and-myanmar-for-displaced-communities-in-rakhine-state/ (accessed 25 April 2018).
16. See http://www.president-office.gov.mm/en/?q=briefing-room/announcements/2018/06/04/id-8827 (accessed 25 April 2018).
17. See https://www.rfa.org/english/news/myanmar/myanmar-signs-mou-with-un-agencies-on-repatriation-of-rohingya-refugees-06062018164116.html (accessed 25 April 2018).
18. See https://www.reuters.com/subjects/myanmar-reporters (accessed 25 April 2018).
19. This proposal was made by then ASEAN Secretary-General Surin Pitsuwan in 2012.

References

Aung, San Suu Kyi. 2018. Democratic Transition in Myanmar: Challenges and the Way Forward. https://www.iseas.edu.sg/images/43rd-Singapore-Lecture-Speech-by-Aung-San-Suu-Kyi-Final-transcript.pdf. Accessed 30 Aug 2018.

Chongkittavorn, Kavi. 2016. Myanmar to Brief ASEAN Amid Alarm over Rakhine. http://asia.nikkei.com/Politics-Economy/International-Relations/Myanmar-to-brief-ASEAN-amid-alarm-over-Rakhine. Accessed 10 Jan 2018.

CHS (Commission on Human Security). 2003. *Human Security Now*. New York: Commission on Human Security.

Corben, Ron. 2017. Myanmar Refugees in Thai Camps Face Repatriation Challenges. https://www.voanews.com/a/myanmar-refugees-thai-camps-repatriation-challenges/3847329.html. Accessed 11 May 2017.

Green Economy Growth. 2018. *Draft Extended Summary Highlights*. http://geggmyanmar.org/draft-extended-summary-highlights/. Accessed 9 Mar 2018.

Hlaing, Kyaw Yin. 2007. Associational Life in Myanmar. In *Myanmar: State, Society and Ethnicity*, ed. N. Ganesan and Kyaw Yin Hlaing. Singapore: ISEAS.

———. 2009. Social Capital, Civil Society Organisations and Cyclone Nargis. Unpublished Paper Presented at Workshop on Lessons from Nargis: Disaster Management in Southeast Asia, 5–6 March 2009, Institute of Southeast Asian Studies, Singapore.

Howe, Brendan M., and Suyoun Jang. 2013. Human Security and Development: Divergent Approaches to Burma/Myanmar. *Pacific Focus* 28 (1): 120–143.

Htut, Ye. 2016. Myanmar's Long Journey to Peace Starts at Panglong. http://www.straitstimes.com/opinion/myanmars-long-journey-to-peace-starts-in-panglong. Accessed 31 Aug 2016.

———. 2017. Myanmar's Elusive Dream of Peace. https://www.iseas.edu.sg/medias/commentaries/item/5479-myanmars-elusive-dream-of-peace-by-ye-htut. Accessed 1 June 2017.

ICRC (International Committee of the Red Cross). 2018. Myanmar: Six Months on into the Rakhine Crisis. https://www.icrc.org/en/document/myanmar six-months-rakhine-crisis. Accessed 18 Mar 2018.

IOM (International Organization for Migration). 2015. Myanmar. http://www.iom.int/cms/en/sites/iom/home/where-we-work/asia-and-the-pacific/myanmar.html. Accessed 6 Jan 2015.

Kyaw, Aye Thida, and Clare Hammond. 2016. Government Reveals 12-Point Economic Policy. http://www.mmtimes.com/index.php/business/21664-nld-12-point-economic-policy-announcement.html. Accessed 14 Aug 2016

Lee, Yimou. 2017. China Draws Three-Stage Path for Myanmar, Bangladesh to Resolve Rohingya Crisis. https://www.reuters.com/article/us-myanmar-rohingya/china-draws-three-stage-path-for-myanmar-bangladesh-to-resolve-rohingya-crisis-idUSKBN1DK0AL. Accessed 27 Nov 2017.

MacDonald, Connor, and Phyu Thiha-Cho. 2016. Rapid Migration and Lack of Cheap Housing Fuels Yangon Slum Growth. https://www.irrawaddy.com/news/burma/rapid-migration-and-lack-of-cheap-housing-fuels-yangon-slum-growth.html. Accessed 15 Dec 2016.

Mar, Aye Aye. 2014. Violent Standoff Continues at Myanmar Mine Protest. http://www.voanews.com/content/violent-standoff-continues-at-myanmar-mine-protest/2570915.html. Accessed 25 Jan 2014.

Maung, U Maung. 1976. *From Sangha to Lait: Nationalist Movements of Burma 1920–1940*. Unpublished Master's Thesis, Australian National University.

Mang, Lun Min. 2016. Pilot Census Lays Groundwork for Citizenship Verification in Rakhine. http://www.mmtimes.com/index.php/national-news/20746-pilot-census-lays-groundwork-for-citizenship-verification-in-rakhine.html. Accessed 10 June 2016.

MM Business News. 2014. Myanmar Spends the Least for Education Among ASEAN Countries: AAM. http://mmbusinessnews.blogspot.sg/2014/03/myanmar-spends-least-for-education.html. Accessed 30 Mar 2014.

Mon, Kyaw Hsu. 2014. $22 Mn in ADB Programs to Reduce Poverty, Improve HIV/AIDS Care. http://www.irrawaddy.org/burma/22mln-adb-programs-reduce-poverty-improve-hivaids-care.html. Accessed 15 July 2014.

Mon, Ye. 2016. Officials Deny Squatter 'Census'. http://www.mmtimes.com/index.php/national-news/yangon/20929-officials-deny-squatters-census.html. Accessed 25 Dec 2016.

Mooney, Paul. 2014. Myanmar Students Protest Against Education Law for Third Day. http://www.reuters.com/article/2014/11/16/us-myanmar-protest-idUSKCN0J00MD20141116. Accessed 29 Nov 2016.

NLD (National League for Democracy). 2015. 2015 Election Manifesto. http://www.burmalibrary.org/docs21/NLD_2015_Election_Manifesto-en.pdf. Accessed 10 Feb 2018.

Nippon Foundation. 2013. Yohei Sasakawa named Japan's Special Envoy for National Reconciliation in Myanmar. https://www.nippon-foundation.or.jp/en/news/articles/2013/1.html. Accessed 20 Feb 2016.

———. 2017. Projects in Myanmar. https://www.nippon-foundation.or.jp/en/what/projects/myanmar/img/5.pdf. Accessed 30 Nov 2017.

Nitta, Yuichi. 2017. Rohingya backlash pushes Suu Kyi toward Beijing. https://asia.nikkei.com/Politics-Economy/International-Relations/Rohingya-backlash-pushes-Suu-Kyi-toward-Beijing. Accessed 30 Nov 2017.

Nitta, Yuichi, and Thurein Hla Htway. 2018. Two Ethnic Groups in Myanmar Sign Ceasefire. https://asia.nikkei.com/Politics-Economy/Policy-Politics/Two-ethnic-groups-in-Myanmar-sign-ceasefire. Accessed 21 Feb 2018.

Obuchi, Keizo. 1998. *Toward the Creation of a Bright Future for Asia*. http://www.mofa.go.jp/region/asiapacific/asean/pmv9812/policyspeech.html. Accessed 30 Dec 2014.

Ogata, Sadako, and Amartya Sen. 2003. Foreword. In *Human Security Now by Commission on Human Security*. New York: Commission on Human Security.

Than, Tin Maung Maung. 2007. Human Security Challenges in Myanmar. In *Myanmar: State, Society and Ethnicity*, ed. N. Ganesan and Kyaw Yin Hlaing. Singapore: ISEAS.

Than, Tin Maung Maung, and Moe Thuzar. 2012. Myanmar's Rohingya Dilemma. https://www.iseas.edu.sg/images/pdf/ISEAS_Perspective_9July2012_Issue_1.pdf. Accessed 25 Oct 2017.

Thant, Htoo. 2017. Defense Expenditure Ranks Third in 2017–18 Union Budget Proposal. https://www.mmtimes.com/national-news/nay-pyi-taw/24755-defence-expenditure-ranks-third-in-2017-18-union-budget-proposal.html. Accessed 10 Feb 2017.

The Economist. 2014. Kidnapped. http://www.economist.com/news/business/21602719-chinese-miner-tries-be-nice-kidnapped. Accessed 10 June 2016.

Thuzar, Moe, and Ye Htut. 2017. Honeymoon over, Suu Kyi Faces Fresh Challenges. http://www.todayonline.com/world/honeymoon-over-suu-kyi-faces-fresh-challenges. Accessed 28 Apr 2017.

Thuzar, Moe, and Lex Reiffel. 2018. ASEAN's Myanmar Dilemma. https://www.iseas.edu.sg/images/pdf/ISEAS_Perspective_2018_3@50.pdf. Accessed 29 Jan 2018.

Toe Lwin, Ei Ei. 2014. Military Spending Still Dwarfs Education and Health. http://www.mmtimes.com/index.php/national-news/10000-military-spending-still-dwarfs-education-and-health.html. Accessed 30 May 2014.

UNDP (United Nations Development Programme). 1994. *Human Development Report 1994*. New York: Oxford University Press.

UNGA (United Nations General Assembly). 2005. *World Summit Outcome*, A/RES/66/290. New York: United Nation.

UNHCR (United Nations High Commissioner for Refugees). 2016. First Myanmar Refugee Returns From Thailand Under Way. http://www.unhcr.org/news/briefing/2016/10/580f1c0d4/first-myanmar-refugee-returns-thailand-under-way.html. Accessed 1 Dec 2017.

UNHSU (United Nations Human Security Unit). 2014. *Strategic Plan 2014–2017*. New York: United Nations.

UNOCHA (United Nations Office for the Coordination of Humanitarian Affairs). 2017. Rohingya Refugee Crisis. https://www.unocha.org/rohingya-refugee-crisis. Accessed 15 Dec 2017.

———. 2018. Rohingya Refugee Crisis. https://www.unocha.org/rohingya-refugee-crisis. Accessed 20 Mar 2018.

Vatikiotis, Michael. 2017. Statesman Who Raised ASEAN's Profile. https://asia.nikkei.com/Viewpoints/Michael-Vatikiotis/Statesman-who-raised-ASEAN-s-international-profile. Accessed 13 Dec 2018.

Wee, Sui Lee. 2015. Myanmar Official Accuses China of Meddling in Rebel Peace Talks. https://www.reuters.com/article/us-myanmar-china/myanmar-official-accuses-china-of-meddling-in-rebel-peace-talks-idUSKCN0S22VT20151008. Accessed 10 Oct 2015.

World Bank. 2017. Myanmar Poverty Assessment 2017: Part One Examination of Trends Between 2004/05 and 2015. http://www.worldbank.org/en/country/myanmar/publication/myanmar-poverty-assessment-2017-part-one-examination-of-trends. Accessed 15 Dec 2017.

Yahya, Yasmine. 2018.ASEAN, Australia Doing Their Best to Help Myanmar Re-establish Stability in Rohingya Crisis. http://www.straitstimes.com/politics/govts-in-region-doing-their-best-to-help-myanmar-re-establish-stability-in-rohingya-refugee. Accessed 20 Mar 2018.

Zarni, Maung. 2005. An Integrated Approach to National and Human Security Issues in Myanmar or Burma. http://www.freeburmacoalition.org/integratedsecurityapproach.htm. Accessed 10 Feb 2017.

———. 2013.Burma/Myanmar: Its Conflicts, Western Advocacy, and Country Impact. http://sites.tufts.edu/reinventingpeace/2013/03/25/burmamyanmar-its-conflicts-western-advocacy-and-country-impact/. Accessed 1 Jan 2015.

Interviews

Government Source #1. 2014. Dr Myint. Economic Advisor to President Thein Sein. Conversation with the author in Singapore, May 29.

Government Source #2. 2015. U Ohn Gyaw, former foreign minister of Myanmar. Interviewed by the author in Yangon, December 27.

Government Source #3. 2015. U Khin Maung Win, former deputy foreign minister of Myanmar. Interviewed by the author in Yangon, July 15.

CHAPTER 8

Human Security in Practice: The Philippine Experience from the Perspective of Different Stakeholders

Maria Ela L. Atienza

8.1 Introduction

Human security, which shifts the definition of security away from a traditional military-oriented, state-centric focus to a people-centric view, has become one of the most important concepts in international relations and development studies since the 1990s. Yet, it is still a contested concept with debates about its actual definition and utility. To contribute to more context-specific and multi-sectoral perspectives about human security, this chapter discusses the Philippine experience. It asks two main questions: How do different stakeholders perceive and interpret the concept of human security? And, how do they perceive human security threats? The specific questions focus on the following: stakeholders and

M. E. L. Atienza (✉)
Department of Political Science, University of the Philippines, Diliman, Quezon City, Metro Manila, Philippines
e-mail: ma_ela.atienza@upd.edu.ph

Y. Mine et al. (eds.), *Human Security Norms in East Asia*, Security, Development and Human Rights in East Asia,
https://doi.org/10.1007/978-3-319-97247-3_8

their institutions' understanding of human security as a concept and its conceptual basis; human security threats (urgent) and risks (long-term) in the Philippines and the East Asian Region; cross-border responses to human security challenges; human security in practice; and the added value of human security.

To answer these questions, the study gathered perceptions of human security and threats from the following sectors: government, academe, civil society, local government officials, and local communities. The following methods were used: a review of the academic literature, relevant policy documents, position papers, and so on; face-to-face interviews; online correspondence with informants; and focus group discussions (FGDs) with *barangay*[1] officials in Manila, transient sidewalk vendors, and farmers.

The Philippines is a study in contrasts. Despite the country's reported sustained economic growth as one of Asia's best economic performers in the last few years, approximately 21.6% of Filipinos (out of about 100 million total population) still live below the poverty line (2015 est.). Many citizens' quality of life has not improved. Thus, the country remains a medium human development country, ranked at 117, behind Singapore, Malaysia, Thailand, and Indonesia (UNDP 2014). It was not able to achieve all Millennium Development Goals (MDGs) in 2015 particularly in poverty incidence, children disadvantaged in terms of performance at school, and access to maternal services (PSA 2017). The causes of this situation include non-inclusive, inequitable growth. Geographically, the country is prone to natural hazards. Politically, long-running conflicts with communist insurgents and several Muslim groups in the South continue to challenge the national government. Political institutions and leaders continue to suffer from inefficiency, poor implementation of well-meaning laws, and poor governance.

This chapter is organized into several parts. Based on the review of literature, Sect. 8.2 traces the history of how human security norms have been incorporated in the work of Philippine institutions and various groups as well as the continuing debates among different stakeholders about the use and interpretation of human security. Section 8.3 discusses the 2014 findings of the author regarding the different perspectives of stakeholders on human security as a concept and the various threats and risks they associate with it. Section 8.4 discusses the conclusions and recommendations based on the findings.

8.2 Debating and Accepting Human Security: A Brief History

Let us begin by discussing how human security came to be a focus in the Philippine context. National security in the Philippines was redefined after the 1986 People Power as "security of the people" instead of security of the state during the efforts to reconcile the viewpoints of the military and civilian agencies (Atienza et al. 2010, 34). The framework contains nontraditional elements like moral/spiritual consensus, cultural cohesiveness, economic solidarity/organicity, sociopolitical stability, ecological integrity, territorial integrity, and external peace (Atienza et al. 2010, 33) but the term human security was not mentioned.

Based on a previous review of literature (Atienza et al. 2010), until 2007 the concept of human security still had to make a concrete impact on national security plans in the Philippines. The concept was first introduced into public consciousness through the conference "The Gathering for Human and Ecological Security," a year after the publication of the landmark Human Development Report (UNDP 1994), which resulted in a commitment to place the protection of people and the environment at the forefront of the national agenda. This commitment was merged with then President Fidel Ramos' Social Reform Agenda.

Before the use of the term human security, some Filipino scholars had already dealt with nontraditional security issues and explored the nexus between development and security. The *Development and Security in Southeast Asia* book series examined how state-society relations are affected by and entwined with the complex security-development nexus in the context of the environment, people, and globalization (Dewitt and Hernandez 2003). Following the UNDP's 1994 HDR, the *Philippine Human Development Report* (PHDR) (HDN 2005) prepared by academics centered on human security, defining it as freedom from fear, want, and humiliation and distinguishing between human security and human development. While "human development is the process that widens the range of people's choices, human security means that people can make those choices safely and freely. Human security is the external pre-condition for human development" (HDN 2005, 1–2).

Among some civil society organizations (CSOs), there is recognition of human security and its use in their advocacy. Assisi Development Foundation, Inc. (ADFI), for example, uses a multi-level development framework for human security in working with, protecting and empowering indigenous peoples (IPs) against threats resulting from poverty and conflicts (Abadiano 2004). *Tabang Mindanaw*, a multisectoral development program launched by ADFI to improve the quality of life and overcome underdevelopment of marginalized groups in Mindanao especially IPs, developed a "justice-based human security framework" in response to the 2005 PHDR. This argues that injustice and not poverty is the root cause of armed conflict and articulates that human security "complements state security, enhances human rights, and strengthens human development" (Dee and Garilao 2005).

Prior to 2007, it is almost impossible to find actual use or acknowledgment of the term human security in government documents. However, the Office of the Presidential Adviser on the Peace Process (OPAPP) became involved in efforts to promote the discourse in government policies when it became the Project Management Office of the UNDP's Conflict Prevention and Peacebuilding Programme until 2010. It also had its own UNDP-supported projects and developed a conflict sensitive and peace-promoting local development planning guide incorporating human security (OPAPP 2009). The Mindanao Economic Development Council (MEDCo), which managed peace programs in Mindanao, also developed human security indicators to monitor local government performance (Atienza et al. 2010, 77). Unfortunately, since 2010, OPAPP's more recent programs and documents have not mentioned human security.

What brought the issue of human security to the public consciousness, albeit only temporarily, was the enactment of the controversial law, Republic Act No. 9372 or *An Act to Secure the State and Protect Our People from Terrorism*, with the short title "Human Security Act of 2007." The law triggered debates between state-centric and people-centric definitions of human security (Atienza et al. 2010; Atienza 2012b). CSOs, particularly human rights and law groups, questioned the law's legality in the Supreme Court, especially its usurpation of the term and possible threats on the people; however, the law was declared constitutional by the High Court in 2010 and with finality in 2011. Since then, human security debates have not been clearly articulated in public.

Despite no formal acknowledgement from the Philippine government of the concept and principles of human security in any major law, with the exception of the controversial Human Security Act, there were a number of national government programs and policies on development, local government performance, peace and security under Presidents Macapagal-

Arroyo and Benigno Aquino that contained certain elements of human security as defined by UNDP and the Commission on Human Security (Atienza 2012a, 56–62; 2015, 10–11).

Regarding government perceptions of human security, interviews with civilian and military officials, as well as CSO representatives, conducted in 2007 by a project headed by the author found that those in the Armed Forces of the Philippines (AFP) view human security as "an intrinsic component of national security" and therefore complementary to it (Atienza et al. 2010, 92). The AFP informants viewed human security as the protection of the people, who are a component of the state. One of the duties of the AFP is to protect the people and at times, they cannot help but perform development functions in assigned areas, especially where local governments are not functional or incapacitated due to conflicts or other contexts. In contrast, representatives of party-lists and national government agencies recognized the evolving nature of security from a purely military perspective to a people-oriented one. At that time, they viewed human security through the lens of human rights (Atienza et al. 2010, 94–95).

In terms of human security threats, AFP officials identified insurgencies, territorial disputes, transnational crime, and international terrorism as threats to both the state and the people. However, representatives from civilian government agencies and the legislature went beyond traditional threats and highlighted poverty, social and cultural conditions, political bickering, corruption and inefficiencies in government institutions, military abuse, and state aggression as threats (Atienza et al. 2010, 95–98).

Interviews with CSO representatives also conducted during the same project in 2007 (Atienza et al. 2010) found that there was recognition of the evolving context and nature of security issues, especially the need to broaden the understanding and scope of security from a primarily military-centric to a more people-oriented concept. Informants emphasized the interlinkages between a rights-based approach and human security to ensure the people's right to an acceptable quality of life. Threats to human security mentioned include: proliferation of small arms, abuses of the military and the police, poverty, "development aggression" due to the state's economic policies and multinational companies, violations of women and IPs' rights, and the United States through the Visiting Forces Agreement. Informants also identified the state, academe, civil society, and communities themselves as stakeholders in promoting human security.

Political scientists did most of the direct work on human security. Carolina G. Hernandez is one of the pioneers in comprehensive security and in linking development and security issues in the Philippines and ASEAN (Hernandez 1995; Dewitt and Hernandez 2003) and has authored studies and led projects on security sector reform and human security (Hernandez 2014; and ISDS 2009) as well as mainstreaming human security in ASEAN (Hernandez 2012; Hernandez and Kraft 2012). Herman Joseph S. Kraft (2006, 2003, 2012) works on human rights and human security in Southeast Asia and ASEAN.

Scholars have also received research support from UNDP to mainstream human security in the country. These projects include the following:

- The University of the Philippines' Third World Studies Center's (UPTWSC) dialogue series with different sectors in 2016 that led to a proposed human security framework (Cabilo and Quinsaat 2007, 117–123);
- The Institute for Strategic and Development Studies' framework for developing a security sector reform index (ISDS 2009);
- UP TWSC's two projects on developing a human security index for the Philippines: (1) developing the index based on eight areas with history of conflict (Atienza et al. 2010), and (2) pilot-testing the index in five municipalities in Luzon and Visayas (Atienza et al. 2011), supplemented by UP funding to pilot-test in Mindanao (Atienza et al. 2013); and
- Lusterio-Rico et al.'s (2009) review of the Mining Act and the Indigenous Peoples' Rights Act.

All these projects used comprehensive definitions of human security with individuals and communities as referent objects.

In terms of local or people's perspectives, 800 respondents in seven provinces and Metro Manila surveyed by the author's project team in 2007 identified top perceived potential threats to security. Common perceived threats include food shortage, environmental disaster, and disease outbreak; but Metro Manila and Surigao del Sur (Mindanao) respondents mentioned high crime rates, while those from North Cotabato and Sulu in Mindanao included ethnic conflict and insurgency. The highest perceived threat is in economic security with the lowest in community security (Atienza et al. 2010, 130–133).

In UP TWSC's pilot-testing studies (Atienza et al. 2011; 2013), local people have a comprehensive understanding of human security, covering peace and development components as well as protection and empowerment approaches. Filipino concepts they relate with human security include *walang gulo* (no conflicts) and *ligtas* (being safe). Economic and environmental threats are usually the major concerns, although they are also linked with other threats. While national government and international agencies can help in addressing threats, they think local governments and the people themselves should be empowered to deal with these. Some local officials said that they do not want dole-outs from the national government, including conditional cash transfers; they prefer capacity and skill building so that they can help themselves (see Atienza 2015, Annexes 1 and 2).

From the abovementioned previous studies, there is a convergence in terms of the primacy of threats to economic and food security, followed by the environment. Data also show a preference for government and non-government sectors working together to respond to these. Individuals and communities must also protect themselves, highlighting the role of local governments and localization in addressing threats.

8.3 Perspectives of Different Stakeholders Based on Interviews and FGDs in 2014

In this section, the outcomes of the 2014 interviews and FGDs are presented. The general outcomes seem to be a continuation of most of the findings from previous studies, both qualitative and quantitative, though the questions for the 2014 interviews and FGDs are more detailed and discuss more clearly the different dimensions (protection and empowerment; freedom from fear and want and freedom to live in dignity; local, national, and regional threats and risks) of human security and prospects for mainstreaming. Freedom to live in dignity was not prominent as a clear component of human security in previous studies, though injustice was already mentioned by some CSOs prior to 2014.

8.3.1 *The Concept of Human Security*

In terms of personal understandings of security, two government sources (Government #2 and #4 2014) affirmed previous findings that those in more traditional government security offices view human security as encompassed or contextualized by national security, which has now evolved with focus on people's well-being and welfare. But two other sources go beyond the national security framework. Carizo (Government #3 2014) said human security means the absence or lowering of fear and exposure to physical, economic, and psychological risks, while Government #1 (2014) thinks that human security is different from traditional security by focusing on the people, though there could be overlaps.

Human security has still not been formally accepted by their respective agencies if this means using the term, though they confirmed that, in varying ways, human security elements are recognized by their agencies. In the Department of National Defense (DND), its Internal Security Operations-Internal Peace and Security Plan (ISO-IPSP) *Oplan Bayanihan* program utilizes both human security and human rights and focuses on community-based peace and development activities with local government units and people in conflict areas. For the National Security Council (NSC), human security has already been incorporated into the national security framework (Government #2 2014). Its closest manifestation is the use of people's "well-being and welfare" in the national security definition. For the Foreign Service Institute (FSI), mandated to provide research for the Department of Foreign Affairs (DFA), there is strong recognition of "nontraditional security" with efforts to include it in training the foreign service corps. In the DFA, consciousness about human security is present in the offices in charge of the United Nations (UN) and international organizations, ASEAN, and policy, but not in other desks. The National Anti-Poverty Commission (NAPC), mandated to focus on poverty and vulnerable sectors, appears to support a more formal recognition of human security elements. Human security is now being mentioned in its research papers (Government #3 2014).

Regarding the conceptual basis of human security and the three elements or freedoms, human security issues in the Philippines are locality based. The dominant issues vary, and hence the type of relevant freedom varies per locality, and thus the appropriate approach(es) should be localized (Government #4 2014). Freedom to live in dignity is also difficult to operationalize. In the case of NAPC, there is an obvious emphasis on freedom from want. However, want may be satisfied but not necessarily fear (of landlords, armed groups, conflicts, and so on); so, fear must also be addressed. In addition, freedom to live in dignity is the highest level of human security. It completes human security and addresses all types of freedoms (Government #3 2014). The NSC official (Government #2 2014) said that all three elements of human security are interrelated. She defines freedom to live in dignity as a state where the basic needs of the people are met. It is indirectly related to welfare and well-being and refers to the liberty to pursue them. All elements of human security are being discussed by FSI as its research emphasis is on nontraditional security issues (Government #1 2014), which reflects the DFA's growing mandate. Freedom to live in dignity can be used to emphasize the importance of addressing poverty issues, which are incorporated in many economic arrangements and groupings through the Philippines' membership.

All academic informants' understanding of human security appeared to be comparable with the comprehensive definition provided by the UN and UNDP. They understand the term in a nontraditional, comprehensive manner encompassing issues like freedom from want, freedom from fear and desire for peace, sustainability of resources and the environment, well-being, fulfillment of basic needs, and absence of discrimination.

In Miriam College's Center for Peace Education, the concept has already been accepted and is being used as one of the core messages in training and teaching activities (Academic #1 2014). At the Polytechnic University of the Philippines (PUP) Mulanay, peace and human security in Mulanay are promoted by integrating human security into the curriculum and leading many multisectoral peace-related projects in the municipality (Academic #6 2014). For Western Mindanao State University (WMSU), human security has already been incorporated into social science subjects, specifically peace and human rights (Academic #2 2014).

In terms of the conceptual basis of human security, academics agree that "freedom to live in dignity" is important like the first two and may be even more basic and comprehensive; however, academics cannot agree about how it should be differentiated from the first two. For Rebullida (Academic #5 2014), there is still "concept stretching with human security encompassing a wide range of concerns," so there is a need to be very clear about the indicators of all these "freedoms." Kraft (Academic #3 2014) said that while the first two more established freedoms are more discrete with clearer issue areas, "freedom to live in dignity" must still be fleshed out to be distinguished from the other two.

All three CSO representatives described human security as encompassing freedom from fear and want. There was also an element of dignity because aside from protection from various threats, individuals and communities must be empowered and equipped with skills to address the causes of threats and vulnerabilities. Regarding whether their respective organizations accept the concept formally or informally, Fuentes (Civil Society #2 2014) confirmed ADFI's use of the justice-based human security framework in developing and implementing peace and development programs that empower IPs. The Sulong Comprehensive Agreement on Respect for Human Rights and International Humanitarian Law (CARHRIHL) focuses on respect for human rights as a path to peace but does not use the words "human security" due to lack of a standard definition (Civil Society #3 2014). While the CBARAD Project uses "community safety and security," the human security approach is very evident in its implementation of community-based disaster risk reduction (Civil Society #1 2014).

In terms of the conceptual basis of human security, all three CSO representatives see the interrelatedness of all three freedoms (Civil Society #1, #2, and #3 2014). Hence, an appropriate approach takes into consideration all three. ADFI uses human security as a guide in pursuing holistic peace and development programs. Sulong CARHRIHL initially focused only on freedom from fear but realized that people are more concerned with basic issues that are development oriented. While working on freedom from fear and want elements, the CBARAD Project gives more weight on freedom to live in dignity as its interventions must be appropriate to local contexts.

Adding freedom to live in dignity in the human security discourse is important. Fuentes said that "freedom from humiliation and to live in dignity" is a crucial element of human security in the Philippines because poverty, marginalization, and discrimination can be a very humiliating experience for affected individuals and communities, particularly Muslims and IPs who are minorities (Civil Society #2 2014). Reyes said that the first two freedoms deal with immediate needs of the people, whereas freedom to live in dignity is long-term, connoting justice, sustainable development, and empowerment (Civil Society #3 2014). For the CBARAD informant, living in dignity means recognizing the basic rights of an individual necessary for his/her survival and development; protection and promotion of dignity should also be based on local culture (Civil Society #1 2014).

For local communities and leaders who participated in the FGDs, their sense of security is, consistent with previous findings, based on their own contexts (see Atienza 2015, Table 4). They also relate Filipino terms like *kaligtasan* (safety), *kasiguraduhan* (certainty), *kapayapaan* (peace), and so on to, security. While not clearly articulated, they do have a comprehensive view of security that is not only individual based but also family based and community based. For them, freedom to live in dignity means the ability to live and work honorably and honestly while also helping others.

8.3.2 Human Security Issues

Interviewees were asked about human security issues in the Philippines and East Asia. Poverty, armed conflicts and disasters were prominently mentioned as both urgent and long-term threats in the Philippines (Atienza 2015, Table 5). According to government respondents, widespread poverty, lack of food, and lack of education are the root causes of many other security issues in the country. Maritime disputes and natural disasters are both urgent and long-term risks because these will likely persist in the future, they are unpredictable, and more resources are needed to address them (Government #1 2014). Most academics and CSO representatives think that many of these urgent threats are linked with each other, with implications for the lives and well-being of people and communities, especially vulnerable sectors. For FGD respondents in local communities, major threats to their security include lack of stable sources of income, criminality, and natural disasters. They also noted state-sourced threats, like corruption and police abuse.

When asked if their respective agencies respond to urgent threats and long-term risks, the government informants said yes. DND's mandate is more focused on freedom from fear threats but food security, together with energy and climate change, are now part of its second set of priorities. FSI gives recommendations to DFA in resolving human security threats, such as arbitration and bilateral negotiations for maritime disputes. NAPC is heavily involved in addressing these threats by providing oversight functions and coordination with other government agencies and international bodies in promoting anti-poverty programs. The NSC concentrates on peace and order issues, but these cannot be totally separated from economic issues; so, it refers them to, exchange information with, and work with relevant agencies regarding economic dimensions of security issues.

To address these threats and risks, academics and civil society representatives emphasize addressing the root causes of conflicts with all stakeholders working together to achieve peace, observing human rights and international humanitarian law, and using indigenous/local systems when possible. They also suggest institutional and governmental reforms, participatory processes, and education campaigns at the local level to strengthen accountability and transparency, and to promote human security and development at different levels grounded on local needs. Academics also suggest capacity building for local governments and communities in disaster risk reduction and management (DRRM) and infrastructure development. Academics have a special role to play here; in fact, some academic institutions are already doing these suggested responses. Civil society respondents also suggested strengthening the role of CSOs to advocate for genuine development reforms and capacity building of basic sectors, to empower local communities to respond to the concerns, and to strengthen local development planning by incorporating awareness of human security.

From the FGD participants in local communities, there was an emphasis placed on self-help, organizing, awareness raising, vigilance, and continued perseverance and industry to make lives more secure. They do accept assistance from government, universities, and lending facilities but they prefer more transparent, effective, and participatory processes to ease security threats. For Manila barangay officials and Nasugbu farmers, the assistance they need covers capacity building, proper information about disasters and livelihood opportunities, and access to schools to help them prepare and improve many aspects of their security.

In terms of urgent threats and long-term risks in the East Asian region (see Table 6 in Atienza 2015, 34), maritime conflicts particularly in the West Philippine/South China Sea, poverty and economic inequality, and disasters and climate change dominate the list of urgent threats and long-term risks. Other threats and risks include terrorism and nontraditional security threats like energy and food scarcity, health pandemics, pollution, and insecurity of migrant workers.

Academics think that these urgent threats and risks have spill-over effects on each other with effects on vulnerable sectors. CSO respondents agree, adding that these threats and risks also affect whole nations and the region in different dimensions of human security. If left unaddressed, these can become more complex and increase in magnitude.

In terms of resolving the threats and risks in the region, the FSI and the DFA favor peaceful settlement of disputes, use of UN mechanisms, cooperation in meeting these regional threats, promotion of more people-to-people exchanges, and sharing of best practices in meeting these threats. Academics and CSOs also recommend regional cooperation and dialogues, especially strengthening ASEAN for these, the use of diplomatic initiatives, mechanisms, and UN processes, building strong and accountable state and non-state institutions, promoting training and research for different sectors' awareness of issues, including DRRM, delivering sustainable and equitable growth planning and policies, harnessing renewable energy appropriately, and the adoption, implementation, and monitoring of international environmental agreements.

8.3.3 Cross-Border Responses to Human Security Challenges

8.3.3.1 Accepting Assistance from Outside

All informants agreed that the Philippines should accept assistance from outside when it is affected by a massive natural disaster. Recalling the experience with Haiyan (local name Yolanda) and other disasters, help was urgently needed during those times, and the country was grateful for the assistance received. However, all agreed that there should be proper mechanisms to improve response and assistance to affected communities, including having no strings attached to assistance. The following were the recommendations:

- Stronger and systematic coordination with the Philippine government being more prepared, leading and considering local conditions and circumstances, and determining the appropriate assistance to be given and the process of distribution;
- Better coordination and partnership system among all state and non-state actors in monitoring assistance;
- Observance of humanitarian assistance protocols, transparency, and accountability;
- Capacity building in DRRM for national and local systems; and
- A greater focus on preparedness and rebuilding assistance instead of just relief.

According to several academics, the fact that there will be help from outside should not make the country complacent. It has enough experience from disasters to strengthen its responses and develop more effective mechanisms to complement any help from outside. Ideally, academics prefer that external assistance be ASEAN driven or more regional and international in nature for greater coordination, efficiency, and transparency. CSO informants also prefer UN-led efforts and agencies with expertise in disasters like the Japan International Cooperation Agency (JICA).

In terms of the Philippines accepting assistance during escalation of violence, this is a more delicate issue compared with disasters because this treads on sovereignty issues. Government informants think that domestic resources and mechanisms should first be exhausted as the Philippine government does not want to be labeled as a failed state and the type of assistance offered must therefore be evaluated. Those providing assistance might also be accused of siding with certain groups, and assistance might further escalate the violence and conflicts. Academics disagree about assistance as some said this is okay, but others expressed reservations due to the sensitive nature of assistance in an internal conflict, unless there is genocide. CSO informants, meanwhile, welcome international assistance.

Should external assistance be accepted, informants said the following should be followed: the Rome Statute's provisions on the jurisdiction of the International Criminal Court over the crime of genocide, crimes against humanity, war crimes, and the crime of aggression; strictly limiting assistance to humanitarian assistance and peacekeeping; invoking Responsibility to Protect principles to prevent various crimes against humanity and prioritize assistance to displaced populations; the use of diplomatic assistance, international arbitration, and UN mechanisms when conflict has an international dimension; and enforcing transparency and accountability.

While some neighboring countries can play mediating roles, assistance from individual donors might become more politicized. Some academics suggested that assistance should be ASEAN led, but since there is no effective mechanism in place yet at this level, UN- or European Union-led operations would be the most practicable, preferred mechanism of assistance. CSO informants also prefer UN-led assistance, because according to them, it is neutral and has a wide network of partners and a broad range of experience. Finally, international pressure on both parties in the conflict is important to make violence stop as government is also conscious of its image internationally (Civil Society #3 2014).

8.3.3.2 Ability and Willingness to Assist Other Countries

All informants agreed that the country has a duty to the international community as a responsible member to help other countries during massive disasters. The Philippines can draw on its own experiences with disasters and the growing expertise of different sectors in DRRM. Despite its limited resources, the country has already assisted other countries during natural disasters in the past. It is able to send quick response teams to assist overseas Filipinos and citizens of affected countries. The government and other sectors can also document their experiences in addressing disasters locally and abroad to provide lessons for appropriate responses that can be useful for both the Philippines and other countries.

In terms of lending assistance when there is escalation of violence in other countries, all informants also said that this is not generally a problem, as the Philippines has a long experience participating in UN peacekeeping operations in different parts of the world, including East Timor, and has also dispatched election-monitoring personnel to Aceh. Philippine CSOs and academics also have worldwide networks working on human rights, conflict prevention, and other issues. In both situations, however, there is preference for providing this assistance under the UN or ASEAN umbrellas, following UN conventions, and prioritizing Filipinos abroad. Assistance should be coordinated and monitored to be more efficient and accountable. The types of assistance should be determined depending on the local conditions and state of diplomatic relations with the countries involved.

8.3.4 *Human Security in Practice*

Government informants agreed that the top-down protection approach and the bottom-up empowerment approach should go together. However, each government agency has a different mandate, so there is sometimes emphasis on one approach over the other. In some cases, the functions require doing both approaches, even with NAPC being the most bottom-up in terms of mandate. For the academic informants, both top-down/protection and bottom-up/empowerment approaches are important and should be balanced. Government agencies and other groups can initially provide services and assistance to protect vulnerable sectors, but empowerment and capacity building should be the long-term goal. As most of their institutions are already doing, empowerment can be done through education and training to develop community potential and capacities. People should also be encouraged to participate in various community processes to address their needs and be organized, aware of their situation, and accountable to their fellow community members.

All CSO informants considered both protection and empowerment approaches to be important. Their organizations focus on empowerment through capacity building, and sustainability of programs and resilience, since their engagement is time-bound, though they start with top-down approaches like assistance and building community awareness.

8.3.5 *The Added Value of Human Security*

Has the concept of human security contributed to consolidating preparedness to mitigate risks and shocks of natural and human-made disasters? Does it have some value added and potential to induce ways of thinking, policy making, and practice? Theoretically, most government respondents said that knowledge of the concept should be able to do this; but right now, awareness of the concept is still too low for it to make a significant difference. For those agencies which have some knowledge or at least recognize some elements of human security, there is now a stronger focus on a more holistic approach involving capacity building and resilience instead of just assistance. More awareness of the concept would definitely help local governments to be more focused on saving constituents' lives and more sensitive to their needs. Quilop (Government #4 2014) notes that knowledge of the concept reinforces the realization that people's well-being is the center of national security, and its usage helps the defense establishment operationalize human security and forces changes in the mindset of people, which are sometimes hard to change.

Generally, academics said that human security has value-added potential because it contributes to consolidating preparation and mitigation of certain shocks. There is now a more broadly based, people-oriented definition of security that is more tangible than development and can be linked with more local concepts. Kraft (Academic #3 2014) notes that it has a political value that fits the agenda of CSOs and covers the vast array of issues that developing countries face. It can prove to be very useful at different levels, especially in prioritizing programs and budgeting.

If people and local authorities are made aware of the concept of human security, CSO informants think this will make them more prepared to prevent and reduce risks, mitigate a variety of shocks, and strengthen their responses because the added value of human security emphasizes urgent, holistic, people-centered approaches in preparing and addressing life-threatening situations (Civil Society #2 2014). Formally introducing the concept in national and local governments will make governments more accountable in formulating informed decisions (Civil Society #1 2014).

However, the concept still faces several problems. It has few advocates, even among donor agencies, and there is low awareness and usage among the public and government offices. It is also too broadly defined, so that while it is considered "experiential" with people facing it daily, it is difficult to define, explain, and operationalize, especially at the grassroots level. Further confusion was created by the Human Security Act. The informants suggested the following to make people more conscious of human security:

- Learning lessons on how human rights advocates succeeded in mainstreaming the concept of human rights in the formal government level and public consciousness;
- Incorporating human security in school curricula;

- Linking it to more popular issues like poverty and natural calamities to highlight the urgency of focusing on people's security;
- Relating it to indigenous or local concepts to avoid criticisms of being too "Western" or foreign and making it easily applicable to everyday, cultural experiences;
- Explaining the concept and differentiating it from older related concepts through indicators or indices;
- Continuously engaging local government leaders, community and CSOs, on the integration of human security in local development planning suitable to local needs;
- Engaging policy makers to increase their awareness of human security;
- Collaborating with CSOs in addressing human security issues; and
- Empowering various sectors at the local level.

8.4 Conclusions

This study has identified several findings regarding the introduction and evolution of human security in the country, as well as the different stakeholders' understanding and operationalization of the concept. First, while human security has not been formally recognized by the national government and its use is not widespread among academics, CSOs, or the public, informants share a more comprehensive view of human security spanning traditional and nontraditional issues. Those in more traditional security offices also acknowledged the evolution of the concept. Some CSOs and tertiary education institutions have already incorporated the human security framework into their research, curricula, and extension/service programs. Agencies and groups that are not formally using the concept argue that they do address some of the elements of human security in their work.

Second, government, academics, and CSOs see all three "freedoms" as interrelated, though emphasis of actual work is based on their specific mandates. A few academics, however, emphasized the need to clarify further the conceptual elements and indicators of human security, especially "freedom to live in dignity," so that it can be distinguished from other concepts. This third freedom could potentially take the human security discourse to a higher level where sustainability of overall security and empowerment are important.

Third, even though many local communities and basic sectors are not aware of the formal debates around human security, their understanding of the components of security is very comprehensive and drawn from local experience. They equate it with local concepts that mean safety, certainty, peace, and order. Their sense of security is not only for themselves but for their families and communities.

There are also findings regarding perceived human security threats and risks in the Philippines and the East Asian region and appropriate responses to them. First, stakeholders identified a wide range of threats that cover all dimensions. Poverty and economic inequality, climate change and disasters, energy and food security concerns, and territorial disputes are prominent responses. Hence, the recommendations include government reforms, more holistic and equitable national and local planning, greater dialogues and genuine cooperation among concerned parties to resolve the threats, and capacity building for affected sectors, and so on.

Second, for cross-border responses to human security challenges, there is agreement that, in principle, the Philippines can be both a recipient and provider with other countries of assistance during massive disasters and escalation of violence. However, the country should be careful about deciding whether to accept assistance or to lend assistance during escalation of violence as this involves more sensitive issues like sovereignty and national pride. Despite limited resources, the Philippines has a long history not only of accepting assistance but also providing peacekeeping and humanitarian assistance to other countries. But based on these experiences, respondents also recommended the following: being better prepared to face all these possible challenges; having strict mechanisms for identifying and prioritizing appropriate assistance, coordinating and distributing assistance; monitoring the transparency and accountability of assistance; giving assistance preferably through the UN, ASEAN, or other international agencies; and observing international humanitarian protocols.

Third, most stakeholders see a more holistic approach to human security by combining both top-down protection approaches (engagement and monitoring) and bottom-up empowerment approaches. Empowerment should be the long-term goal as assistance and interventions are limited and temporary. Hence, capacity building, participation in political processes and organizing are also important in the quest to improve human security, especially in the dignity aspect.

In the future, human security has the potential to help stakeholders become better prepared in both planning for and coping with regular and massive challenges. If introduced properly, it can induce changes in ways of thinking, policy making, and practices. However, the concept is poorly understood in the Philippines and has not yet become mainstream. Hence, for human security to make relevant contributions to the activities of stakeholders, it has to be defined properly, discussed with different sectors who have roles to play in its mainstreaming, popularized so that it can be linked with actual experiences that people can readily understand, and incorporated into formal and informal capability building activities. The participation of different stakeholders, especially from the basic groups like local communities, women, farmers, IPs, and fisherfolks most vulnerable to threats and risks, should be the focus so that plans and programs are appropriate and localized.

In conclusion, the discourse on human security in the Philippines has been enriched by perceptions of different sectors, although the lack of consensus is understandable given the different contexts and mandates of the informants' groups and institutions. However, understanding of and debates about the concept itself remain mainly among a limited group of people. Academics and CSOs have a crucial role to play in conducting research to clarify the concept, situating it within the local context and, in the process, empowering local governments and communities to deal with human security threats and vulnerabilities. At present, the persistence of threats and risks makes it more urgent for human security advocates to use the concept not only for theoretical clarifications but also to assist communities and people in finding appropriate solutions to these problems.

A new administration is now in place in the Philippines, several years after this research was completed. Economic, food, and environmental issues are still urgent issues, but new developments like the administration's war on drugs, threats of terrorism, the declaration of martial law in Mindanao, threats to democratic processes and institutions, human rights violations, and President Duterte's declaration of communist insurgents as terrorists have added new urgent threats in the other dimensions of human security. This makes the mainstreaming of human security even more urgent.

Acknowledgments The author acknowledges the help of Assistant Professor Reynold Agnes and Assistant Professor Jan Robert Go for conducting and documenting the 2014 focus group discussions; ISDS for administrative support; and Professor Emeritus Carolina G. Hernandez for her unwavering support.

Note

1. The lowest/most basic local government unit at the village level in the Philippines.

References

Abadiano, Benjamin. 2004. Development on the Margins: How Indigenous People Chart their Own Progress. Paper presented at the 2004 Magsaysay Awardees' Lecture Series, Magsaysay Center, Manila, August 27.

Atienza, Maria Ela L. 2012a. Achieving the Millennium Development Goals in the Philippines: Localization of the MDGs and Implications for Mainstreaming Human Security. In *Mainstreaming Human Security in ASEAN Integration Volume II: Lessons Learned from MDGs Implementation in Southeast Asia*, ed. Herman Joseph S. Kraft, 53–90. Quezon City: ASEAN Institutes of Strategic and International Studies and Institute for Strategic and Development Studies.

———. 2012b. Filipino Conceptions of Human Security: Developing a Human Security Index Based on an Exploratory Study in Conflict Areas. In *Mainstreaming Human Security: Asian Perspectives*, ed. Chantana Banpasirichote, Philip Doneys, Mike Hayes, and Chandan Sengupta, 215–232. Bangkok: Chula Global Network in collaboration with International Studies Development Program, Chulalongkorn University.

———. 2015. *Human Security in Practice: The Philippine Experience(s) from the Perspective of Different Stakeholders*, JICA-RI Working Paper 98. Tokyo: JICA-RI.

Atienza, Maria Ela L., Clarinda L. Berja, and Elinor Mae K Cruz. 2011. *A Pilot Study on the Human Security Index in Five Municipalities in the Philippines*, Unpublished report of the Third World Studies Center, University of the Philippines, Diliman.

———. 2013. *A Pilot Study on the Human Security Index in One Municipality in Mindanao: The Case of Indanan, Sulu*, Unpublished Report submitted to the Office of the Vice Chancellor for Research and Development, University of the Philippines, Diliman, Quezon City.

Atienza, Maria Ela L., Clarinda L. Berja, D. Cabilo Zuraida Mae, Mara Yasmin S.P. Baviera, and Dina Marie B. Delias. 2010. *Developing a Human Security Index: An Exploratory Study in Selected Conflict Areas.* Quezon City: University of the Philippines' Third World Studies Center, in partnership with the Office of the Presidential Adviser on the Peace Process and UNDP-CPPB.

Cabilo, Zuraida Mae D., and Sharon M. Quinsaat. 2007. Towards a Human Security Framework in the Philippine Context. In *Defining the Human Security Framework in the Philippine Context (Proceedings of the Third World Studies Center Policy Dialogue Series 2006)*, ed. Zuraida Mae D. Cabilo, Sharon M. Quinsaat, and Trina Joyce M. Sajo, 117–123. Quezon City: Third World Studies Center in partnership with UNDP-CPPB.

Dee, Howard, and Ernesto Garilao. 2005. A Justice-based Development as a Fundamental Right. Paper presented as a reaction during the presentation of the highlights of the 2005 Philippine Human Development Report, Heritage Hotel, Pasay City.

Dewitt, David B., and Carolina G. Hernandez, eds. 2003. *Development and Security in Southeast Asia, Volumes I–III*. Aldershot: Ashgate.

Hernandez, Carolina G. 1995. Linking Security and Development in Southeast Asia: A Concept Paper. In *Southeast Asia: Security and Stability*, 33–47. Manila: Konrad Adenauer Stiftung Philippines Occasional Papers.

———., ed. 2012. *Mainstreaming Human Security in ASEAN Integration Volume I: Regional Public Goods and Human Security*. Quezon City: Institute for Strategic and Development Studies.

———. 2014. Peacebuilding and Security Sector Governance in the Philippines. In *Peacebuilding and Security Sector Governance in Asia*, ed. Yuji Uesugi, 49–75. Geneva: Geneva Centre for the Democratic Control of the Armed Forces and Hiroshima University Partnership for Peacebuilding and Capacity Development.

Hernandez, Carolina G., and Herman Joseph S. Kraft, eds. 2012. *Mainstreaming Human Security in ASEAN Integration Vol. III: Human Security and the Blueprints for Realizing the ASEAN Community*. Quezon City: Institute for Strategic and Development Studies.

HDN (Human Development Network). 2005. *The Fifth Philippine Human Development Report: Peace, Human Security and Human Development in the Philippines*. Quezon City: HDN and UNDP.

ISDS (Institute for Strategic and Development Studies). 2009. *Developing a Security Sector Reform Index in the Philippines towards Conflict Prevention and Peacebuilding*. Quezon City: ISDS.

Kraft, Herman Joseph S. 2003. Human Rights, Security, and Development in Southeast Asia: An Overview. In *Development and Security in Southeast Asia, Vol. III (Globalization)*, ed. David B. Dewitt and Carolina G. Hernandez, 115–135. England: Ashgate.

———., ed. 2012. *Mainstreaming Human Security in ASEAN Integration Volume II: Lessons Learned from MDGs Implementation in Southeast Asia*. Quezon City: ASEAN Institutes of Strategic and International Studies and Institute for Strategic and Development Studies.

———. 2006. 11 September 2001 and Human Security. *OSS Digest* 1st -2nd Quarter: 11–20.

Lusterio-Rico, Ruth R., Rolando S. Fernando II, Maria Anna Rowena Luz G. Layador, Gianna Gayle H. Amul, and Farrah Grace V. Naparan. 2009. *Promoting Peace, Development and Human Security: The Mining Act of 1995 and the Indigenous Peoples' Rights Act (IPRA)*. Quezon City: Philippine Social Science Council.

PSA (Philippine Statistical Authority). 2017. Statistics at a Glance of the Philippines' Progress Based on the MDG Indicators, November.

OPAPP (Office of the Presidential Adviser on the Peace Process). 2009. *Guidebook on Conflict Sensitive and Peace-Promoting Local Development Planning*. Pasig City: OPAPP and the Surveys, Training, Research and Development Services (STRIDES) with the Support of UNDP-CPPB.

UNDP (United Nations Development Programme). 1994. *Human Development Report 1994*. Oxford: Oxford University Press.

———. 2014. *Human Development Report 2014*. Oxford: Oxford University Press.

Focus Group Discussions (FGDs)

FDG #1. 2014. Barangay Officials, Barangay 395, Sampaloc, Manila. Conducted by Reynold Agnes, July 10.

FGD #2. 2014. Transient Sidewalk Vendors, C.M. Recto, Manila. Conducted by Reynold Agnes, July 19.

FGD #3. 2014. Sugarcane and Rice Farmers, Barangay Dayap, Nasugbu, Batangas. Conducted by Jan Robert Go, 26 July.

Interviews

Academic Source #1.2014. Loreta N. Castro, Program Director of Center for Peace Program, Miriam College. E-mail correspondence with author in Quezon City, June 14.

Academic Source #2. 2014. Rosalyn R. Echem, Director of Gender Research and Resource Center, Western Mindanao State University. E-mail correspondence with author in Zamboanga City, June 15.

Academic Source #3. 2014. Herman Joseph S. Kraft, Associate Professor of Political Science, University of the Philippines Diliman. Interview by author in Quezon City, June 4.

Academic Source #4. 2014. Dennis Quilala, Assistant Professor of Political Science, University of the Philippines Diliman. Interview by author in Quezon City, May 27.

Academic Source #5.2014. Maria Lourdes G. Rebullida, Professor of Political Science, University of the Philippines Diliman. Interview by author in Quezon City, June 6.

Academic Source #6. 2014. Adelia Roadilla. Director of Polytechnic University of the Philippines Mulanay Campus. E-mail correspondence with author in Mulanay, May 29.

Civil Society Source #1. 2014. A project coordinator of the Community-Based Adaptation and Resilience against Disasters Project. E-mail correspondence with author in Iloilo City, August 9.

Civil Society Source #2. 2014. Pio Fuentes, Program Manager of Assisi Development Foundation, Inc. E-mail correspondence with author in Davao City, July 8.

Civil Society Source #3. 2014. Joeven Reyes, Executive Director of Sulong CARHRIHL (Comprehensive Agreement on Respect for Human Rights and International Humanitarian Law). Interview by author in Quezon City, June 13.

Government Source #1. 2014. An Official at the Foreign Service Institute, Department of Foreign Affairs. Interviewed by Author in Pasay City, June 25.

Government Source #2. 2014. An Official at the National Security Council. Interviewed by Author in Quezon City, June 18.

Government Source #3. 2014. Jay Carizo, Technical Consultant at the National Anti-poverty Commission. Interviewed by Author in Quezon City, July 8.

Government Source #4. 2014. Raymund Jose Quilop, Assistant Secretary at the Department of National Defense. Interviewed by Author in Quezon City, June 9.

CHAPTER 9

Human Security in Singapore: Where Entitlement Feeds Insecurity

Belinda Chng and Sofiah Jamil

9.1 Introduction and Development of Human Security

In 2014, when asked about Singapore's development plans for the next ten years, Prime Minister Lee Hsien Loong replied: "The purpose of life is not assurance and security (...but) to use that security to go and achieve something new and different and do better than the people who came before you." (Lee 2014). This remark is reflective of two things. First, it acknowledges the efforts of Singapore's pioneer generations, which set the foundations for the high living standards that most Singaporeans enjoy. Since becoming independent in 1965, the country has made impressive strides in healthcare and education, achieving a literacy rate of 100 percent, an average life expectancy of 83 years, and average schooling of 11 years

B. Chng (✉)
Asia Center, Milken Institute, Singapore, Singapore
e-mail: bchng@milkeninstitute.org

S. Jamil
Australian National University, Canberra, Australia
e-mail: sofiah.jamil@anu.edu.au

Y. Mine et al. (eds.), *Human Security Norms in East Asia*, Security, Development and Human Rights in East Asia,
https://doi.org/10.1007/978-3-319-97247-3_9

(UNDP 2016). In 2016, Singapore was ranked fifth in the global Human Development Index, above the Netherlands, the United States, and Sweden.

Second, the remarks reflect Prime Minister Lee's thoughts that Singapore's current generation can do better by overcoming the country's physical challenges through innovation and creativity. But doing more may imply desiring and expecting more in return. As development levels increase, so do consumption patterns and expectations of higher living standards. As a result, basic human security is insufficient, and those with higher order needs may not be sensitive to the concerns of the vulnerable and minority populations who have not necessarily had access to these taken-for-granted basic needs. These issues have become more acute in recent years because of Singapore's predominantly pro-economic growth strategies, particularly since the 1980s, which in a bid to create efficiency and meritocracy have inadvertently perpetuated a culture of elitism and entitlement. Given this context, the study highlights the paradoxical development of human security in Singapore, where despite having achieved a high level of human security provision nationwide, the heavy top-down approach has not sufficiently empowered the Singaporean society to cope with risks at the community level.

This study is divided into the following sections. The latter half of this first section presents a brief background on Singapore's efforts to achieve high levels of human security. Second, the study discusses whether the downside risks or inadvertent policy implications for human security are the result of uneven access to, or provision of, protection by the state and a lack of empowerment (i.e., actions that enable people to cope with risks). Third, it presents a snapshot of the Singapore government's efforts to mitigate downside risks, particularly after the 2011 General Elections, in which the ruling People's Action Party (PAP) garnered 60.1 percent of the popular vote (the lowest in the party's history), and for the first time lost a multi-member constituency to an opposition party (Adam and Lim 2011). Fourth, the study discusses Singapore's policies in mitigating transnational human security risks. Given Singapore's small size and proximity to other states, it is aware of its vulnerabilities and takes steps to mitigate transnational risks that have the potential to spill over into Singapore.

An important caveat needs to be noted which relates to the research methodology used in the study. In terms of data gathering, attempts to conduct one-on-one interviews with high-level Singapore government officials were challenging. This was due to two main factors. First, when approaching the Prime Minister's Office (PMO) and its coordinating offices, the researchers were directed to resource persons who would speak on specific dimensions of human security that related to the "freedom from want" but were reluctant to comment on the implications of the human security concept as a whole. This observation is interesting as it indicates that the government prefers to manage human security based on specific issues that come under the scope of various ministries and statutory boards. This approach is perceived to be a pragmatic way of operationalizing a multifaceted and complex academic concept such as human security.

The second factor is that the difficulty contacting potential interviewees within the government was exacerbated by timing the research to coincide with Parliamentary Budget sessions—a busy period for government officials. However, this void could be filled by other sources of primary and secondary data, such as the publicly viewable Facebook pages[1] of Singapore ministers and other politicians, government press releases, and news reports. Five interviews were conducted with mid-level civil servants as well as members of academia and civil society. The issues covered in this study, such as human trafficking, economic inequality, and social marginalization, were chosen as they are aspects of human security. These issues have gained greater traction in recent years, given the attention brought by social media to their ramifications for society, and their consequences for political stability and the credibility of the ruling party.

In a nutshell, Singapore's efforts in meeting human security needs contain some paradoxes. While the term human security does not feature in Singapore's policymaking lexicon, an examination of Singapore's development trajectory reveals that the limited use of human security language has not prevented the state from providing strong basic protection for its citizens in the first two pillars: freedom from fear and freedom from want. The PAP, which has been in power since the country's independence in 1965, is highly regarded for transforming Singapore from a Third to a First World nation in one generation. Given the circumstances surrounding Singapore's forced exit from the Federation of Malaya and the country's lack of natural resources, the government adopted a mix of strong authoritarian leadership and corporatist-style governance for political survival. The ruling party subsequently anchored its political legitimacy to the country's economic performance and focused on providing citizens with the means for upward mobility, largely through an open economic and business environment, and progressive education, health, and housing policies.

Although Singaporeans appear to be "fulfilled and secure" in their needs, there are underlying insecurities that belie its stellar achievements. While these insecurities may appear "less serious" when compared to the larger human security challenges faced by neighbors in Southeast Asia, they nonetheless have the potential to destabilize Singapore's economy and reduce social cohesion. Similarly, even though Singapore's gross national income per capita nearly doubled from $27,428 to $54,040 (in current US dollars) between 2005 and 2013 (World Bank n.d.) and with median household income in 2017 grew by 2 percent (Tang 2018), a PAP grassroots leader noted that "the freedom from want is a moving target and can always be interpreted in varying degrees depending on the state of development of a particular economy" (Political Grassroots #1 2014).

Furthermore, recent developments in Singapore have demonstrated challenges in meeting the third human security pillar, the "freedom to live in dignity," a consideration of often-ignored discriminatory actions within existing human security issues (Annan 2005). This relates to how a sense of entitlement has bred a sense of insecurity among Singapore citizens as well as some migrant communities. The sense of insecurity has particularly acute effects on marginalized groups, as there are limitations on the freedom to live in dignity, which compromise the quality of some dimensions of human security. The following section on the downside risks of Singapore's development policies provides further explanation of these insecurities.

9.2 The Downside Risks of Singapore's Development Policies

While the abovementioned policies have certainly put Singapore in good stead in relation to human security, there are limitations to its predominantly state-driven development policies. What emerges as a dominant thread in these limitations or downside risks is the fact that while Singapore's development policies have meant the meeting of human security needs at the national level, uneven access to, and provision of, protection by the state, and the lack of community empowerment have resulted in varying degrees of quality and end-point provision of human security among Singaporeans. This is exacerbated by a rapidly changing global landscape and the increasing inter-connectedness of a world to which age-old policy thrusts may be poorly equipped to adapt. The following downside risks reflect some of the major grievances in Singapore society, many of which became rallying points by candidates in the 2011 General Elections and/or were validated by members of civil society organizations and the civil service.

9.2.1 *Uneven Access to Protection by the State: Growth for Whom?*

A sense of entitlement that stems from Singapore's success is feeding into the insecurities of the younger generations. There is a question of uneven protection when one examines the state's capacity to meet their higher-order expectations. The acquisition of material wealth and the promise of upward social mobility are no longer a given regardless of how hard one works. The top-down approach by the government and the growth-at-all-cost strategy, coupled with a narrow definition of success over the past four decades, have thus contributed to increased inequality.

Similar concerns have been raised by members of parliament (MPs). During the re-opening of the second parliamentary session in May 2014, MP Inderjit Singh described the growing inequality as a shift "away from growing through motivating and encouraging Singaporeans, to importing talent that the government feels will contribute to the nation's bottom-line, our GDP" (Singh 2014). The growth strategy, which focused more on outcomes than means, has led to Singapore being the fastest place in the world to accumulate wealth and the country with the fifth highest concentration of millionaires (Barclays Wealth and Investment Management 2013).

This uneven provision of state protection is reflected by the increasing rate and visibility of economic inequality. Statistics from the Ministry of Manpower (MOM) showed that wages from 2008 to 2013 have been stagnant, as slight increases in median gross monthly income were offset by a corresponding rise in inflation (MOM 2013). Instead of enjoying a higher standard of living as the economy grew, the population is now faced with the prospect of working past the age of 65 and foregoing their current lifestyles as increases in the cost of transportation, healthcare, education, housing, and leisure outpace wages (Singh 2013). More recently, despite the increase in household incomes in 2017, income growth for the bottom 50 percent of households was much slower, thus implying a "widening" gap between the poor and the rich (Tang 2018).

The sense of feeling worse off is exacerbated by international surveys and reports that reaffirm Singapore's high cost of living. In 2013, Singapore was ranked 26th out of 136 countries for income inequality (UNDP 2013), and in 2014, became the world's most expensive city to live in (Economist Intelligence Unit 2014). These survey results came at a time when the middle-class majority in Singapore was facing increasing pressure from a widening income gap, higher costs of living, and increased competition for jobs, schools, and housing. These pressures are largely attributed to the government's open immigration and employment policies in the past decade, which have drawn criticism from several former senior policymakers for its perceived pursuit of economic growth at the expense of the people's interests. The problem is compounded by the lack of adequate social safety nets due to the government's long-standing emphasis on self-reliance with minimal assistance from the state.

Growing public discontentment with the national compulsory savings scheme known as the Central Provident Fund (CPF), a key social security pillar in Singapore, is one such example where state-led protection lacked an effective feedback loop to understand the livelihood concerns of Singapore's aging population. CPF account holders, comprising most, if not all, of Singapore's workforce, are required to set aside an estimated 20 percent of their monthly income. The CPF Board is entrusted by the government to manage and invest the monies on behalf of account holders who may finance home mortgages and healthcare needs by drawing down these funds or withdrawing their savings at the age of retirement. According to Yee Ping Yi, chief executive officer of the CPF Board, the CPF system is faced with the "global challenge of remaining financially sustainable with an ageing population and navigating a more challenging and volatile investment environment" (IPS 2014). As a means of managing Singaporeans' higher life expectancy, citizens past the age of 60 are strongly encouraged by the government to continue working on annual contracts, in many cases for lesser pay and as cleaners or kitchen help, while employers are incentivized through subsidies and various schemes to retain and train older workers.

9.2.2 Uneven Protection Causing Imbalance Between Market Efficiency and Resilience

The emphasis on growth through market efficiency principles has served Singapore well in the past. In recent years, however, public services, infrastructure, and social integration have come under stress given changes to Singapore's social landscape and pressures from a burgeoning population. In the past decade, emphasis was placed on de-nationalizing public goods such as transportation, healthcare, and telecommunications, among others. The performance of companies and public institutions is also measured against gains in efficiency and productivity, thereby creating systems that tend to be compromised when unexpected events occur. A former

Singaporean civil service scholar has noted that Singapore prides itself on market efficiency, which is predicated on minimizing redundancies in the system (Civil Service #1 2014). One may therefore argue that Singapore's emphasis on market efficiency has led to the removal of redundancies that may in fact be necessary if systems are to remain resilient to downside risks.

A case in point is the series of breakdowns in train services run by the SMRT Corporation due to shortcomings in its maintenance regime. More than 127,000 commuters were affected in consecutive service disruptions in December 2011. SMRT was strongly criticized by the government and commuters for managing the situation poorly. A Committee of Inquiry established to investigate the disruptions revealed that Singapore did not have an integrated Land Transport Emergency Plan that articulates response strategies and defines the roles of various stakeholders and coordination protocols (MOT 2012) and said that this situation resulted in the poorly coordinated response.

9.2.3 Uneven Protection for Local Companies

From the mid-1960s to the late 1980s, Singapore's growth model was largely focused on foreign multinational corporations (MNCs) as an engine of growth, arguably at the expense of local enterprises. Local enterprises were developed as a supporting industry to supply products and services to MNCs and received no domestic protection from foreign competition. For decades, despite comprising over 90 percent of all businesses, small and medium enterprises (SMEs) employed just half the workforce and contributed to one-third of the value added (Chia 2005). After the 1985 economic recession, due to concerns that MNCs might withdraw operations in future crises, the government began to take steps to strengthen SMEs by promoting entrepreneurship and technology transfer programs. Nonetheless, the emphasis on providing support to MNCs continued until 1998 (Chia 2005).

As the world moves toward a knowledge-based economy, the government realized the importance of local enterprises in building economic resilience, innovation, and entrepreneurship. Since 2000, the government has turned toward nurturing SMEs to build up their capacity to compete internationally, and to encourage productivity enhancements through restructuring, grants, and subsidies, as well as create a pro-enterprise environment by supporting innovation. These efforts have shown results, with a handful of local enterprises becoming regional brand names. Nonetheless, many local enterprises in Singapore remain weak. A recent study of local enterprises showed 80 percent of SMEs have seen a rise in business costs and continue to experience high rentals and a shortage of labor that impact their competitiveness and productivity negatively (ASME 2012).

9.2.4 *Meritocracy: A Cause for Uneven Protection?*

In the realm of policymaking, a meritocratic approach toward talent scouting for individuals to be recruited into the civil service has inadvertently led to elitism within the civil bureaucracy, with some impact on the quality of policymaking. Academically gifted students from the age of 18 are routinely identified and offered government scholarships that fund their education at premier overseas universities. The scholarships typically come with a contractual bond of three to ten years. Upon graduation, the scholars are assigned to "fast-track" postings among various ministries, with each stint lasting an average of two to three years. Upon the completion of each stint, the scholars are assessed on their suitability to move up the rungs of the elite civil service based on stringent key performance indicators. Those who reach the apex of the prestigious Administrative Service would enter the "Superscale G" salary where those with the lowest entry grade, SR9, are paid an annual salary of US$319,000 (PMO 2007). This fast-track system has cultivated a brand of elitism in the civil service, which has contributed to a growing disconnect between policymakers and the average Singaporean.

Instead of training policymakers to craft effective long-term policies that affect a majority of the population, this system runs the risk of "group-think," producing policymakers who lack depth of knowledge and the ability to empathize with inflationary cost pressures felt by ordinary Singaporeans. One may also argue that the pressure to produce sterling results before the end of each stint may run counter to long-term planning. MP Inderjit Singh spoke in favor of a bottom-up approach to policymaking and pointed to the tendency for policymakers to "fire-fight," noting that the constant need to manage crises could be a result of policies that do not reflect a diversity of perspectives (Singh 2014). Additionally, there is an observably unhealthy division within the civil service, where the differentiation between scholars and non-scholars has created a strong sense of dissatisfaction, as scholars are perceived as being promoted more rapidly simply because they are on the scholar track (Civil Service Source #1 2014).

9.2.5 *Personal and Community Security: Protection for Whom?*

Another consequence of the uneven provision of protection by the state is that protection for some has inadvertently created insecurity for others. Incidents relating to personal and community security reflect this dynamic, whereby society feels more protected, but specific communities and interest groups feel a lack of protection. This is particularly the case for minority groups and those that have limited means of representation and expression in the Singaporean society.

The challenge to personal security comes to the fore when one examines the extent to which migrant workers feel a sense of personal security. While Singapore is touted as having relatively low crime rates (Singapore Police Force 2014), there have been recent reports of increased crime and violence, several of which have implicated foreign workers in Singapore as both contributors and victims of the crimes. First, there had been concerns over the growing number of foreigners engaged in criminal acts such as illegal gambling, drug sales, and prostitution in the red-light district of Geylang. According to the commissioner of the Singapore Police, Geylang presented a "clear and present danger to public order" (Banu 2014) as offences increased from 34 in 2011 to 38 in 2013 and 49 in 2014 (Banu 2014).

Second, there was the Little India riot on December 8, 2013, which was sparked by the death of a foreign worker who was killed instantly after being hit by a bus along Race Course Road, an area where large groups of South Asian foreign workers congregate on their rest days (MHA 2014). In a bid to assure Singaporeans of tighter public security after the riot, the government issued a Public Order Act, which banned the sale of alcohol and curtailed the freedom of foreign workers to congregate in the Little India precinct. Two months after the incident, a five-week Committee of Inquiry was convened. Among their findings, alcohol was the main contributing factor causing the riot to escalate into violence, and not the alleged widespread abuse of foreign workers.

These two cases led to the belief that government officials and agencies had been prioritizing traditional security measures (it was managed as a law enforcement issue) over other efforts to ease the concerns of migrant workers and civil society advocates (Au 2014). Moreover, referring solely to media reports on these issues would portray foreign workers in a negative light, thus augmenting the degree of stigmatization that is sometimes experienced by these foreign blue-collar laborers.

9.2.6 *Downside Risks from the Lack of Empowerment*

Downside risks also emerge when the space in which civil society can express its concerns is curtailed. This is reflected in the limited advocacy abilities of most Civil Society Organisations (CSOs) in Singapore, as the degree to which the government engages the CSOs is based on their ability to complement the government as service providers. Community self-help groups, for instance, are viewed as complementing the state's efforts to provide protection to vulnerable groups. While there are several ground-up community organizations, state-driven community self-help groups have been formed explicitly along racial lines: the Singapore Indian Development Association (SINDA) for Indians, the Yayasan Mendaki for Malays, and the Chinese Development Assistance Council (CDAC). The rationale for such distinctions is that each community would be able to support itself and better attend to its own specific needs.

This arrangement of communities looking after themselves, however, has led to downside risks, particularly among Singapore's Malay-Muslim minority community, which has experienced a degree of community insecurity. For instance, retrospective statistics have shown that the highest rate of poverty and school dropouts come from the Malay community, as well as high rates of drug abuse in the 1980s to 1990s (MSFD 2014). This large incidence was found to be disproportionate to the funding that is available from within the community itself, thus making the issue more difficult to address. These trends, amplified by mainstream media reporting, created a stigma that prolonged limited social progress is inherently a Malay problem.

The lack of empowerment and the inability of CSOs to express their views also result from the fact that CSOs that are seen to be taking stances deemed undesirable by the government are co-opted or given stern warnings. Drawing from the experience of the Association of Muslim Professionals (AMP), members of this Malay-Muslim Organization (MMO) have been active in voicing concerns from within the community. AMP's vocal stance was particularly evident during its 2nd National Convention in 2000, when it criticized the lack of autonomy that the existing Malay-Muslim leadership faced. It argued that the "way in which the Malay political leadership were hand-picked and imposed upon the community was not sustainable as such leaders would lack legitimacy in Malay eyes" (Mutalib 2012). AMP also pushed the envelope further by suggesting the formation of an independent, non-partisan collective leadership in the Malay community (AMP 2000). The outcomes of the convention did not sit well with government interests and resulted in heavy punitive action taken against members of AMP, including a cut in funding from government sources, for challenging existing political structures (CSO Source #1 2014). In this regard, the freedom to live in dignity has not been ensured for Singapore's Malay minority, and to an extent has been curtailed by the state.

The lack of empowerment is also because many CSOs in Singapore struggle to achieve financial independence, which invariably limits the extent of their activities. Many MMOs, for instance, get a substantial proportion of funding from the government. While it would be within their comfort zone to refrain from seeking funding from non-governmental sources, financial dependence on the government could prevent MMO members from voicing concerns that would "rock the boat" and threaten a cut in government funding (CSO Source #1 2014).

Recent years have seen a higher level of community empowerment using social media. Issues that were previously unaddressed have now come to the forefront. Because of this increased ability for self-expression, there are more voices competing to be heard in the limited social space. The inability of the Singaporean government to engage, maneuver, and address the issues expressed in cyberspace can potentially therefore lead to both online and offline downside risks. The growth of the gay movement in Singapore is one such example. The developments can be traced to Prime Minister Goh Chok Tong's term in office, where he spoke about allowing gays to take up jobs in the civil service and attracting the "Pink dollar" in the early 2000s. In this regard, it can be suggested that Singapore's top-down approach in enhancing development has also included efforts to be more accepting of the gay community and tap into their creative talents to support the economy. Fast-forward to a decade later, the Pink Dot Movement, a non-profit movement open to both straight and gay individuals who support the belief that everyone deserves the freedom to love, has gained traction since 2009, and congregates annually for its Pink Dot event at Hong Lim Park. In 2014, however, the Pink Dot Movement met with overt opposition, particularly from religious groups. The "Wear White" movement, initiated by a small group of Muslims and headed by a young Islamic teacher, Ustaz Noor Deros, expressed the view that laws of nature should not be violated.

The incident created two polarizing views of being for or against the lesbian, gay, bisexual, and transgender (LGBT) movement, and an impression that the more religious sections of society were intolerant of differences. An example of this was the fact that the Pink Dot 2014 campaign video was criticized online for its inclusion of a hijab-wearing Muslim girl (Pink Dot SG 2014). Some "keyboard warriors" questioned the girl's religiosity and condemned her for misrepresenting Singapore's Muslim community (Chua 2014). This incident pushed the religious authorities in Singapore to issue a comment on the matter. The Council of Islamic Scholars in Singapore (MUIS), a government body administering matters pertaining to the Muslim community, called on Muslims to adopt a non-confrontational stance toward homosexuality and the Pink Dot Movement (*Channel NewsAsia* 2014). The Catholic Church, too, reiterated its stance on non-discrimination but also disagreement with homosexual relationships (Kwara 2014). In this regard, we begin to see a more complex web of understanding of community security emerging where on the one hand, the gay minority is afforded increased security to exercise their rights in society, but on the other hand, is perceived by some sections of religious groups as a threat to their community security.

The burgeoning civil society space also has implications on the extent of intellectual freedom and space in Singapore. A debate ensued when a member of the public wrote to the Forum section of *The Straits Times* and complained that there were books on the shelves of the children's section in the public library he perceived to be advocating homosexuality (Campbell 2014). In what appeared to be a knee-jerk reaction, the National Library Board of Singapore (NLB) immediately removed the three books off the shelves preparatory to their being discarded. This, however, resulted in a downside risk where the wider section of Singapore society became upset with the removal of the books as it reflected literary censorship (*The Straits Times* 2014; Poh 2014). Following several events indicating protest over the NLB's decision, the board decided to reinstate the books in the adults' section, and noted that it would re-examine the review process of books containing controversial themes.

Most pertinently, the uneven provision of, and access to, protection and the lack of empowerment led to downside risks such as a lack of social cohesion and community resilience, with consequences for the credibility of the ruling government. The most acute of these downside risks is best reflected in the 2011 General Elections, when Singaporeans voiced their discontent over the growing economic inequality. The 2011 General Elections saw the ruling party's poorest performance since 1963, where its overall share of the votes declined by more than 15 percentage points compared to the 2001 elections, which it had won by 75.3 percent

(Elections Department Singapore 2014). The poor showing that prompted "soul-searching" was largely attributed to a growing sense of alienation between the government and the electorate (The Economist 2011). George Yeo, former minister of foreign affairs and PAP member, said that the resentment toward the PAP was the result of its arrogance and high-handedness (The New Paper 2011; AsiaOne 2011). A former civil service scholar observed that the election result signaled the fraying of the social contract because the government has not delivered sufficiently on its promise to provide the population with opportunities for upward social mobility (Civil Service #1 2014).

9.3 Mitigating Domestic Downside Risks

Following the 2011 General Elections, the Singaporean government acted to mitigate the domestic downside risks, namely through better engagement with Singaporeans to understand their concerns, and gradual reforms within the public service sector. To better understand ground sentiments, the government launched a one-year national survey known as the Singapore Conversation in August 2012. The report published by the Singapore Conversation Secretariat revealed that the aspirations and concerns of Singaporeans revolved around the themes of community security, health security, and economic security. These include the ability to access and afford basic needs, increased economic opportunities, strengthened social bonds and community spirit, and open and sincere engagement with policymakers (Our Singapore Conversation Secretariat 2013).

These aspirations have also been supported by various academics and commentators on Singapore politics. In a co-written article, three notable Singaporean economists, Yeoh et al. (2012), noted that "Singapore also needs to reconstruct its social compact to one led by a more activist and redistributive state, one that strikes a better balance between growth and equity, between social protection and individual responsibility."

As the Singaporean government attempts to transform its governance approach from an authoritarian top-down style to one that is more consultative and engaging, it is necessary that the initiatives be seen to be genuine efforts for long-term sustainable change. In 2012, the government addressed housing issues for the elderly, through the Enhancement for Active Seniors (EASE) program, "to improve safety and comfort of seniors living in Housing Development Board (HDB) flats" (Chan 2014). These efforts have culminated in the launching of the pioneer generation packages in 2014 for Singaporeans over the age of 65, which include rebates for healthcare and other social services. In addition to providing senior citizens with improved social benefits, there has been a greater recognition of pioneering communities that helped to build Singapore in its formative years.

Effective public communication, however, does need to meet the challenge of managing various public perspectives and determining to what degree those perspectives are substantive or just "noise." Permanent Secretary of the Law Ministry, Dr. Beh Swan Gin, for instance, noted the importance of listening to the silent majority to avoid having the very loud minority voice determine policy directions. This point is crucial given the increasing activities in cyberspace. It is therefore necessary for the government to better formulate strategies to block out "noise," while ensuring that it listens to important views from Singapore's civil society.

Efforts to mitigate domestic downside risks have also included progressive changes in the civil service. Human resources management, for one, continues to evolve over the years. In a move to improve policy implementation, Peter Ong, Head of the Civil Service, noted that it was also vital to tap into the wisdom of public-sector specialists with in-depth knowledge (Chan 2014). A new management scheme has been introduced to enhance skills and capabilities in five specialized areas: (1) economy building, (2) infrastructure and environment, (3) security, (4) social work, and (5) central administration. Under this public-sector leadership program, civil servants are no longer just generalists but will be equipped with sector-relevant capabilities and preparedness to address contemporary issues (Civil Service #3 2014).

Another area of reform has been the development of programs to expose administrative officers in the civil service to operational jobs. An example of this is a six-month community attachment program, which has seen a gradual increase in the annual number of participants. It is said that by the end of 2014, 70 percent of administrative officers are expected to have undergone such a program in their first 15 years (Chan 2014). However, this begs the question: to what extent would these temporary "hardship postings" change the quality of the civil service?

The situation following the 2011 elections has also precipitated a growing internal discussion on the compromises needed to make effective progress on political security. There is a sense within the civil service that the Singaporean government will need to get used to sharing power with members of civil society that are deemed credible. At the same time, there is a sense that Singaporeans themselves ought to reduce their dependence on the government and exercise more agency over their lives, as the government cannot realistically meet nor sustain higher-order needs (Civil Service #3 2014).

The 2015 General Election was perceived by the PAP that their reform efforts had paid off—although many analysts have suggested that the PAP's victory rode on the passing of Singapore's founding father, Lee Kuan Yew. Nevertheless, it remains to be seen to what extent the PAP will be able to sustain these reforms and genuinely listen to the needs and aspirations of Singaporeans. This is particularly critical for the next generation of leaders (commonly known as the 4G leaders) who are poised to take over from Prime Minister Lee Hsien Loong and senior members of his cabinet.

9.4 Mitigating Transnational Risks

Several efforts have been made by the Singaporean government to address transnational risks. These efforts can be seen in both the Singaporean government's domestic and international policies. First, there have been efforts to address human trafficking in Singapore. What was initially a private member's bill, mooted by MP Christopher De Souza in 2008, started to receive government support through the establishment of an inter-ministerial task force in 2010. Second, in terms of migrant worker policies, legislation requiring an official day off for domestic helpers was passed and began to be enforced in January 2013 (Hodal 2012). In addition to this, tougher penalties can be brought against employers if the payment of salaries to foreign workers is delayed. This has, however, generated some negative reactions due to the perception that enhancing the human security needs of migrant workers may compromise the security of their Singaporean employers. Some sections of the Singaporean society have raised concerns that allowing their domestic helper a day-off might potentially expose her to undesirable influences, which may risk the security of the employer's home should the helper bring acquaintances into the house without the permission of her employer (Francesca 2012). The issue of "protection for whom" therefore needs to be discussed and debated not only from the perspective of the migrant workers but also the issues faced by employers, and the effects of cultural perspectives and stereotypes in influencing employer-employee relations (*Kiasu* Parents n.d.; Singapore Motherhood n.d.).

Third, Singapore marked a milestone in efforts to address the trans-boundary haze. The acute health and economic effects of the haze in mid-2013, however, said to be worse than the peaks in 1998 and 2006, prompted the Singaporean government to take more decisive action. The Singapore Parliament passed the *Trans-Boundary Haze* Bill in August 2014, which allows enforcers to impose fines of up to US$2 million on companies that cause or contribute to trans-boundary haze pollution in Singapore (Kotwani 2014).

Fourth, Singapore plays an important role in supporting disaster preparedness and relief capabilities in the Southeast Asian region. Through its military as well as humanitarian organizations such as the Red Cross and Mercy Relief, Singapore has provided assistance following many, if not all, of the major disasters in East Asia. Similarly, there has been a concerted effort to socialize the Southeast Asian region to the threat of infectious diseases and contribute to the development of regional crises-management mechanisms. To this end, the Ministry of Home Affairs (MHA) funded a series of three international and regional conferences on pandemic preparedness between 2009 and 2011. On behalf of Association of Southeast Asian Nations (ASEAN), Singapore was responsible for holding the regional stockpile of antiviral drugs and personal protection equipment such as masks and isolation gowns and to distribute the stockpile in a rapid containment operation if a human-to-human transmission pandemic was confirmed in the ASEAN region.

Finally, in ensuring freedom from fear for its citizens, the Singaporean government's approach to addressing terrorism and extremism is twofold. First, it takes a primarily hardline stance on persecuting individuals deemed to be supporting terrorist activities and transnational militant movements, such as the Islamic State in Syria and Iraq (ISIS), and the Jemaah Islamiyah network in Southeast Asia. Following the discovery of Singaporeans joining the fight in Syria, Deputy Prime Minister Teo Chee Hean noted that such persons pose "a real threat to Singapore's national security and will be dealt with in accordance with our laws" (Salleh and Asyqin 2014). This hardline stance is complemented by a second softer approach that involves counseling and religious rehabilitation for the suspects. In addition to this, the government is aware of the importance of maintaining the social fabric, thereby specifically avoiding the association of terrorism with Singapore's Muslim minority population.

9.5 Conclusions

Singapore is held in high esteem for overcoming the challenges of being a small nation with no natural resources and meeting human security goals that other countries in the region continue to struggle with. It is often perceived as a development model by governments who look toward its corporatist style of governance under which the citizenry willingly relinquishes some levels of personal freedom for basic protection and growth in terms of income and material wealth. In recent years, however, the thrust of Singapore's age-old social compact has been questioned, and the demand for greater freedoms has become a major challenge for the government. As Benny Lim, Permanent Secretary, Prime Minister's Office and Ministry of National Development puts it, "Our level of tolerance for security problems is very low largely because we've been blessed by peace, stability, and safety" (PMO 2012). As such, the heavy top-down approach must be complemented with a bottom-up approach to build up the resilience of society to downside risks and to empower society with the means to resolve or manage a range of diverse and complex issues that challenge Singapore's human development.

This study has highlighted that Singaporeans are demanding the missing human security aspects as manifested through a series of events, particularly in the last ten years. Such citizen-led advocacy will likely be a feature of Singapore's future development and will keep the Singaporean government vigilant in understanding the perspectives on the ground. A lesson that can be drawn from Singapore's experience is that a social compact anchored to a country's economic performance is unsustainable. In this information age, issues are brought to the fore instantly, and governments are pressured to respond just as rapidly. While Singapore's authoritarian and corporatist style of governance has provided the majority population with basic levels of human security, the time has come to change its governance style to one that is consultative and involves more actors in the process of decision-making.

Note

1. Politicians in Singapore, including Prime Minister Lee Hsien Loong, have increasingly been utilizing social media to engage the public and to provide personal views on issues.

References

Adam, Shamim, and Weiyi Lim. 2011. Singapore's Lee Retains Power with Smallest Margin Since 1965. *Bloomberg*, May 8.

Au, Alex Waipang. 2014. Manpower Director Makes Incredible Claims about How Well Migrant Workers Are Treated by Ministry. *Yawning Bread*, March 24.

Annan, Kofi. 2005. *In Larger Freedom: Towards Development, Security and Human Rights for All*. New York: United Nations Publications.

AsiaOne. 2011. George Yeo Not Standing for Elections in 5 Years. *AsiaOne*, May 11.

AMP (Association of Malay Professionals). 2000. Malay Professionals Rebut LKY's Policy on Malay Leadership. *Think Centre*, November 1.

ASME (Association of Small and Medium Enterprises). 2012. The Sentiments from the Ground. http://www.asme.org.sg/downloads/ED%2045%20COMPLETE%20SET.23.pdf. Accessed August 7, 2014.

Banu, Yasmeen. 2014. Geylang—MP Expresses Frustration, Wants 'Major Clean Up'. *The Online Citizen*, April 2. http://www.theonlinecitizen.com/2014/04/geylang-mp-expresses-frustration-wants-major-clean-up/. Accessed 7 Aug 2017.

Barclays Wealth and Investment Management. 2013. Origins and Legacy: The Changing Order of Wealth Creation. https://wealth.barclays.com/en_gb/home/research/research-centre/wealth-insights/volume-17.html. Accessed August 10, 2017.

Campbell, Charlie. 2014. Singapore Provokes Outrage by Pulping Kids' Books About Gay Families. *Time*, July 11.

Chan, Robin. 2014. Policy, Implementation Both Vital: Civil Service Chief. *The Straits Times*, March 27.

Channel News Asia. 2014. Don't Be Confrontational on LGBT Issues: MUIS. June 20.

Chia, Siow Yue. 2005. The Singapore Model of Industrial Policy: Past Evolution and Current Thinking. Paper presented at the Second LAEBA Annual Conference, Buenos Aires, November 28–29.

Chua, Trinity. 2014. Pink Dot and Muslims. *The Independent Singapore*, June 27.

Economist Intelligence Unit. 2014. *Worldwide Cost of Living Survey 2014*. London: EIU.

Elections Department Singapore. 2014. *Parliamentary Election Results*. http://www.eld.gov.sg/elections_past_parliamentary.html. Accessed 7 Aug 2014.

Francesca. 2012. *Domestic Workers Cheer New Day-Off Rule, Struggle with Memories of Work Without Rest*. http://twc2.org.sg/2012/03/08/domestic-workers-cheer-new-day-off-rule-struggle-with-memories-of-work-without-rest/. Accessed 7 Nov 2017.

Hodal, Kate. 2012. Singapore's Maids to Get a Day Off. *The Guardian*, March 6.

IPS (Institute of Policy Studies). 2014. *Summary Report from the Forum on CPF and Retirement Adequacy*. Singapore: NUS.

Kiasu Parents. n.d. *About Full-Time Maids*. http://www.kiasuparents.com/kiasu/forum/viewtopic.php?p=263924. Accessed 7 Nov 2017.

Kotwani, Monica. 2014. Parliament Passes Transboundary Haze Pollution Bill. *Channel NewsAsia*, August 5. http://www.channelnewsasia.com/news/singapore/parliament-passes/1297832.html. Accessed 6 Nov 2014.

Kwara, Michelle. 2014. *Catholic Church in Singapore Reiterates 'Consistent' Position on LGBT Issue in Reply to Wijeysingha*. https://sg.news.yahoo.com/vincent-wijeysingha-hits-out-at-singapore-archbishop-s-open-letter-about-lgbt-individuals-030444396.html. Accessed August 7, 2017.

MHA (Ministry of Home Affairs). 2014. *Report of the Committee of Inquiry into the Little India Riot on 8 December 2013*. Singapore: Ministry of Home Affairs.

MOM (Ministry of Manpower). 2013. *National Wages Council (NWC) Guidelines 2013/2014*. Singapore: Ministry of Manpower.

MOT (Ministry of Transport). 2012. *Report on the Committee of Inquiry (COI) into the Disruption of MRT Train Services on 15 and 17 December 2011*. Singapore: Ministry of Transport. https://www.mot.gov.sg/news/COI%20report%20-%20Executive%20Summary.pdf

MSFD (Ministry of Social and Family Development). 2014. *Progress of the Malay Community in Singapore since 1980*. Singapore: Ministry of Social and Family Development.

Mutalib, Hussin. 2012. *Singapore Malays: Being Ethnic Minority and Muslim in a Global City-State*. New York: Routledge.

Pink Dot SG. 2014. For Family, For Friends, For Love. https://www.youtube.com/watch?v=3iGKeIbxDoQ. Accessed 7 Aug 2017.

Poh, Eileen.2014. Reading Event in Response to NLB Book Withdrawal Draws a Crowd. *Channel NewsAsia*, July 13.

PMO (Prime Minister's Office, Singapore). 2007. *Administrative Officers, Political, Judicial and Statutory Appointment Holders to Get 4% to 21% Pay Increase*. Singapore: Prime Minister's Office.

———. 2012. Life is More Complicated Than Black and White. http://issuu.com/challengeonline/docs/challenge-mar2012-single/22. Accessed 7 Nov 2017.

———. 2014. Transcript of Prime Minister Lee Hsien Loong's Dialogue at IIMpact Gala Dinner. Singapore: Prime Minister's Office. https://www.pmo.gov.sg/newsroom/transcript-prime-minister-lee-hsien-loongs-dialogue-iimpact-gala-dinner. Accessed 30 Sept 2014.

Our Singapore Conversation Secretariat. 2013. *Reflections of Our Singapore Conversation*. Our Singapore Conversation Secretariat: Singapore, October 2013. http://www.reach.gov.sg/Portals/0/Microsite/osc/OSC_Reflection.pdf. Accessed 7 Nov 2014.

Salleh, Mohamad, and Nur Asyqin. 2014. Parliament: Singaporeans Planning to Support or Join ISIS Will Be Dealt with Under the Law. *The Straits Times*, October 7.

Singapore Motherhood. n.d. Bad Maid? Post Here!!!. http://singaporemotherhood.com/forum/threads/bad-maid-post-here.4207/. Accessed 6 Nov 2014.

Singapore Police Force. 2014. Crime Rate Falls to 30-Year Low. *Annual Crime Brief*, February 14.

Singh, Inderjit. 2013. Speech on the White Paper on Population. https://www.facebook.com/100000502271288/posts/598891680137569/. Accessed 7 Mar 2018.

———. 2014. Response to the President Address at the Re-Opening of 2nd Session of Parliament May 2014. https://www.facebook.com/kbinderjit/posts/864760460217355. Accessed 8 Aug 8 2017.

Tang, See Kit. 2018. Singapore's Household Income Grew in 2017, Income Inequality Unchanged: Singstat. *Channel NewsAsia*, February 8.

The Economist. 2011. A Win-Win Election? *The Economist Online*, May 8. http://www.economist.com/blogs/banyan/2011/05/singapores_election. Accessed 7 Aug 2017.

The New Paper, RazorTV. 2011. George Yeo: PAP Must Change. *The New Paper*, May 6.

The Straits Times. 2014. NLB 'Saddened by' Reaction over Its Removal of Three Books with Homosexuality Themes, Says Chief Executive. *The Straits Times*, July 13.

UNDP (United Nations Development Programme). 2013. *Human Development Report 2013*. New York: UNDP.

———. 2016. *Human Development Report 2016*. New York: UNDP.

World Bank. n.d. *Singapore*. Washington, DC: The World Bank.

Yeoh, Lam Keong, Donald Low, and Manu Bhaskaran. 2012. Rethinking Singapore's Social Compact. *Globalis Asian,* 13 (January–March). Singapore: Institute of Policy Studies.

Interviews

Political Grassroots Source #1. 2014. Interviewed by author in Singapore, May 19.

CSO Source #1. 2014. Interviewed by author in Singapore, April 7.

Civil Service Source #1. 2014. Interviewed by author in Singapore, April 11.

Civil Service Source #2. 2014. Interviewed by author in Singapore, April 10.

Civil Service Source #3. 2014. Interviewed by author via email, March 17.

TIP Participatory Observation. 2014. Authors at Public Consultation for Trafficking in Persons (TIP) Bill in Singapore, April.

Dialogue Session at the IIMPACT Gala Dinner. YouTube video, 2:53. Posted by 'Prime Minister's Office, Singapore,' August 28, 2014. https://www.youtube.com/watch?v=-i0_zuGEow0&index=5&list=PLqvAkd0-laMfuTGK5KeJMrwr61v4PrE0p. Accessed November 6, 2017.

National Day Rally 2014 - Full Speech in English. YouTube video, 1:25:41. Posted by 'Prime Minister's Office, Singapore,' August 17, 2014. https://www.youtube.com/watch?v=x2wsTopymmk. Accessed November 6, 2017.

CHAPTER 10

Human Security in Practice: The Case of South Korea

Eun Mee Kim, Seon Young Bae, and Ji Hyun Shin

10.1 Introduction

South Korea became a member of the Organization for Economic Co-operation and Development-Development Assistance Committee (OECD-DAC) in 2010 and joined the ranks of advanced industrialized country donors. In this chapter, we examine whether South Korea's development cooperation has focused on human security, given its own experience of being a recipient of a large amount of development assistance after World War II and the Korean War. Even today South Korea continues to face human security threats, with nuclear threats from North Korea as well as natural disasters. However, this chapter focuses on whether

E. M. Kim (✉)
Graduate School of International Studies, Ewha Womans University, Seoul, Republic of Korea
e-mail: emkim@ewha.ac.kr

S. Y. Bae
International Committee of the Red Cross, Seoul, Republic of Korea

J. H. Shin
Ewha Womans University, Seoul, Republic of Korea

Y. Mine et al. (eds.), *Human Security Norms in East Asia*, Security, Development and Human Rights in East Asia,
https://doi.org/10.1007/978-3-319-97247-3_10

South Korea has identified human security as an important element in its official development assistance (ODA).[1]

The concept of human security was introduced in the 1990s by the United Nations Development Programme (UNDP) and was later adopted by Japan and Canada as a priority in their ODA programs. According to the discussion on the definitions of human security in this book, we focus on three components: (1) freedom from fear, based on efforts to address the causes of conflict and to improve governance; (2) freedom from want, gained by extending assistance to developing countries to provide basic services including water, food, and shelter; and (3) freedom to live in dignity, gained through assistance in improving basic conditions that ensures individual human rights and dignity. These are delivered by means of two approaches: (1) protection, the top-down "protection of those who suffer," in which institutions play a major role in the recovery or development of social safety; and (2) empowerment, which is the "empowerment of people to make them cope with risk and threats by themselves," and emphasizes the capacity building of individuals, preparing them to be more resilient to potential risks.

We examined the use of human security by key stakeholders in the South Korean ODA community using the following three questions: (1) Have the stakeholders used the term "human security" in their official documents? (2) Have the stakeholders embraced the meaning/concept of human security even if the term was not used explicitly in their policies and practices, in other words have they implicitly used the term "human security"? and (3) What are the implications of human security for South Korea's ODA? We reviewed relevant government documents for the explicit as well as implicit use of the term, "human security," and interviewed key stakeholders in the ODA community.

This chapter is organized as follows: Sect. 10.2 presents the research design and key stakeholders in the South Korean ODA community; Sect. 10.3 includes the research findings based on a review of documents and interviews; and the final section provides concluding remarks.

10.2 Research Design

10.2.1 Research Methodology

We conducted empirical research to determine whether human security has been explicitly or implicitly used in South Korea's ODA in two stages: (1) a review of government documents related to ODA[2] and (2) the interview of key stakeholders in that community. Key stakeholders in the ODA community include: (1) The President, the Prime Minister's Office (PMO), the line Ministries in charge of ODA, and the ODA-implementing agencies for the Government; (2) the National Assembly and political parties; (3) Civil Society Organizations (CSOs); (4) International Organizations (IOs); and (5) Academia. Private sector businesses have not yet emerged as major stakeholders although many businesses participate in ODA projects, and the public would not appear to be a major stakeholder either. Thus, the private sector and the public were not surveyed.

For a more in-depth analysis, interviews were conducted with a few of the key stakeholders (see interviews in references): (1) Government sector—officials from the PMO, and the Ministry of Strategy and Finance (MOSF); (2) CSOs—World Vision Korea; (3) IOs—the UN World Food Programme (UN WFP) and the International Organization for Migration (IOM); and (4) Academia.

The following six questions were asked during the in-depth interviews:

1. Do you think the concept of human security is used in South Korea's ODA?
2. Do you think human security is considered important in South Korea's ODA?
3. Do you think human security requires greater emphasis in South Korea's ODA?
4. How is human security reflected in South Korea's ODA?
5. Do you think the three components of human security are currently realized in South Korea's ODA?
6. Which do you think is closer to South Korea's ODA policies and practices—protection or empowerment?

All six questions were asked to government officials and those from academia. Questions 1–4 were asked to CSOs and IOs, and questions 5 and 6 were asked to interviewees from academia. We asked interviewees from CSOs and IOs about whether human security was used in their organizations using questions 1–4, and finally, we asked about the use of the elements of human security, the three components and the two approaches, in all the interviews.

10.2.2 Key Stakeholders in South Korea's ODA

10.2.2.1 Government

Government stakeholders included: (1) the President; (2) the PMO, which coordinates aid institutions, and the Committee for International Development Cooperation (CIDC) under the PMO, which oversees overall policy direction, and coordinates aid policies and implementation among ministries and aid implementing institutions; (3) the Ministry of Foreign Affairs (MOFA), which sets the policy direction of grants, and supervises grant implementing agencies including the Korea International Cooperation Agency (KOICA), line ministries and local governments, as well as international humanitarian assistance; (4) the MOSF, which sets the national budget, including that for MOFA, and oversees the aid implementing agency of the Economic Development Cooperation Fund (EDCF) in charge of concessional loans; and (5) the major aid implementing agencies KOICA (grant aid agency), and EDCF (concessional loans agency).

10.2.2.2 The National Assembly[3]

The National Assembly promulgates legislation, and reviews and approves the national budget including ODA. Among the Standing and Special Committees of the National Assembly, the Foreign Affairs and Unification Committee reviews the laws, budgets, and other related matters involving the Ministries of Unification, Foreign Affairs, and the National Unification Advisory Council based on the *National Assembly Law*, Articles 36 and 37 (Foreign Affairs and Unification Committee 2014). This Committee reviews the ODA laws, policies, and budget before they are submitted to the National Assembly for voting. Thus, we reviewed the official website of this Committee including official meeting minutes, agenda items, country reports, public hearing proceedings, and policy documents.

Two major political parties in the National Assembly were selected to participate in the research: the Saenuri Party (incumbent party; conservative), and the New Politics Alliance for Democracy (NPAD; the opposition party; liberal). The Saenuri Party was the incumbent party for two Presidents (Lee Myung-bak [2008–2013] and Park Geun-hye [2013–2017]). We reviewed party documents including meeting minutes and briefings.

10.2.2.3 Civil Society Organizations (CSOs) and International Organizations (IOs)

IOs and international CSOs, which have been important in South Korea's ODA implementation, policy advice, advocacy, and international humanitarian assistance, were included for document review and interviews. These included UN WFP, which provides food supplies and ensures food security; IOM, which provides refugee assistance, advocates on immigrant rights, and manages refugee camps; and World Vision Korea, which is one of the largest international CSOs in South Korea's development cooperation and humanitarian assistance.

10.2.2.4 Academia

University professors and researchers have been important in South Korea's ODA community and the CIDC. Professor A of Ewha Womans University is an expert on international relations and non-traditional and human security. Professor B of Korea University is an expert on human security with a focus on North Korean defectors and refugees. Professor C of Kyung Hee University is an expert on South Korea's ODA and global governance on development cooperation. These three professors were elected due to their research/policy interests in South Korea's ODA and human security. Their publications were reviewed, and Professors A and C were interviewed.

10.3 Human Security Discourse and Practice in South Korea

This section presents findings from our research based on the examination of documents and in-depth interviews. Table 10.1 presents the list of government documents regarding ODA that were reviewed.

Table 10.2 presents a summary of the explicit use of the term "human security" by various stakeholders, and which elements of human security were used in the documents. We examined both the explicit and implicit use of human security. The cells were left blank when there were no relevant laws or documents to be reviewed. The findings on the review of documents and speeches show that there were only a few cases when human security was explicitly used, but in most cases the concept of human security was implicitly used. The findings showed that the government rarely uses the term human security, but the concept of human security is implicit in its ODA policies and projects. We found that the emphasis on

Table 10.1 South Korea's ODA documents by government office

Government office	*Document title (Year of publication/Presentation)*	*Classification/ Source*
PMO & MOFA	Framework Act on International Development Cooperation (Promulgated in 2010; Revised in 2013)	Law
PMO	ODA White Paper (2014)	Policy document
	Strategic Plan for International Development Cooperation (October 2010)	Policy document
	Mid-term ODA Policy for 2011–2015 (2010)	Policy document
MOFA	Opening Speech at the International Conference "New Strategic Thinking: Planning for Korean Foreign Policy" (Minister of MOFA, 2013)	Speech
	MOFA Official Website (2012)	Website
	Overseas Emergency Relief Act (2007)	Law
MOSF	"South Korea as the Top Country with the Highest Increasing Rate of ODA Size among the OECD DAC Members in the Last 5 years" (2014)	News article
	MOSF Official Website (2012)	Website
KOICA	KOICA Official Website (2014)	Website
	Glossary of International Development Cooperation Terms (2012)	Website
EDCF	2013 EDCF Annual Report (2014)	Policy document
	EDCF Official Website (2011)	Website
	Glossary of Humanitarian Aid Terms (2011)	Website

the components of human security has changed over time, from freedom from fear in the earlier documents (MOFA 2008) to freedom from want and freedom to live in dignity, in more recent documents. The empowerment approach has been emphasized over time (MOFA 2008).

Table 10.3 presents the summary of the interview results, which show that while there was no explicit use of human security in South Korea's ODA, all the interviewees noted that the term was used implicitly. We further examined which of the elements of human security were in both the explicit as well as the implicit use of the term. One interesting finding is that a few interviewees in CSOs, IOs, and academia were skeptical of the implementation of human security in South Korea's ODA, while the government representatives tended to perceive that it had been implemented. A more detailed discussion of findings from the review of documents and interviews of key ODA stakeholders is presented in the following section.

Table 10.2 Summary of review of documents

Sector	*Institutions/Name*		*Explicit use of the term "Human Security"*				*Elements of "Human Security"*				
			Law	*Policy document*	*Practice*	*Speech*	*Components*[a]			*Approach*[b]	
							F1	*F2*	*F3*	*P*	*E*
Government	President		–	–	–	O	–	–	–	–	–
	PMO		X	X	X	X	O	O	O	O	O
	MOFA		X	X	O	O	O	O	O	O	O
	MOSF		–	X	X	X	X	O	X	X	O
	KOICA		–	X	O	X	O	O	O	O	O
	EDCF		–	X	X	X	X	O	O	X	O
National Assembly	Political Parties	Saenuri	–	X	X	O	X	O	X	O	O
		NPAD	–	X	X	O	O	X	O	X	X
	Foreign Affairs and Unification Committee		X	X	X	X	X	O	X	X	O
Academia	A		–	–	–	–	O	O	O	O	X
	B		–	–	–	–	O	O	O	O	X

[a]F1 refers to freedom from fear; F2 refers to freedom from want; and F3 refers to freedom to live in dignity
[b]P refers to protection; and E refers to empowerment

Table 10.3 Summary of interviews

Sector	*Institution*	*Use of the term "Human Security"*			*Elements of "Human Security"*				
		Explicit use of the term	*Implicit use of the term*	*Policy implementation*	*Components*			*Approach*	
					F1	*F2*	*F3*	*P*	*E*
Government	PMO	X	O	O	O	O	O	O	O
	MOSF	X	O	O	O	O	O	X	O
Civil Society Organizations	World Vision Korea	X	O	X	X	O	X	O	O
International Organization	UN WFP Korea	X	O	O	O	O	O	O	O
	IOM Korea	X	O	X	O	O	O	O	O
Academia	A	X	O	X	O	O	O	O	O
	C	X	O	X	X	X	X	X	X

10.3.1 Government

We examined whether the South Korean government used human security explicitly in various documents, and whether the other elements of human security were used explicitly or implicitly.

In South Korea, the Presidents set the overall tone of ODA policy directions, and thus plays a significant role in ODA policy and implementation. Presidents Roh Moo-hyun (2003–2008), Lee Myung-bak (2008–2013), and Park Geun-hye (2013–2017) all supported ODA, South Korea's ascendance to OECD/DAC, and an increase in the volume of ODA. President Park, for example, used the term during her presidential campaign speech on foreign policy, national security, and unification (November 5, 2012), saying: "I will promote sustainable development and enduring peace in Northeast Asia. I will cooperate with all nations interested in this vision in building trust, cooperation in national security, social and economic relations, and human security" (Geun-hye 2012).

10.3.1.1 The Prime Minister's Office (PMO)

The PMO has been playing an important role in the coordination of various ODA policies, in particular regarding two important modalities of development cooperation in South Korea: grant aid and concessional loans. The CIDC is the oversight committee under the PMO, which reviews and votes on South Korea's overall ODA policy direction and helps with the coordination of grant aid and concessional loans. The PMO and the Ministry of Foreign Affairs put together the *Framework Act on International Development Cooperation* (2010), which was ratified by the National Assembly in 2009. The PMO was put in charge of presenting the Mid-term ODA Policy for 2011–2015 (2010), and the Strategic Plan for International Development Cooperation (2010). To improve the coordination of grant aid and concessional loans, the PMO subsequently published the first ODA White Paper in 2014 (PMO 2014), which was endorsed by all relevant ministries, and presented an overall vision for South Korea's global role for the Millennium Development Goals (MDGs), poverty reduction and development based on its history as a recipient-turned donor. We reviewed the above documents since they included major guidelines for ODA policies.

The Framework Act defines the missions, goals, and principles of ODA. Article 3 of the Framework Act identifies the basic principles of international development cooperation as: reduce poverty in developing countries, improve the human rights of women and children, and achieve gender equality, realize sustainable development and humanitarianism, promote cooperative economic relations with developing partners, and pursue peace and prosperity in the international community.

The Mid-term ODA Policy for 2011–2015 presents policy directions and annual ODA targets, ODA allocation guidelines by region and by income group, and partnership strategy with major developing countries. It includes plans to distribute 40 percent of grants to the least developed countries (LDCs) and fragile states, and 30 percent to countries in conflict (PMO 2010a). The government aims to provide humanitarian assistance in disaster-affected areas, reflecting the freedom from fear (PMO 2014, 65). Its aim to reduce poverty and improve the quality of life in developing countries, which is the freedom to live in dignity (PMO 2014, 52). Bringing hope to recipient countries and emphasizing poverty eradication and self-help reflects the freedom from want and empowerment (PMO 2010b, 13).

The ODA White Paper (2014) included assistance policies and practices, and the aims of international humanitarian assistance and support for fragile states. The ODA White Paper shows that South Korea's ODA aims to reduce poverty in developing countries and promote sustainable development based on humanitarianism. It aims to improve the human rights of women, children, and the handicapped, as well as gender equality in developing countries as stated in Article 3 (PMO 2010b, 52). Emphasis on economic development and human rights refers to the approach to freedom from want and freedom to live in dignity. South Korea's ODA includes infrastructure for development, improvement of relations with developing countries, and solutions for global problems (PMO 2010b).

10.3.1.2 The Ministry of Foreign Affairs (MOFA)

MOFA sets the policy directions for grant aid and coordinates the grant aid projects of line ministries and local government. MOFA affirms the goals for ODA as economic development and poverty reduction of developing countries (MOFA 2014a), and commitments based on humanitarianism and sustainable development (MOFA 2014c). South Korea has endorsed international humanitarian assistance for the protection of basic human rights and freedom from fear (MOFA 2014e). MOFA has included human security in ODA projects and policies based on humanitarianism and human rights for poverty reduction and sustainable development. MOFA and KOICA were two government institutions that used human security in their official documents, but that was only in the reference section explaining ODA terminology. In other words, MOFA used human security in policy documents in 2008, but it was used in broader discussions on foreign policy without an explicit focus on ODA.

MOFA stated that human security has become very important given that we are faced with non-traditional security threats including terrorism, environmental degradation, transnational crimes, internal conflict, poverty, and disasters. And it further discussed the concept of human security as follows: "Individual security and safety, protection of human rights, and protection of an individual's basic necessities" (MOFA 2008). Protection of individual safety and human dignity are seen as important for international peace and security. Thus, the government affirms the basic goals of human security and the international community's emphasis on human security, and "common value of humanism" (MOFA 2008). MOFA has stated that "there is a need to cooperate at the regional and global levels to deal with traditional as well as non-traditional security threats" (MOFA 2008). This is in line with the freedom from fear component of human security.

Minister Yun Byung-se of MOFA used human security at an international conference in 2013, *New Strategic Thinking: Planning for Korean Foreign Policy*, which was the first time a Minister of MOFA had used the term human security (Yun 2013). He stated that the global policies of the Park Administration "reflect the belief that peace and prosperity of South Korea and the world are indivisible, and that there has been a global paradigm shift which emphasizes the importance of human security" (Yun 2013). For further clarification, the lead author of this chapter asked Minister Yun whether his use of the term was deliberate and referred to human security in ODA. He responded that this was based on his firm conviction about human security in South Korea's international development cooperation.[4]

In terms of international humanitarian assistance, MOFA's *Overseas Emergency Relief Act* 2007 details the law and implementation guidelines for international humanitarian assistance (F2). MOFA has affirmed its implementation of the UN Security Council Resolution 1325 on Women, Peace and Security (MOFA 2014b), and emphasized empowering women in conflict prevention, conflict resolution, and peacebuilding. MOFA's documents show a strong interest in human security in all three components and both approaches although the term is not used explicitly. In addition, the Framework Act's Article 3 highlights: reduction of poverty (freedom from want); human rights of women, children, and the handicapped, and gender equality (freedom to live in dignity); and sustainable development, humanitarianism, and peace (MOFA 2014f). MOFA included "strengthening of humanitarian assistance and peace building effort for the regions in conflict" in the six strategic goals of its ODA (freedom from fear). It aims to gradually increase ODA for human security and humanitarian assistance.

The South Korean government has been expanding international humanitarian assistance through active participation with UNDP, UN WFP, UNICEF, and International Committee of the Red Cross (ICRC). It has raised the effectiveness of humanitarian assistance by working closely with international humanitarian organizations and consultative groups (MOFA 2014f). The government embraces both the protection and empowerment approaches in humanitarian assistance and tries to link short-term humanitarian assistance and long-term reconstruction efforts with disaster risk reduction (DRR) (MOFA 2014f). MOFA announced the *Strategic Plan for International Humanitarian Assistance* (May 2010) and the *Strategic Plan for International Development Cooperation* (October 2010), and expanded the emergency relief budget and trained and dispatched humanitarian assistance professionals in humanitarian crises. These efforts reflected the government's effort to expand international humanitarian assistance and improve the overseas emergency relief system (MOFA 2014d).

10.3.1.3 The Ministry of Strategy and Finance (MOSF)

MOSF supervises concessional loans and provides policy advice to developing countries based on its development experience. The MOSF website states that South Korea has been noted to have the highest rate of increase in ODA volume among OECD/DAC members, and that it has provided aid tailored to the needs of partner countries in Africa and Asia (MOSF 2014). The website shows that this policy consultation and technical assistance reflected South Korea's economic development. Interviews with a MOSF official showed that the three freedoms of human security, as well as protection and empowerment, were embraced in concessional loans, although the term was not explicitly used.

10.3.1.4 The Korea International Cooperation Agency (KOICA)

KOICA provides grant aid projects and programs to developing countries. The former refers to economic and technical cooperation projects with a single focus, while the latter refers to multi-faceted programs for nationwide development. Both aim to provide the foundation for economic development in developing countries (freedom from want) (KOICA 2014e). Its aid is based on the universal value of humanitarianism including democracy and human rights for poverty reduction and follows the freedom from want and freedom to live in dignity (KOICA 2014d).

KOICA recognizes that extreme poverty still exists even with the massive social development that has occurred since World War II, and that people in developed countries have a moral obligation to assist other countries that are unable to provide for the basic livelihood of their people (KOICA 2014c). These efforts are linked to the freedom from fear and freedom to live in dignity. KOICA refereed to the 1961 Pearson Report, which argued that the world community is a singular world where everyone is dependent on others for survival (KOICA 2014c). For example, KOICA's food aid is an important example for freedom from want and takes two forms: (1) food to countries with food shortages due to famine, wars, and lack of capability; and (2) cash to countries for food purchases (KOICA 2014c).

In terms of human security, KOICA stated that this can be achieved when individuals are protected from various threats to their lives. Thus, we can see that KOICA uses the concept of human security in terms of freedom from fear as well as protection and empowerment (KOICA 2014b). KOICA provides emergency and distress relief to developing countries that have experienced disasters that cannot be handled with their own resources. These include natural, man-made, and complex disasters (KOICA 2014a), all of which can lead to human suffering and loss of crops and livestock.

KOICA's approach on gender equality and empowering women reflects the empowerment approach to human security (KOICA 2014a). For example, the Ewha-KOICA Master Degree Program in Gender and Development is jointly implemented by KOICA and Ewha Womans University in South Korea. The program accepts female government officials from developing countries. It has been implemented since 2007, and has produced over 250 graduates from sub-Saharan Africa, Asia, and Latin America. The goal is to educate and empower women so that they can contribute to gender equality and achieve poverty reduction and development in their home nations. In sum, KOICA embraces the three freedoms of human security as well as protection and empowerment in its grant aid programs and projects.

10.3.1.5 *The Economic Development Cooperation Fund (EDCF)*

The EDCF provides concessional loans in the spirit of reciprocal economic cooperation and universal value of humanity with developing countries as partners for economic development, which is in line with freedom to live life in dignity in human security (EDCF 2014a). The EDCF includes support for economic and social infrastructure, public health, education, and environment to meet basic human needs, which is in line with freedom from want and freedom to live in dignity in terms of human security (EDCF 2014a). In addition, EDCF provided technical cooperation to Indonesia for the "National Information and Communication Technologies (ICT) Human Resources Development Project" for IT infrastructure and E-government (EDCF 2014b), which contributed to the empowerment of the people.

10.3.2 *The National Assembly*

Review of official documents from the National Assembly, including laws, policies, and by-laws, showed that it does not explicitly use the term human security. However, the two leading political parties used human security when referring to the overall direction of the government's foreign policy, although the reference was not directly to ODA. Our review of the National Assembly's official documents showed that the concept of human security was implicitly used by the two leading parties and the Foreign Affairs and Unification Committee. However, the findings show that neither the political parties nor the National Assembly Committee used the term explicitly, and reference to the elements of human security is therefore quite mixed.

10.3.2.1 *The Foreign Affairs and Unification Committee*

The Foreign Affairs and Unification Committee (referred to as "the Committee" in this section), which is one of the committees of the National Assembly, oversees the budget and activities of MOFA and the Ministry of Unification, including foreign policy, ODA, and national security. We reviewed the meeting minutes and relevant documents of this committee, since this is the only committee that oversees ODA in the National Assembly.

The Committee members argued for a shift in the paradigm for ODA projects toward respecting the developing countries' ownership and their needs at a current affairs briefing on June 18, 2013. This reflects the empowerment approach to human security, which focuses on self-help and independence (Foreign Affairs and Unification Committee 2013a). The Committee also stated that South Korea as a donor should reflect its own history as a long-term recipient of aid. As an example of such an experience, it recommended that the Saemaul Undong (New Village Movement), which is considered to be a successful rural village development project from South Korea's experience in the 1970s, could be introduced to developing countries to promote self-reliance, autonomy, and development (Foreign Affairs and Unification Committee 2013a). In the current affairs brief (summary notes) dated December 1, 2013, the Committee promoted a "can do" spirit, and capacity building based on customized assistance for the recipient countries rather than a donor-driven assistance project, which are in line with the empowerment approach in human security. In sum, the Committee's various recommendations on ODA reflect its understanding in line with the freedom from want and empowerment in human security (Foreign Affairs and Unification Committee 2013b).

10.3.2.2 The Saenuri Party

The incumbent Saenuri Party worked hard to improve South Korea's global role with development cooperation. The Saenuri Party worked with relevant government ministries, including the Ministry of Education, MOFA, and the Ministry of Culture, Sports and Tourism, to educate and train personnel from developing countries for advanced degrees and job training related to empowerment in human security.

On December 21, 2007, then President-elect Lee Myung-bak stated that he would provide strong support for ODA and Peacekeeping Operations (PKO) to the UN Secretary-General Ban Ki-moon.[5] The Saenuri Party, quoting President Lee, stated in 2007: "the government will focus on economic diplomacy and will pay greater attention to human security, including the environment, human rights, poverty and illnesses."[6] Mr. Park Hee-tae, who was the Saenuri Party's Supreme Council member, stated in his 2008 speech that the party would support an ODA budget expansion to US$3 billion by 2015, increase food aid to US$100 million, and promote agricultural productivity growth. These commitments are in line with the freedom from want perspective in human security. He also stated that PKO activities should be expanded.[7] In sum, there was support for all three freedoms as well as the empowerment approach within the Saenuri Party.

10.3.2.3 The New Politics Alliance for Democracy (NPAD)

The NPAD was the leading opposition party and President Roh Moo-hyun (2003–2008) was a member. The NPAD stated in the position paper "Peace Diplomacy and Public Diplomacy Contributing to the Global Community," that it will promote peace diplomacy based on the universal values of humanity, democracy, and anti-terrorism (New Politics Alliance for Democracy 2014). These reflect an endorsement of freedom from want, freedom from fear as well as the freedom to live in dignity.

NPAD's presidential candidate Mr. Moon Jae-in used the concept of non-traditional security during the 2012 presidential campaign: "I will uphold the vision of international cooperation based on global norms.[8] I will promote international cooperation to deal with non-traditional security issues including climate change, human security, and natural disasters" (Moon 2012). The NPAD has been a progressive party and supported the expansion of ODA volume and promoted an active global role for South Korea in global poverty reduction and development.

10.3.3 Civil Society Organizations (CSOs) and International Organizations (IOs)

We interviewed representatives from World Vision Korea from the CSOs, and UN WFP Korea and IOM Korea among the IOs. We asked questions about the use of human security (explicit and implicit), and which of the elements of human security were reflected in their human security. All three interviewees noted that the term human security was not used explicitly in statements on South Korea's ODA. The interviewees from World Vision Korea and IOM Korea stated that they felt that the concept of human security was not implemented in the South Korean ODA, while the UN WFP Korea interviewee felt that the concept was implemented in the South Korean ODA. Their interview responses are summarized in Table 3.

10.3.4 Academia

Members of the academic community have played a very important role in South Korea's ODA community. Thus, we selected three professors whose research and/or policy advice have been critical in shaping South Korea's ODA, which has a special focus on human security. Interviews with Professors A and C showed that the term human security has not been used explicitly, but implicitly in the South Korean ODA. Professor A noted that South Korea's ODA is in line with the protection approach in human security (Howe 2012), and draws on the UNDP's holistic approach to human security, which deals with all three freedoms in human security (Howe 2013). Professor B argued that South Korea's ODA activities, as based on its own history of successful development, can present a role model for developing countries and shows the importance of building the capability of empowerment (Lee 2013).

10.4 Concluding Remarks

South Korea's different institutions have shown varying levels of reception of human security. Government ministries and aid implementation agencies have embraced the concept of human security in their official documents and policies but have not fully implemented human security in their ODA programs. The Government, National Assembly, and political parties favor the concept of human security in terms of freedom from fear, freedom from want, and freedom to live in dignity. Both the protection and empowerment approaches are recognized in the official documents reviewed. On the other hand, the academic experts were skeptical about the government's use of human security in ODA policies and practices. The CSOs and IOs were also mixed in their perception of how the government has used human security in ODA, although they agreed that human security was implicitly used.

In conclusion, the South Korean government has not explicitly but has implicitly used the term human security in its official documents and policies. All three freedoms of human security and the protection and empowerment approaches can be found in ODA-related government documents. Further empirical research is needed to examine if human security is being realized in ODA activities, and whether the emphasis on human security will be strengthened. President Moon Jae-in, who took office in May 2017, is from a more progressive party, and was active in the NPAD. Thus, it will be important to examine whether a more progressive government will have a stronger focus on human security in its ODA policies and projects. But, while it appears that the concept as well as practice of human security may be important in South Korean ODA, it also appears to be domestically even more important since the Korean peninsula itself is faced with nuclear threats among other natural and man-made disasters.

Notes

1. South Korea's ODA does not include its assistance to North Korea, since South Korea's constitution includes North Korea as part of a larger Korea, and not as a separate country. OECD/DAC defines ODA as international development cooperation between nation-states. Thus, South Korea's assistance for North Korea cannot be counted toward its ODA. Hence this chapter does not deal with South Korea's assistance to North Korean refugees or other types of humanitarian support for North Korea.
2. Implicit use refers to when the meaning of human security is embraced without explicit use of the term.
3. Political parties have changed their names, and a more progressive government has taken office in 2017. Please note that the party's name and political position—incumbent versus opposition party—is based on the empirical research in 2014.
4. Eun Mee Kim, 2014, asked the Minister for clarification of his use of the term *human security* in his speech, and he confirmed his knowledge of the term and meaning.
5. President-elect Myung-bak Lee, 2014, telephone communication with the Secretary-General Ban Ki-moon of the UN.
6. Lee Myung-bak, 2008, Focus on Environment and Human Rights as Part of Human Security.
7. The Saenuri Party's Supreme Council member Hee-tae Park, 2014, comments made at the luncheon with the ambassadors from combatant nations of the Korean War commemorating United Nations Day.
8. Although Moon lost the 2012 election, he was elected President in May 2017.

References

EDCF (Economic Development Cooperation Fund). 2014a. About EDCF: Policy Direction of EDCF. Accessed 19 July 2014. http://www.edcfkorea.go.kr/edcf/intro/idea.jsp

———. 2014b. About EDCF Projects. http://www.edcfkorea.go.kr/edcf/job/kind/fund_devel.jsp. Accessed 19 July 2014.

Foreign Affairs and Unification Committee. 2013a. MOFA Current Affairs Report. Working Paper from 316th Provisional Meeting (MOFA). http://uft.na.go.kr/site. Accessed 19 July 2014.

———. 2013b. National Auditing Report of the Committee (Summary Report). http://uft.na.go.kr/site?siteId=site000001025&pageId=page000002431&bd_mode=read&bd_pageNumber=1&bd_searchTerm=&bd_searchKeyword=&bd_recordId=2014010040520. Accessed 26 June 2014.

———. 2014. Overview of the Committee. http://uft.na.go.kr/site?siteId=site000001025&pageId=page000002317. Accessed 30 July 2014.

Geun-hye, Park. 2012. Presidential Candidate of the Saenuri Party, Park's Policies on Foreign Policy, National Security and Unification. *News 1*, November 5. http://news1.kr/articles/?880552.

Howe, Brendan. 2012. Lessons Learned for Promoting Human Security in North Korea. *The Korean Journal of Defense Analysis* 24 (4): 483–489.

———. 2013. *The Protection and Promotion of Human Security in East Asia*. Hampshire: Palgrave Macmillan.

KOICA (Korea International Cooperation Agency). 2014a. KOICA Projects. http://www.koica.go.kr/. Last Accessed 20 July 2018.

———. 2014b. ODA: Glossary of International Development Cooperation Terms. http://www.koica.go.kr/. Last Accessed 20 July 2018.

———. 2014c. ODA: History of Development Aid. http://www.koica.go.kr/. Last Accessed 4 Apr 2018.

———. 2014d. ODA: Objective of Development Aid. http://www.koica.go.kr/. Last Accessed 4 Apr 2018.

———. 2014e. ODA: Strategy of South Korea's Development Aid. http://www.koica.go.kr/. Last Accessed 4 Apr 2018.

Lee, Myung-bak. 2008. Focus on Environment and Human Rights as Part of Human Security. *Dailian*, January 17. http://www.dailian.co.kr/news/view/98118

Lee, Shin-wha. 2013. Analysis of South Korea's Contribution to Peace-Keeping Operations. *The Journal of Asiatic Studies* 56 (2): 188–225.

MOFA (Ministry of Foreign Affairs of South Korea). 2008. The South Korean Government's Views on Human Security. http://www.mofa.go.kr/webmodule/htsboard/template/read/korboardread.jsp?typeID=6&boardid=102&seqno=316170&c=&t=&pagenum=1&tableName=TYPE_DATABOARD&pc=&dc=&wc=&lu=&vu=&iu=&du=. Accessed 14 July 2014.

———. 2014a. Development Cooperation. http://www.mofa.go.kr/trade/development/index.jsp?menu=m_30_130. Accessed 1 June 2014.

———. 2014b. Establishment of National Action Plan for the United Nations Security Council Resolution 1325 on Women, Peace and Security. http://www.mofa.go.kr/news/pressinformation/index.jsp?mofat=001&menu=m_20_30&sp=/webmodule/htsboard/template/read/korboardread.jsp%3FtypeID=6%26boardid=235%26tableName=TYPE_DATABOARD%26seqno=350441. Accessed 5 June 2014.

———. 2014c. ODA Propelling System and Support Status. http://www.mofa.go.kr/trade/development/propulsion/index.jsp?mofat=001&menu=m_30_130_20. Accessed 1 June 2014.

———. 2014d. Overseas Emergency Relief. http://www.devco.go.kr/contents.do?contentsNo=45&menuNo=255. Accessed 5 June 2014.

———. 2014e. Policy Direction of South Korea's Development Cooperation. http://www.mofa.go.kr/trade/development/policy/index.jsp?mofat=001&menu=m_30_130_10. Accessed 1 June 2014.
———. 2014f. The Framework Act on International Development Cooperation. http://www.law.go.kr/lsInfoP.do?lsiSeq=142005&efYd=20140101#0000. Accessed 5 June 2014.
Moon, Jae-in. 2012. The New Politics Alliance for Democracy. Speech by the Presidential Candidate, Jae-in Moon at the Press Interview with the Seoul Foreign Press Club. http://news.naver.com/main/read.nhn?mode=LSD&mid=sec&sid1=123&oid=305&aid=0000010342. Last Accessed 19 July 2018.
MOSF (Ministry of Strategy and Finance). 2014. South Korea as the Top Country with the Highest Increasing Rate of ODA Size among the OECDDAC Members in the Last 5 Years. *Policy Briefing*. http://www.korea.kr/policy/diplomacyView.do?newsId=148776676&call_from=naver_news. Accessed 8 Apr 2014.
New Politics Alliance for Democracy. 2014. Doctrine, Platform Policies. http://npad.kr/?page_id=265. Accessed 20 June 2014.
PMO (Prime Minister's Office). 2010a. Mid-term ODA Policy for 2011–2015. http://odakorea.go.kr/ODAPage_2012/T02/L01_S04.jsp. Last Accessed 21 Dec 2017.
———. 2010b. Strategic Plan for International Development Cooperation (Strategic Plan). http://odakorea.go.kr/hz.blltn.PolicySl.do?bltn_seq=105&sys_cd=&brd_seq=9&targetRow=31&blltn_div=oda&searchKey=01&keyword=. Last Accessed 25 Oct 2017.
———. 2014. ODA White Paper. http://odakorea.go.kr/hz.blltn.PolicySl.do?bltn_seq=158&sys_cd=&brd_seq=9&targetRow=&blltn_div=oda&searchKey=01&keyword=. Last Accessed 20 Apr 2018.
Yun, Byung-se. 2013. Opening Remarks. Speech at the New Strategic Thinking: Planning for Korean Foreign Policy Conference. http://www.mofa.go.kr/webmodule/htsboard/template/read/korboardread.jsp?typeID=9&boardid=749&seqno=301856. Accessed 28 Apr 2013.

Interviews

Government Source #1. 2014. Expert Advisor from the Prime Minister's Office. Interviewed by the author (mailed questionnaire), July 9.
Government Source #2. 2014. Deputy Director of the Ministry of Strategy and Finance (MOSF). Interviewed by the author (mailed questionnaire), July 11.
Academia Source #1. 2014. Professor at Ewha Womans University. Interviewed by the author in Seoul, July 10.
Academia Source #2. 2014. Professor at Kyung Hee University. Interviewed by the author in Seoul, July 7.

Civil Society Organization Source #1. 2014. Director of Advocacy team at World Vision Korea. Interviewed by the author in Seoul, July 7.
International Organization Source #1. 2014. Head of the UNWFP Korea Office. Interviewed by the author in Seoul, July 7.
International Organization Source #2. 2014. Head of IOM Korea. Interviewed by the author in Seoul, July 4.

CHAPTER 11

Human Security in Practice in Thailand

Surangrut Jumnianpol and Nithi Nuangjamnong

11.1 Introduction

This chapter examines the practice of human security in the Thai polity. In doing so, the researchers realize that, while necessary, an analysis of the policy content as well as the perceptions of the policy stakeholder may be insufficient to grasp the overall picture of human security. The current unprecedented chaotic dynamism in Thai politics, moving back and forth within a closed circuit of democratic elections, polarization within civil society, and a series of vehement protests (red and yellow shirts) and coups (September 2006 and May 2014), best demonstrates how the political context can badly erode the human security situation in a community. This research, then, analyzes human security policy in relation to its political context.

In attempting to elaborate on why and how Thai policymakers have imported and embraced the concept of human security in the Thai polity, as well as how they perceive the values and challenges related to human security issues, the authors primarily employ qualitative research methods.

S. Jumnianpol (✉)
Social Research Institute, Chulalongkorn University, Bangkok, Thailand
e-mail: surangrut.j@chula.ac.th

N. Nuangjamnong
Faculty of Social Sciences, Naresuan University, Phitsanulok, Thailand

Y. Mine et al. (eds.), *Human Security Norms in East Asia*, Security, Development and Human Rights in East Asia,
https://doi.org/10.1007/978-3-319-97247-3_11

Data were gathered from a variety of sources, both primary and secondary. First, we focus on the roles of policy actors that can be observed from various sources, such as government publications, policy statements, speeches, feasibility studies, newspaper interviews, and policy-related activities. We also pay equal attention to other variables, such as the roles and positions of stakeholders and other actors in civil society, and the changing international and domestic context, which may affect policy outcomes as well.

Apart from the content analyses resulting from documentary research, it is equally necessary to gather information from in-depth and informal interviews with key informants. Basically, we have identified two groups of key informants: first, key actors or direct policy stakeholders; and second, observers or those who may not be direct actors in the human security policy network but have some close connection with this policy issue. The first group of key informants includes officials from the Ministry of Social Development and Human Security (MSDHS) and other related agencies, such as the Office of the National Economic and Social Development Board (NESDB). The second group consists of academics, independent organizations, such as the National Human Rights Commission, civil society organizations, and an independent policy consultant.

This study is organized into five parts. The first and second parts cover the conceptualization and institutionalization of human security in Thailand. The history of human security in Thailand can be analytically divided into two periods, namely, human security as foreign policy and human security as social welfare.[1] The first part focuses on the first stage, while the second demonstrates the significant deviation of the human security approach toward social welfare. The third part elucidates how the concepts have been operationalized and perceived by key policy actors in Thailand. This section aims to compare human security as perceived by policy actors with the human security that appears in the policy papers and policy actions of agencies. The fourth part of the chapter examines human security in practice in Thailand through the case study of human trafficking. Finally, the chapter raises some critical observations about the characteristics of human security in Thailand.

11.2 Human Security as Foreign Policy

It is difficult to pinpoint exactly when the concept was first employed in Thailand. One Thai academic work that was seemingly akin to the concept of human security was the book, *Environment and Security: State Security and Citizens' Insecurity* (Samudavanija and Snitwongse na Ayudhaya 1992). This book, however, was first published in 1992, two years before the official launch of the human security concept by the United Nations Development Programme (UNDP 1994). What we can say for certain is that human security became increasingly popular in the aftermath of the 1997 Asian economic crisis, and the most vocal presenter of this concept at that time was Surin Pitsuwan, who was then the Minister of Foreign Affairs. Yet the first official Thai statement on human security did not aim primarily to develop the concept on home soil but rather represented an attempt to promote this concept within the regional forum of the Association of Southeast Asian Nations (ASEAN).

By the time Thailand proposed the human security initiative at the regional level, the concept had become increasingly contested, particularly among the middle powers. Apart from the conceptualization of human security as "freedom from fear and freedom from want" by UNDP, some states, notably Canada and Japan, began to promote their own styles of human security; the political and developmental approach, respectively (Tadjbakhsh and Chenoy 2007, 28–34). For its part, the Thai government adopted a balanced but comprehensive approach to human security that incorporated both political and developmental dimensions. This is clearly reflected in Surin Pitsuwan's statement at the 1999 Lysoen Meeting that, "whichever way we conceive it [human security]...fears and wants must be accommodated."[2] This position was in line with the UNDP's first version of human security.

During this stage, it seemed that Thailand employed two strategies for promoting human security, namely bending with the wind depending on the human security initiatives of the middle powers at the international level and taking the lead at the regional level. Thailand started with the latter strategy first. At the ASEAN Post-Ministerial Conference (PMC) in Manila in July 1998, Surin Pitsuwan proposed the idea of setting up the ASEAN-PMC Caucus on Human Security. The main rationale for this was that regional cooperation on human security could ameliorate various aspects of human suffering that resulted from severe economic crises, such as unemployment, poverty, and a lack of social safety nets and welfare (Pitsuwan 1998). Nevertheless, Thailand's first endeavor to promote human security at the regional level received only a lukewarm response from other ASEAN members, as most of them were uncomfortable with the language and implications of "human security," believing that it might adversely affect state sovereignty. As a result, the title of the caucus was accordingly changed to Social Safety Nets (Capie and Evans 2002, 144).

This failure induced Thai policymakers to alter their human security approach, giving rise to the "bamboo in the wind strategy." Between the competing camps of human security led by Canada and Japan, Thailand did not take a specific side. It participated in both sides of the activities. In 1999, Thailand joined a coalition of the Human Security Network (HSN), an initiative of Canada and Norway. Thailand played an active role in this network as its chairman in 2002 (MFA 2012). Apart from its involvement in the Human Security Network, Thailand also supported the R2P agenda promoted by the Canadian government (Kraisoraphong 2012). Thailand also took part in various Japanese-led human security initiatives. When Japan launched the Commission on Human Security in 2001, the then Thai Minister of Foreign Affairs Surin Pitsuwan was appointed as one of its ten distinguished commissioners. Later, Surin Pitsuwan and Vitit Muntarbhorn, a law professor from Chulalongkorn University, were also appointed as members of the Advisory Board on Human Security.

Three observations can be made regarding the introduction of the human security concept into Thailand in the first stage. First, the post-1997 crisis context provided an almost perfect setting for both policymakers and academics to import or invent new reform ideas. At that time several ideas, such as social capital, social safety nets, good governance, and civil society, appeared and became popular buzzwords in Thai society. Second, policy architects or reform importers of human security were mostly from the Ministry of Foreign Affairs. It was Surin Pitsuwan, the then Thai Foreign Minister, who assumed the key role as a human security policy architect and steered the direction of policy during the first stage. Finally, Thailand's human security campaign in this first stage seemed to seek external rather than internal reform impact. The underlying objective might have been to achieve status as a norm leader, at least at the regional level, and as an active member of the progressive camp in international society (Cheeppensook 2007).

11.3 Human Security as Social Welfare

It should also be noted that during the first stage, there was another remarkable attempt that could have potentially become a monumental accomplishment in human security in Thailand, namely the formation of the MSDHS. This ministry was established after major bureaucratic reform. Thai officials and academics often proclaim that it was perhaps the first human security ministry in the world. The work of this ministry portrays the defining characteristics of the second stage of human security in Thailand.

Before considering how human security has been institutionalized in this second period, it would be worthwhile examining the background of the MSDHS in brief. The MSDHS was the product of major bureaucratic reform in 2002 that reorganized several agencies responsible for social affairs into a single ministry. An interesting point to note in this regard is that the idea of having a human security ministry was deliberated on in a workshop on social policy rather than one on security.[3] At first, there was a proposal to relocate the social welfare functions of the Ministry of Labor and Social Welfare to the newly created ministry, which was initially named the Ministry of Social Development and Quality of Life (Lokwanne 2001). Later, at a workshop in September 2011, the phrase "quality of life" in the Ministry's name was replaced by "human security." Although there is no clear evidence pinpointing who first proposed the use of the words "human security,"[4] one thing that is certain is that state officials, academics, and civil society actors were not involved in the process. According to Professor Surichai Wun'Gaeo, one of the commissioners on the Commission on Bureaucratic Reform, in the two or three months before it finalized the bureaucratic reform plan, the Thaksin government never convened meetings of the commission; instead, there were only high-level meetings among key members of the cabinet (Krungthep Turakit 2002).

Another interesting fact is that there is only one department in the MSDHS, the Department of Social Development and Welfare, which stands at the Ministry's core.[5] This department is the reincarnation of the Department of Public Welfare (DPW), which was previously under the Ministry of Interior and then the Ministry of Labor and Social Welfare. The key mandate of this department was to address what the Thai state considered to be social ills, such as beggars, homeless persons, and prostitutes, and to provide basic relief to vulnerable groups, such as orphans, the handicapped and disabled, and senior citizens. This department, which had long been regarded as a C-grade department in the Ministry of Interior, was criticized for lacking policy direction and the resilience needed to adapt to new social challenges (Vichit-Vadakan 1989).

The working philosophy of the DPW originated from the Thai-style Buddhist philanthropic value that the rulers and "the haves" should help "the have-nots" (Department of Public Welfare 2000, 28). This implies the existence of hierarchical relations between rulers and the ruled and is clearly reflected in the name of the department as expressed in the Thai language, *prachasongraha*. The first word, *pracha*, means people. The second word, *songraha*, gives the sense of helping those in need. In earlier times, the function of *songraha* was bound up with temples, which were usually under the patronage of the haves, whether members of the royal family, the nobility, or merchants. When the modern nation state was formed, this function was gradually centralized and institutionalized under bureaucratic agencies (Department of Public Welfare 2000, 28). The key point illustrated by this research is that the newly founded MSDHS inherited the organizational culture and worldview of the DPW or, to put it idiomatically, the old wine of traditional Thai-style social welfare has been put in the new bottle of human security.[6] The possible problem stemming from this situation is that the old culture may not be compatible with the new norm.

This was definitely the case when MSDHS officials started working under the new ministry. According to three informants who had worked for the DPW before being transferred to the MSDHS, about two-thirds of the officials in the MSDHS could not comprehend what was meant by the term human security (Government #3; #4; #5 2014). One of their very first tasks, therefore, was to research the definition, scope, and ways of operationalizing this concept in practice.[7] Their challenge was compounded by the fact that at that time, there was virtually no research on human security in the Thai language, and there was no course on human security in the Thai university curriculum (Saracharas 2002).

In terms of operationalizing the concept of human security, MSDHS officials seem to have adopted a two-pronged strategy. First, they sought and received technical support from actors outside the ministry, particularly from the academic sector and international organizations. It is worth pointing out that most of the support the MSDHS received from these actors was primarily aimed at mainstreaming human security into Thai public policymaking and habituating the MSDHS to the new concept. Second, there also seemed to be a return to DPW's basic philosophy of *songraha*, which emphasized the functions of social welfare for vulnerable groups.[8] Key informants from MSDHS considered this concept unenthusiastically as a discourse whose essence did not substantially differ from its predecessors, such as social security, social protection, social work, and social welfare (Government #4; #5 2014). This is probably why the very broad concept of human security was simply narrowed down to social welfare issues by MSDHS officials. This is clearly reflected in the MSDHS's organizational design, official policy papers, and action plan.

The narrow focus of the ministry on the provision of welfare for vulnerable groups was indeed reflected in a speech made by Prime Minister Thaksin on its establishment: "In October [2002], we established a new ministry, the Ministry of Social Development and Human Security, to take care of some helpless people in society and certain groups, such as the handicapped, the poor, women and children…." (Saracharas 2003). In addition to the interpretation of human security as social welfare, two other interrelated values also defined the meaning and direction of the ministry: self-sufficiency and communitarianism.

It was Thai King Rama IX who had proposed the idea of self-sufficiency on various occasions since the 1970s. The idea became crystallized in a speech made by the King in December 1997 as a guideline for economic recovery in the wake of the 1997 economic crisis. Since then, it has become a hegemonic ideology in Thailand (Elinoff 2014). Consequently, Thai public policy circles since then have witnessed an increasing use of the "self-sufficiency" bottle, or key word, to contain and probably legitimize policy content, notwithstanding some considerable incompatibility and incoherence between certain policies and the self-sufficiency principle (Chambers 2013; Table 11.1).

Although all Thai governments in this second period tended to equate human security primarily with social welfare, there were nevertheless some variations in policy direction from each. During the period of the Thaksin government, in addition to social welfare and communitarianism, another

Table 11.1 Evolving key words and core values of MSDHS under various Thai regimes

Period	*Key words and core values*
Thaksin government (2001–2006)	Social welfare for vulnerable groups, populist policies (housing for the poor), communitarianism, anti-human trafficking
Military regime (2006–2007) and Abhisit government (2008–2011)	Social welfare for vulnerable groups, good society or society with morality, self-sufficiency, communitarianism, anti-human trafficking
Pheu Thai government (2011–2014)	Social welfare for vulnerable groups, anti-human trafficking, communitarianism
Military regime (2014–present)	Social welfare for vulnerable groups, society with morality, self-sufficiency, communitarianism, anti-human trafficking

key mandate of the MSDHS was to implement the so-called populist policy of providing 1 million units of housing for the poor. In contrast, the popular key words of the MSDHS during the military regimes (2006–2007 and 2014–Present) and the Abhisit government were "good society" or "society with morality and self-sufficiency" (Pinprateep and Ubonsawat 2006). Interestingly, the change from a military to a civilian regime under the Abhisit administration was not accompanied by a significant policy departure but instead featured policy continuity, especially regarding the strategic focus on "society with morality." When politics returned temporarily to a state of normalcy under the elected civilian government of the *Pheu Thai* Party, however, the core values of the ministry reverted to social welfare and communitarianism (MSDHS 2014a).

11.4 Local Definitions and Perceptions

According to an official policy paper, the MSDHS defines human security in the broadest sense as a "person who has self-reliant [sic] and can access to basic need as dignity and sustainable including live in society as normal and happiness life" (MSDHS 2013, 50).[9] This official definition of human security reflects an attempt to localize the alien concept of human security to suit the Thai context. First, it opts for "basic needs" instead of "(freedom from) want," which is considered a problematic concept because of its subjectivity and all-inclusive character (Government #5 2014). Second, the definition officially incorporates the idea of "freedom to live with dignity." The reason for this, according to a key informant in the MSDHS, is that notwithstanding its vagueness and abstraction, it enables practitioners to relate human security to social concepts that are familiar to them, such as public welfare, social development, and the social safety net (Government #4 2014). Third, by putting the words "self-reliance" at the beginning of the definition, there seems to be a marriage of convenience between the human security concept and the local hegemonic ideology of the self-sufficiency philosophy. Finally, the MSDHS's version of the definition intentionally omits "freedom from fear," one of the core components of human security.

Regarding the major challenges to human security, the MSDHS derives its perspective from the 11th National Economic and Social Development Plan, which identifies major threats such as globalization, regionalization, aging society, drug addiction among youth, weakness of Thai identity, and weakness of family (MSDHS 2014b).[10] Based on the scope of human security and the interpretation of threats to human security, the MSDHS has specified action plans focusing on the four particular target groups, namely youth, women, elderly, and people with disabilities. The MSDHS also utilizes and operationalizes this concept through the development of a monitoring and reporting mechanism on human security standards and the *Annual Social and Human Security Report*. It should be noted that even though the standards were based on the UNDP's seven dimensions of human security, the Thai human security standards were slightly different because of the expanded agenda that human security in the Thai context encompasses, as shown in Table 11.2.

Although a concrete version of human security has been operationalized in the form of the Human Security Standards/Human Security Index, there is still no guarantee of actual implementation. As mentioned

Table 11.2 Comparing human security standards

UNDP (1994) 7 essential dimensions of human security	*Major elements of MSDHS human security standards*		
	2003 11 dimensions at personal level	*2005 10 dimensions at personal and community level*	*2011 12 dimensions at personal level*
Economic security	Economic security	Employment and income	Employment and income
Food security	Food security		Food security
Environmental security	Environmental security		Environment/ resource and energy
Health security	Health security	Health security	Health
Personal security	Personal security	Personal security	Life and assets safety
Community security	Community security	Social support	Community and social support
Political security	Political security	Rights and Justice	Rights and Justice
		Politics and governance	Political security
	Shelter and inhabitants	Shelter and inhabitants	Shelter and inhabitants
	Education	Education	Education
	Family	Family	Family
	Religion and culture	Religion and culture	Religion and culture

above, the MSDHS action plan narrowly focuses on providing welfare and support to target groups, which directly covers only four dimensions of human security, namely employment and income, community and social support, shelter and inhabitants, and family. There is virtually no implementation plan for the remaining eight dimensions, which are under the jurisdiction of other ministries and agencies.

Moreover, some of the indicators developed in the Human Security Standards have never been shown. To cite one example, in the environmental security dimension there are five indicators, yet only three of them are associated with data in the 2011 Thai *Human Security Report* (MSDHS 2011; Government #3 2014). This is partly attributable to the fact that the MSDHS depends mostly on secondary data from other agencies and is not equipped with the authority to order them to gather needed information. In this sense, the Human Security Standards resembles a rather luxurious reporting tool that has virtually no policy impact.

These shortcomings in official human security definitions and standards partially correspond with perceptions from various policy actors namely bureaucrats from the MSDHS and the Office of the NESDB, an academic, a non-governmental organization (NGO) leader, and a policy consultant (Table 11.3). First, regarding the definition and core values of human security, most actors tended to agree that the major limitation of this concept is its elusiveness. However, different actors perceive the core values of human security differently. While the bureaucrats saw it as another academic jargon having no difference from other social concepts, an academic considered it as an opportunity to open policy space to marginalized policy stakeholders. Intriguingly, a key informant from civil society did not enthusiastically embrace this concept and felt that the discourse of human rights has been much more powerful.

Second, while government officials considered poverty as the most daunting challenges of human security, other actors were concerned more about such political and transnational issues as the protracted political conflicts, unjust power structure, disasters, and environmental degradation at the regional level. Third, as for the approach to achieve human security, all actors astonishingly realized in the same way the necessity to find a balance between the top-down protection and bottom-up empowerment approaches. Last, regarding cross-border challenges to human security, all informants were supportive of intervention for the sake of humanitarianism but not in situations of violent conflict.

Table 11.3 Policy actor perceptions of human security

	Definition/Core values	*Major challenges*	*Approaches*	*Cross-national issues*
MSDHS (Government #3; #4; #5 2014)	Freedom from the lack of basic needs Social welfare Vagueness of the concept Not different from other social concepts	Poverty	Balanced approach between top-down and bottom-up Recognition of limited capacity of the bottom-up approach	Supportive of intervention for the sake of humanitarianism but not in situations of violent conflict
	Officially MSDHS defines human security as freedom from fear, freedom from want, and human dignity Policy action focuses exclusively on provision of social welfare	Officially MSDHS identifies various challenges, such as globalization, regionalization, aging society, political conflict, global warming, and environmental degradation		
NESDB (Government #1; #2 2014)	Well-being Vagueness of the concept Not different from other social concepts	Poverty and income inequality	Balanced approach between top-down and bottom-up Recognition of limited capacity of the bottom-up approach	Supportive of intervention for the sake of humanitarianism but not in situations of violent conflict
	NESDB has not officially adopted this concept	Similar to MSDHS		
Academic (Academic #1 2014)	Realized elusiveness of the concept but considered it as an opportunity to open policy space and to induce cross-sectoral dialogue	Political conflicts and natural and man-made disasters	Balanced approach Recognition of various problems of top-down approach	Supportive of intervention in case of natural disaster but not in the case of political conflict

(*continued*)

Table 11.3 (continued)

	Definition/Core values	*Major challenges*	*Approaches*	*Cross-national issues*
NGOs (NGOs #1 2014)	Freedom from fear and freedom from want Too broad and less powerful than human rights concept in pushing for reform	New types of fear arising from unjust power structure Side effects of development projects	Balanced approach between top-down and bottom-up	Supportive of intervention in case of natural disaster but not in the case of political conflict
Policy consultant (Consultant #1 2014)	Freedom from want and freedom from fear	Poverty Political conflict in Thailand including political instability in the region Environmental degradation in the ASEAN countries and no regional institution to cope with it	Balanced approach In the bottom-up approach, focus on empowering community awareness of risk management, because most threats are national, regional, or global, and communities themselves cannot cope with them	Supportive of intervention in case of natural disaster but not in the case of political conflict

11.5 Human Security in Practice: The Case Study of Human Trafficking

The first real test of human security in Thailand since institutionalization of the concept is perhaps the human trafficking problem. This issue was increasingly coming under the spotlight due to rising international awareness and mounting pressure from major powers such as the United States and the European Union. Owing largely to this pressure, the Thai government felt perhaps uncomfortably obliged to respond to this issue. In the past, Thai governments addressed these kinds of issues primarily with a "national security" or "national interests" approach, which tended to give priority to the nation's political and economic interests of controlling borders, while also securing sources of cheap labor, over safeguarding the human rights of victims (Kenny 2013, 86). Without a central body to orchestrate policy directions on human trafficking, relevant agencies such as the Royal Thai Police, the Royal Thai Army, the Ministry of the Interior, and the Ministry of Labor had to work under their own jurisdictions and organizational mandates, which were irrelevant to the principles of human security.

The rising current of the human security paradigm in international society thus indirectly forced Thai governments to change their approach to human security. In 2003, two years after the US Department of State launched its annual Trafficking in Persons (TIP) Report, the Thai government established operation centers on human trafficking at three different levels—international, national and provincial—with the MSDHS as the focal point for coordination. One year after Thailand was listed in the Tier 2 list (Watch List) in the 2004 TIP Report, the Thaksin administration hastily responded with a declaration of war on human trafficking (August 2004). It was the first time that a Thai government had responded in such a manner. Since then, successive governments have prioritized human trafficking issues. In 2008, a new anti-trafficking law was enacted, and new principles as well as institutional mechanisms were established accordingly. A new institution, the Office of Anti-Trafficking in Persons Committee, was established under the MSDHS with the primary responsibility of coordinating policy on human trafficking with other agencies. However, despite these legal and institutional reforms, the situation of human trafficking in Thailand, according to the TIP Report, has not much improved. The country has moved back and forth between Tier 2 (Watch List) and Tier 3 since 2010.

More recently, in early 2015, a new wave of influential pressure has further compelled the Thai government to accelerate reform measures, especially with respect to the trafficking of fishermen. This started from a series of reports from major news outlets since 2014. For instance, the Guardian noted the extensive use of slave labor in Thailand's seafood industry (Hodal et al. 2014), and the Associated Press (AP) reported on the 4000 slave fishermen stranded on remote Indonesian islands. Almost all of these were men of Thai, Myanmar, Cambodian and Laotian nationalities working for Thai-owned fishing vessels (McDowell et al. 2015). It should be noted that these reports would not be possible without the support from various actors, especially local and international NGOs and international organizations. Notable among them was the Labor Rights Promotion Network which first uncovered the tragic story of thousands of stranded fishermen and thereafter led rescue missions. In the next month, the European Commission under the Illegal, Unreported and Unregulated Fishing (IUUF) scheme issued a yellow card to Thailand as a warning for illegal fishing.

The very first reaction came from the seafood industry, which took the lead in mid-2014 in solving the problem by establishing the Shrimp Sustainable Supply Chain Task Force as an open platform for multi-stakeholders including various international NGOs, with an overarching mission to tackle the IUUF problem (Shrimp Sustainable Supply Chain Task Force 2017). Later, the Thai government stepped in. To improve the country's status in both the TIP report and the IUUF scheme, the Prayuth administration has adopted a three-pronged strategy. First, it prioritized the repatriation of stranded fishermen on the far-flung islands of Indonesia. Shortly after the publication of the AP report, it dispatched a C-130H military transport plane to Indonesia. Nevertheless, most of these people were deported back by Thai fishing companies. Second, it tightened control over the marine traffic through the close inspection of both sea workers and fishing boats entering and departing ports. Certainly, the focal organization in this mission was the Thai Navy. Third, it enforced more stringent measures for the registration of all migrant workers (Marschke and Vandergeest 2016; Vandergeest et al. 2017).

Although these responses were seemingly sufficient to temporarily lift the pressure from major powers, it fell far short of addressing urgent and structural problems. The jury is still out on the restorative justice for the repatriated fishermen. Only 57 of the over 1800 returnees were identified as the victims of trafficking (Royal Thai Government 2016). Most of them received only a small remuneration from due salary. The roles played by the MSDHS during this process were trivial; the Ministry provided temporary shelters and a small amount of money to send them back home. This case essentially demonstrates several weaknesses in the human security regime. Most importantly, the Thai government seems to pay a lot of attention to legal and institutional reform and the country's image, but less on addressing victim grievances and the exploitative structures conducive to human trafficking. All of this appears to suggest that human security is still secondary to state security as far as the issue of Thai "national security" is concerned.

11.6 Conclusions: Implications of the Human Security Concept in Thailand

Some interesting points can be drawn from examining the way that Thailand has imported and embraced "human security." These points are summarized in the following discussion. First, there is a huge gap between the human security principles and the actual functions of the MSDHS. The statement of the former foreign minister and one of the key architects of human security in Thailand, Surin Pitsuwan, best mirrors this gap and is therefore worth quoting at length:

> We have perhaps the first human security ministry in the world but, unfortunately, with the understanding that human security equals human welfare/social welfare. Human security is more than social welfare… there is an element of fulfillment, there is an element of human rights, there is an element of human development, there is an element of fuller freedom. (Pitsuwan 2007, 68)

Since its inception, even though political bosses and administrations might have added some auxiliary values and political mandates, such as populist policies or the rhetoric of "the good society," the core value of the MSDHS has remained the same: *songraha* or the provision of social welfare for vulnerable groups. This interpretation falls short of capturing the real spirit of human security. In this sense, Thai-style human security is far from being balanced and comprehensive, as proclaimed by Surin Pitsuwan in the first phase. Instead it is rather unbalanced, fragmented, and not comprehensive. Compared to other versions of human security, whether UNDP, Canadian or Japanese, the Thai approach is the narrowest in focus. By focusing on social welfare, it covers only a small portion of "freedom from want." Omitted from the Thai version of human security is the whole component of "freedom from fear" and some elements of "freedom from want," such as environmental security and economic security. All of this seems to suggest that human security has never been mainstreamed in the Thai public policy process. It has rather been depoliticized by strictly demarcating human security issues as belonging within a C-grade ministry.

Second, there was virtually no linkage between policy architects in the first stage and policy implementers in the second stage. Because the main actors in the first stage were in the Ministry of Foreign Affairs, while those in the second stage were in the MSDHS (the reincarnated form of the DPW), there seems to have been an unbridgeable cultural gap between the two. A gap also existed in the bureaucratic reform process when the proposal for establishing the MSDHS was placed on the table. While the reform initiators, who were mainly high-level cabinet members, directed and thoroughly controlled the process of reform, the policy practitioners themselves had only a negligible role. Nevertheless, the policy architects in the first stage and the reform drivers during the bureaucratic reform process found the concept of human security intriguing and promising in terms of promoting their organizational missions, which in turn helped elevate the status of Thai diplomacy in the eyes of the international community.

Yet, while promotion of a foreign concept abroad is one thing, actual implementation of that concept on home soil is an utterly different thing. This was certainly the case for the importation of human security into the Thai polity. The problem in this case was complicated even more by the fact that the policy architects (Ministry of Foreign Affairs) and the policy implementers (DPW) had completely different policy orientations, and bureaucrats in the DPW, who constituted the core of the newly created human security ministry, were not significantly involved in its establishment (Government #3; #4 2014). When they found that the concept of human security was too abstract, broad, ambiguous, and elusive to operationalize into bureaucratic functions, they seemed to return to their old working philosophy of providing social welfare to needy people.

Third, the introduction of the human security concept into the Thai polity unfortunately did not engender the necessary debate and discussion about security structures, not to mention security policy shifts or security sector reform. As alluded to earlier, the Ministry of Foreign Affairs employed the concept of human security in a way that was aimed primarily at improving Thailand's diplomatic image rather than driving an internal reform agenda. In the same vein, when the Thaksin administration gave the newly established ministry the label "human security," it had no intention of pushing for security reform and instead limited deliberation exclusively to the area of social issues rather than including security issues. In the end, state or national security seems to be as dominant as ever, untouched by the arrival of human security.

Fourth, according to the UNDP's approach, human security encompasses a wide range of dimensions, including health security, food security, political security, economic security, environmental security, personal security, and community security. Yet the integration of all these aspects into a single ministry seems unfeasible, both on paper and in practice. Thailand is a case in point. The jurisdiction of the human security ministry in Thailand only includes small portions of the overall concept of human security, covering merely community security, shelter and inhabitants, family, and some aspects of economic security. Other dimensions of human security fall under the jurisdiction of various other ministries and agencies, including some A or B-grade ministries, such as the Ministry of Interior, Ministry of Defense, and the economic ministries.

Fifth, numerous problems arise from this situation. Notably, various vulnerable groups, such as migrants, informal laborers, and victims of human trafficking, are left outside the protective cover of human security. Moreover, there is a lack of coordination among different agencies with different mandates under the rigid vertical structure of the Thai bureaucracy. Even worse, when policy objectives and organizational interests are in conflict, human security always remains secondary to national economic interests and national security. This holds true not only for the MSDHS but also for other agencies that deal with certain dimensions of human security. The crisis of human trafficking is a case in point. Various governments seem to prefer a piecemeal approach as being sufficient to lessen the immense pressure in this area from major powers.

Finally, according to key informants, the major cause of the failure to mainstream human security in Thailand may stem from its ambiguity and the vagueness of the concept. For academics, the elusiveness of the concept seems to be more of an appealing feature than a shortcoming, as it enables new types of challenges to be included in the policy stream. However, for policy practitioners, it is a source of confusion, since they do not know how to prioritize policy problems or how to transform the concept into practical operation. For NGOs, the abstraction of the concept makes it much more difficult to gather bottom-up support for campaigns around human security. Therefore, they have opted instead to privilege the human rights concept, which they regard as more practical and powerful than the human security one.

Notes

1. The division of the history of human security into two periods is purely for analytical purposes. The authors realize that in the real world, the periods may overlap and policies in the first period may continue into the later stage.
2. See quotation of Surin's statement in Capie and Evans (2002, 144).
3. In the bureaucratic reform workshop, the Thaksin administration further divided participants into three mini-workshops grouped around three different functions, namely, economic, security, and social affairs. See Lokwanne (2001).
4. When asked who put the words "human security" into the name of the newly created ministry, key informants voiced different opinions. While officials from the National Economic and Social Development Office thought that it was Paiboon Wattanasiritham, an NGO leader who later became Minister of the MSDHS during the Surayud government (Government #1; #2 2014), one university professor suggested that it might have been Surakiart Sathirathai, the then Minister of Foreign Affairs (Academic #1 2014). According to an official MSDHS document, however, the initiator of the Ministry of Social Development and Human Security was Prime Minister Thaksin Shinawatra. See Saracharas (2003).
5. Most recently the number of departments has been expanded into five. The former four divisions of women, child and youth, elderly, and persons with disabilities were elevated to department level.
6. Interestingly, most of the key informants pointed out in the same way that there is nothing new in the concept of human security. One of the very first articles about human security in the Thai language also indicated this point. See Srisirirojnakorn (2002).
7. This point was confirmed by an interviewee who was posted at an MSDHS provincial office. He also mentioned that the first task his boss assigned him was to research the definition of human security. He admitted that he (and his boss) had not previously known about this concept (Government #5 2014).
8. This point was also raised by Sora-Ath Klinpratoom, the second minister, who wrote, "We (officials in the MSDHS) are still stuck to the old framework of *songraha*." See Klinpratoom (2003).
9. Note that this is a direct quotation from the bilingual book published by the MSDHS without any revisions or modifications.

10. Note that the overall list of threats that appeared in the 11th National Economic and Social Development Plan includes political uncertainty and protracted conflict, and environmental degradation from global warming and climate change (National Economic and Social Development Board 2012).

References

Capie, David, and Paul Evans. 2002. *The Asia-Pacific Security Lexicon*. Singapore: Institute of Southeast Asian Studies.

Chambers, Paul. 2013. Economic Guidance and Contestation: An Analysis of Thailand's Evolving Trajectory of Development. *Journal of Current Southeast Asian Affairs* 32 (1): 81–109.

Cheeppensook, Kasira. 2007. The ASEAN Way on Human Security. Paper presented at the International Development Studies Conference on Mainstreaming Human Security: The Asian Contribution, Bangkok, October 4–5.

Department of Public Welfare. 2000. *60 Years Anniversary of the Department of Public Welfare (1940–2000)*. Bangkok: Department of Public Welfare.

Elinoff, Eli. 2014. Sufficient Citizens: Moderation and Politics of Sustainable Development in Thailand. *PoLAR: Political and Legal Anthropology Review* 37 (1): 89–108.

Hodal, Kate, Chris Kelly, and Felicity Lawrence. 2014. Revealed: Asian Slave Labor Producing Prawns for Supermarkets in US, UK. *The Guardian*, June 10, 2014. https://www.theguardian.com/global-development/2014/jun/10/supermarket-prawns-thailand-produced-slave-labour

Kenny, Edith. 2013. Securitizing Sex, Bodies and Borders: The Resonance of Human Security Frame in Thailand's War against Human Trafficking. In *Gender, Violence and Human Security: Critical Feminist Perspective*, ed. Christina Ewig, Myra Marx Ferree, and Aili Mari Tripp, 79–108. New York: New York University Press.

Klinpratoom, Sora-Ath. 2003. Offering to Clean the MSDHS. *Matichon*, December 10, 2003.

Kraisoraphong, Keokam. 2012. Thailand and the Responsibility to Protect. *Pacific Review* 25 (1): 1–25.

Krungthep Turakit. 2002. Nakvichakarn Rum Ad Rat Patiroob Sanong Karnmuang [Academics Criticize Government that Reform Serves Political Interests]. *Krungthep Turakit* [Bangkok Business News], January 28, 2002.

Lokwanne. 2001. Sarubpol Workshop Patiroobrabobratchakarn: Euk Kwamhwang Khong Kon Thai Chak Rattabarn Thaksin [Conclusion of the Bureaucratic Reform Workshop: Another Hope of Thai Citizens to Thaksin Administration], *Lokwannee* [Global Today], August 13, 2001.

Marschke, Melissa, and Peter Vandergeest. 2016. Slavery Scandals: Unpacking Labor Challenges and Policy Responses within the Off-shores Fisheries Sector. *Marine Policy* 68: 39–46.
McDowell, R, M. Mason, and M. Mendoza. 2015. AP Investigation: Slaves May Have Caught the Fish You Bought. *The Associated Press*, March 25, 2015. http://www.ap.org/explore/seafood-from-slave-/ap-investigation-slaves-may-have-caught-the-fish-you-bought.html
MFA (Ministry of Foreign Affairs of the Kingdom of Thailand). 2012. Human Security Network-HSN. http://www.mfa.go.th/main/th/issues/9895-เครอขายความมนคงมนษย.html. Accessed 10 Jan 2013.
MSDHS (Ministry of Social Development and Human Security). 2011. *Kwammankong Khong Manut Pratet Thai 2554* [*Human Security in Thailand*]. Bangkok: Ministry of Social Development and Human Security.
———. 2013. *Human Security Standards*. Bangkok: Bureau of Social Development and Human Security Standards.
———. 2014a. Kwam Chiamyong Pankollayut khong Kraxuang Pattana Sangkom Lae Kwammankongkhong Manut Tangtae 2546 (BE)-Patjuban [Linkage between Strategic Plan of the Ministry of Social Development and Human Security from 2003 to the Present]. http://www.m-society.go.th/ewt_news.php?nid=12502. Accessed 15 Jan 2015.
———. 2014b. *Strategy of Ministry of Social Development and Human Security 2012–2016 (2014 revision)*. Bangkok: Ministry of Social Development and Human Security.
National Economic and Social Development Board. 2012. *The 11th National Economic and Social Development Plan*. Bangkok: National Economic and Social Development Board.
Pinprateep, Poldej, and Patchara Ubonsawat. 2006. *Sangkom Thai pen Sankom Tee Dee Ngam lae Youyen pen Suk Ruamkan* [Thai Society is a Good Society Living Together Peacefully]. Bangkok: Ministry of Social Development and Human Security.
Pitsuwan, Surin. 1998. *Statement at the PMC 9+10 Session, Agenda Item 2 (a) – (c) Manila, July 28, 1998*. Association of Southeast Asian Nations (ASEAN): Manila.
———. 2007. Human Security in South-East Asia and the Experience of the Commission on Human Security. In *Proceedings of the ASEAN-UNESCO Concept Workshop on Human Security in Southeast Asia*, 67–70. Jakarta: ASEAN and UNESCO.
Royal Thai Government. 2016. *Update Trafficking in Persons Report 2015: The Royal Thai Government response 1 January-31 March 2016*. Bangkok: Royal Thai Government.

Samudavanija, Chai-Anan, and Kusuma Snitwongse na Ayudhaya. 1992. *Sing waedlom kap khwam mankhong: Khwam mankhong khong rat kap khwam mai mankhong khong Ratsadon* [Environment and Security: State Security and Citizens' Insecurity]. Bangkok: Institute of Public Policy Studies.

Saracharas, Supachai. 2002. *Tidtang Mai Kwammankongmanut nai Pratate Thai* (New Direction of Human Security in Thailand). Bangkok: Ministry of Social Development and Human Security.

———. 2003. Preface to *Ruam Patakatha darn Sangkom Prime Minister Thaksin Shinawatra* [Collection of Speeches on Social Policy by Prime Minister Thaksin Shinawatra], ed. Supachai Saracharas. Bangkok: Ministry of Social Development and Human Security.

Shrimp Sustainable Supply Chain Task Force. 2017. *Driving Oversight and Continuous Improvement: People, Product and Process.* Bangkok: Shrimp Sustainable Supply Chain Task Force, Inc.

Srisirirojnakorn, Nithirat. 2002. Kwammankongkhongmanut kab kwamsiangth-angsankom (Human Security and Social Risks). *Karnprachasongraha* (*Public Welfare*) 45 (2): 59–64.

Tadjbakhsh, Shahrbanou, and Anuradha Chenoy. 2007. *Human Security: Concepts and Implications.* London: Routledge.

UNDP (United Nations Development Programme). 1994. *Human Development Report 1994.* New York: Oxford University Press.

Vandergeest, Peter, Olivier Tran, and Melissa Marschke. 2017. Modern Day Slavery in Thai Fisheries: Academic Critique, Practical Action. *Critical Asian Studies* 49 (3): 461–464.

Vichit-Vadakan, Juree. 1989. *Krom Pracha Songraha* [The Department of Public Welfare]. Bangkok: Thailand Development Research Institute.

Interviews

Government Source #1. 2014. Official from the NESDB. Interviewed by the author in Bangkok. (July 25).

Government Source #2. 2014. Official from the NESDB. Interviewed by the author in Bangkok. (July 25).

Government Source #3. 2014. Official from the MSDHS. Interviewed by the author in Bangkok. (June 26).

Government Source #4. 2014. Official from the MSDHS. Interviewed by the author in Bangkok. (June 30).

Government Source #5. 2014. Official from the MSDHS. Interviewed by the author in Chiang Mai. (July 7).

Academic Source #1. 2014. Interviewed by the author in Bangkok. (April 11).

NGO Source #1. 2014. Interviewed by the author in Bangkok. (July 18).

Consultant Source #1. 2014. Interviewed by the author in Bangkok. (July 3).

CHAPTER 12

The Concept of Human Security in Vietnam

Lan Dung Pham, Ngoc Lan Nguyen, Bich Thao Bui, Thi Trang Ngo, and Thu Giang Nguyen

12.1 Introduction

Human security is understood as the "right of all people to live in freedom and dignity, free from poverty and despair." According to the United Nations (UN), "all individuals, in particular the vulnerable people, are entitled to freedom from fear and freedom from want, with an equal opportunity to enjoy all their rights and fully develop their human potential" (UNGA 2005). As such, human security aims at ensuring the survival,

L. D. Pham (✉)
Foreign Service Training Center, Diplomatic Academy of Vietnam, Hanoi, Vietnam

N. L. Nguyen
School of Law, Utrecht University, Utrecht, The Netherlands

B. T. Bui
The Ministry Office, Ministry of Foreign Affairs, Hanoi, Vietnam

T. T. Ngo
Faculty of International Law, Diplomatic Academy of Vietnam, Hanoi, Vietnam

T. G. Nguyen
National Boundary Commission, Ministry of Foreign Affairs, Hanoi, Vietnam

Y. Mine et al. (eds.), *Human Security Norms in East Asia*, Security, Development and Human Rights in East Asia,
https://doi.org/10.1007/978-3-319-97247-3_12

livelihood, and dignity of people in response to current and emerging threats that are often widespread and complex. In order to flesh out its contents, the human security concept can be divided into seven securities (UNDP 1994): economic security, food security, health security, environmental security, personal security, community security, and political security. These securities are useful to make an initial examination of the situation and perceptions of human security in a given country.

Therefore, this chapter reviews related laws, policies, research and media comments, and then discusses a series of interviews with key informants in order to clarify the concept, threats, and responses related to human security in Vietnam. A total of 35 legal and policy pieces, including the Constitution, codes, laws, resolutions, decisions of the Prime Minister, decrees of the government, and national strategies are analyzed, which provide an idea of how the state has been reacting to different challenges.[1]

The review of the law and policies of Vietnam shows that even though the concept of human security is not brand new or unheard of, it is not provided for, explained, or endorsed in laws or other legally binding documents. This does not mean, however, that the concept is unknown in Vietnam. At the 15th Asia-Pacific Economic Cooperation (APEC) Summit Meeting (September 2007), the then President of the Socialist Republic of Vietnam H.E. Nguyễn Minh Triết stated that "human security is of vital importance and is closely connected with the stability and prosperity of every nation and every economy" (M.T. Nguyen 2007). The fact that human security was mentioned by the Head of State in an international forum indicates that this concept was not unheard of.

In the next section, the understanding of the human security concept in Vietnam, as well as the perception of the threats to human security and the range of responses to such threats, will be analyzed in view of each of the components of human security listed above, namely, (i) economic security, (ii) food security, (iii) health security, (iv) environmental security, (v) personal security, (vi) community security, and (vii) political security.

12.2 Perceptions of Human Security in Vietnam

12.2.1 Understanding the Concept, Threats, and Responses to Threats to "Human Security" Through Official Documents

12.2.1.1 Economic Security

Vietnam's recent economic development has raised the people's standards of living. However, development has also brought major threats to economic security such as unemployment, rampant uncontrolled inflation, economic depression, and financial crises. In response, the government has enacted and promulgated many laws and policies. For example, Article 4 on Labor Policy of the amended Labor Code stipulates that the Government shall provide favorable conditions to activities that can generate jobs, self-employment, vocational training, and manufacturing operations. The Vietnamese government also introduced an Unemployment Insurance Policy, established labor market forecasts and information centers, implemented the National Fund for Employment; and developed state-owned job placement centers.

12.2.1.2 Food Security

The importance of ensuring food security is recognized in Government Resolution No. 63/NQ-CP. This resolution clearly states that national food security is an issue about which the Communist Party and the state should have the highest concern in both the short and long term. Ensuring food security strives to be in line with the overall socio-economic development strategy, in conjunction with industrialization and modernization of the country, as well as the resolution of issues relating to agriculture, farmers, rural areas, poverty reduction, and hunger eradication.

Regarding the threat of starvation, central and provincial level governments have been revising and fine-tuning policies on poverty reduction as a key and regular task. The National Congress of the Communist Party of Vietnam confirms that hunger eradication and poverty reduction continue to be a major policy and long-term objective, and a specific task in the country's socio-economic development. The Platform on National Construction in the Period of Transition to Socialism (revised and supplemented in 2011) sets out the task of "promoting legal richness in parallel with sustainable poverty reduction to narrow the rich-poor differences between regions, areas, and classes and fine-tune the social welfare system." In the Strategy on Socio-economic Development 2011–2020, sustainable poverty reduction is the key priority.

The legislation that puts these policy orientations into practice includes Government Resolution 30a/2008/NQ-CP on Fast and Sustainable Poverty Reduction in 62 Poor Districts. In relation to this resolution, Prime Ministerial Decision 1489/QĐ-TTg on the National Targeted Program on Sustainable Poverty Reduction from 2012 to 2015 sets certain targets for the period 2011–2015. These include increasing gross domestic product (GDP) by 1.6 times compared to 2011 and decreasing the number of poor households by an average of 2 percent per year in accordance with the national poverty standard. Vietnam also has several laws and policies to ensure the quality of food, including Law No. 55/2010/QH12 on Food Safety and Law No. 05/2007/QH12 on Product and Goods Quality.

12.2.1.3 Health Security

There have been remarkable improvements in the quality of the disease prevention and health care system in Vietnam, indicated by lower infant, maternal, and adult mortality rates, and longer life expectancy than most other countries with the same GDP. However, Vietnam still faces significant disease problems, including infectious diseases such as HIV/AIDS, tuberculosis, and malaria. In addition to these problems, cancer, heart disease, traffic accidents, and new variants of flu have loomed larger, becoming the new threats to health security.

Recognizing these threats, the government set up the National Strategy for Health Protection, Health Care and Health Promotion, aimed at ensuring every citizen's access to the health care system as well as a safe physical and mental environment for people to live in. Legislation has also been passed, including Law No. 40/2009/QH12 on Medical Examination and Treatment, and Government Resolution 87/2011/NĐ-CP on guiding the implementation of this Law. As part of the effort to combat infectious diseases, the National Assembly passed Law No. 03/2007/QH12 on the Prevention and Control of Infectious Diseases, and the Government issued Resolution 92/2010/NDD-CP on guiding its implementation. Moreover, there are national strategies to improve health care policies, including the National Strategic Policy on Fighting and Preventing HIV/AIDS to 2020, with a Vision to 2030.

12.2.1.4 Environmental Security

A growing population and the related increase in economic activity have put pressure on the stock of natural resources, particularly forests, waters, and marine resources in Vietnam. According to the Communist Party of Vietnam's Resolution No. 24/NQ-TW, threats to environmental security include: first, increasingly unusual natural disasters that cause significant damage to people and assets; second, environmental pollution that is becoming increasingly serious in some places and slowing environmental recovery from the effects of war; and third, a decline in biodiversity, with the risk of ecological imbalances happening on a large scale. All these negatively affect social and economic development, people's health, and their lives. The Ministry of Natural Resources and Environment has also confirmed that the consequences of climate change for Vietnam are highly serious, posing an apparent threat to poverty eradication, the implementation of the Millennium Development Goals, and the overall sustainable development of the country (Ministry of Planning and Investment 2013, 29).

To tackle threats from pollution and the shortage of natural resources, the government enacted the *Law on Environmental Protection* (52/2005/QH11) in 2005. This law clearly states that the policy of environmental protection is to ensure rational use of natural resources, the development of clean and renewable energy, and the promotion of reduce, reuse, and recycling of waste. Moreover, the Government also set the National Strategy on Environmental Protection to 2020, with a Vision to 2030, and the National Program on Green Growth. The Prime Minister issued Decision No. 2139/QĐ-TTg, dated December 5, 2011, on the National Strategy on Climate Change, with a view to preparing responses to possible threats from future changes. To prevent threats arising from instability of the physical environment including natural disasters, the National Assembly passed the Law No. 33/2013/QH13 on Preventing and Combating Natural Disasters in 2013.

12.2.1.5 Personal Security

Personal security means protection against violence and the deprivation of basic freedoms. For vulnerable groups such as women and children, protection of personal security also includes protection from domestic violence and human trafficking. The Ministry of Public Security reports that human trafficking, especially that of women and children, is becoming more complicated, and an apparent threat not only in Vietnam but also globally.

In response to domestic violence, which is one of the major threats to the personal security of women, specifically women in the rural areas of Vietnam, the Government passed Law No. 02/2007/QH on Preventing and Combating Domestic Violence, Government Resolution No. 08/2009/ND-CP on Guiding the Implementation of Some Articles of the Law on Prevention and Combating Domestic Violence, Government Resolution No. 110/2009/ND-CP on Sanctions for Administrative Violations in The Field of Domestic Violence, and Directive No. 16/2008/CT-TTg on the Implementation of the Law on Prevention and Combating Domestic Violence.

With regard to human trafficking, Vietnam is often a source, sometimes a transit, but rarely a destination country. Nevertheless, the government has established an institutional framework to tackle this problem in a more concerted manner. The legislation includes: Law No. 66/2011/QH12 dated March 29, 2011, on Human Trafficking Prevention and Combat; Prime Ministerial Decision 1427/QĐ-TTg dated August 18, 2011, for the Action Program on Prevention and Fighting Crimes in Human Trafficking; Prime Ministerial Decision 1217/QĐ-TTg dated September 6, 2012, for the National Targeted Program on prevention and fighting crime in the period 2012–2015; and Prime Ministerial Decision No. 130/2004/QĐ-TTg for the Action Program on prevention and fighting crimes relating to the trafficking of children and women.

Moreover, Vietnam has participated in the Coordinated Mekong Ministerial Initiative against Trafficking (COMMIT), and coordinated with UN agencies such as the United Nations Children's Fund (UNICEF), the United Nations Office on Drugs and Crime (UNODC), the International Organization for Migration (IOM), the United Nations Inter-Agency Project on Human Trafficking (UNIAP), and World Vision (WV), as well as concluding many bilateral agreements and treaties with Laos, Cambodia, China, and Malaysia, with a view to effectively strengthening the fight against human trafficking in the region.

12.2.1.6 Community Security

Community security allows people to live safely in their own places without fear of any conflict. Thus, threats to community security might include intra-community strife, tensions, or hurtful practices directed against certain members of the community, such as women. Regarding community security, Article 5 of the Constitution 1992 (as amended in 2013) stipulates that: "The Socialist Republic of Vietnam is a unified nation of all ethnicities living together in the country of Vietnam. All ethnic groups are equal and unified, and respect and assist one another for mutual development; and all acts of discrimination against and division of the ethnicities are prohibited."

Although it is not a legal document, the Resolution of the 7th Concentrator Photovoltaic Systems Conference confirming the strategic importance of ethnic issues and national unity plays a role as an orientation in all policy-making activities. Prime Ministerial Decision 449/QĐ-TTg on the Strategy for Ethnic Affairs to 2020, dated March 12, 2013, then puts this orientation into the practices of authorized bodies of the government.

12.2.1.7 Political Security

Political security is ensured when people are protected from political violence including war, civil unrest, and systematic torture and human rights violations. Regarding the promotion of human rights, the newly amended Constitution confirms in Article 14 that in the Socialist Republic of Vietnam, political, civil, economic, social, and cultural rights are respected and provided for in the Constitution and laws. In particular, the Constitution also provides in Article 20 that everyone has rights and is protected by law, and is not to be subjected to torture, violence, coercion, corporal punishment or any form of treatment harming his or her body and health or offending his or her honor and dignity. The Platform on National Construction in the Period of Transition to Socialism (revised 2011) also concentrates on creating prosperous people, a strong country, and an equitable and civilized society.

To meet international standards on human rights protection, Vietnam has signed, ratified, and acceded to more than 30 international treaties, and participates in international and regional organizations in guaranteeing human security.

12.2.2 Perception of Human Security in the Academic Community

In general, "human security" is not a common topic of research in Vietnam. Still, there are some scholars who engage in the analysis of the concept and related aspects, illustrating the different levels of understanding among the academic community. For the purposes of this study, research on this issue can be categorized into two types: (1) in-depth research directly addressing the concept and related aspects of human security; and (2) works that address human security indirectly through related aspects of human security, without acknowledging the concept directly.

There have only been a handful of studies by Vietnamese experts concentrating on analyzing the concept or specific aspects of human security. The authors of these studies generally share an adequate level of understanding and awareness of the concept of human security. However, the approaches taken in these works vary from one another, ranging from analyzing basic concepts, delving into aspects of human security, and/or studying the concept in the situation of Vietnam and the world. This section of the report looks into some of the most prominent works on this topic to date.

In his PhD dissertation "Human Security in Modern International Law," Chu Manh Hung places the analysis of human security within the framework of international law and human rights. His analysis focuses on the concept of human security as discussed in the general literature and introduces the provisions of international law and Vietnam on human security (Chu 2012). The application of the concept of human security is not mentioned or studied in detail. This work serves as an introduction to the concept of human security for the Vietnamese academic community.

Also looking at human security in terms of the clear correlation with human rights and human development, Nguyen Hong Hai examines the concepts in the context of poverty reduction in Vietnam (H.H. Nguyen 2007). From the viewpoint that human development, human security, and human rights are important pillars of human protection, the author argues that none should take precedence over the others as they are all intertwined. With this approach, human security issues are included in the overall relationship across the board, but still address the practical problems of Vietnamese society.

In discussing the threats posed to human security, Ta Minh Tuan analyzes the global threats to human security posed by uncontrolled population increases, inequalities in economic opportunities, pressure from migration, environmental degradation, drug trafficking, international terrorism, and weapons of mass destruction. The author also proposes measures to protect human security in Vietnam's current condition (Ta 2008). In his article "Human Security and Insecurities in Modern Society," Vu Duong Ninh, while also focusing on threats to human security, analyzes the underlying causes of war, the ethnic and religious conflicts leading to food insecurity, and the risk of natural resource scarcity and energy shortages in Southeast Asia and highlights the necessity for a sustainable development strategy (Vu 2009). It seems quite clear that both these articles endeavor, somewhat successfully, to place the abstract concept of human security in the context of Vietnam and Southeast Asia, and to use the concept as a starting point for certain solutions.

The viewpoints of Vietnamese scholars can also be ascertained through workshops and conferences organized specifically on human security issues. However, most of the presentations at these events focus on only one element of the concept of human security in connection with an aspect of social life. For example, in the Second National Workshop on Human Security held by the Institute for International Relations in Hanoi in 2002, the presentations analyzed the problem with respect to five aspects: human rights, society, economy, religion, and culture. Participants also reconfirmed the necessity of researching the human security concept in Vietnam and made some specific recommendations in each of their respective fields to promote the application of the concept of human security in Vietnam. However, only a few references were made to the concept of human security, mostly defined as freedom from want, despite the fact that the authors themselves may not have acknowledged it as such. Freedom to live in dignity was hardly touched upon (Institute for International Relations 2002).

Apart from this research, there have been multiple efforts that have indirectly addressed the human security issues discussed above that did not use the concept, or at least it was not directly acknowledged. One prominent example is the *2013 Workshop on Water and Food Security in Vietnam*, part of a series of workshops and dialogues on food security in the Mekong River Basin (Water Governance Facility 2013). This workshop dealt with the situation of alteration/reductions of water flow, or salt water intrusion which may lead to serious changes in local food security, in the political economy of food production, and to trade in the region. This, overall, is shaped from the perspective of food and water security, which correlates with the concept of human security. However, hardly any of the presentations incorporated the concept of human security in their analyses. This type of study is more common than those directly using the human security concept but they are beyond the scope of our present research.

12.2.3 Perception of Human Security in the Media

In the Vietnamese media, human security per se is not a topical issue. In fact, the concept is hardly mentioned at all, and has only appeared in a few online articles. On the other hand, the media focuses more on reporting issues concerning human rights, and the different facets of people's lives. The concept of human security has nevertheless been mentioned in a few online newspapers (T. Nguyen 2013; Hong 2014). However, the articles usually do not provide a clear definition or background explanation of the term. The concept is used as a platform from which each article goes on to focus on other existing problems in Vietnamese society. Although such articles clearly display an inadequate level of awareness of the term "human security," they play an important role in increasing the understanding of the public in general of the threats to their daily lives.

12.3 Findings from Interviews

12.3.1 Background of the Interviews

Eleven interviewees were selected from five main sectors, namely the government, civil society, scholars/academics, the media, and businesses. For each of these sectors, the research team managed to interview representatives from the following institutions:

- For the government: The Ministry of Public Security, Ministry of Defense, and Ministry of Foreign Affairs;
- For scholars: Vietnam National University;
- For civil society: The Women's Union, the Youth Union, and East Meets West (non-governmental organization [NGO]);
- For the media: Vietnam News Agency, and the Vietnam Television Corporation; and
- For private businesses: Mai Linh Taxi Corporation, and the Cuu Long Joint Stock Company.

The interviewees were selected using two key selection criteria. The first important consideration was the representativeness of the interviewees. Apart from choosing interviewees working in different sectors, those from each sector were selected to represent the people most likely to be involved with works that concern human security issues. For example, representatives from the Ministry of Public Security, Ministry of Defense, and Ministry of Foreign Affairs were invited, since these Ministries are associated with ensuring security, public order, and social welfare for the people. Second, in selecting the interviewees, the team was also mindful that not all of them, even if they had agreed to meet us, would be willing to have an open discussion on an issue that might be deemed sensitive. Therefore, we had to identify those who were either within our network of connections or those put into contact with us through our colleagues and acquaintances. This would allow us to approach them in a somewhat less formal way to make it easier for the interviewees to share their opinions with us.

The research group encountered various difficulties in conducting interviews, as follows: first was the translation problem. Not all the interviewees spoke or were fluent in English, and the team encountered some difficulties in finding the equivalent terms in Vietnamese for some of those in the original research design. For example, the word "empowerment" does not have a Vietnamese equivalent. Therefore, the team had to use long phrases to explain the term to give the interviewee a general understanding. Other concepts such as "freedom from fear" and "freedom from want" have equivalents in Vietnamese, but a literal translation does not convey the whole meaning of the concepts, and this called for further clarification as well.

Second, there was reluctance from the interviewees. As the concept of human security is not widely known in Vietnam, it is not uncommon that when people hear the term "human" it is usually associated with "human rights," which up until now, has been considered a rather sensitive topic of discussion. This mentality has to a certain extent contributed to a situation where some people, especially those in higher positions, refused to be interviewed, or if they did agree, were prevented from freely and candidly voicing their views. Therefore, even though these people may have had sufficient experience in their respective fields to be able to provide sound and meaningful answers to the questions, it was not always easy or possible to persuade them to share their opinions.

Finally, geographical limitation was a limiting factor. Due to financial constraints, most of the interviews were conducted in Hanoi, not in other provinces and cities. The advantage of conducting interviews in Hanoi is that, as the capital city of Vietnam, it is reasonably convenient to approach representatives from the identified sectors, especially governmental agencies, since they are all based there. However, Vietnam is a rather diverse country in terms of both culture and customs, which in turn certainly could have profound impacts on people's understanding of the relevant aspects of human security. Therefore, the findings discussed in this report are limited in terms of geographical representativeness.

12.3.2 *Findings from the Interviewees*

The questionnaire was designed based on the central questions of the overall research, as explained in this book's introductory chapter, with some modifications in terms of the choice of words and expressions used, to make the questions more comprehensible to laymen as well as experts (see Annex 1).

12.3.2.1 Perception and Understanding of Human Security

In this part, we cover information concerning whether the interviewees were aware of the concept of "human security," and their level of understanding of its elements. In general, the majority of interviewees had not heard of the term 'human security' before the study with the exceptions being the human rights expert from Vietnam National University, the interviewees from the Youth Union who had previously attended a training course on traditional and non-traditional security, and the interviewee from the Vietnam News Agency who had stumbled upon the term in a news article. This implies that the concept of "human security" is rather new in Vietnam for people hailing from many different backgrounds.

Some interviewees approached the concept by dividing it into two components: human and security, and then taking security as the starting point, later linking it with human. Therefore, the concept of human security was very frequently understood in connection to or in contrast to traditional national security. Others started with human and almost immediately associated it with "human rights," but from a more general perspective. Sometimes, interviewees found it hard to differentiate between human security and human rights. Also, as the word security in Vietnamese bears close resemblance to the word safety, most interviewees perceive human security as the state in which an individual can lead a safe and comfortable life, both physically and mentally. One interviewee thought that human security should be seen more as an approach rather than a concept with normative content. This means that human security does not carry with it any rights on the part of the individual nor obligations on the part of the state, but rather is a way to approach the issue of ensuring human rights.

When briefly introduced to the concept and its constituent elements, most of the interviewees were able to quickly connect the abstract concepts of "freedom from fear," "freedom from want," and "freedom to live in dignity" to specific examples in their lives. The examples given by the interviewees correspond quite well with the basic understanding of human security. On the relationships among these three constituent elements of the human security concept, all interviewees agreed that they cannot be understood independently or separate from one another. Instead, a holistic approach to understanding these three elements should be taken, meaning that the promotion of one of the three freedoms will enhance the other two, and vice versa.

However, when asked to rank the three freedoms in order of importance, the interviewees were divided in their answers. Around half of the interviewees held the opinion that the three freedoms are of equal importance and thus cannot be ranked. Nonetheless, their opinions do acknowledge that, depending on the conditions of each individual, for example, age, health condition, culture, and economic status, one freedom may take priority over the others. The answers of the remaining half of the interviewees varied from choosing freedom from fear as the most important factor, the reason being that unless and until people are free from any fear or persecution, they will not be able to freely want and freely live in dignity. It seems the answers to this question are heavily dependent on the background of interviewees; for example, the younger ones tend to place emphasis on the freedom to live in dignity, without which they say they cannot exist as an individual with personal integrity and identity in society, while others say that the importance of any element is subject to how well they understand it. In short, most of the interviewees had not heard of the term human security per se. However, most had a good grasp and understanding of the core contents of the concept when asked to give specific examples of the three freedoms.

12.3.2.2 Perception of Threats to Human Security

Questions in relation to perceptions of threats were designed to gather information regarding the interviewees' sense of safety, and the threats perceived by interviewees to themselves, their communities, to Vietnam in general, and to Southeast Asia.

Most of the interviewees indicated that they feel safe in their lives even though they acknowledge that their lives are not free from all threats. This sense of safety and security derives from the fact that Vietnam is not currently facing any war, threats of aggression, or terrorism, and security is generally ensured in their communities. As wars and conflicts have been a prominent feature in Vietnam's history, the consequences of which can still be seen today, the fact that the country is now at peace brings a great sense of safety and security to most people. Some also pointed to having a stable income and a sound education, such that they would be able to face any threats and adapt to new circumstances. Two of the interviewees indicated that they no longer feel as safe as before and expressed concerns over recent developments. For example, they were concerned about the tensions caused by events in the South China Sea, which according to them could potentially bring about unpredictable unrest and instability in the country and the region.

Regarding the perceived threats, those that were identified by all the interviewees include poverty, natural disasters, pollution, corruption, and political distrust and economic regression. Other threats voiced by some interviewees were traffic safety, food safety, poor law enforcement, and community conflict. Even though the interviewees were asked about threats posed at different levels, to themselves, their community, Vietnam and/or Southeast Asia, in the end the answers they provided do not differ that much. This seems to indicate that the sense of security perceived by individuals is very closely tied to that of community or country.

12.3.2.3 Responses to Perceived Threats

As mentioned above, there is no Vietnamese term equivalent to "empowerment," therefore, the phrasing of the questions focused more on how people would respond to threats to human security, whether by the individuals themselves or through government assistance, as well as which approach was given greater relative importance. In connection with this, the questionnaire also asked interviewees about their preparedness for future risks.

In response to the question of who should bear the responsibility to tackle the threats posed to human security, all interviewees answered that both the state and the individual must share the burden. However, when it comes to the question of who should be primarily responsible, all except one indicated that the state should take the lead. The state is considered to play a more important role in tackling threats to human security because it passes the laws and policies and holds the tools and powers to enforce the provision of more comprehensive and long-term protection to the people. It is expected that if the state can address the threats in an appropriate and concerted manner, it can maintain order and create a safer environment for people to thrive in. Nevertheless, individuals should certainly take steps and find ways to ensure their own safety, as each is in the best position to understand the threats posed to himself/herself.

Only one interviewee suggested that the primary role in dealing with the risks should not be generalized but should be understood in relation to the specific threat in question. That is, some threats can be more effectively combatted by an individual being proactive, while others are more suitably addressed by the state. For instance, that interviewee believes that threats from road accidents or traffic safety in general may be tackled mainly by individuals, through increasing their awareness and sense of obedience. It is also interesting to note that the interviewee from the Ministry of Public Security stated that, in addition to the government and the individual, the role of NGOs in ensuring human security should also be recognized and enhanced. The suggested reason is that NGOs have a broader reach and can directly impact the lives of groups who may not be as adequately protected by the law and overlooked by society as a whole: for instance, ethnic minorities or the LGBT (lesbian, gay, bisexual, and transgender) community.

In terms of the level of preparedness for future risks, most interviewees felt that they are prepared to deal with future risks, but only to a certain extent. All the interviewees have a job with a stable income and are relatively well educated. Therefore, they felt that financially and intellectually they are somewhat prepared for the risks that may appear in the near future. They also attributed their feeling of preparedness to the fact that potential threats are well reported in the mass media to which easy access is available, and more importantly, the fact that individuals are aware of the risks has contributed to their preparedness to deal with them. However, they also find it very difficult to say with certainty that they are all well prepared, since threats may strike randomly, and bring about consequences beyond human prediction.

On the other hand, the level of preparedness of Vietnam varies depending on the type of risk. Most interviewees agree that Vietnam is adequately prepared for natural disasters, as these occur every year, and the state as well as the people have gathered enough experience and invested resources to deal with them. Regarding threats such as corruption, political distrust, poverty, and economic recession, certain steps have been taken but they are not being carried out in an effective manner, and thus are not able to address the problems. In this regard, most of the interviewees feel that Vietnam is not well prepared for these other types of threats.

12.3.2.4 Added Value of Human Security

This part seeks to grasp the opinions of the interviewees on the usefulness of understanding the concept of human security, both for themselves and for the government in dealing with threats to human security.

The interviewees were rather united when it came to acknowledgment of the added value of understanding the concept of human security in promoting the actual state of human security. Except for two interviewees who believed that the understanding of such a concept would not contribute much, all interviewees expressed the opinion that a sound and proper understanding of the concept would both help individuals to better prepare themselves, and induce the state to bring about changes in policy to protect and promote human security. This is because when people are equipped with a better understanding of the concept of human security, they will use it as an intellectual tool to help prepare themselves mentally, and as a relevant approach to assist in practically equipping themselves with skills to combat the threats. At the same time, they will be able to demand that the state takes more action and be more proactive in protecting human security. In turn, this will force governments to put in place laws and policies that are more human centered, rather than state centered as used to be the case, thereby focusing on improving the lives of the people. It will also lead to the government paying greater attention to international cooperation and collaboration to confront global threats.

The two dissenting interviewees said that the awareness of the human security concept would not play a significant role, pointing to the fact that even if the existing laws and policies do not acknowledge the term, they still embrace and implement aspects of it. Thus, increased understanding will not make too much of a difference. The other reason is that while understanding the concept may help in theory, putting the concept to use in practice heavily depends on other factors, such as the capacity of the individual. Therefore, increased understanding may not induce a significant change in the mindset of either the individual or the state.

12.3.2.5 Cross-Border Issues

In response to the hypothetical scenarios of disasters and conflicts, there seems to be a strong consensus among the interviewees in their answers. All the interviewees believe that in the event of a natural disaster that exceeds the capacity of the country to respond, Vietnam should receive assistance from other countries along with international organizations such as the UN, or NGOs like the Red Cross, provided that this comes from trustworthy sources, and the assistance is not accompanied by any political conditions. Also, when another country needs assistance in the event of a natural disaster, Vietnam should lend a helping hand, as this is considered a humanitarian act and it would be immoral to refuse to help. However, Vietnam should only help with the consent of the host state and within its capacity.

On the other hand, when it comes to military conflicts and internal unrest, the interviewees were much more hesitant. The majority believe that external assistance should not be accepted to help resolve internal violence, as it may be used as an excuse for military or political intervention. The few interviewees that did approve of such assistance still hold the reservation that such assistance should only be called for when absolutely necessary, and be limited to medical or provision of food from those who are either allies or have had traditional and long-term relationships with Vietnam. In the reverse scenario, Vietnam should only provide assistance when the affected country directly requests it, or if the situation may negatively affect Vietnam. Some suggest that assistance could be made through regional or international organizations, such as sending troops to United Nations Peacekeeping Operations.

12.4 Conclusions

Human security is a new concept in Vietnam, demonstrated by the lack of acknowledgement of the concept in official governmental documents or mainstream media. While elements of the concept can be distilled from Vietnamese law and policies, there is no clear-cut connection between these elements and the concept of human security. Likewise, the amount of media coverage on the issue is low; few articles directly discuss the concept or address threats using the human security concept. Even within the academic community, there are few articles on this topic, most merely discussing threats to human security in a general manner, as opposed to analyzing the threats in detail in the context of Vietnam.

The information gained from interviewing representatives with different backgrounds also reveals a lack of awareness of the concept. The term human security is frequently associated with the term human rights. The interviewees have different perceptions of the term human security, but they believe it to be the state in which an individual can lead a safe and comfortable life, or the conditions based upon this, both physical and mental. Most interviewees seem to grasp the concepts of freedom from fear and freedom from want, which explains why most believed that these two should be given priority.

The threats to human security that were identified also varied slightly among the interviewees; however, the most common threats agreed upon were those concerned with economic security, environmental security, and political security. Most interviewees placed great reliance on the state and believed that it is the government that should be responsible and will do a better job in protecting the people from threats to human security. They believed that human empowerment could only be possible and effective if the state has already been able to create a safe and fair environment for its people. In terms of cross-border collaboration to combat threats to human security, they indicated a much higher willingness to accept assistance, and to assist other countries in the event of natural disasters; but when it comes to political issues, there was much greater reluctance toward giving and receiving external help.

In short, the concept of human security itself is not meaningfully understood in Vietnam. However, constituent elements are reflected in the law and policies of the state, as well as in the mindset of the people. As such, human security in Vietnam can be said to be a jigsaw puzzle, in which the pieces are identified, but have not been put together. Therefore, there is potential for further promotion of the concept and its value to Vietnam.

Annex 1 Interview Questions

The Concept of Human Security

- Have you ever heard of the term "human security?" If yes, in what context did you hear of this term?
- How do you understand the term? What comes into your mind when you hear this term?
- When did you first hear of the term "human security?" In what context does the concept of human security consists of three elements: "freedom from fear," "freedom from want," and "freedom to live in dignity." Can you think of an example for each of these elements?

Threats to Human Security

- What do you think are the major threats to human security in Southeast Asia? By governmental protection of those who suffer or by capacity building for the people so that they can cope with risks and threats by themselves?
- What do you think are the major threats to human security in Vietnam in both the short and long term?
- How do you think such issues should be tackled?
- Do you (or does your organization) engage in resolving such issues in some way?

The Value of the Concept of "Human Security"

- If you and the people around you were equipped with a better understanding of "human security," do you think that there would be any change in policy, making and the protection of human security in Vietnam?
- Do you think a better understanding of the term "human security" helps to tackle global issues today?
- What do you think are *major obstacles* to the use of human security? How can we overcome such difficulties?

Scenarios

Four specific scenarios were discussed with the interviewees, namely (i) Receiving Assistance in Case of Natural Disasters; (ii) Receiving Assistance in Case of Escalation of Violence; (iii) Providing Assistance in Case of Natural Disasters, and (iv) Providing Assistance in Case of Escalation of Violence.

For the first two scenarios, the interviewees were placed in the specific hypothetical situation that his/her country is being affected by each of the above-mentioned scenarios. The question normally asked was whether he/she thinks that his/her country should accept assistance from outside. And then, if the answer was positive, what kind of *organizations* and what *methods* did they think would be acceptable to such operations and why?

For the latter two scenarios, the affected area was expanded to the surrounding region of his/her country or another country and its magnitude is supposed to be beyond the control of a single government, risking the lives of many people, and whether the organizations of his/her own country would be able to give effective support. The question is how he/she or their organizations should deal with this situation in the case that the government of the affected country is reluctant to accept foreign assistance.

Annex 2 Relevant Vietnamese Legislation

1. The *Constitution 1992* (as amended in 2013).
2. The *Penal Code* (as amended in 2009).
3. The *Labor Code* (as amended in 2013).
4. The *Criminal Procedure Code (19/2003/QH12).*

5. Law 52/2005/QH11 of November 20, 2005, on *Environmental Protection*.
6. Law 03/2007/QH12 of November 21, 2007, on *Prevention and Control of Infectious Diseases*.
7. Law 05/2007/QH12 of November 21, 2007, on *Product and Goods Quality*.
8. Law 40/2009/QH12 of November 23, 2009, on *Medical Examination and Treatment*.
9. Law 55/2010/QH12 of June 17, 2010, on *Food Safety*.
10. Law 66/2011/QH12 of March 29, 2011, on *Human Trafficking Prevention and Combat*.
11. Law 33/2013/QH13 of June 19, 2013, on *Natural Disaster Prevention and Control*.
12. Resolution of the 7th Vietnamese Communist Party Conference, 2004.
13. Resolution of the Government 30a/2008/NQ-CP of December 27, 2008, *The Support Program for Fast and Sustainable Poverty Reduction in 61 poor districts*.
14. Resolution of the Government 63/NQ-CP of December 23, 2009, on *National Food Security*.
15. Resolution of the Government 80/2011/NQ-CP of May 19, 2011, on *Directions for Sustainable Poverty Reduction (2011–2020)*.
16. Resolution of the 13th National Assembly 10/2011/QH13 of November 8, 2011, Approving the *Five-year Socio-economic Development Plan for the 2011–2015 period*.
17. Resolution of the Vietnamese Communist Party 24/NQ-TW of June 3, 2013, on *Actively Coping with Climate Change, Increasing Natural Resources Management and Protecting the Environment*.
18. Decision of the Prime Minister 138/1998/QD-TTg of July 31, 1998, Approving the *National Program on Crime Prevention and Combat*.
19. Decision of the Prime Minister 130/2004/QD-TTg of July 14, 2004, Approving the *Action Program on Prevention and Combat of Women- and Children-Trafficking Crimes* from 2004 to 2010.
20. Decision of the Prime Minister 172/2007/QD-TTg of November 16, 2007, on the *National Strategy for Natural Disaster Prevention, Response and Mitigation to 2020*.

21. Decision of the Prime Minister 1427/QD-TTg of August 18, 2011, Approving the *Program of Action to Prevent and Combat the Human Trafficking Crime* during 2011–2015.
22. Decision of the Prime Minister 2139/QD-TTg of December 5, 2011, on the *National Strategy for Climate Change.*
23. Decision of the Prime Minister 1489/QD-TTg of October 8, 2012, Approving the *National Targeted Program for Sustainable Poverty Reduction* in the period of 2012–2015.
24. Decision of the Prime Minister 449/QD-TTg of March 12, 2013, Approving the *Ethnic Monitory Affairs Strategy* through 2020.
25. Decree of the Government 92/2010/ND-CP of August 30, 2010, Detailing the Implementation of the *Law on Infectious Disease Prevention and Control*, Regarding Biosafety in Laboratories.
26. Decree of the Government 87/2011/ND-CP of September 27, 2011, Detailing and guiding a number of articles of the *Law on Medical Examination and Treatment.*
27. *National Strategy on Climate Change*, issued by Prime Minister Nguyen Tan Dung in Decision 2139/QĐ-TTg of December 5, 2011.
28. *National Strategy on Environmental Protection to 2020*, with *Vision towards 2030*, Approved by Prime Ministerial Decision 1216/QĐ-TTg on September 5, 2012.
29. *National Strategy on Food Safety in the period 2011–2020*, with *Vision towards 2030*, approved by the Prime Minister on December 12, 2013.
30. *National Green Growth Strategy*, approved by Prime Ministerial Decision 1393/QD-TTg on September 25, 2012.
31. *National Strategy for Natural Disaster Prevention, Response and Mitigation to 2020*, approved by Prime Ministerial Decision 172/2007/QD-TTg of November 16, 2007.
32. *Platform on National Construction in the Period of Transition to Socialism* (Revised and Supplemented in 2011).
33. *Strategy for People's Health Care and Protection 2001–2010*, approved by Prime Ministerial Decision 35/2001/QD-TTg on March 19, 2001.
34. Unemployment Insurance Policy (effective in 2009).
35. Vietnam's *Ten Year Socio-Economic Development Strategy* (SEDS) for 2011–2020.

Note

1. The most important legal document in the Vietnamese legal system is the Constitution passed by the National Assembly in 1992 and amended in 2013. Under the Constitution there are laws, ordinances, decrees, and other affiliated legal documents, including orders issued by the State President, government decisions issued by the Prime Minister, and circulars issued by individual ministries. Also, the resolutions of the Communist Party of Vietnam are considered to provide guidelines for all laws and regulations to be adopted by the authorities, even though they are not legal documents and have no binding effect.

   Besides the law, Vietnamese policies can be ascertained in national action plans, national targeted programs, and national strategies issued by the Government to set specific goals for the implementation of each policy. Although these are not legal documents, they are still strictly followed and implemented by governmental organs in specific localities. For the full list of laws and policies analyzed in this chapter, please see annex 2.

References

Chu, Manh Hung. 2012. *Vấn đề an ninh con người trong luật quốc tế hiện đại* [Human Security in Modern International Law]. PhD Diss., Hanoi Law University.

Hong, Ha. 2014. Climate Change Threatens Human Security. *Binh Dinh Online*, March 31.

Institute for International Relations. 2002. *Report for the Second National Workshop on Human Security*. Hanoi, July.

Ministry of Planning and Investment. 2013. *Millennium Development Goals Full Report 2013: Achievements and Challenges in the Progress of Reaching Millennium Development Goals of Vietnam*. Hanoi: New Technology Printing Joint Stock Company.

Nguyen, Hong Hai. 2007. *Assessing the Inter-relationship of Human Development, Human Security and Human Rights in Poverty Reduction in Vietnam*. Paper Presented at Workshop on Mainstreaming Human Security: The Asian Contribution Bangkok, October 4–5.

Nguyen, Minh Triet. 2007. APEC 2007 Closing Ceremony. *Online Journal of the Communist Party of Vietnam*, September 10. Accessed June 20, 2017. http://123.30.190.43:8080/tiengviet/tulieuvankien/tulieuvedang/details.asp?topic=1&subtopic=104&leader_topic=174&id=BT1090731013.

Nguyen, Thang. 2013. Hydroelectricity: From Energy Security to Human Security. *One World E-News*, November 14.

Ta, Minh Tuan. 2008. An ninh con người trong mối đe doạ toàn cầu [Human Security and Global Threats]. *Tạp chí Cộng sản* [Communist Journal] 12. http://www.tapchicongsan.org.vn/Home/Nghiencuu-Traodoi/2008/1178/An-ninh-con-nguoi-va-nhung-moi-de-doa-toan-cau.aspx. Accessed 24 Feb 2018.

UNDP (United Nations Development Programme). 1994. *Human Development Report 1994.* New York: Oxford University Press.

UNGA (United Nations General Assembly). 2005. *2005 World Summit Outcome, A/RES/60/1.* New York: United Nations.

Vu, Duong Ninh. 2009. *An ninh con người và sự bất an trong cuộc sống hiện nay* [Human Security and Insecurities in Modern Society]. *Tạp chí Phát triển khoa học & công nghệ* [Journal of Science and Technology Development] 12(1): 5–16.

Water Governance Facility (Stockholm International Water Institute). 2013. *Workshop on Water-Food Security in Cambodia and the Vietnam Delta – Assessing Risk and Alternatives under an Altered Flow Regime.* Can Tho, December 5–6. Stockholm: SIWI and UNDP.

Interviews

Academic Source #1. 2014. Vietnam National University. Interviewed by author in Hanoi, April 25

Civil Society Source #1. 2014. East Meets West (NGO). Interviewed by author in Hanoi, April 19

Civil Society Source #2. 2014. The Ho Chi Minh Communist Youth Union of the Diplomatic Academy of Vietnam. Interviewed by author in Hanoi, July 8

Civil Society Source #3. 2014. The Women's Union. Interviewed by author in Nam Dinh Province, July 1

Government Source #1. 2014. Ministry of Defense. Interviewed by author in Hanoi, July 20

Government Source #2. 2014. Ministry of Foreign Affairs. Interviewed by author in Hanoi, April 16

Government Source #3. 2014. Ministry of Public Security. Interviewed by author in Hanoi, June 11

Media Source #1. 2014. Vietnam News Agency. Interviewed by author in Hanoi, July 20

Media Source #2. 2014. Vietnam Television Corporation (VTC). Interviewed by author in Hanoi, April 18

Private sector Source #1. 2014. Cuu Long Joint Stock Company. Interviewed by author in Hanoi, April 15

Private sector Source #2. 2014. Mai Linh Taxi Corporation. Interviewed by author in Hanoi, July 15

Private sector Source #3. 2014. Mai Linh Taxi Corporation. Interviewed by author in Hanoi, July 15

CHAPTER 13

What Is at Stake in Localizing Human Security Norms in the ASEAN+3?: A Comparative Analysis of 11 Qualitative Regional Review Surveys

Oscar A. Gómez

13.1 Introduction

Two decades after its formal introduction to the world of ideas on global governance, surveying perceptions of human security remains a paradoxical exercise. As a concept, deep understanding of human security remains limited to a narrow community of scholars and practitioners, contested even in those societies in which specific efforts to flesh it out locally have advanced the most (see Chaps. 5, 8, and 11 on Japan, the Philippines, and Thailand). Nonetheless, the fundamental changes to the concept of security that are implied by human security are widely recognized. Interviewees accept that individuals and communities should be at the heart of security practice, and that the insecurities people experience go beyond the purely militaristic. They also see multiple offices of the government and several

O. A. Gómez (✉)
Research Institute, Japan International Cooperation Agency (JICA), Tokyo, Japan
e-mail: oagomez@apu.ac.jp

Y. Mine et al. (eds.), *Human Security Norms in East Asia*, Security, Development and Human Rights in East Asia,
https://doi.org/10.1007/978-3-319-97247-3_13

other social actors as active in trying to protect and empower people from a wider range of threats, and even describe how there is an international dimension for those problems and their solutions. Inquiry about human security results in a comment that seems to be common to practitioners everywhere: "we already do human security, we just don't call it that" (Kaldor et al. 2007, 274). At first sight this is the general trend found in the reports on each of the Association of Southeast Asian Nations +3 (ASEAN+3) countries covered by this research, suggesting that the idea of human security is not alien to anyone, just that its components are spread across other many constructs through which people understand insecurity and security.

However, the "we already do human security, we just don't call it that" stance can have important implications when we approach human security as an emerging norm that is being localized. Localization is defined as "the active construction … of foreign ideas by local actors, which results in the former developing significant congruence with local beliefs and practices" (Acharya 2004, 245). Acharya suggests a trajectory that starts with prelocalization, when local actors resist and contest new norms on the grounds of existing beliefs and practices. Then a local entrepreneur must push for the adoption of the norm, which is in turn followed by a process of adaptation between the external norm and existing beliefs and practices. Finally, new instruments and practices result from the new normative framework that amplify and make universal the now localized norm. From the point of view of this localization process, the "we already do human security" position could be understood as suggesting that the norm life cycle is over and that there is nothing new to add; or conversely, it could also be a strategy for prelocalization resistance. The chapters in this collection thus offer a great opportunity to appraise the advance of human security localization across the region.

A useful guide to estimate localization progress in the ASEAN+3 can be found in the work of Mary Kaldor and colleagues. She is perhaps the most important human security norm entrepreneur in Europe, having pursued ways to influence the European Security and Defence Policy with human security thinking for over a decade (Human Security Study Group 2004, 2007, 2010, 2016). In this process, Kaldor et al. (2007) encountered very early the "we already do human security" resistance to norm localization and identified its source in a series of practices and principles that practitioners perceived as already covering human security—mainly related to crisis management, civil-military coordination, and conflict prevention.

Kaldor and colleagues found that these practices and principles lacked a bridging concept encompassing short-term and long-term objectives after crises, and that also put "in place a coherent and innovative policy tailored to the complex needs of contemporary global security" (Kaldor et al. 2007, 288). Therefore, they focused on these weaknesses in order to advance renovated versions of human security norms, better tailored to the European context. The previous 11 case study chapters can be read as offering a similar analysis, distinguishing normative areas in which specific human security proposals are in the process of localization or encountering resistance as perceived by ASEAN+3 stakeholders.

Aiming to understand what lies behind the "we already do human security" position and discern the progress made in human security norms localization, I identify four trends that stood out as the most relevant throughout the chapters, namely: (1) the different ways in which human security is seen as an essential part of state security; (2) the beliefs underlying security provisions that would come into play when localizing human security; (3) the paradox of empowerment in practice; and (4) the strong connections between development, threats, and insecurities. These trends flesh out in each country the relations between the basic elements of security narratives (Gomez et al. 2016): the state as the provider of security is at the center of all the chapters, followed by the means for security available and how people, the referent of security, are active or passive about the provider and its means. The threats and the values underlying those threats also are important through the chapters. In the following sections, I discuss each one of these trends and then come back to the question of localization as a guide for future research on human security theory and practice.

13.2 Human Security Norms as the *Raison d'Être* of the State?

In the introduction, we stated that "the normative message of human security boils down to a powerful proposition that the ultimate objective of governance at all levels is to provide security (or ensure freedoms) for every individual." Is the understanding of human security any different in the ASEAN+3? When respondents express that human security is being considered or taken care of, what they usually refer to is that the protective, and to a certain extent also the empowering, functions and institutions of the state are in place, at least nominally. In other words, all chapters identify different forms of state action as aiming to provide human security, which are engrained in the state's conception of its role. This starts from the constitutions of Cambodia and Japan, through which the authors identify a commitment to "the security of the people." Embracing the rule of law is also seen as a pillar of human security provision, as the case of Malaysia in Chap. 6 makes explicit. Human security measures are also to be found in a broad range of legislation covering sectors associated with the freedoms from want, fear, and to live in dignity, as described in detail in the Indonesian and Vietnamese contexts in Chaps. 4 and 12, in regard to health, social welfare, migration, and disaster management, among those specific to the seven securities suggested by the Human Development Report of 1994 (UNDP 1994).

It is in the sense of all these government offices playing a role in the provision of human security that some interviewees from Thailand as quoted in Chap. 11 view with concern the existence of a Ministry of Human Security. When all branches of government already do human security, creating a single ministerial roof for the concept appears contradictory or unnecessary. The authors observe how: "The jurisdiction of the human security ministry in Thailand includes only small portions of the overall concept of human security, covering merely community security, shelter and inhabitants, family, and some aspects of economic security. Other dimensions of human security fall under the jurisdiction of various other ministries and agencies, including a number of A or B-grade ministries, such as the Ministry of Interior, Ministry of Defense, and economic ministries." The observation suggests how difficult it is to constrain human security ideas to a single institution or community in practice. Still, the authors note how this Ministry became a focal point for coordination on action against human trafficking. So, despite being presented as "a C-grade ministry," with all the remaining challenges, it still manages to offer a window of opportunity for action in areas that are not a public policy priority.

Human security at the core of state action also includes foreign policy and international cooperation, particularly mentioned in Chaps. 3, 5, 10, and 11 on China, Japan, South Korea, and Thailand, respectively. These states have a commitment to help protecting humans beyond borders, for instance, by upholding the principle of "the common value of humanism" and promoting humanitarian action and human rights, as in South Korea, or by "shifting to handling foreign affairs for the people," as in China. For all those chapter authors that included questions on accepting and receiving cooperation after crises, particularly disasters, in their surveys, the replies were positive about both, although in the case of conflicts the answers were less enthusiastic. There were also cases of transnational risk management in which domestic exposure could be evidenced within international action. For instance, in Singapore, the problem of infectious diseases motivated different types of activities by the government in an effort to contribute to regional protection, including "a series of three international and regional conferences on pandemic preparedness" and "holding the regional stockpile of antiviral drugs and personal protection equipment such as masks and isolation gowns."

Importantly, the vision of the state evoked by human security perceptions in all the surveys is not static. Surveys make multiple references to the evolution of institutions to deal with the problems inherent in challenging old policies or developing new strategies to cope with these problems, such as the consolidation of a new government in Myanmar (Chap. 7), changes in international cooperation in Japan (Chap. 5), new ways to deal with trans-boundary haze in Singapore (Chap. 9), the creation of the Ministry of Human Security in Thailand (Chap. 11) among others. Human security visions of the state are thus based on history and change that implies normative changes as well. They include the story of changes that have not materialized yet, as in the case of Myanmar, and the hurdles in changing the focus of human security policy and practice from civic and humanitarian action to addressing developmental needs. But it is also the story of the modern state formation in Singapore, in which a social compact anchored exclusively to the country's economic performance appears unsustainable. That is also the case in Chap. 3, which describes the evolution of the Chinese role in world affairs as one now engaged and enhancing human security, as it can be seen in its country work through the UN, its support to the Millennium Development Goals (now the Sustainable Development Goals), and the Paris Agenda for Climate Change.

Some of these changes imply a redefinition of the roles assigned to traditional security institutions. In the Philippines (Chap. 8), the changes after the Marcos regime gave rise to the redefinition of security "as security of the people instead of security of the state." The resulting framework included moral/spiritual consensus, cultural cohesiveness, economic solidarity, and ecological integrity, besides the established values of territorial integrity, sociopolitical stability, and external peace. Chap. 4 also describes a broad vision of security in Indonesia's Bill for the National Security Act, covering a wide range of threats including "pandemics, extreme hunger, natural disasters resulting in mass casualties, abject poverty, crimes against humanity, and extreme stress," and covering both Indonesian citizens and foreigners. The setting of transition in Myanmar (Chap. 7) also suggests movement in the same direction of wider, developmental threats becoming more relevant as traditional threats are dealt with. All these cases suggest that human security offers an appealing framework to rethink traditional security doctrine after the fall of authoritarian regimes.[1] The appeal is not, however, universal, despite its widespread use. In Thailand, human security ideas have not had any local impact on traditional security policy, for instance.

Interestingly, Chap. 3 on China also makes mention of the connection between human security ideas and the evolution of national security institutions, such as the creation of the National Security Commission. In the case of Malaysia (Chap. 6), the authors even suggest that human security ideas can be seen locally as a menace to the national ownership of security policy, and thus "non-traditional security" is preferred there, a trend common to the ASEAN institutions reluctant to embrace human security language. The chapter on China offers a more optimistic prospect, affirming that the inclusion of non-traditional security implies that people and human development are regarded as ultimate goals.

While the impact of human security on the evolution of the traditional security apparatus remains a pending issue, the wide range of institutions identified by the authors in this volume suggests that the ultimate objective of human security provision has begun to be placed at the core of the state conception of security in East Asia. The country surveys suggest that multiple institutions of the government play a role in providing security to the people. Thus, surveying perceptions on human security in general stresses the overlap between state security and human security and, at the same time, highlights the many challenges remaining, which are discussed below. The case studies maintain in their essence the urge for "sovereignty as responsibility" associated with the origins of the Responsibility to Protect (Deng et al. 1996). This balance between remaining domestic challenges and recognizing the central role of the state provides further hints on what is at stake in localizing human security norms.

13.3 Security Provision, Paternalism, and Responsibility

The central role of the state in the provision of security, as discussed in the previous section, is nothing new. Human security proponents repeatedly point out how human security is supposed to complement, not replace, traditional security (CHS 2003). It should be noted that the threats covered throughout the chapters in this book were largely domestic and, thus, did not contest the national interest from a point of view of international relations. In other words, the traditional situations in which state security and human security have been in conflict were scarcely raised. This could suggest that there is no contestation against human security because it is fully compatible with existing constitutions, legislations, policies, and institutions. Nonetheless, the chapters also showed that even when looking at the national level, the underlying beliefs and practices associated with state-provided human security involve resistance and adaptation. One major case was the embracing of state paternalism, and another was the paradoxical views on empowerment discussed in this and the following section.

Paternalism is the attitude of a person of power (normally males) to the task of protecting people but not giving them freedom of choice. It is assumed that parents know what the best is for their children. Although this term is supposed to have negative connotations, the respondents used the term descriptively for the most part. The most straightforward presentation comes from Chap. 3 on China, which deserves being quoted in full:

> Government as a "necessary evil" is very much a Western invention and it is not a Chinese idea. Traditionally, people in China often have wishes for government and they want the government to do good things for them. Compared to the Western political culture, they have less vigilance and more expectations for the government. One revealing example is the use of the term "parent officials" (*fumu guan*) to refer to government officials, and people expect them to play a *paternalistic role* (Italics added).

Such a view connecting the embracing of the government's paternalistic role and traditional values can be found in other chapters. The authors writing about the Cambodian case (Chap. 2) mention the non-Western values underlying security provision by the state, with a particular twist. Through their survey:

> Several people likened the state to a parental figure whose duty it is to protect the population: "Whenever the children have an argument, the parents have to reconcile and that is the responsibility of the government" (journalist). This recalls the paternalism that the former popular Cambodian King Sihanouk played to and suggests a cultural value of a benign paternalistic monarch that does not necessarily mesh with Western ideas of empowerment.

In that chapter, several interviewees perceived political rivalry emerging from the democratization process of the country as a threat to human security, rather than a sign of progress, or at least as the way the system should work. This may be a consequence of the recent violent past and most people's wish to avoid any further confrontation and instability, something that respondents from Vietnam in Chap. 12 also mentioned; Chap. 2 authors consider this "suggests that Western notions of democratic leadership may not be understood in the same way in this very different cultural and historical context." The authors also found that the strengthening of such leadership depends not only on institutions, norms, and laws, but also on Buddhist values of morality. They include the voice of a monk who describes these values as including: "(1) avoid taking the life of beings; (2) avoid stealing; (3) avoid sexual misconduct; (4) avoid telling lies; and (5) avoid taking intoxicating substances."

From a different perspective, the Thailand case in Chap. 11 also suggests a connection between Buddhism and the conception of the state, particularly in relation to welfare. Authors present the philosophy of the Department of Public Welfare, the heart of the Ministry of Human Security, as originating "from the Thai-style Buddhist philanthropic value that rulers and the haves should help the have-nots," which entails a hierarchy of social relations and duties. Such hierarchy gives shape to the accepted understanding of society and state relationships, describing how the traditional "patronage of the haves, whether members of the royal family, the nobility, or merchants" moved through modernization to bureaucratic agencies. In both Cambodia and Thailand, the deterioration of morals was thus considered a threat to human security.

Such a distinct view of traditional values and security provision also has ramifications beyond the domestic sphere. The chapter on Myanmar sees some peculiarity in the actions of the region with regard to its reaction to the sanctions imposed on the military junta governing Myanmar (Burma), from 1988 until recently. Despite international pressure, ASEAN governments "did not join the sanctions regime and instead advocated constructive engagement as the approach to bringing about change in Myanmar." Only Japan applied some sanctions, but it remained a major source of foreign aid. The author sees this attitude as being connected to the human security philosophy promoted through Japan's foreign policy, one that finds greater traction among the region policy elite. Such respect to the state is also seen in the reaction to Cyclone Nargis in 2008, after which

Western menaces of intervention were counterproductive, while ASEAN and UN negotiations gave a way to ease tensions and a productive engagement with international support.

It should be noted that these beliefs and attitudes are not uniformly Eastern and were not homogeneous among interviewees in a single chapter, or across chapters. The description of China is linked to Confucian ideas which directly address the art of government, while Buddhism is in principle more spiritual and moral. Yet, even in the latter cases, connection to Buddhism is identified as being part of the values necessary to provide security and to understand the obligations of the government toward society. In this sense, it is worth noting how Amartya Sen in his *Idea of Justice* (2009, 205) draws from Buddhism a conception of responsibility that is derived from the asymmetry of power, illustrated by Gautama Buddha through an analogy of the relationship between mother and child. This radically differs from the most conventional Western idea of responsibility derived from a social contract among hypothetically equal individuals. While he staunchly opposes Asian exceptionalism (Sen 1999), it is possible to foresee such a conception of responsibility of protection implying that the role of government in providing parental protection can be positive, or at least normal in certain circumstances.[2]

There are at least two alternative explanations to the dominant view of the paternalistic role of government from other chapters. One is the strong linkage between state *responsibility* and the provision of human security. Chapters 4 and 12 on Indonesia and Vietnam, for example, describe in detail such a role, and frame security in the traditional terms of state responsibility toward its citizens, particularly as legislation establishes such duties for the government. Interviewees in Vietnam found that "when it comes to the question of who should be primarily responsible [to tackle the threats posed to human security], all except one indicated that the state should take the lead."[3] The perceptions in Cambodia and Thailand that are framed in terms of traditional values also emphasize responsibility toward those in trouble. The emphasis on the rule of law in Malaysia also points to the importance of responsibility and the center-stage position of the state in security provision.

Another alternative explanation is the extent to which *welfare* provision is associated with human security. Welfare is at the heart of the Thai Ministry of Human Security, to the point that both concepts are mutually interchangeable. Chapter 7 on Myanmar also places emphasis on the important role of welfare organizations when trying to move human security practice beyond the merely humanitarian. In Chap. 4 on Indonesia, the author points out how "The term '*kesejahteraan*' (welfare) is also used as equivalent for security since '*keamanan*' generally refers to hard security with a heavy military emphasis"; therefore, legislation identified as covering human security belongs to a good extent to the realm of welfare. Chapter 5 also mentions welfare policy in discussions about the possible domestic application of human security ideas in Japan. Welfare is also used in the new definition of security in the Philippines. Therefore, as welfare provision is also strongly related to state action, this approach would necessarily result in an emphasis on the paternalistic role of government.[4]

All these elements can be found mixed in Chap. 9 about Singapore. While the authors do not use welfare nor responsibility language to explain human insecurity in that country, they emphasize certain non-religious values held by the government that result in observed insecurities, and the over-dependency on the state as part of this problem. They describe how a "culture of elitism and entitlement" has resulted in a "heavy top-down approach [that] has not sufficiently empowered Singaporean society to cope with risks at the community level." Interestingly, they describe at the same time "the government's long-standing emphasis on self-reliance with minimal assistance from the state,"[5] which prevents the creation of social safety nets, and the struggle of civil society organizations (CSOs) to achieve financial independence, particularly because they "get a substantial proportion of funding from the government." Indeed, a civil service officer who was interviewed remarks that "there is a sense that Singaporeans themselves ought to reduce their dependence on the government and exercise more agency over their lives, as the government cannot realistically meet nor sustain higher-order needs." This chapter thus portrays a specific form of paternalism, successful in meeting basic needs, yet confronted with new challenges deriving from its success. Are all countries in the region following the same path? Of course not, but the case of Singapore gives a hint of what the interviewees in other countries could be striving for.

The emphasis in the conclusion of Chap. 9 about Singapore nurturing bottom-up approaches to human security provision highlights a weakness in the case studies: the role of the other possible providers of security. The association between security and responsibility seems to obscure the role of families, communities, and other organizations in providing welfare, which common knowledge suggests should be more prominent. Perhaps this is because those networks of support are not conceived in terms of responsibility in the legal sense, but as solidarity.[6] Non-governmental organization (NGO) representatives across chapters voice their preference for human rights frameworks, which place special emphasis on state responsibility, so they also do not see themselves as providers, although Chaps. 6, 7, 8, 9, and 12 on Malaysia, Myanmar, the Philippines, Singapore, and Vietnam suggest NGOs may or could be in this position. In theory, promoting empowerment is supposed to help balance the over-emphasis on protection underlying traditional state security, giving room for all other actors to locate themselves as providers of human security in practice. Whether that is the case is discussed in the following section.

13.4 The Paradox of Empowerment in Practice

The dominant emphasis through the surveys of the central role of the state and the positive views about the paternalistic provision of security has important implications when inquiring about empowerment. On the one hand, many of the chapters refer to some conventional, abstract form of empowerment, contrasting this to the protection approach that emanates from human security definitions. It is associated with action in the sectors of education, as in Chap. 3 on China, and health, as in Chap. 4 on Indonesia and Chap. 7 on Myanmar. Minorities are also populations mentioned as requiring empowerment in Indonesia, the Philippines, and Singapore, although communities in general are also seen as actors to be empowered. Such approaches to insecurity are linked to ideas of bottom-up capacity development, resilience, and the ability to cope with threats.

On the other hand, empowerment is seen across different chapters as something that the government provides. In Chap. 4, Indonesian respondents suggest that the government does not provide enough support to empower the society in a similar vein to Vietnam (Chap. 12), where "[i]t is believed that human empowerment can only be possible and effective if the State has already been able to create a safe and fair environment for its people." Also, in the Chap. 4 on Indonesia "Respondents alluded to the government's resources and capacities as main modalities that allow it to empower civil society, so that the latter might work alongside the government in addressing challenges." Even so, legislation there defines empowerment for social welfare as aiming at "assisting citizens in meeting basic needs." The interviewees from Cambodia also saw "the need for the state to promote empowerment."

Chapter 7 on the Philippines is the only exception, presenting a more standard view of empowerment. This may be related to the long tradition of civil society work in that country and its greater familiarity with human security ideas. Even there, people's empowerment was a pillar of President Fidel Ramos' "Social Reform Agenda." Besides, that chapter observes how "Academics and NGOs have a crucial role to play not only in conducting research to clarify the concept but also by situating it within the local context and, in the process, empowering local governments and communities to deal with human security threats and vulnerabilities." The urge to empower local governments is justified in the case of disaster response, where "local officials commented that they do not want handouts from the national government, including conditional cash transfers; they prefer capacity and skill building so that they can help themselves."

Whether focusing on collectives is the right way to promote empowerment is a contentious issue. Following the human rights tradition, human security propositions often put individuals at the center, trying to reach the most vulnerable and those left behind; but it is not unusual to find people in general and/or specific communities mentioned as well. To some extent, empowerment becomes an empirical question of coverage and priority. However, under a positive view of paternalist provision of security, the size of the collective being empowered could grow to the point of becoming one with protection. Conflating protection and empowerment deserves special attention in the context of international cooperation. For instance, in South Korea the "Foreign Affairs and Unification Committee members argued that there should be a shift in the paradigm for ODA projects, and that development cooperation projects should be based on developing countries' ownership and its perceived needs. This statement reflects the empowerment approach to human security since there is a strong focus on self-help and independence." Such understanding of empowerment could accommodate any actor in developing countries as the one to be empowered.

It is important to observe that not all chapters discussed empowerment in detail. Responses from interviewees in Thailand (Chap. 11) were mostly limited to contrasting protection with empowerment, but no substance was added. In discussing Myanmar in Chap. 7, the author makes almost no mention of empowerment, despite much emphasis on the role of the civil society in dealing with human insecurities. In Vietnamese, there is no direct translation of the word, which forced researchers to explain the questions to the interviewees. In Indonesia, "Very few respondents responded to the question on empowerment." In Japan, the author also detects some particularities in Japanese practitioners' understanding of protection in contrast with empowerment: some see that "JICA, as an implementation agency for ODA, has mainly focused on the improvement of people's daily lives, based on 'empowerment' approaches," what the author contrasts with protection from armed conflict, which Japan International Cooperation Agency (JICA) does not do. However, the assumption that JICA's work is mainly based on empowerment does not reflect the fact that most of the agency's cooperation is carried out in conjunction with partner governments. Besides, the only concrete example of empowerment provided is "sending specialists to long-term projects," which is open to different interpretations.

The surveys, nonetheless, offer other possible explanations or entry points to illuminate what lies underneath this relation between people, states, protection, and empowerment. Chapters 6, 7, 8, and 9 on Malaysia, Myanmar, the Philippines, and Singapore give special attention to the role of CSOs and their connection to empowerment. In Thailand, human security ideas open the way for a broader range of actors to be involved in policy, although this is weak in comparison to human rights. The Malaysian and Singapore cases in Chaps. 6 and 9 describe the struggle to confront top-down measures resulting in insecurities that reflect a more conventional view on empowerment as activism. Even Chap. 3 on China sees "local autonomous grassroots organizations" contributing through "assistance to ordinary people who encounter difficulty and they also, for example, mobilize donations to help people in the regions that have been struck by earthquakes or other natural disasters. The work of these local self-help organizations has proved to be useful and reassuring in terms of social governance."

Yet, even in these cases some contradictions arise: for instance, the provision of hand-outs and other resources from the government to CSOs is seen as creating dependency in vulnerable populations, making it difficult to protest; on the other hand, safety nets are also seen as the means required for alleviating insecurities. Besides, support for advocacy as empowerment is not necessarily shared across the region. Democratic rivalry is seen as a threat in Cambodia, while respondents in Indonesia and Thailand describe some limitations of those advocacy and bottom-up approaches that do not provide solutions. In any case, CSOs as a stakeholder capable of practical empowerment in the region deserve further attention, especially if information and communication technologies keep being game changers, as Chap. 9 on Singapore shows.

It is also the case that empowerment is seen by some authors and interviewees as linked to human rights, which offer important means for vulnerable populations to get protection. A CSO in Malaysia would prefer human rights over human security in as much as they have been working for a long time with this concept, it seems to have a larger scope, and it seems to be useful in terms of tools for advocacy, a preference voiced in other chapters as well. For these actors the operationalization of human security is not well understood. Yet, human rights activism such as in Malaysia and the Philippines does combine protection or empowerment, as well since CSOs act as providers of protection and eventually move into empowerment through capacity building because they cannot accompany vulnerable populations forever.[7] On the other hand, in Vietnam, connecting human security and human rights was deemed sensitive, hindering the willingness of respondents to speak. Is this the case for empowerment as well? Exploring the interconnection between human security and human rights in practice would offer additional hints about how empowerment is conceived in the region.

13.5 Development, Threats, and Insecurities

Looking at the threats included in the different surveys and the underlying logic of human insecurity offers additional nuance to the discussion. However, we need to bear in mind that the only classification of threats that was common to all surveys was the one drawn from the three freedoms, fear, want, and to live in dignity, and not even this construct was used systematically throughout the surveys. Some authors referred to the seven securities outlined in the 1994 Human Development Report (UNDP 1994), while others included previous surveys or polls that were available. Also, the model questionnaire, described in Chap. 12, included hypothetical cases on disasters and conflict inside the country or elsewhere, which could have biased responses toward these kinds of threats. Because the aim was to enumerate threats, it was not possible to discern how these threats are interlinked and prioritized, beyond the common statement that all of them are important. Yet, despite of the lack of uniformity and the limitations, several trends can be observed.

Most of the threats mentioned in the surveys have a strong connection with trade-offs relating to development.[8] Suffering from some kind of "development aggression" was expressed in seven of the 11 surveys. This can occur in different ways, in the shape of modernization and land appropriation in Chap. 3 on China, the destruction of forests in Chap. 4 on Indonesia, and land grabbing in Chap. 2 on Cambodia, so the perpetrators can be the state, but also the private sector. Environmental pollution and its effects on health are also considered to be a source of concern regionally, closely linked to urbanization, and of a transboundary nature in Singapore. Corruption may as well be included here as a trade-off of development in the context of growth. Finally, if we include inequality, and the social marginalization resulting from it, as one of the tradeoffs of development, then the downside risks of development are mentioned in all the country surveys.[9]

At the same time, the surveys report several threats derived from development not taking place or development gains being fragile. Poverty and unemployment are frequent proxies for economic security, and health and education are two frequently mentioned sectors in which deficiencies are seen as threats. So, after identifying these contradictory sets of threats resulting from lack of development and because of development aggression in Cambodia, the authors concluded that the protection-empowerment duality of human security may not be appropriate when trying to understand the "more complex and sometimes conflicting range of ideas about how their [people in Cambodia's] future well-being may be secured." They suggest that the added value of human security is in enabling communication around needs and people's conflicting aspirations. Yet, they recognize that addressing these contradictions in practice is a totally different matter and a remaining challenge.

I believe that human security norms can be of help in addressing the conflicting aspirations described in the chapter on Cambodia, mainly through the promotion of a renovated understanding of the connection between responsibility and security. A hint can be found in Chap. 12 about Vietnam. One interviewee there did not consider the state to be a priori *responsible* for human security, observing that "the primary role in dealing with the risks should not be generalized, but should be understood in relation to the specific threat in question." In other words, asking the question "who is responsible" before understanding the threat and the best possible security means to cope with it may inhibit the power of human security analyses to inform possible solutions. For that, focusing on specific threats and crises is necessary, as the second phase of the project that this book belongs to is striving for (Hernandez et al. 2018). Once again, despite multiple weaknesses, the case of the Ministry of Human Security at least gives an example of a contribution in the pursuit of a solution to human trafficking in Thailand.

A different question is to what extent framing all these issues as human security threats is of any help. Interviews related to traditional security institutions in Indonesia in Chap. 5 raised concerns about the involvement of the armed forces in dealing with problems beyond their scope of work. Still, several chapters suggest that the connection between a wider set of threats and *dignity* resonates with people's claims and their relationship with the state. For example, Chap. 3 on China stresses how change converging through human security ideas includes "the persistent value … that people should not be sacrificed for national goals"; that is, government should respect their dignity. The chapter on Japan also highlights dignity as connoting respect and the integration of a wider view of people beliefs and ways of life, so "Putting aside exceptional humanitarian crises such as genocide and massive violations of human rights, when cooperating through the provision of assistance, we should not violate the feelings of people in recipient societies and should respect what they believe and the ways that they organize their cultural, religious, and social lives." Similarly, in the Philippines adapting international aid to local customs was also regarded as an issue of dignity. Let me add that dignity was also of use in pointing out the people being left behind. These populations were not seen as threats, although instability following migrant workers' protests in Singapore was a matter of concern; the threat was failing to attend to their needs. Issues underlying migration, human trafficking, LGBT (lesbian, gay, bisexual, and transsexual) communities, and aging societies were also mentioned through the surveys. In sum, the wider framing of threats allows us to integrate the complexity underlying social problems, and even the possibility of solutions being incomplete or backfiring. Dignity is, however, another idea difficult to conceptualize, and was not explored in depth through the current surveys, thus its meaningfulness requires further research.

Lastly, interviewees did include in their responses threats in the more classic sense of the word.[10] Natural disasters were the most frequent occurrences discussed, probably because of the research design, but also reflecting a well-known problem in the region. Climate change was mentioned as well, although it is not always clear whether this related to disasters or to something else. These two threats were followed by concerns about political instability and distrust in governments, showing that the relationship with the state can be problematic. Some respondents included traditional security threats such as interstate conflict and nuclear security; while, particularly in the Philippines case, concerns about direct aggression from the state and the military were explicitly named. Nevertheless, a regional profile of threats is difficult to synthesize from the surveys, given that most of the specific issues were expressed in only one or two countries. This shows a methodological weakness when approaching human security in general, since the selection of threats for each country reflected the specific backgrounds of the respondents, or problems recently reported in the news that may not have appeared as concerns if the survey was held on a different date or country. These are common issues in the approach to the study of human security, which require periodic quantitative surveys complemented with crisis-specific analyses to increase their significance. Our survey is thus just one preliminary step in this iterative process.[11]

In this sense, it is worth highlighting how the team in Vietnam found that respondents "do feel safe in their lives even though they acknowledge that their lives are not free from all threats." Besides not perceiving there to be major threats now, the authors point out that given the turbulent past of Vietnamese society, the present prosperity "brings great sense of safety and security to most people." In contrast with a troubled past, the present stability is welcome, and any destabilizing forces are seen as dangerous; that does not mean that everything is fine, and dissatisfactions emerge with the government that is primarily responsible for human security. In Cambodia, a critical shift against top-down security comes from "the huge cohort of young people who have no memories of the Khmer Rouge period or even of civil war." Two observations can be made: one, asking for security perceptions will always result in the enumeration of multiple threats, even if respondents feel secure; and, two, not only new threats but also new expectations modify perceptions of insecurity. Those two observations need to be balanced, through the analysis of the resistance and adaptation of human security propositions, to effectively manage expectations.

13.6 Conclusions

The collection of country studies in this book offers multiple insights on how stakeholders of the ASEAN+3 region perceive the process of the localization of human security norms. First, by examining the institutions involved in the provision of security, through which the state strives to protect and empower populations against multiple threats, scholars and practitioners from each of these countries see their polities and their constitutive norms as compatible with human security as a whole.[12] Thus, all of them reaffirm the important overlap between human security and state security, and explain its evolution within the permanent balance of satisfying needs and dealing with downside risks associated with the aggression brought about by development. Despite multiple and conflicting challenges for the provision of human security, stability is praised, and these states are seen as decent members of the international community sharing the goal of "sovereignty as responsibility." This implies that, at least in principle, human security norms are not perceived as requiring a change of regime or having any fundamental incompatibility with present structures.

Second, narratives presented through the country studies evidence overall a strong association between human security norms and the primary responsibility of the state, particularly in relation to welfare provision. The paternalist relation is explicitly embraced in several chapters, associated in some cases with traditional values, but also implicit in the emphasis on the question of "who is responsible for human security provision?" Therefore, it appears that in principle human security norms are being embedded in the expansion of state duties toward the populations living in their countries. Only the case of Singapore reflects the situation in which a successful state seems to have reached the limits of the provision model of human security to the point that what seems to be lacking is mainly bottom-up empowerment. Yet, even in that case solutions pass through the government, so there seems to be a dilemma in the domestic application of human security, which is different from the case of state security and deserves further attention.

This centrality of the government deeply influences the view of empowerment across the different countries and how it differs to or complements protection. While empowerment remains not well understood and lacks proper translation into local languages, the general view is that it is something the state provides. This is done as part of services such as education and health, or by encouraging participation of underrepresented sectors. There is much openness about who is empowered, as strengthening national governments was part of the response to our surveys. Since empowerment is a fundamental tenet of human security propositions, repeated almost every time the idea is introduced, further exploration seems urgent. An option emerging from the surveys is to undertake in-depth studies about the role of CSOs and the experience of human rights promotion, which are conventionally related to bottom-up activities. This is particularly crucial because interviewees belonging to these organizations did not see in the human security idea much added value, posing a question mark for who could be the possible norm entrepreneur in each context. The examples of Thailand, the Philippines, and Japan suggest that it is government officials and academics who see opportunities in the concept, recognizing that it could reinforce the state-centric and technocratic perception of human security. Dignity, as a reflection of the moral and spiritual expectations of people, can also be of help in understanding empowerment against downside risks and the dark side of development.

Finally, the cases suggest that the meat of human security norm localization is to be found in the approaches to specific problems, so further in-depth studies should be conducted. One option for this is to focus on welfare provision; however, given the great amount of attention and work on welfare from the point of view of development studies and economics, it is not clear how much an impact focusing on human security can have in this approach. Instead, a focus on different types of crises as catalyzers of social change may have better prospects. Crisis and dealing with threats is where criticisms emerge and solutions are looked for. The lack of actual solutions associated with human security promotion could be addressed through a better understanding of specific threats (Hernandez et al. 2018). Still, even this book's general take on human security ideas is important in as much as it provides room for stakeholders to communicate and find opportunities for joint work. It should be also born in mind that the risk of politicization of human security ideas was voiced by long-term supporters and like-minded interviewees; alternatives to counter such situations, particularly worrisome given how state-centric the idea is perceived, deserve attention. Human security as a concept can be useful when other concepts fail; for instance, when racial and religious factors hinder impartiality, as it is suggested in the chapter on Malaysia. That does not mean that human security ideas are otherwise inconsequential. The deep reflections gathered in the surveys attest to the importance of human security norms as a *raison d'être* of the State and, thus, highlight how crucial the understanding of security is and how the study of human security perceptions promises to be an important method of gauging each society's condition.

Notes

1. I have suggested elsewhere that this may also have been the case in Latin American countries (Gomez 2015), as part of what Huntington (1991) called the third wave of democratization.
2. For instance, in the management of crises (Gomez 2014).
3. The only different answer is discussed in Sect. 13.5.
4. National human development reports using human security to understand countries in transition have also shown this particular emphasis on welfare—Chile (UNDP 1998) and Macedonia (UNDP 2001).
5. Self-sufficiency, together with communitarianism, is also a value pushed through the Ministry of Human Security in Thailand, and it is part of the Japanese Development Assistance Charter.
6. Interestingly, the private sector company interviewed in Chap. 5 on Japan is involved in human security through its corporate social responsibility strategy.
7. Thanks to Professor Maria Ela L. Atienza, University of the Philippines, Diliman, for this clarification.
8. This connection in the region has been discussed in relevant detail by Umegaki (2009).
9. Another framing of this kind of threats is "the dark side of development," which is commonly used through the global Human Development Reports to understand human security in relation to human development; see Gomez et al. (2016).
10. These are of course not totally unrelated to development but, for the sake of the analysis, I treat them separately.
11. In Gomez et al. (2013) and Gomez and Gasper (2013) we identify the strengths and limitations of different approaches to human security reporting.
12. For a discussion on constitutive norms, see Katzenstein (1996).

References

Acharya, Amitav. 2004. How Ideas Spread: Whose Norms Matter? Norm Localization and Institutional Change in Asian Regionalism. *International Organization* 58 (2): 239–275.

CHS (Commission on Human Security). 2003. *Human Security Now*. New York: Commission on Human Security.

Deng, Francis, Sandikiel Kimaro, Terrence Lyons, Donald Rothchild, and I. William Zartman. 1996. *Sovereignty as Responsibility: Conflict Management in Africa*. Washington, DC: Brookings Institution.

Gómez, Oscar A. 2014. What Can the Human Development Approach Tell Us about Crisis? An Exploration. *International Journal of Social Quality* 4 (2): 28–45.

———. 2015. Alternative Views of Security in Latin America: Towards a Global Contribution to Human Security. *Regions and Cohesion* 5 (1): 26–53.

Gómez, Oscar A., and Des Gasper. 2013. *Human Security Guidance Note*, Human Development Report Office. New York: UNDP.

Gómez, Oscar A., Des Gasper, and Yoichi Mine. 2013. *Good Practices in Addressing Human Security Through Human Development Reports*, Report for the Human Development Report Office. New York: UNDP.

———. 2016. Moving Development and Security Narratives a Step Further: Human Security in the Human Development Reports. *Journal of Development Studies* 52 (1): 113–129.

Hernandez, Carolina, Eun Mee Kim, Yoichi Mine, and Ren Xiao, eds. 2018. *Human Security and Cross-Border Cooperation in East Asia*. New York: Palgrave Macmillan.

Human Security Study Group. 2004. *A Human Security Doctrine for Europe*. The Barcelona Report of the Study Group on Europe's Security Capabilities. http://www.lse.ac.uk/internationalDevelopment/research/CSHS/humanSecurity/barcelonaReport.pdf. Accessed 20 Oct 2017.

———. 2007. *A European Way of Security*. The Madrid Report of the Human Security Study Group. http://eprints.lse.ac.uk/40207/1/A_European_Way_of_Security%28author%29.pdf. Accessed 21 Oct 2017.

———. 2010. *Helsinki Plus: Towards a Human Security Architecture for Europe*. The First Report of the EU-Russia Human Security Study Group. http://www.lse.ac.uk/internationalDevelopment/research/CSHS/humanSecurity/HelsinkiPlusEnglish.pdf. Accessed 21 Oct 2017.

———. 2016. *From Hybrid Peace to Human Security: Rethinking EU Strategy Towards Conflict*. The Berlin Report of the Human Security Study Group. https://europa.eu/globalstrategy/en/file/424/download?token=VFwH62WJ. Accessed 20 Oct 2017.

Huntington, Samuel P. 1991. *The Third Wave: Democratization in the Late twentieth Century*. Norman: University of Oklahoma Press.

Kaldor, Mary, Mary Martin, and Sabine Selchow. 2007. Human Security: A New Strategic Narrative for Europe. *International Affairs* 83 (2): 273–288.

Katzenstein, Peter J. 1996. *Cultural Norms and National Security*. Ithaca: Cornell University Press.

Sen, Amartya. 1999. Human Rights and Economic Achievements, Chapter 4. In *The East Asian Challenge for Human Rights*, ed. Joanne R. Bauer and Daniel A. Bell. New York: Cambridge University Press.

———. 2009. *The Idea of Justice*. Cambridge: The Belknap Press of Harvard University Press.

Umegaki, Michio. 2009. Introduction: East Asia in a Human Security Perspective. In *Human Insecurity in East Asia*, ed. Michio Umegaki, Lynn Thiesmeyer, and Atsushi Watabe, 1–19. Tokyo: United Nations University Press.

UNDP (United Nations Development Programme). 1994. *Human Development Report 1994: New Dimensions of Human Security*. New York: UNDP.
———. 1998. *Chile Human Development Report—Paradoxes of Modernity: Human Security*. Santiago: UNDP.
———. 2001. *Macedonia Human Development Report—Social Exclusion and Human Insecurity in the FYR Macedonia*. Skopje: UNDP.

CHAPTER 14

The Way Forward: The Power of Diversity

Ako Muto and Yoichi Mine

14.1 Introduction

The case studies in this volume have dug deep into the process of localization of the human security norm-complex in the 11 countries of East Asia. As indicated in Chap. 1, there are three major characteristics that stand out in these case studies. First, the surveys uncover a wide variety of issues that are locally considered critical and pervasive threats to human security; political conflict and repression are included in this list, but we have found that the range of perceived human security threats is much wider than that. Second, human security consists of clusters of norms, and each component (freedom from fear and want, freedom to live in dignity, protection and empowerment) has been well understood, accepted, and put into practice in East Asian countries. Thus, the parts are already there, but another push seems necessary to elevate human security to a full-fledged international norm.

A. Muto (✉)
Research Institute, Japan International Cooperation Agency (JICA), Tokyo, Japan
e-mail: Muto.Ako@jica.go.jp

Y. Mine
Graduate School of Global Studies, Doshisha University, Kyoto, Japan
e-mail: ymine@mail.doshisha.ac.jp

Y. Mine et al. (eds.), *Human Security Norms in East Asia*, Security, Development and Human Rights in East Asia,
https://doi.org/10.1007/978-3-319-97247-3_14

Third, in many countries, the national government is expected to assume the role of guarantor of human security. As meticulously discussed in the comparative analysis in Chap. 13, this protective role of the state is generally appreciated by scholars and practitioners of human security in the region. In fact, wedding the idea of human security to the expected functions of national governments may be the most salient feature of the localization of the human security norm in East Asia. The same chapter also indicates that there is a shared perception that a host of serious human insecurities is caused by the process of rapid economic development in the region. It is imperative for us to pay closer attention to the quality of growth especially because the East Asian region is still a major engine of growth for the world economy.

Based on the findings in regionwide surveys and insightful comparison, this final chapter, a slightly long epilogue to the book, attempts to provide some food for thought not only for scholars but also for practitioners of human security and development in East Asia and worldwide. While this book presents constructivist perspectives such as norm dynamics and security communities, its core message is meant to reach beyond the scholars of international relations (IR), as it is part of an endeavor to find the conditions to create a "community of practice" (Wenger 1998; Adler 2005) of human security in the East Asian region. Such a community will provide the normative and epistemic grounds for concerted action to realize human security.

In 2013, the United Nation Secretary General (UNSG) released a document on global human security practice, which is presented according to the three levels of governance: national (and sub-national), regional, and international (UNSG 2013). The discussion in the rest of this chapter is presented according to these three dimensions. While the UNSG document was based on questionnaire surveys covering the broad UN member states, the present book complements it by advancing a focused inquiry targeting the East Asian region in more depth. At the end of this book, we will return to the definition of human security and discuss why human security eventually had to be separated from its "sibling," the responsibility to protect (R2P).

14.2 Empowerment and Capacity Development: The National Dimension

Human security is practiced by combining top-down protection with bottom-up empowerment. Although people may empower themselves without waiting for intervention from domestic authorities or international donors, our comparative analysis (Chap. 13) argues that in East Asia, governments are widely expected to extend parental care and lead people to the right path; we may call this "guided empowerment." Some case studies in this volume review this function in a positive light, while others envision the promotion of civil society that will act as a democratic counterbalance to authoritarian governments. Although empowering people while protecting them appears to be a contradiction, those holding power may practice both in the passage of time in a similar way to the process in which parents protect and bring up children: the young will eventually take control of their own life and may challenge, and even protect, their parents. The notion of paternalism invites mixed, sometimes emotional reactions.[1]

By definition, empowerment "aims at developing the capabilities of individuals and communities to make informed choices and to act on their own behalf. Empowering people not only enables them to develop their full potential, but it also allows them to find ways and to participate in solutions to ensure human security for themselves and others" (UNHSU 2009, 7). In short, empowered people will possess enhanced levels of problem-solving capacity. If the capacity of individuals and communities to make informed choices is weak, the government may have to set up institutions and provide resources to assist them in making their own decisions. Then, if the capacity of the government to empower people is weak, deficiencies could be filled by means of international aid. The practice of empowerment and that of capacity development are thus closely related.

The concept of capacity development gained currency among international donors in the early 2000s (Fukuda-Parr et al. 2002). Under the presidency of Sadako Ogata, the Japan International Cooperation Agency (JICA) took up the task of operationalizing capacity development at the same time as it absorbed the idea of human security. In its capacity assessment handbook, JICA distinguished three elements of capacity at each of the individual, organizational, and societal levels: the first element is the "technical capacity," which takes the form of particular skills and knowledge (including tacit knowledge); the second is the "core capacity," which refers to leadership capabilities and motivation to utilize the technical capacity; and the third is the "enabling environment," which makes target organizations produce results with an increased capacity. JICA emphasizes the significance of nurturing the core capacity at the organizational level, which is supposed to be the leverage point in many cases (JICA 2008, 14–22). International donors including the World Bank, the Asian Development Bank, the United Nations Development Programme

(UNDP), the European Commission, the Department for International Development (DfID), and Deutsche Gesellschaft für Internationale Zusammenarbeit (German Society for International Cooperation—GIZ) GmbH have developed their principles and programs with regard to capacity development.

The initiative to develop people's problem-solving capacity may be taken by national governments or international donors. The process of empowerment can also proceed in the private economy or intimate spheres independently of the authorities. In any case, if citizens are sufficiently empowered, they may want to change their environments and courses of life from bottom up or begin to resolve local problems collectively by themselves. Empowered individuals may also demand more of government authorities, and if the delivery is short of their expectations and perceived as unjust, they may want to "punish" the national authorities through democratic mechanisms. Otherwise, the same citizens may want to sacrifice themselves voluntarily as "unknown soldiers" to preserve their own imagined (national) community in face of threats posed from the outside (B. Anderson 1983). In East Asia, the time of "oriental despotism," in which obedient rural subjects were mobilized from top down for public works (Wittfogel 1957) is definitely over, as people now think and act on their own. Thus, the path of East Asia's further empowerment and democratization is not predetermined.

The concept of freedom to live in dignity is related to the cultural aspect of human life. In the process of post-war decolonization, people in the newly independent nations called for the restoration of national dignity. The prevalence of dignity in the culture of the UN is closely related to the expansion of the territories in which people are regarded as members of legitimate sovereign nations to which the sacred right of self-determination has been conferred. In Northeast Asia, the concept of national dignity possessed by all formally sovereign and equal nations came into existence with the rise of modern nationalism in the twentieth century, resulting in entangled discourses of equality and hierarchy (Fitzgerald 2006). From the human security perspective, national dignity and individual dignity are both highly esteemed: human security requires international donors to pay respect to national self-determination and obliges national governments to respect the intrinsic value of individual citizens. The challenge is thus dual. The principle of ownership has become part and parcel of human security practice by incorporating the concept of dignity into the norm-complex.

14.3 Diversity of the East Asian Nations: The Regional Dimension

The chapters of this volume have provided a comprehensive list of non-traditional and traditional threats: natural disasters (earthquakes and typhoons/cyclones), environmental pollution, climate change, epidemics, violent conflict, political repression, religious tensions, human trafficking, minority issues, unemployment, conditions of migrants, food crises, lingering poverty, and so on. In a given country, people are exposed to a certain set of threats due to their geographic location, the state of economic development, and other unique factors. The land-locked country of Laos will never experience a tsunami, for example.

The East Asian nations are extremely diverse. In terms of territory and population size, one may hesitate to lump China and Singapore together in the same category of nation states. In this region, presidential or parliamentary republics, constitutional monarchies, and communist regimes coexist side by side. Countries like Indonesia, Malaysia, and China are rich in natural resources, while Singapore, Thailand, South Korea, and Japan are less endowed. Before anthropologists discovered the notion of cultural relativism, East Asians were long accustomed to this way of thinking; the region has accommodated diverse indigenous and exogenous cultures and religions like Confucianism, Buddhism, Christianity, Islam as well as various sorts of animism. Hundreds of languages are spoken in Indonesia while basically one language is used in a country like Japan. However, such diversity has never hindered the economic development of East Asia. More than two decades after the publication of the *East Asian Miracle*, which attributed the rapid economic growth of the East Asian tigers to good education and appropriate industrial policies (World Bank 1993), most national economies continue growing with the strong backing of relatively efficient bureaucracies and capable administrations. It is noteworthy that the capacity development of government institutions by means of knowledge transfer has always been an important component of Japan's development assistance.

In the meantime, China has become the second largest economy in the world, and South Korea is now a member of the Organisation for Economic Co-operation and Development-Development Assistance Committee (OECD-DAC). Despite the miraculous economic successes and deepening value chains in the region, a common security arrangement has not taken shape in East Asia, where sovereign nations still compete against each other openly. Since the 1950s, the North Atlantic world have nurtured layers of regional organizations, called "security communities" by Karl Deutsch and his colleagues, in which all community members expect that disputes among the states will be settled in peaceful, non-military ways (Deutsch et al. 1957). Given that the emergence of such security communities followed the deepening of economic and cultural ties rather than the formation of military alliances (Ruggie 1996, 85), the time for a security community in East Asia where we witness a remarkable degree of economic integration may already be ripe. However, a political community that would share sovereignty is not preferred in this region, and as shown in the case study chapters and discussed later in this chapter, most are also skeptical about the R2P style intervention within the region. Nevertheless, in East Asia, it may not be difficult to reach a consensus to organize multiple cooperative platforms[2] to address particular human security challenges, thereby building a pluralistic "human security community" in which member states collaborate while retaining national sovereignty (Hernandez et al. 2018).

Regarding the prospect of the regional cooperation for human security, the Association of Southeast Asian Nations (ASEAN) stays one step ahead. On top of the accelerated effort to consolidate the ASEAN community in its political-security, economic and socio-cultural aspects, ASEAN is taking concerted action to address non-traditional security issues (Acharya 2014; Caballero-Anthony 2016). Among the five world regions (Asia, Africa, Americas, Europe, and Oceania), from 2006 to 2015, 40 percent of natural disasters took place in Asia, and 51 percent of the related total casualties were people who lived in the region (IFRC 2016, 232–3). As Southeast Asia is a specifically disaster-prone area, ASEAN has advanced regional cooperation in disaster management in the framework of the ASEAN Agreement on Disaster Management and Emergency Response (AADMER), which is "a legally-binding, regional multi-hazard and policy framework for cooperation, coordination, technical assistance, and resource mobilization" (UNOCHA-ROAP 2013). While Japan contributes to this initiative, ASEAN also succeeded in collaborating with China, with the support of the World Health Organization (WHO), when the Severe Acute Respiratory Syndrome (SARS) broke out. In responding to the SARS crisis, the ASEAN Plus Three (China, Japan, and South Korea) framework was utilized (Acharya 2014, 217–8).

Depending on the choice of criteria, East Asian states can be classified into several groups with asymmetric power configurations. It is widely known that hierarchical regimes with centralized power structures historically developed in the plain regions of the Eurasian continent, while flexible, amorphous, and network-based polities prevailed largely in mountain areas as well as islands and archipelagoes in the Pacific (see, e.g., Geertz 1980; Scott 2009). Today, we face an intriguing paradox: while traditionally centripetal governments in China, Japan, and South Korea develop strained relationships among themselves, relatively centrifugal governments in Southeast Asia have steadily and tenaciously advanced the community formation of ASEAN. The future of a human security community in East Asia hinges upon whether equal partnership can be matured between these two asymmetric powers, namely, between ASEAN and the "Plus Three." A positive aspect is that, despite the political rivalry, a culture of mutual respect is gradually fostered, and there are active collaborative networks in civil society, business, and academia across the region. If East Asia can sustain growth while assuming the responsibility to address global human security issues, the region may give rise to an Asian version of the OECD in the future.

14.4 The Sustainable Development Goals (SDGs) and Human Security: The Global Dimension

It is very clear from the case studies that East Asian experts of human security share a view that multilateral assistance is much preferable to unilateral intervention. Presently, the most important multilateral framework to solve global problems is the SDGs. The "2030 Agenda for Sustainable Development" was adopted at the UN Summit in September 2015, and the 17 SDGs of the Agenda were released in January 2016. The SDGs build on the success of the Millennium Development Goals (MDGs), but "the new Goals are unique in that they call for action by all countries—poor, rich, and middle-income—to promote prosperity while protecting the planet." Moreover, "while the SDGs are not legally binding, governments are expected to take ownership and establish national frameworks for achievement of the 17 Goals."[3] East Asian countries have already started to elaborate their own programs to meet these goals by 2030, and their efforts will be accelerated as the target year draws nearer.

There are two critical points that link the human security perspective with the practice to realize the SDGs. The first relates to the role of the government. Although the SDGs seek a strong alliance with the private sector and civil society, Article 41 of Agenda 2030 notes that the state can play a significant role: “We recognize that each country has primary responsibility for its own economic and social development.” Second, the SDGs appear to pay less attention to risks and resilience that feature the discourses of human security, and this gap is expected to open a new field of complementary action. As Fig. 14.1 shows, the process of human development cannot be a linear progress. If development is the process of expanding people’s freedom, human security aims at removing sources of people’s unfreedom. Calamities such as wars, armed conflicts, outbreaks of infectious diseases, and natural and human-made disasters pounce upon a wide swath of people at a time. The focus on these “downside risks” is part of the theoretical underpinnings of the human security concept (Sen 2014). In the risk-prone societies of our time, even though both haves and have-nots are equally exposed to cross-border threats such as air pollution, multiple risks compel the most vulnerable people to suffer most, intensifying their insecurities (Beck 1992). These are the people who need to be protected and empowered most urgently.

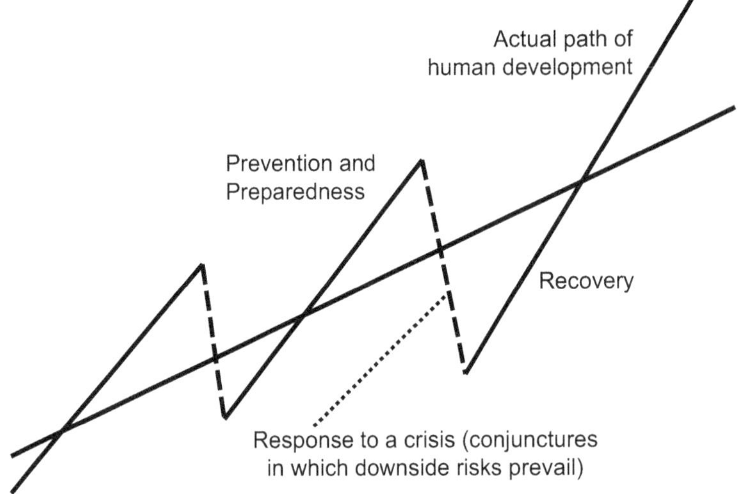

Fig. 14.1 Human security and development. Adapted from Mine (2007, p. 72)

Let us use some illustrative examples. When violent conflict breaks out, those civilians who do not possess resources to evacuate or emigrate become easy targets of warring parties. In refugee camps, strong men often monopolize distributed foods and deprive women, children, and the weak of their food entitlements. The socially excluded persons living with human immunodeficiency virus infection and acquired immune deficiency syndrome (HIV/AIDS) may not have access to effective treatment even though the government provides such a service. In debt-laden households, young voiceless children fall prey to human trafficking. People who have no choice but to live in a wetland delta have their houses swept away by deluges caused by global climate change. People who cannot but choose the cheapest foods are exposed to the risks of dangerous food additives. And finally, those who have decided to sacrifice their lives for others may be tortured and "disappear" when the government turns against its own citizens. These are all human security issues, and simultaneously, it is these sufferings that must be addressed by the SDGs.

Downside risks, or critical and pervasive threats to human security, may hinder sustainable human development and exert grave impact on specific groups of vulnerable people. Traditionally, the UNSG regarded inter-state wars as the central threats to peace and security of the world, but the UN has already begun to discuss ways to address global risks other than classic wars, such as economic and social threats (including poverty, diseases, and environmental degradation), violent conflict within the nation, new weapons, terrorism, and transnational organized crime (UN 2004). While the SDGs aim to reach a set of prescribed goals, human security strives to deal with the obstacles in the way of these shared goals and examines who are affected most adversely by those obstacles. Amartya Sen proposed a methodology of disaggregation in his *Poverty and Famine*, a classic analysis of famine crises in South Asia and Africa (Sen 1981): even when the total food supply seems to be sufficient in the nationally aggregated data, specific groups (including landless people) can starve to death, especially when they are wracked by ferocious market forces. Focusing attention on such variables as gender, generation, occupation, and geographic location, we should be able to clearly understand the differential vulnerability of particular communities and individuals to human security threats.[4]

In East Asia, people often refer to natural disasters, infectious diseases, and political conflict as typical human security issues. In the list of the SDGs, these issues are featured in Goal 11 (Make cities and human settlements inclusive, safe, resilient, and sustainable), Goal 3 (Ensure healthy lives and promote well-being for all at all ages), and Goal 16 (Promote peaceful and inclusive societies for sustainable development, provide access to justice for all and build effective, accountable and inclusive institutions at all levels). We can also check how many times the keywords of human security such as want, fear, dignity, protection, and empowerment appear in the text of the SDGs; for example, empowerment is explicitly used in Goal 5 (Achieve gender equality and empower all women and girls). However, these exercises to find thematic overlaps may be misleading, as an international norm is not just a set of issues and keywords but a certain collective expectation for appropriate action. The idea and practice of human security have unique potential to contribute to the overall achievement of the SDGs through its focus on risks, vulnerability, and an ethical imperative of "no one left behind" as a global concern.

14.5 Human Security and the Responsibility to Protect

Finally, let us revisit the definition of the human security norm-complex. In 2012, the United Nations General Assembly (UNGA) adopted a resolution on the definition of human security (UNGA 2012; see also Chap. 1 of this volume). According to this document, a common understanding of human security includes: "The right of people to live in freedom and dignity, free from poverty and despair. All individuals, in particular the vulnerable people, are entitled to freedom from fear and freedom from want, with an equal opportunity to enjoy all their rights and fully develop their human potential." In this text, freedom is defined in terms of the duality of peace (absence of fear) and development (elimination of want), and juxtaposed with the right to live in dignity, with special emphasis given to the rights of vulnerable people. Development of "human potential" resonates with the idea of human development, which was originally defined as the process of enlarging people's choices. The resolution fleshes out the concept further in subsequent paragraphs that begin with: "(b) Human security calls for people-centred, comprehensive, context-specific and prevention-oriented responses that strengthen the protection and empowerment of all people and all communities."

As discussed in Chap. 1, human security is a norm-complex that consists of a cluster of related norms, and this hybridity allows for different interpretations of human security. This is one of the reasons why the title of this book is *Human Security Norms* in the plural, rather than the human security norm in the singular (the other reason lies in a variety of interpretations of the concept in different countries in East Asia). Since the introduction of the concept to the UN discourse around 1994, human security has been regarded by some as a sort of "patchwork" of norms. Human security was criticized by Paris (2001) and others as a "vague" and "useless" concept in a series of debates that largely took place in the North Atlantic region.[5] The definition of human security in the 2012 UNGA resolution was agreed upon as a compromise among diplomats from the UN member states with starkly different backgrounds. As such, the latest definition also appears to remain elusive.

In fact, however, the message of human security redefined in the 2012 UNGA resolution seems powerfully comprehensive and far from ambiguous. The purport becomes clear when we contrast human security with its adversarial "sibling," the R2P, which was originally born as a sharp-edged, narrow interpretation of the human security concept (ICISS 2001). The UNGA resolution redefined human security as an opposite of the R2P approach: "(d) The notion of human security is distinct from the responsibility to protect and its implementation." It also specifies the role of the state and international community engaged in assistance in case of humanitarian crises: "(e) Human security does not entail the threat or the use of force or coercive measures. Human security does not replace State security." In addition, "(f) Human security is based on national ownership (…)," and "(g) Governments retain the primary role and responsibility for ensuring the survival, livelihood and dignity of their citizens. The role of the international community is to complement and provide the necessary support to Governments, upon their request, to strengthen their capacity to respond to current and emerging threats. Human security requires greater collaboration and partnership (…)."

When applied to a humanitarian emergency, the R2P approach is supposed to simplify the problem, react to the crisis, mobilize the military, enter the sovereign territory, and protect citizens. In contrast, the priority of the human security approach in the UN is now understood to contextualize the problem, prevent the crisis, coordinate activities of various actors, respect national sovereignty, and empower citizens from the bottom up. In every respect, human security as defined in the 2012 resolution is the antithesis of the conventional interpretation of the R2P.[6] The action to address humanitarian crises has been discussed much in the analogy of medical practice such as "do no harm," a phrase in the Hippocratic Oath (M.B. Anderson 1999). While the R2P is like a "surgical" or "invasive" therapy targeting troubled society, human security seems closer to an "internal" or "oriental" medicine designed to promote the resilience of an organism. When multilateralism flourishes, the ideas of human security and the R2P, as well as their confrontation, complementarity and entanglements, attract keen public attention. However, when the enthusiasm for multilateral thinking recedes, it appears that both ideas tend to be sidelined.

Still, it is noteworthy that most respondents in our case studies did not confuse human security with the R2P, indicating that the comprehensive approach to human security is taking root in the region. After having witnessed how the R2P was applied and not applied since the Libyan case in 2011, thinkers seriously started to wonder if "the old ghost of the standard of civilization, exorcised after 1945 by the United Nations, had risen from the grave (Mazower 2012, 396)." In response, ASEAN's team of scholars headed by Surin Pitsuwan stated that the regional organization is "already" equipped with relevant mechanisms and instruments to carry out the R2P (High-Level Advisory Panel on the Responsibility to Protect in Southeast Asia 2014). Given that human security challenges posed by nature and humans continue to confront the region and that East Asian people prefer the holistic approach to address them, the "oriental" way of securing freedom will never cease to exist.

Notes

1. The paternalist norm of governance prevalent in some Asian countries should be distinguished from the controversial modalities of intervention such as technocratic "libertarian paternalism" in behavioral economics (Thaler and Sunstein 2008) and paternalistic humanitarianism (Barnett 2011).
2. Trilateral collaboration between China, South Korea and Japan in the field of development assistance was gaining momentum by 2011. Accessed August 26, 2017. https://www.jica.go.jp/english/news/opinion/2012/120702_01.html
3. See the United Nation's Sustainable Development Knowledge Platform. Accessed August 26, 2017. https://sustainabledevelopment.un.org/sdgs
4. Many of the individual chapters of this book discuss this aspect. For a more detailed issue-based study of human security in East Asia, see Hernandez et al. (2018).

5. As for a mapping of the pros and cons *vis-à-vis* the human security concept, see various articles in the special section on "What is 'Human Security'" in *Security Dialogue* 35(3), 2004. Tadjbakhsh and Chenoy (2007) tried to shift the gravity of the human security discourse to the "South" by capturing its holistic vigor.
6. Note that this is based on how the R2P is commonly perceived (and this perception is reflected in the 2012 UNGA resolution). As a statutory norm, the R2P consists of three pillars: (1) every state has the responsibility to protect its populations, (2) the international community has the responsibility to assist every state in assuming that responsibility, and (3) when a state fails to protect citizens, the internal community should be prepared to take collective action. It is evident that the first two pillars resonate with the idea of human security. For a nuanced review of the entanglements of the two norms of non-intervention and intervention, with a relative commitment to the former, see Doyle (2015).

References

Acharya, Amitav. 2014. *Constructing a Security Community in Southeast Asia: ASEAN and the Problem of Regional Order*. 3rd ed. London: Routledge.

Adler, Emanuel. 2005. *Communitarian International Relations: The Epistemic Foundations of International Relations*. London: Routledge.

Anderson, Benedict. 1983. *Imagined Communities: Reflections on the Origin and Spread of Nationalism*. London: Verso.

Anderson, Mary B. 1999. *Do No Harm: How Aid Can Support Peace - or War*. Boulder: Lynne Rienner Publishers.

Barnett, Michael. 2011. *Empire of Humanity: A History of Humanitarianism*. Ithaca: Cornell University Press.

Beck, Ulrich. 1992. *Risk Society: Towards a New Modernity*. Trans. Mark Ritter. London: Sage.

Caballero-Anthony, Mely, ed. 2016. *An Introduction to Non-Traditional Security Studies: A Transnational Approach*. Los Angeles: Sage.

Deutsch, Karl W., Sidney A. Burrel, Robert A. Kann, Maurice Lee Jr., Martin Lichterman, Raymond E. Lindgren, Francis L. Loewenheim, and Richard W. Van Wagenen. 1957. *Political Community and the North Atlantic Area: International Organization in the Light of Historical Experience*. Princeton: Princeton University Press.

Doyle, Michael W. 2015. *The Question of Intervention: John Stuart Mill and the Responsibility to Protect*. New Haven: Yale University Press.

Fitzgerald, John. 2006. Introduction: The Dignity of Nations. In *The Dignity of Nations: Equality, Competition, and Honor in East Asian Nationalism*, ed. Sechin Y.S. Chien and John Fitzgerald, 1–22. Hong Kong: Hong Kong University Press.

Fukuda-Parr, Sakiko, Carlos Lopes, and Khalid Malik, eds. 2002. *Capacity for Development: New Solutions to Old Problems*. London/New York: Earthscan/ United Nations Development Programme.

Geertz, Clifford. 1980. *Negara: The Theatre State in Nineteenth-Century Bali*. Princeton: Princeton University Press.

Hernandez, Carolina, Eun Mee Kim, Yoichi Mine, and Ren Xiao, eds. 2018. *Human Security and Cross-Border Cooperation in East Asia*. New York: Palgrave Macmillan.

High-Level Advisory Panel on the Responsibility to Protect in Southeast Asia (Chaired by Dr. Surin Pitsuwan). 2014. *Mainstreaming the Responsibility to Protect in Southeast Asia: Pathway Towards a Caring ASEAN Community*. Report of the Advisory Panel Presented at the United Nations, New York, September 9.

ICISS (International Commission on Intervention and State Sovereignty). 2001. *The Responsibility to Protect: Report of the International Commission on Intervention and State Sovereignty*. International Development Research Centre (IDRC): Ottawa.

IFRC (International Federation of Red Cross and Red Crescent Societies). 2016. *World Disasters Report 2016*. Geneva: IFRC.

JICA (Japan International Cooperation Agency). 2008. *Capacity Assessment Handbook: Project Management for Realizing Capacity Development*. Tokyo: JICA Research Institute.

Mazower, Mark. 2012. *Governing the World: The History of an Idea*. New York: Penguin Press.

Mine, Yoichi. 2007. Downside Risks and Human Security. In *Protecting Human Security in a Post 9/11 World: Critical and Global Insights*, ed. Giorgio Shani, Makoto Sato, and Mustapha Kamal Pasha, 64–79. Basingstoke: Palgrave Macmillan.

Paris, Roland. 2001. Human Security: Paradigm Shift or Hot Air? *International Security* 26 (2): 87–102.

Ruggie, John Gerard. 1996. *Winning the Peace: America and World Order in the New Era*. New York: Columbia University Press.

Scott, James C. 2009. *The Art of Not Being Governed: An Anarchist History of Upland Southeast Asia*. New Haven: Yale University Press.

Sen, Amartya. 1981. *Poverty and Famines: An Essay on Entitlement and Deprivation*. Oxford: Clarendon Press.

———. 2014. Birth of a Discourse. In *Routledge Handbook of Human Security*, ed. Mary Martin and Taylor Owen, 17–27. Abingdon, Oxon: Routledge.

Tadjbakhsh, Shahrbanou, and Anuradha M. Chenoy. 2007. *Human Security: Concepts and Implications*. Abingdon, Oxon: Routledge.

Thaler, Richard H., and Cass R. Sunstein. 2008. *Nudge: Improving Decisions about Health, Wealth, and Happiness*. New Haven: Yale University Press.

UN (United Nations). 2004. *A More Secure World: Our Shared Responsibility: Report of the High-Level Panel on Threats, Challenges and Change*. New York: United Nations.

UNGA (United Nations General Assembly). 2012. *Follow-up to Paragraph 143 on Human Security of the 2005 World Summit Outcome*, September 10, A/RES/66/290.

UNHSU (United Nations Human Security Unit). 2009. *Human Security in Theory and Practice: Application of the Human Security Concept and the United Nations Trust Fund for Human Security*. New York: Human Security Unit, Office for the Coordination of Humanitarian Affairs, United Nations.

UNOCHA-ROAP (United Nations Office for the Coordination of Humanitarian Affairs, Regional Office for Asia and the Pacific). 2013. II. International Humanitarian Architecture. Disaster Response in Asia and the Pacific. *Disaster Response in Asia and the Pacific*. Thailand: UNOCHA-ROAP.

UNSG (United Nations Secretary General). 2013. *Follow-up to General Assembly Resolution 66/290 on Human Security*. Report of the Secretary-General, A/68/685, December 23.

Wenger, Etienne. 1998. *Communities of Practice: Learning, Meaning, and Identity*. Cambridge: Cambridge University Press.

Wittfogel, Karl A. 1957. *Oriental Despotism: A Comparative Study of Total Power*. New Haven: Yale University Press.

World Bank. 1993. *The East Asian Miracle: Economic Growth and Public Policy*. New York: Oxford University Press.

Index[1]

A

[1] Note: Page numbers followed by 'n' refer to notes.

Y. Mine et al. (eds.), *Human Security Norms in East Asia*, Security, Development and Human Rights in East Asia,
https://doi.org/10.1007/978-3-319-97247-3

I

T

CPSIA information can be obtained
at www.ICGtesting.com
Printed in the USA
LVHW070004171218
600703LV00020B/1109/P

9 783319 972466